CHINESE HERBS

CHINESE HERBS

Their Botany, Chemistry, and Pharmacodynamics

中
草
藥

by JOHN D. KEYS

WITH
SPECIAL SECTIONS ON:

- Mineral Drugs
- Drugs of Animal Origin
- 300 Chinese Prescriptions
- Toxic Herbs

CHARLES E. TUTTLE COMPANY
Rutland • Vermont : Tokyo • Japan

Published by the Charles E. Tuttle Company, Inc.
of Rutland, Vermont & Tokyo, Japan
with editorial offices
at 2-6 Suido 1-chome, Bunkyo-ku, Tokyo 112

LCC Card No. 75-35399
ISBN 0-8048-1667-0

First edition, 1976
First paperback edition, 1990
Fifth printing, 1997

PRINTED IN SINGAPORE

TO MY MOTHER AND FATHER

who watched the preparation of this work
over the years

TABLE OF CONTENTS

FOREWORD

by Ilza Veith, Ph.D.
Professor, History of Health Sciences
University of California

EVER SINCE its first contact with the Far East, the Western world has been irresistibly fascinated by the *materia medica* of China, by its promise of health, longevity, increased sexual potency, fertility, and rejuvenation.

It is for this reason that John D. Keys's work *Chinese Herbs: Their Botany, Chemistry, and Pharmacodynamics* is such a welcome publication. It provides an excellent and scholarly insight into most practical aspects of the herbal lore of China. Although not a complete description of all Chinese herb medications, it is a selection of those that appear most important to the author; these, incidentally, have become best known to the Western world.

In making his selection, the author has not failed to include ginseng root, which is said to cure all ills, to return youth and beauty, and even to confer the latter if it had not previously existed. A further *sine qua non* in all descriptions of Chinese herb medicine is the legendary Ma Huang, which was avidly accepted in the West, where it came to be known by its botanical name *Ephedra sinica*, and was synthesized as ephedrine to furnish an indispensable drug for the treatment of asthma and allergic reactions.

Many readers will view the extraordinary richness of the Chinese herbal pharmacopoeia with wonder, and question how it came into being. The secret of this development lies in the beginning of Chinese medicine, which is veiled in legend. Important in this legendary background is the personality of an emperor of the third millennium B.C.

This emperor, Shen Nung or "The Divine Husbandman," was deified by the people as the God of Agriculture for having given China its healing medicines, its rice and other foodstuffs, and all its agriculture.

To Shen Nung is also attributed the authorship of the first *Pen Ts'ao*, generally translated as the "Great Herbal." This vast book, which has been analyzed and annotated more than any other Chinese medical volume, is actually of anonymous authorship. It contains descriptions of vegetable, animal, and mineral medicines and foodstuffs, and it was the forerunner of all later Chinese herbals.

The contemplation of the antiquity and anonymity of the *Pen Ts'ao* evokes certain parallels with *Chinese Herbs* here before us. It is well possible that the unknown Chinese herbalist who compiled the first Chinese pharmacopoeia was, like John D. Keys, an amateur in the true sense of the word: He loved to study plants for their healing virtue, but he was not a pharmacologist or a pharmacist. It is to be assumed that the earlier author was Chinese and familiar by birth with the spoken and written language of China. Mr. Keys early in life developed a passionate interest in things Chinese, particularly Chinese herbs. So strong was his interest that he studied the language—an endless undertaking so far as time and effort are concerned—and in eighteen years of single-minded devotion produced this interesting work.

At a time when Chinese culture, civilization, and particularly Chinese medicine occupy the forepoint of interest of the Western world, John D. Keys's contribution is bound to occupy an important place in the literature concerning the healing herbs of the immense country behind the Great Wall.

San Francisco

PREFACE

I CAN RECALL strolling as a child down the streets of San Francisco's Chinatown and passing by at least one herb shop in every block. They always did intrigue me, especially when I would pause before an open door and inhale the alluring smells of odoriferous woods and spices which drifted from the dim interior. Almost always an ancient Chinese, wearing a pair of immense spectacles, would be peeping out over the half-curtains in the window, and I must confess he struck me as looking rather sinister.

The window itself would be arranged with small porcelain saucers, each containing a small mound of some herb or another. There were chips of various woods, shriveled rootlets, bunches of frizzly grasses that looked like miniature tumbleweeds, rodents stretched and dried on small wooden frames, and delicate seeds. Several tall apothecary jars, almost opaque with the accumulation of years of dust, contained lengths of viper steeped in who knew what.

Small boxes covered with Chinese characters and wrapped in cellophane were arranged here and there, all of them bearing the words, "Made in Hong Kong." These were obviously modern manufactured pills which utilized the traditional medicaments of the Chinese pharmacopoeia.

After a while I became a little bolder, and would step into the doorway of one of these shops, adjusting my eyes to the darkness within. Against the wall would be a massive, ornate counter, running the length of the store. The wall itself contained row upon row of tiny drawers, each filled with a certain dried herb or other medicine. These drawers possessed no labels or other identifying marks, yet the Chinese druggists could at a second's notice locate the desired item. Sometimes they had to use a ladder, for the drawers went up to the ceiling, and back into the shop as far as one could see.

On the counter stood a scale-beam for weighing out the herbs and other medicines. Beside the scale lay a pile of rectangular pieces of paper, in which the medicines were wrapped. The druggist, following the instructions of a written prescription, would first grind the dried herbs to a powder in an earthenware mortar. Lastly, the deft fingers of the clerk would slip over the black teakwood beads of the abacus which lay at the front of the counter, to determine the amount due.

Against the other wall stood a row of high-backed, rather elegant carved chairs which were mounted on a low platform. Here the customers would sit and chat as they waited for their prescriptions. It was a symbol of prosperity to be seen leisurely passing one's time in the herb shop, for the Chinese take medicaments not only to cure illness, but also as a preventative and general tonic. And many of these wonder drugs were not cheap.

And thus began an overwhelming desire on my part to learn more about Chinese herbs, a subject so little understood by the Western world. Was the interest primarily botanical or medical? At that time I could not answer this question, but whatever inherent drive launched me on what was to become a very extensive study indeed, I immediately took the first logical and necessary step, namely the study of the Chinese language.

After several years of linguistic preparation, I undertook the translation of Chinese pharmaceutical works. Until recently, analyses in the English language of Chinese *materia medica* have been the result of translations from the ancient and traditional native works. Because of the vagueness of expressions and terms used by the Chinese authors, and their inclination to the marvellous, these existing translations left much to be desired, from the scientific viewpoint. My goal was the writing of something more concrete.

True, most of traditional Chinese medicine is based solely on superstition and fancy. The Chinese are much addicted to the doctrine of signatures, which is based on the belief that an external mark or character on a plant indicates its suitableness to cure particular diseases. Thus they employ a decoction of the thorns of *Gleditschia* or *Zizyphus* to accelerate the bursting of abscesses. The yellow bark of *Berberis* is used for jaundice. Emmenagogue properties are ascribed to the red root of *Rubia cordifolia*. And the well-known ginseng, whose branching root resembles the human figure, appears to be a panacea for nearly all ills.

On the other hand, Western medical science continues to discover important constituents in botanicals employed in the so-called "folk" medicines of various countries. As far as the folk medicine of China is concerned, the difficult and ambiguous language barrier has kept this area from being extensively studied. Perhaps the Japanese have made the greatest headway in this respect.

I needed to find a way to relate the many age-old plant remedies of China to today's scientific procedures, in the hope that I might open the door to further study by those more specifically qualified in the field of pharmacology. I was finally fortunate enough to locate several recent works in Chinese on the subject, recent enough to include a sufficient content of modern chemical analysis and botanical identification, together with traditional therapeutic usage as related to Occidental medical terminology. My work had just begun.

The preparation of this book, which has occupied my interest for the past twenty years, has taken me by necessity through the studies of not only the Chinese language, but also of Japanese and French, as well as the subjects of botany, chemistry, and medical science. It has been an exhausting labor of love, and yet I feel the surface has been merely scratched. The greatest feeling of accomplishment shall come only when I determine that my efforts, purely those of a layman in all the subjects above mentioned, have been of actual assistance to more legitimate research.

JOHN D. KEYS

ABBREVIATIONS USED IN THIS BOOK

m.p.	melting point
b.p.	boiling point
mm.	millimeter
cm.	centimeter
gm.	gram
ml.	milliliter
dm.	decimeter
c.c.	cubic centimeters
q.s.	*quantum sufficit* (L., as much as suffices)
ad lib.	*ad libitum* (L., without restraint or limit)
gen.	genus, genera
sp.	species
fam.	family
b.i.d.	*bis in die* (L., twice a day)
t.i.d.	*ter in die* (L., thrice a day)
q.i.d.	*quater in die* (L., four times a day)

All temperatures given are in degrees centigrade.

EXEGESIS

UPON COMPLETION of the individual monographs which comprise this book, the author was faced with the decision on the manner in which they should be organized. Three alternatives presented themselves, namely (1) alphabetization by the romanized Chinese name; (2) over-all alphabetization by generic plant name; and (3) classification by traditional botanic procedure of division, class, subclass, order, and family, the genera within each family being arranged alphabetically. The latter arrangement was chosen as the most logical, for it had become evident through all my researches and wanderings that this work was indeed of botanical foundation.

At this point I should like to explain to the reader the basic form used in the treatment of each botanical:

1. The Latin botanical name (and family)
2. The common English name, if any
3. A complete botanical description (index numbers throughout the text refer to bibliographical entries on p. 361)
4. The natural habitat
5. Botanical synonyms, if any
6. The pharmaceutical description of the drug, including physical description, taste, odor, and toxicity
7. Phytochemical analysis
8. Pharmacodynamic investigations, together with any related use of the same drug in other pharmacopeias, as well as any references to related plants

9. Chinese therapeutic usage of the drug
10. Dosage given by the Chinese herbals (These figures have to be accepted as extremely generalized, for the particular drug may or may not be taken in conjunction with other medicament. Basically, the dosages given are intended to represent the daily dosage to be made into a single decoction or tea, divided into two or three drafts. On the other hand, many medications are meant to be given in powder or pill form, in which case these dosage figures would not at all coincide. A subject of constant ambiguity to the author, these figures are given merely as hypothetical reference.)
11. Incompatible drugs, if any
12. Lastly, related plants of the same genera used for the same purpose, if any

Note: Each plant description is accompanied by a small illustration, except for a few plants for which illustrations were not available. The larger illustrations give a closer or more detailed view, but where a large picture of a certain plant was not available a related plant of the same genus used for the same purpose is shown. The Chinese characters given with the illustrations are read from right to left.

I : THALLOPHYTA

ALGAE

昆布

LAMINARIA JAPONICA Aresch.

(Laminariaceae)

A massive seaweed of the giant kelp family. Holdfast well-developed, branched; growing attached to shoreline rocks. Stalk flexuous, slender, short. Blade well-developed, several meters long, brown, leathery. The plants are collected after they have detached from the rocks. Coasts of China, Japan.

The dried seaweed contains iodine, alginic acid, mannite, iron, calcium, arsenic.[140] The taste is bitter and salty. In Japan *L. japonica* is known as *kombu*; it is used extensively in Japanese and Chinese cuisine. The ancient Chinese, who had no knowledge of the iodine which gives seaweeds their particular efficacy against goiter, prescribed for this disease a tincture and powder of these plants.[153]

Employed as alterative in the treatment of goiter and other iodine deficiencies. Dose, 10–40 gm.

(Also used, *L. angusta* Kjellm., *L. cichorioides* Miyabe, *L. religiosa* Miyabe, *L. longipedalis* Okam.)

SARGASSUM SILIQUASTRUM J. Ag.

(Sargassaceae)

海藻

A rockweed with branching thallus; leaf-like parts equipped with round, swollen bladders. An expanded holdfast attaches the plant to partly submerged rocks between high- and low-tide waters; when covered, the thallus is buoyed up by the bladder-like floats. The seaweed also lives for some time as a free-floating plant, after detaching from the rocks. The color is dark brown, becoming greenish when added to hot water. Gathered December through May. Coasts of China, Japan.

The plant contains 0.2% iodine, iron, calcium, arsenic.[140] The taste is saline and bitter.

Used as *Laminaria japonica* for iodine deficiencies, also as diuretic. Dose, 5–8 gm.

DIGENIA SIMPLEX Wulf.

(Rhodomelaceae)

A red alga, growing attached to shoreline rocks. It is a slender, filamentous plant, randomly branching. The texture is pliable but tough, and the color is purplish black, becoming yellowish brown when dried. Length, 1–2 m. Coasts of China, Taiwan.

The various analyses of this drug by Japanese differ in the determination of the active principle, which has been identified variously as a glycoside and alkaloid. However, all agree that the plant possesses anthelmintic properties similar to those of *santonin,* being strongly effective against *Ascaris.* The taste of the alga is saline, the odor mildly fetid.

Employed as pediatric ascaricide and laxative. Dose, 4–10 gm.

FUNGI

馬勃

LYCOPERDACEAE (fam.)

Various members of the puffball family are employed in the Chinese pharmacopoeia. They grow in wooded areas, and consist of a more or less spherical fruiting body which varies in size from a golf ball to a basketball. They are white when young and are attached to the ground by a cord-like structure, a rhizomorph. The interior of the puffball, known as the gleba, is cottony when young and consists of the spores and capillitium; at maturity this interior becomes a fine, dry powder which is released through a hole in the upper wall. They are gathered in autumn, and the reddish brown dust is extracted for medicinal use.

The spore dust of puffballs has a pungent taste and is characterized by a rather fetid odor, especially after it has been applied to wounds. The dust of *L. bovista* was found to yield 0.57% ash consisting of 72% sodium phosphate, 16% aluminum, 3% magnesium, and 0.44% silicic acid.[140] The dust, mixed with honey or syrup, has been used with success in the treatment of throat infections, as expectorant, and also emmenagogue.[146] Applied externally to wounds, the dry powder promptly arrests hemorrhage.[150]

Used internally as astringent, antiphlogistic, and antitussive in laryngitis, tonsillitis, mucitis; as hemostatic in hematemesis, epistaxis. Dose, 1–2 gm. Externally, for hemorrhage of incised wounds.

雷丸

MYLITTA LAPIDESCENS Horan.

(Polyporaceae)

A subterranean fungus which apparently grows in association with the roots of the bamboo. It occurs as small, irregular globules, often joined together by a slender peduncle at one or both extremities. The size varies from that of a soybean to that of a chestnut. The surface is finely reticulate, while the interior is compact, granular, somewhat farinaceous, and of a dirty brown or reddish color. The odor is faint. "They are produced by thunder and the metamorphoses of the subtle vapors of plants; they have the power of destroying worms and driving out evil spirits."[138] When dried, the fungus takes the form of small, shriveled nodules, very hard, and of a brownish gray color. They are ground to a gray, odorless powder which is used medicinally. Northern China.

The drug has a bitter taste, and is mildly toxic. It contains 3% of an odorless, tasteless, ash-brown substance which is soluble in water and glycerine and insoluble in ether and alcohol; this has been identified as a proteolytic enzyme, which is responsible for the vermicidal action of the drug.[140] Administered orally, the powder has been used effectively against *Taenia*, with few side effects. Heat destroys the efficacy of the drug.

Employed as taeniafuge. Dose, 18 gm. b.i.d. or t.i.d., following meals.

PORIA COCOS Wolf.

(Polyporaceae)

A subterranean fungus which grows in association with the roots of various conifers, particularly *Pinus sinensis, P. longifolis*, and *Cunninghamia*. It occurs as large, ponderous tuberiform bodies, with a reddish brown covering. The interior consists of a compact mass of considerable hardness, varying in color from cinnamon brown to pure white. These

苓 茯

bodies are actually considered to be an altered state of the root of the tree, occasioned by the presence of a fungus whose mycelium penetrates the ligneous substance; these bands of mycelium appear under the microscope to be intertwined with irregular bodies which apparently are the remnants of the ligneous tissue.[40] (Syn. *Pachyma cocos* Wolf.)

The interior portion of this fungous body is odorless and slightly sweet; it is barely soluble in water or cold alcohol but more easily soluble in a dilute solution of sodium carbonate, which when treated with an acid yields a light gelatinous principle, presumably pectin.[153] The American counterpart of this fungus, known variously as tuckahoe, Indian bread, and Virginia truffle, was found to consist of pure pectin.

Employed as diuretic and sedative in the treatment of oliguresis, insomnia, tachycardia, gastrointestinal atony. Dose, 5–10 gm. Incompatibles: *Ampelopsis serjanaefolia, Sanguisorba officinalis, Justicia gendarussa.*

II : PTERIDOPHYTA

EQUISETINAE

草賊木

EQUISETUM HYEMALE L.

(Equisetaceae)

A perennial herb of the horsetail family, known as scouring rush because of its tough, wiry stems which are used for polishing. Stem evergreen, 0.5–1.0 m., simple or slightly branching, swollen between nodes, very rough, with 10–30 even longitudinal furrows, large central cavity. Leaves reduced to sheaths, short, as wide as long, closely set, awl-shaped, teeth 10–30, scariose, after falling leaving a round black projection lined with a ridge provided with protuberant tubercles in two regular rows. Spikes terminal, 8–15 mm. long by 4–6 mm. across, cone-like, ovoid, compact, pointed, bearing spores. North Temperate Zone.

The stems, after having been stripped of their sheaths, are ground to a powder for medicinal use. The taste of the drug is bittersweet and astringent. The plant contains silica, starch, a volatile oil and resin, and equisetic (aconitic) acid. Its action is hemostatic and diuretic.[120]

Used internally as an astringent hemostatic in dysentery, enterorrhagia, hemorrhoidal hemorrhage. Dose, 5–10 gm. Externally, in cataplasm for hemorrhoids and anal fistulae; as ophthalmic lotion in treatment of epiphora, leukoma.

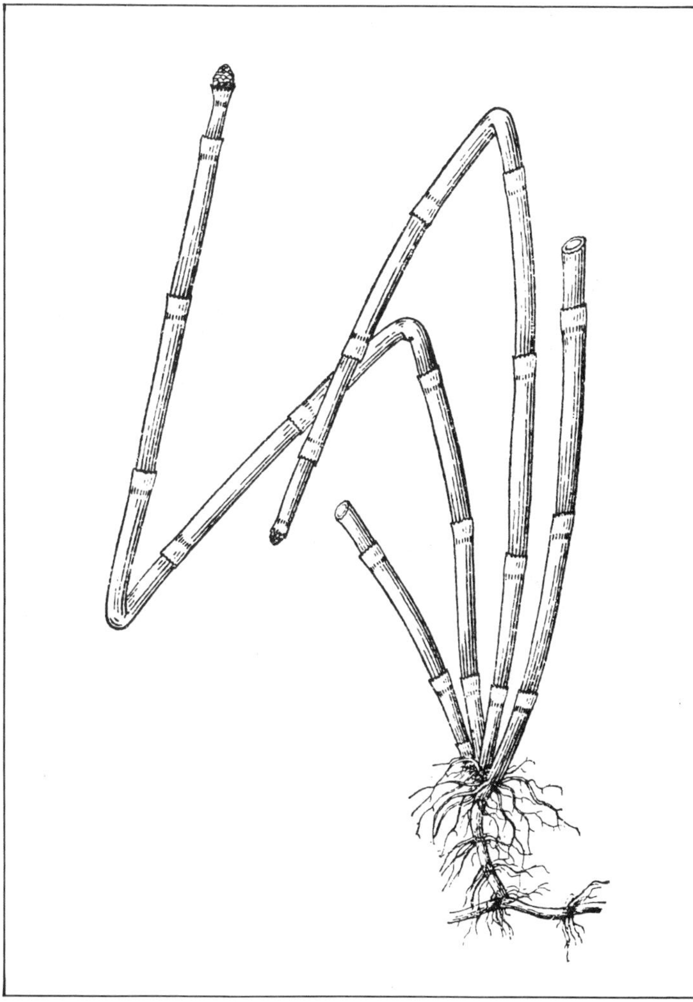

Equisetum hyemale

FILICINAE

沙金海

CIBOTIUM BAROMETZ J. Smith.

(Cyatheaceae)

An arborescent fern. Fronds tripinnate, the inferior pinnae oval-lanceolate, 30–60 cm. long by 16–30 cm. wide. Pinnulae linear-acuminate, segments linear-oblong, acute, nearly falciform. Sori 2–12 per lobe, nearly regular; valves transversal, oblong. Southern China, India, Malaysia. (Syn. *Dicksonia Barometz* Link., *Phrymatodes hastata* Ching)

The root is of a black color, 7–10 cm. long, with many protuberances, resembling the backbone of a dog, the interior of a greenish color. The taste is bittersweet. The rhizomes contain a large amount of starch.[140]

Prescribed as tonic and analgesic in rheumatism, lumbago, myospasm. Dose, 5–10 gm.

(In Japan, *Woodwardia japonica* Sw. is employed.)

DRYNARIA FORTUNEI J. Smith.

(Polypodiaceae)

A polypody with two forms of fronds. The sterile fronds are sessile, without chlorophyll and of a brown color, oval, 5–8 cm. long by 3–6 cm. wide, base cordate, lobate, veins protu-

金毛狗脊

berant. The fertile fronds are green, glabrous, pinnate, 25–40 cm. long; petiole winged; lobes oblong, tip obtuse, 5–8 cm. long, reticulate. Sori rounded, without indusia, numerous. Fructification April–November. Central China. (Syn. *Polypodium fortunei* Kze.)

The thick rhizomes are covered with bright yellow scales. The taste is bitter.

Employed as analgesic in arthralgia, lumbago, myalgia, bruises and contusions. Dose, 5–15 gm.

骨碎補

POLYPODIUM LINGUA Sw.

(Polypodiaceae)

A fern which grows plentifully on rocks and in crevices, known as the tongue fern or felt fern. Rootstock slender, scaly. Fronds 12–15 cm. long, half of which is stalk, broadly lanceolate, undivided, soft and pliable like leather; underside rust-colored, covered with conspicuous, circular spore cases. Southern China, Taiwan, Japan. (Syn. *Niphobolus lingua* Spr., *Cyclophorus lingua* Desv., *Acrostichum lingua* Thunb., *Polycampium lingua* Presl.)

The fronds are employed medicinally. The taste is bitter.

Used as astringent and diuretic in gonorrhea, menorrhagia, urethrorrhagia, cystitis. Dose, 5–10 gm.

LYGODIUM JAPONICUM Sw.

(Schizaeaceae)

A vine-like fern of the family Schizaeaceae. Stem long, slender, climbing. Fronds much-divided, soft, light green;

葦 石

ultimate segments pinnate, about 25 mm. long, variously toothed. Sporangia yellowish brown at maturity. The fronds are collected and dried on sheets of paper; the sand-like spores are collected from the surface of the paper and used medicinally. Asia to Austria.

The spore powder is very fine, yellowish, and ignites like amadou. The taste is bittersweet. The powder contains a fatty oil.[140] It is employed in the treatment of various disorders of the urinary tract.

Employed as antiphlogistic and diuretic in cystitis, urethritis, hematuria, dysuria of gonorrhea, urinary calculus. Dose, 5–10 gm.

III : SPERMATOPHYTA

GYMNOSPERMAE Ginkgoales

銀杏

GINKGO BILOBA L.

(Ginkgoaceae)

The only living representative of the order Ginkgoales, once a widely distributed group throughout the Mesozoic Era. It is a tall, resinous tree, growing to 35 m. Leaves deciduous, alternate, lengthily petiolate, fan-shaped, bilobate, base wedge-shaped, 6–9 cm. broad, turning yellow in autumn; venation dichotomously branching, seemingly parallel. Staminate and ovulate strobuli on separate trees; staminate strobuli consisting of naked pairs of anthers in catkin-like clusters; ovulate strobuli in the form of long, slender, fused stalks bearing a single naked ovule which is fertilized by motile sperm cells, developing into two seeds. Seeds yellow when mature, foul-smelling, drupe-like, the middle layer of integument becoming hard, the outer layer fleshy. China. (Syn. *Salisburia adianthifolia* Smith., *S. macrophylla* C. Koch)

The ripe fruits, macerated in vegetable oil for 100 days, have been used in the treatment of pulmonary tuberculosis in China, but there has not been sufficient indication to classify the drug as specific. The outer fleshy portion of the fruit is very stimulating to the epidermis and mucous membrane, inducing inflammation and exanthema. The kernels are used as aliment in China, however large amounts may be toxic, inducing convulsions, pyreticosis, emesis, and dyspnea.

The kernels are used as astringent, sedative, antitussive in asthma. Dose, 5–10 gm., shelled and cooked. The outer pulp of the fresh fruit is employed as vesicant.

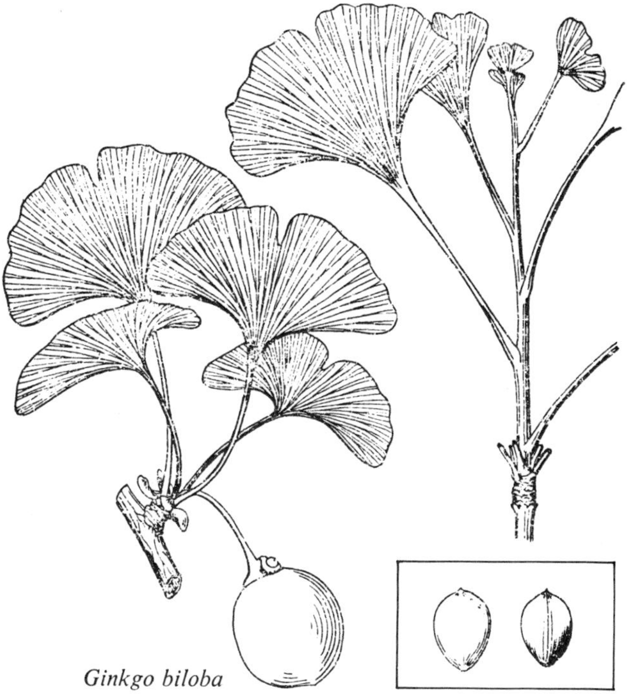

Ginkgo biloba

GYMNOSPERMAE: Coniferales

THUJA ORIENTALIS L.

(Pinaceae)

A shrub pyramidal in form, the branches compressed. Leaves opposite, small, scaly, imbricate, those of the extreme twigs obtuse, those of the larger branches acute or awl-shaped. Flowers monoecious, in catkins, April; male flowers globular, isolated, stamens 3–6; female flowers terminal. Cone ovoid, 1.5–2.5 cm. long, scales 6, spines oval-obtuse; two

側柏葉

seeds per scale, ovoid, brownish; August–September. China, Japan, India. (Syn. *Biota orientalis* Endl., *B. chinensis* Hort., *Thuja chinensis* Hort.)

Both the leaves and the seeds are employed medicinally. The plant contains a volatile oil comprising pinene and caryophyllene; the bitter principle pinipicrin $C_{22}H_{18}O_{11}$; thujin $C_{20}H_{22}O_{12}$, a yellow, astringent and crystallizable coloring principle; tannin; resin. The taste of the leaves is bittersweet and astringent; that of the seeds, sweetish.

The leaves are employed as astringent, antipyretic, emmenagogue. Dose, 5–10 gm. The seeds are used as sedative in neurasthenia, palpitation, insomnia; as lenitive in enterostenosis. Dose, 5–15 gm.

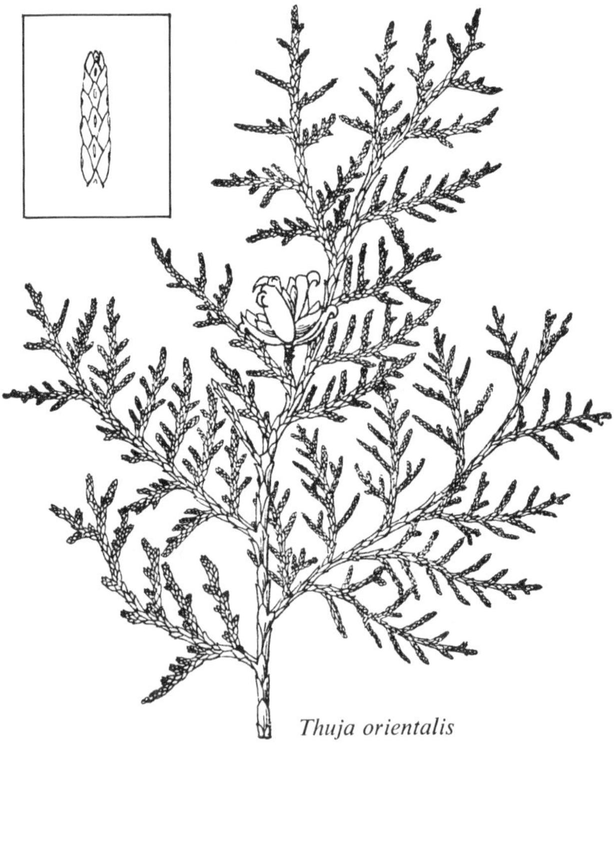

Thuja orientalis

子 榧

TORREYA GRANDIS Fortune

(Taxaceae)

An evergreen tree growing to 20 m., branches yellowish green at 2 years. Leaves stiff, 1.5–2.5 cm. long, nearly round at the base, acute, prickly at the tip, surface lightly convex, dark green, underside marked with 2 discolored streaks, median vein indistinct above. Flowers dioecious; the male in catkins formed of stiff imbricate scales; the female in pairs, axillary, globular, surrounded with 4 large scales, a single terminal ovule. Fruit oblong-elliptical; September. Central China. (Syn *T. nucifera* var. *grandis* Pilger.)

The seeds are elongate, pointed at the tip, round at the base, 35 mm. in length, 15 mm. in diameter, of a light brown color. They contain a large amount of fatty oil, torreyol, which comprises linoleic, oleic, palmitic, and stearic acids. Injected into the lymphatic sac of frogs, the oil induces motor inhibition, paralysis, and death.[70] The oil acts as a nerve poison. An infusion of the seed is anthelmintic to *Ascaris, Enterobius, Taenia*, and *Ancylostoma*.

The seeds are employed as vermifuge. Dose, 10–35 gm.

GYMNOSPERMAE: Gnetales

EPHEDRA SINICA Stapf.

(Gnetaceae)

Ma Huang. An erect or prostrate undershrub, 30–50 cm. tall. Branches erect, short, glaucous green, somewhat flat, 1.0–1.5 mm. thick, lightly striate lengthwise, fasciated at the nodes. Leaves opposite, reduced to scales barely 2 mm. Male flowers pedunculate or nearly sessile, grouped in catkins composed of 4–8 pairs of flowers with about 8 anthers; female flowers biflorous, pedunculate with 3–4 pairs of

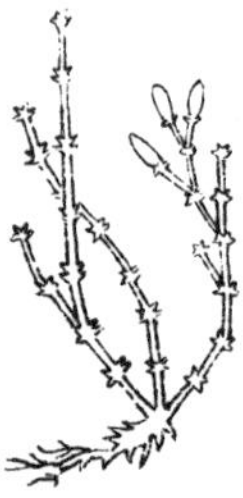

黃 麻

scales. Fruit red, globular, fleshy, 6–7 mm. long. Northern China, Mongolia, Europe. (Syn. *E. distachya* L.)

The roots and stems contain up to 1% of the alkaloid ephedrine $C_{10}H_{15}NO$, along with variable quantities of isomers. Ephedrine dilates the bronchi, stimulates the respiratory center, and acts as a preventive in bronchial asthma.[16] Its vasoconstrictive action shrinks congested mucous membrane. The heart muscle is stimulated, inducing palpitation and hypertension; the blood pressure is raised. It stimulates the cerebral cortex and results in nervous excitability. A 1–2% solution produces mydriasis when applied locally to the iris.

The stem and root are used in bronchial asthma, hay fever, trachitis. Dose, 3–10 gm.

(*E. equisetina* Bunge. is also employed.)

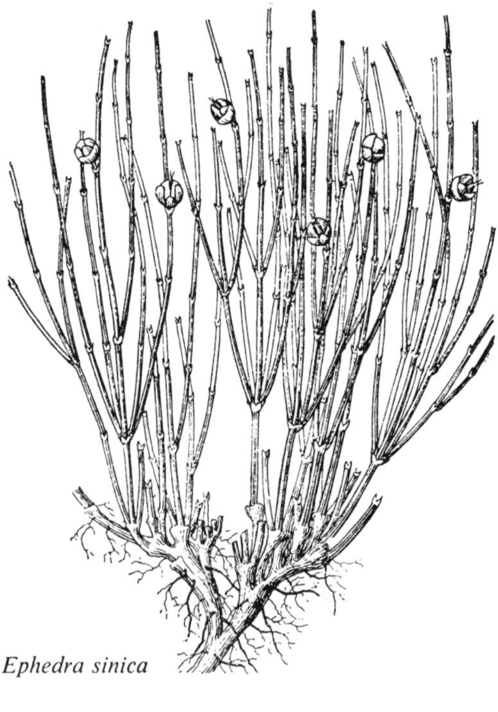

Ephedra sinica

ANGIOSPERMAE **Monocotyledonae**

瀉 澤

ALISMA PLANTAGO L.

(Alismaceae)

Water plantain, a perennial marsh herb 0.1–1.0 m. tall. Stem erect. Leaves basal, petiolate, simple, lanceolate, base cordate or round. Inflorescence in verticillate divisions, large, paniculate, bracteal. Flowers red or white, small; May–September; sepals 3; petals 3, larger than the sepals; stamens 6; carpels numerous, laterally compressed. Seeds glossy, compressed laterally. Northern Hemisphere. (Syn. *A. cordifolia* Thunb.)

The root is officinal. It occurs as ovoid, whitish, with circular depressions. The taste is bitter. It contains a highly volatile oil, 23% starch, and a very acrid resin.[151] An extract of the root increases urinary excretion.[50] The drug is believed by the Chinese to stimulate the female genitalia.[146]

Employed as diuretic. Dose, 5–15 gm.

Alisma plantago

CURCULIGO ENSIFOLIA R. Br.

(Amaryllidaceae)

A biennial herb with a tuberous root. Stem to 40 cm. Leaves basal, petiolate, lanceolate, 15–40 cm. long by 12–35 mm. wide, acuminate at both extremities. Inflorescence sessile, in the floral sheaths. Flowers yellow, close to the ground;

仙茅

perianth tubular with 6 regular lobes; stamens 6; ovary inferior, rostrate, 3-celled; stigmas 3. Fruit bacciform, surmounted with the persistent perianth tube. Southern China, Indochina, India, Malaya. (Syn. *C. malabarica, C. stans* Labill., *C. orchioides* Gaertn., *Hypoxis minor* Seen., *H. orchioides* Kurz.)

The tubercles are used medicinally. They occur the size of the small finger, the epidermis coarse, dark brown, interior yellowish white. The taste is bittersweet and pungent. The drug is slightly poisonous. It contains 4% tannin, fat, resin, and starch.[140]

Used as stimulating tonic in premature senility, to increase virility, for nerve tone, in neurasthenia, also as digestant and to stimulate the appetite. Dose, 4–7 gm.

石蒜

LYCORIS RADIATA Herb.

(Amaryllidaceae)

A perennial, bulbous herb. Leaves basal, developing in spring and dying down in summer. Floral axis appearing in autumn; flowers terminal, red; petals 6; stamens and style protruding. The bulb is tunicate, with black epidermis. China, Japan. (Syn. *Amaryllis radiata* L'Herit., *A. sarniensis* Thunb., *Nerine japonica* Miq.)

The bulb is used medicinally. The taste is sweet and pungent. It is poisonous. The drug contains the alkaloids lycorine $C_{16}H_{17}NO_4$ (white prismatic crystals; m.p. 275°; insoluble in water; slightly soluble in alcohol, ether), lycoramine $C_{17}H_{25}NO_3$ (plates; m.p. 121°; soluble in water, alcohol, acetone), sekisanine $C_{16}H_{19}NO_4$ (crystals; m.p. 207–209°; insoluble in water; soluble in alcohol, ether), and other minor alkaloids.[148] The action of lycorine is similar to that of emetine, with less toxicity and greater emetic action; it is also antipyretic.[140]

Used as expectorant and emetic. Dose, 1.5–3.5 gm.

水仙根

NARCISSUS TAZETTA L. var. CHINENSIS Roem.

(Amaryllidaceae)

Polyanthus narcissus. Leaves basal, flat, linear, about 45 cm. long and 2 cm. wide. Floral stalk appearing in late autumn, the terminal membranous spathe breaking to reveal the flowers. Flowers fragrant, in clusters of 4–8; corolla in 6 segments, white; corona much shorter than the segments, about 2.5 cm. long, pale yellow; stamens 6. China, Japan.

The tunicate bulbs are used medicinally. They occur as ovate or spherical, epidermis black. The taste is bitter; the drug is poisonous. It contains the alkaloids lycorine and tazettine $C_{18}H_{21}NO_5$ (m.p. 210–211°).[151] In animals the drug induces gastralgia, gastroenteritis, accelerated pulse, and pyrexia, larger doses producing convulsions, paralysis, and death; toxic doses in humans induce hidrosis and collapse.[140]

The fresh bulbs are chopped and used externally as antiphlogistic and analgesic to boils, abscesses, mastitis.

石菖蒲

ACORUS GRAMINEUS Ait.

(Araceae)

A perennial marsh herb; rhizome creeping, 0.5–0.75 cm. thick. Leaves sheathed, extending 1.0–1.5 dm. outside the sheath, attaining 3–5 dm. in length by 2–4 mm. in width, green or whitish, without distinct median vein. Scape supporting the axillary inflorescence, a cylindrical spadix. Spadix 0.3–1.0 dm. by 3–4 mm., section above spathe 0.75–2.0 dm. long by 2–3 mm.; perianth in 6 divisions, the outer three larger; stamens 6. Fruit a long berry, 2 mm. thick. Southern China, Japan, Himalayas, India. (Syn. *A. calamus* Lour.)

Acorus gramineus

The rhizomes are officinal. The surface is yellowish brown and marked with longitudinal wrinkles where leaves were attached; the interior shows the scars where the radicles originated. The odor is aromatic. The drug contains 0.5–0.8% essential oil and the bitter principle asarone $C_{12}H_{16}O_3$ (crystals; m.p. 67°, b.p. 296°; insoluble in water; soluble in alcohol, ether, chloroform). The action is similar to that of *A. calamus* L., aiding digestion and regulating gastrointestinal fermentation.[140]

Employed as aromatic bitter and stomachic in dyspepsia and hyperacidity. Dose, 2.5–5.0 gm.

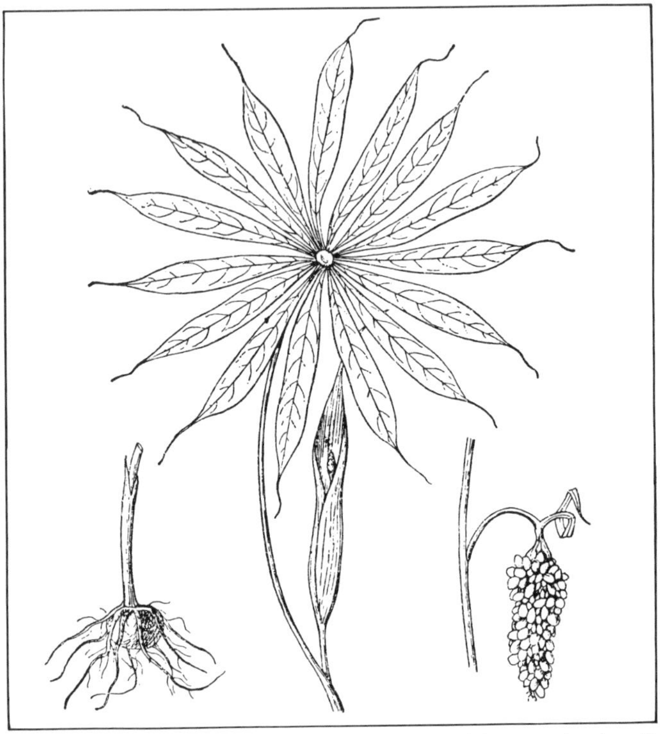

Arisaema thunbergii

星南天

ARISAEMA THUNBERGII Blume.

(Araceae)

A perennial, alpine herb. Leaves 1–2, 11-segmented, the intermediate segment 10 cm. long by 2.5 cm. wide, the lateral segments gradually becoming shorter and narrower; petiole 15–30 cm. long. Peduncle 25 cm. long; spathe an elongate tube 10 cm. long; spadix exceeding the tube by half. Flowers sessile, without perianth; May; stamens 3–4. Northern China, Korea, Japan. (Syn. *Arum dracontium* Thunb.)

The tubercles are used medicinally. They occur as roundish, flat, yellowish brown or whitish; the central portion consists of an umbilicus from which grow other tuberous roots equally containing an umbilicus; the texture is firm. The taste is bitter. The fresh root is very toxic; when cooked the poison dissipates. The tubercles contain a saponin, benzoic acid, and a large amount of starch. The extracted juice of the fresh root, injected into rabbits, induces intense convulsions, paralysis, and death.[140]

A decoction of the fresh root in beef bile is used internally as analgesic and antispasmodic. Dose of the decoction, 3–5 gm. Employed externally for insect bites, abscesses, and swellings.

夏 半

PINELLIA TUBERIFERA Tenore

(Araceae)

A tuberous perennial herb. Petiole often tuberiferous at base and top. Leaflets 3, segments oblong-elliptical, acute at both ends, the middle segment 5.0–7.5 cm. long by 2.5 cm. wide, the lateral segments 4.5 cm. long by 1.0–1.5 cm. wide. Peduncle solitary, 25–30 cm. long. Spathe persistent, cylindrical, narrow, emarginate at the extremity, 5 cm. long, appendix of spadix filiform; May–June. Southern China, Japan. (Syn. *Arum macrourum* Bunge., *A. ternatum* Thunb., *Atherurus, ternatus* Blume., *Pinellia ternata* Tenore)

The tubercles are officinal. They occur as spherical or pyriform, 1–2 cm. thick; the surface is white or yellowish white, with small brown fossettes around the depressed umbilical portion; the interior is perfectly white, solid, and amylaceous. The taste is faintly bitter. The drug contains an essential oil, a fatty oil, phytosterols, and a toxic alkaloid.[76] The alkaloid is similar in sedative and antispasmodic action to coniine; oral administration of the powdered drug restrains apomorphine-induced emesis in dogs.[49]

Used as antiemetic, sedative, antitussive in nausea, pharyngalgia, singultus, chronic gastritis. Dose, 3–7 gm.

Pinellia tuberifera

CYPERUS ROTUNDUS L.

(Cyperaceae)

A perennial grass-like herb, 20–40 cm. tall, glabrous. Rhizomes slender, swollen here and there with blackish, ovoid-oblong tubercles 1 cm. in diameter. Stem slender, erect. Leaves numerous, 5–15 cm. long by 2–6 mm. broad, carinate. Inflorescence umbelliferous; pedicels 4–10, erect, very irregular. Spikelets reddish brown, linear, 10–20 mm. by 1–2 mm., in short umbelliferous fascicles; axis winged. Scales densely imbricate, nearly acute, faintly veined, the margin

附 香

pale. Stamens and stigmas 3; June–October. Achene triquetrous, half as long as the scale. Asia, Australia, southern Europe, America.

The tubercles are 5 cm. long, reddish brown, marked with circular parallel rings, the epidermis fibrous; the interior is white, ligneous; the odor and taste are slightly aromatic.[153] They contain 0.5% of an essential oil comprising cyperene, cyperol, cyperone, pinene, and sesquiterpenes.[151]

Used as aromatic stomachic in nervous gastralgia, dyspepsia, diarrhea; as emmenagogue, sedative, and analgesic in dysmenorrhea, amenorrhea, chronic metritis. Dose, 5–8 gm.

Cyperus rotundus

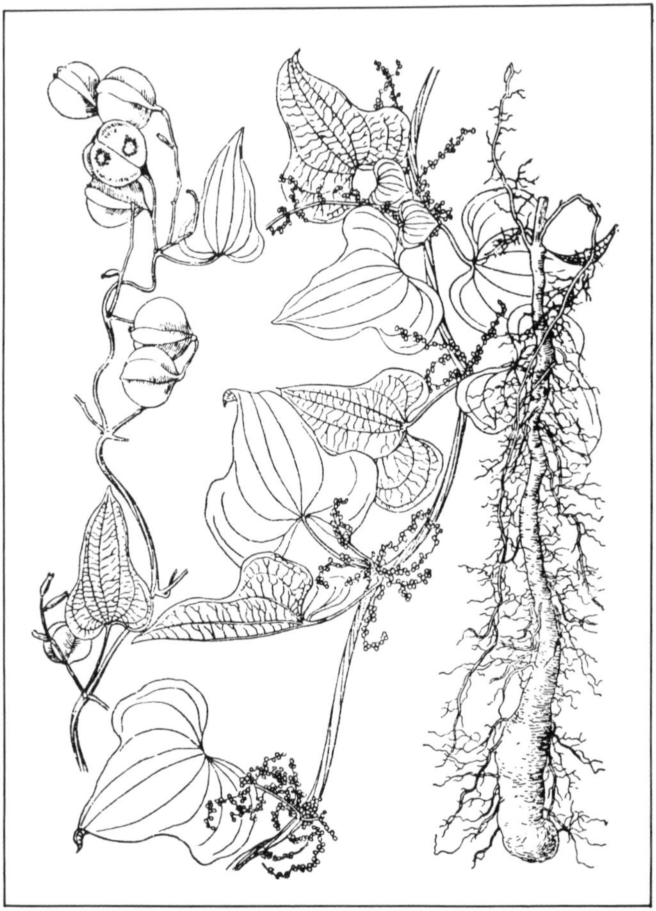

Discorea batas

DIOSCOREA JAPONICA Thunb.

(Dioscoreaceae)

The Chinese yam. Root tuberous, flat, more or less ramiform. Stem volubilate, angular. Leaves opposite, petiolate,

山藥

rarely alternate, oval or oblong, entire, deeply cordate, auricles lightly oblique, 8 cm. by 5–6 cm., acuminate, with numerous glands, petiole 4–5 cm. long. Flowers dioecious, in axillary spikes, solitary or geminate; September–October; male flowers with perianth in 6 segments, stamens 6; female in 6 segments, ovary inferior, 3-celled. Capsule triquetrous, compressed, winged. China, Japan.

The tubers contain 16% starch, mucilage, amylase, albuminoid matter, fat, sugar, amino acids (arginine, leucine, and tyrosine), and glutamine.[140, 151]

The tubers are employed as a nutrient tonic and digestant in chronic enteritis and diarrhea; also prescribed in nocturnal enuresis, spermatorrhea, neurasthenia. Dose, 10–30 gm.

(*D. batatas* Decne. is similarly employed.)

薏苡仁

COIX LACRYMA-JOBI L.

(Graminae)

Job's tears. An annual grass 1–2 m. high, the stem branching. Leaves 10–40 cm. long, 2–4 cm. wide, lanceolate-acuminate, margin coarse, auriculate, ligule very short. Spikelets monoecious, in panicles consisting of pedunculate spikes, partly concealed in the leafy sheaths; August. Male biflorous, numerous, at the end of the spike. Female uniflorous, solitary at the base of the spike, enclosed in a hard involucre, ovoid-conical, bluish white, glossy, 8 mm. long, narrowly open at the top. Glumes and glumelles nearly regular, stamens 3, stigmas terminal, rather short. Caryopsis hemispherical. Central and western China, India, tropical Africa, America. (Syn. *C. agrestis* Lour., *C. chinensis* Tod., *C. lachryma* L.)

The seeds are globular, split longitudinally, 5 mm. long, 4 mm. in diameter, white. They contain 52% starch, 7% fat, a sterol, vitamin B, and 17% protein including the amino acids leucine, tyrosine, lycine, glutamic acid, arginine, and histidine.[68]

An infusion of the seeds is considered nutritive, refrigerant, and diuretic; it is prescribed in bronchitis, pulmonary abscess, pleurisy, hydrothorax. Dose, 10–25 gm. An alcohol fermented from the seeds is considered antirheumatic.

白茅根

IMPERATA CYLINDRICA Beauv.

(Graminae)

A perennial grass, the stalk 30–90 cm. high, thick. Sheath rather loose, glabrous. Leaves linear, erect, 15–30 cm. long by 3–6 cm. wide, rigid, acuminate, surface scabrous, the underside smooth. Ligule short, ciliate. Panicle spiciform, 5–20 cm. long, slender, compact, silvery; June. Spikelets in pairs, each with two flowers of which only one is fertile, the other reduced to a glumelle, 3–4 mm. long, covered with very long, flexible hairs. Glumes longer than the flowers, dentate, glabrous; glumelles fringed at the top. Stamens 2. Southern China, India, Sri Lanka, Indochina, Japan, Africa, Oceania. (Syn. *I. arundinaceae* Cyrill., *Lagurus cylindricus* L.)

The root, flowers, and young sprouts are all used in the Chinese pharmacopoeia. "The root is white, very long, flexible like a tendon, provided with joints, and of a sweet taste."[138] "The sprouts are edible and are good for children."[142]

The root is employed as antipyretic, diuretic, and hemostatic. Dose, 10–35 gm. The flowers are used in hemoptysis and epistaxis of pulmonary disease. Dose, 5–10 gm. The young shoots are diuretic. Dose, 5–10 gm.

Coix lacryma-jobi

Imperata cylindrica

糯米

ORYZA SATIVA L.

(Graminae)

Common rice. An annual, water-inhabiting grass with a fibrous root. Stem erect, 50 cm.–1.5 m. high, smooth, angled, mostly hidden in the long leaf-sheaths. Leaves 15–30 cm. long, attaining 2 cm. in width, rough, with oblong ligule, entire or divided. Inflorescence paniculate, branches erect, reaching 25 cm. in length; June–September. Spikelets hermaphrodite, uniflorous, compressed laterally, villous, caducous, 7–9 mm. long; glumes very small, nearly regular, lanceolate, single-veined; glumelles large, very cartilaginous, nearly regular, carinate, the inferior often mucronate or aristate, 5-veined, the superior 3-veined; stamens 6; stigmas exserted laterally. Caryopsis yellowish white, oblong, compressed, narrowly enclosed in the glumelles. Cultivated in the Old and New World.

The germinated seeds contain 90% starch, the highest of all the cereals, and vitamins A, B, C, D, and E.[151] Rice is taken freely as stomachic and tonic. The rootlets are also officinal, being astringent and anhidrotic. Dose, 10–20 gm.

蘆根

PHRAGMITES COMMUNIS Trin.

(Graminae)

Reed grass. A perennial marsh grass, 1–4 m. tall, glabrate, rhizomes creeping. Leaves 30–50 cm. long and 1–3 cm. wide, margin coarse, ligule consisting of a row of short regular hairs. Panicle terminal, 10–30 cm. long, compact, erect, purplish brown or reddish, often blackish. Spikelets 10–12 mm. long, flowers 2–7; glumes very irregular, entire, lanceolate-acute, glabrous, shorter than the flowers; stamens 1–3. Caryopsis oblong. Cosmopolitan. (Syn. *Arundo phragmites* L.)

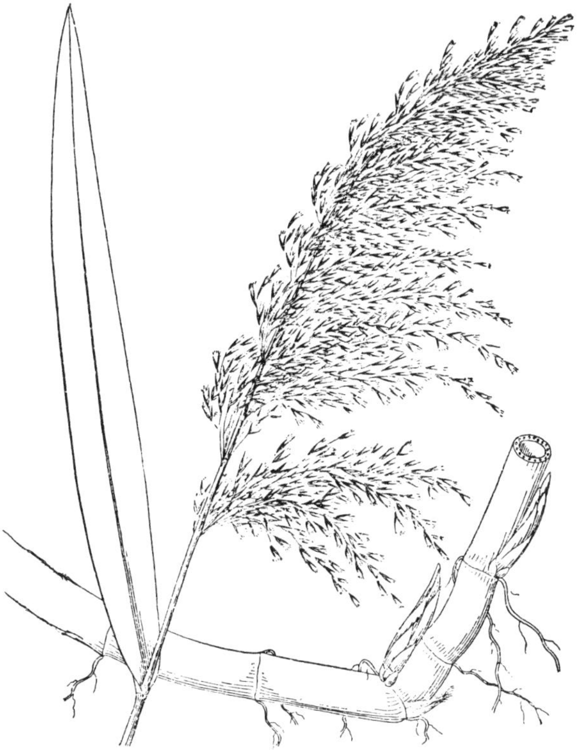

Phragmites communis

The root is used medicinally. "The root is like that of the bamboo, but the joints are at a greater distance apart; that part of the root which is below the water, in the mud, is sweet and pungent; that which is in the water is not good for use."[142] The root contains 51% glycosides, 5% protein, 0.1% asparagin.[151]

Employed as stomachic, antiemetic, antipyretic; in acute arthritis, jaundice, pulmonary abscess, food poisoning. Dose, 20–40 gm.

竹葉

PHYLLOSTACHYS (gen.)

(Graminae)

Various of the bamboo-like grasses of the above genera are used medicinally by the Chinese, especially *P. nigra* Munro. var. *henonis Mak*. and *P. bambusoide* S. et Z. The roots are considered astringent, styptic, and antipyretic. The leaves are antipyretic and diuretic, decoctions being prescribed in stomatitis, pharyngitis, head and chest colds. The epidermis of the young stems is regarded as sedative and antiemetic. The extracted juice of the stem is used as sedative and antipyretic in catarrhal, bronchial, and cerebral infections. Young shoots of the bamboo were found to contain 0.23% benzoic acid.[36] Siliceous concretions which occur inside the inferior internodes, and which are known as *tabaschir*, are also esteemed medicinally. They often attain the size of a chicken egg, are opaque, angular, hard but fragile. This concretion contains 70–90% silica, 1.1% potassium hydroxide, 0.9% aluminum oxide, 0.9% iron oxide, calcium.[140] It is used as antipyretic and antispasmodic in catarrh, infantile chorea, paralysis, rheumatism.

Dose of the leaves or epidermis, 7–10 gm. Of the succus, 35–70 gm. Of the tabaschir, 5–10 gm.

浮小麥

TRITICUM VULGARE Vill.

(Graminae)

Common wheat. An annual grass 8–15 cm., with fibrous roots. Leaves flat, abruptly acuminate, 30–40 cm. long by 13 mm.; sheaths smooth; ligules short, truncate. Floral spike erect, bent at maturity, more or less compact, rarely loose. Spikelets sessile, solitary, imbricate on the two sides opposite the rachis, compressed laterally, ovoid, glabrous or villous, whitish or reddish, containing 3–5 flowers, most often 4, the topmost sterile. Glumes 1 cm., shorter than the flowers situated directly above, nearly regular, broadly oval, corpulent, truncate, rounded on the back to one-half their height, carinate at top only. Glumelles corpulent; one oval-rounded on the back, carinate at the top, laterally compressed, venation faint near the base; the other two with ciliate carina. Stamens 3, ovary villous at top. Caryopsis free, oval or oblong villous at top, internal side furrowed. (Syn. *Triticum sativum* Lam.)

The entire wheat kernel contains 13.8 % protein, 1.9 % fat, 71.9 % carbohydrate, vitamins A, B, E, and G, 1.6 % ash.[154]

Wheat is prescribed by the Chinese as sedative and antipyretic in night sweats and insomnia. Dose, 15–30 gm. Infusions of the bran of wheat are given in diarrhea, hematuria, and high fever.[153]

干 射

BELAMCANDA CHINENSIS DC.

(Iridaceae)

Blackberry lily, leopard flower. A perennial herb with creeping rhizome. Stem erect, 0.6–1.2 m. tall. Leaves sword-shaped, shortly sheathed, 30 cm. long by 2–3 cm. wide. Inflorescence a dichotomous corymb, 20–40 cm. long; August–October; spathes multiflorous; pedicels articulate at the top; bracts scariose. Perianth rotate, in 6 unguiculate segments, light yellow spotted with red; stamens 3, shorter than the perianth; ovary 3-celled; stigmas 3. Fruit an obovoid capsule, 3-valved, 23–25 mm. long. Seeds blackish blue, globular, 5 mm. in diameter, glossy. Southern China, Japan, Korea, northern Vietnam, Laos. (Syn. *B. punctata* Moench., *Ixia chinensis* L., *Pardanthus chinensis* Van Houtte, *Moraea chinensis* Thunb.)

The rhizomes are flat, divaricate, brownish, carrying scars of the resinous stem on the surface. The taste of the fresh drug is acid; it is poisonous. It contains shikanin; belamcandin $C_{24}H_{24}O_{12}$; and iridin $C_{24}H_{28}O_{13}$.[113]

The rhizome is employed as expectorant, antipyretic, stomachic, purgative; in throat and upper respiratory inflammations, pharyngitis, tonsillar abscess; in constipation, dyspepsia, asthma, halitosis. Dose, 3–6 gm.

燈芯

JUNCUS EFFUSUS L.

(Juncaceae)

Bog rush. A perennial herb 40–80 cm. high, green, the rhizomes running. Stem grass-like, glossy when fresh, becoming striate upon drying, easily broken, pith continuous, rarely hollow. Leaves reduced to basilar, reddish sheaths, not glossy. Flowers greenish, in a lateral, ramose panicle, more or less loose and diffuse, arranged on upper part of stem; perianth in acute lanceolate divisions; stamens 3. Capsule obovoid, truncate-flattened, without mammilla at top, greenish, slightly shorter than the perianth. Cosmopolitan. (Syn. *J. communis* Mey.)

The pith is officinal. It contains arabinose and xylan.[151] Used as diuretic and antiphlogistic. Dose, 5–10 gm.

大蒜

ALLIUM ODORUM L.

(Liliaceae)

Chinese chive. Bulbs clustered, conical, nearly cylindrical, with a fibrous, reticulate envelope. Stalk cylindrical or angular at top, leaved at the base, 15–50 cm. high. Leaves narrowly linear or linear-flat, carinate near the top, 1–6 mm. wide. Inflorescence umbelliferous, spathe scariose, whitish, shortly mucronate, eventually divided or lacerate, shorter than the pedicel. Pedicel filiform, angular, two to four times longer than the perianth, attaining 2 cm., 3 cm. during fructification. Perianth whitish, in 6 petaloid divisions. Stamens 6; ovary superior, nearly globular, trigonal. Fruit obovoid, obcordiform. China, Tibet, Japan, western Nepal. (Syn. *A. uliginosum* G. Don., *A. tuberosum* Roxb., *A. chinense* Max., *A. tartaricum* Ait.)

The bulbs of the genus *Allium* contain a volatile oil consisting mainly of diallyl sulfide $(C_3H_5)_2S$, upon which the bactericidal action depends. The oil has been shown to be

Juncus effusus

Allium bakeri

strongly effective against various microorganisms; it increases gastric and intestinal secretion.[137] It acts as a tonic and carminative, and is supposed to have a special influence upon bronchial secretion.[150] Large doses often produce gastric irritation, hemorrhoids, headache, and fever.

The bulbs are employed as tonic and stomachic, and as bactericide in the treatment of amebic and bacillary dysentery, pertussis, tuberculosis, and cutaneous diseases. Dose, 5–10 gm.

(Also used, *A. scorodoprasum* L., *A. bakeri, A. fistulosum* L.)

薈 蘆

ALOE VERA L.

(Liliaceae)

Curaçao aloe, Barbados aloe. A stemless succulent plant. Leaves basal, in a rosette, grayish green, 30–60 cm. long, erect, juicy, margins spinose. Flowers yellow, 2.5 cm. long, tubular, the tip separated into spreading segments, in a dense nodding cluster on a stalk somewhat longer than the leaves. Fruit a triquetrous capsule. Africa, West Indies, India, Mediterranean.

Aloes is the inspissated juice of the leaves. It occurs as irregular solidified pieces 2 cm. thick by 3 cm. long, of waxy texture, the surface dull, color varying from orange brown to blackish brown. The odor is strongly aromatic, the taste very bitter and pungent. It contains anthraquinone derivatives, especially aloins (18–25%), which yield emodin upon cleavage in the intestine. Doses of 10–30 mg. act as a bitter stomachic; 60–200 mg. as laxative; 300–1,000 mg. as purgative. It is moderately irritating, and has a tendency to cause griping; it does not lose its efficiency on continued use, and is especially useful in correcting constipative action of iron medication.[152]

Prescribed as laxative, stomachic, emmenagogue.

Anemarrhena asphodeloides

知母

ANEMARRHENA ASPHODELOIDES Bunge.

(Liliaceae)

An herbaceous plant with thick rhizome. Leaves basal, linear, 20 cm. long by 5 cm. wide. Stalk 1 m., simple, terminated by a long spiciform cluster of small flowers; October. Flowers purplish inside, yellowish on the exterior, odoriferous, opening in the evening. Pedicel very short; perianth pink, in 6 divisions in 2 rows, lightly united at the base, 3-veined, radiating. Stamens 5, with a very short filament; ovary 3-celled, style filiform. Fruit a hexagonal capsule; seeds 1–2, triangular, black. Northern China.

The rhizomes occur as flat pieces 10 cm. long by 18 mm. thick, covered with reddish or yellowish erect hairs. The interior is yellow, fleshy. The odor is pleasant, the taste bitter. The rhizomes contain the saponin asphonin, which has been shown to be antipyretic.[52] The drug is toxic in large doses, due to inhibition of the nerve centers. In small doses there is no action on the heart, while moderate doses weaken the contraction. A large amount of mucilage is present in the drug.[140]

Prescribed as antipyretic and expectorant in typhoid fever, scarlet fever, pneumonia, chronic bronchitis, pulmonary tuberculosis. Dose, 3–7 gm. Iron preparations are incompatible.

天門冬

ASPARAGUS LUCIDUS Lindl.
(Liliaceae)

Shiny asparagus. A much branching, creeping undershrub. Branches cylindrical, with numerous midribs barely projecting; spines reflected, 6 mm. and longer, thicker at the base. Branchlets slender, deeply furrowed, without spines; cladophylls flat, linear, barely arched, 15–25 mm. by 1.0–1.5 mm., finely acuminate, arranged in pairs, the median midrib apparent. Flowers polygamous, white, solitary or in pairs, rarely 3, in the axils of the cladophylls. Perianth in 6 linear-navicular segments, 3.5 mm. long by 6 mm. wide; stamens 6; ovary amphora-like; style very short; stigmas deltoid, extended. Fruit a white berry, globular, 7 mm. in diameter; seed globular, black, finely vermiculate, 4 mm. in diameter. Southern China, Japan. (Syn. *A. falcatus* Benth., *A. insularis* Hance.)

The roots are officinal. They occur as translucid, yellowish pieces 7–8 cm. long. The taste is bitter. The drug contains asparagin, starch, sucrose, and mucilage.[140]

Used as diuretic and expectorant. Dose, 5–10 gm.

Asparagus lucidus

母 貝

FRITILLARIA VERTICILLATA Willd.
(Liliaceae)

A bulbous perennial. Bulb with 2 thick scales, orbicular. Stem 30–60 cm. Leaves verticillate, 6–12 mm. long by 2–5 mm. wide, the superior leaves curled at the tips like tendrils. Flowers axillary, solitary, drooping; pedicel short; perianth campanulate, in 6 segments, greenish yellow with purplish spots; style barely longer than the ovary; stigmas 3. Fruit a capsule, 6-lobed, winged. Central China, Japan. (Syn. *F.*

thunbergii Miq., *F. collicola* Hance., *Uvularia cirrhosa* Thunb.)

The bulbs are used medicinally, occurring in the Chinese pharmacy as white fragments 4.5 cm. long. They contain the alkaloids verticin ($C_{18}H_{33}NO_2$ or $C_{19}H_{35}NO_2$; m.p. 224°), verticillin ($C_{19}H_{33}NO_2$; m.p. 149–150°), fritillin ($C_{25}H_{41}NO_3 \cdot H_2O$; m.p. 214°), and fritillarin ($C_{19}H_{33}NO_2$; m.p. 130–131°). The alkaloids are toxic, inducing paralysis of the central nervous system, with inhibition of respiratory and autonomic functions; the action upon respiratory movement is similar to that of morphine; lethal doses produce cardio-inhibition and hypotension.[119]

Used as antitussive and expectorant in chronic trachitis, bronchitis, bronchial asthma. Dose, 5–10 gm.

(Also used, *F. roylei* Hook., *F. maximowiczii* Freyn)

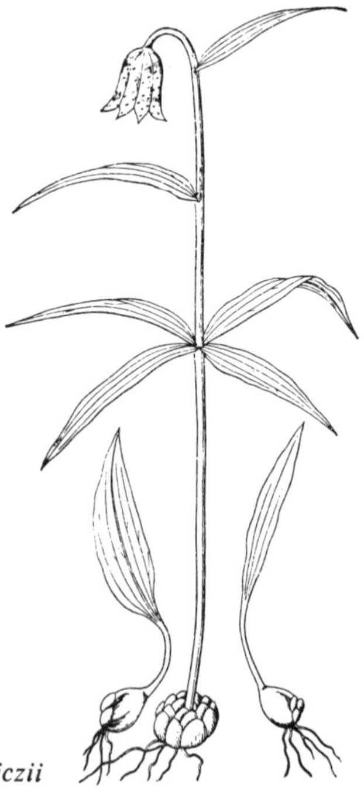

Fritillaria maximowiczii

土茯苓

SMILAX CHINA L.

(Liliaceae)

China root. A climbing shrub, the stem provided with thorns. Leaves alternate, oval or orbiculate, 0.6 cm. long, cartilaginous and shiny, with tendrils at the base of the petiole. Flowers small, very numerous, in axillary umbels, solitary, dioecious, yellow green; summer. Perianth in 6 free segments. In the male flower, 6 stamens; in the female, 6 staminodes. Ovary 3-celled. Fruit a berry, red at maturity, spherical. China, Taiwan, Korea, eastern India, Nepal. (Syn. *S. ferox* Wall, *S. japonica* A. Gray, *Coprosmanthus japonicus* Kunth.)

The roots are officinal, occurring in pieces 15–20 cm. long, 4–5 cm. thick, generally flat, more or less gnarled, brown on the outside, pinkish white inside, the texture sometimes light and spongy, sometimes compact and very hard, sometimes resinous. The drug is odorless and slightly bitter. It contains the crystalline saponin smilacin ($C_{45}H_{74}O_{17}$; soluble in water and hot alcohol), tannin, and resin.[151]

Employed as alterative and diuretic in syphilis, gout, skin disorders, rheumatism.

(In Japan, *Heterosmilax japonica* Kunth. is used.)

麥門冬

LIRIOPE SPICATA Lour.

(Liliaceae)

Creeping lily-turf. A perennial herb with a short, thick root-stock. Leaves bushy, stiff, 30 cm. long by 5 mm. wide. Floral stalk simple, rigid, angular, greenish violet, longer than the leaves. Flowers terminal, violet-blue, showy; September. Pedicel rarely solitary, slightly longer than the flowers, erect, articulate with the flowers; bracts herbaceous, acuminate; perianth in 6 segments, free, regular; stamens 6, shorter than the perianth; ovary orbiculate, depressed. Fruit a blue berry,

Liriope spicata

ovoid-subglobular; seeds few. China, Japan. (Syn. *L. graminifolia* Bak., *Draceana graminifolia* L., *Convallaria spicata* Thunb., *Fluggea spicata* Schult, *Ophiopogon japonicus* Wall., *Oph. longifolius* Decne., *Oph. spicatus* Ker-Gawl., *Oph. gracilus* Kunth.)

The rhizomes are used, occurring as oblong, 4 cm. long, 5 mm. in diameter, light yellow. They contain mucilage.[140]

Used as antitussive, expectorant, and emollient. Dose, 5–10 gm.

休 蚤

PARIS POLYPHYLLA Smith

(Liliaceae)

A perennial plant with annulate root. Stem 75–90 cm. high. Leaves verticillate 4–9, petiolate, oblong or lanceolate, acuminate, generally rounded at the base, 7.5–15.0 cm. long. Perianth in 4–7 segments; the exterior segments oval-lanceolate, acuminate, green; the interior segments filiform, yellow. Stamens fairly numerous; ovary nearly globular. Fruit a green capsule, glabrous, 6 cm. in diameter, valves 3–6; seeds elongate, ovoid, scarlet. China, Himalayas.

The roots occur in the pharmacy in pieces 4 cm. long, curved, with numerous purplish brown rootlets, the exterior nearly black, the interior pinkish. They contain 7.9% sucrose, the crystalline glycoside paridine, and the amorphous glycoside paris-typhnine.[151] The physiological action of the amorphous glycoside is considerable, being analagous to that of paraptiphnine isolated from *P. quadrifolia.*[27] The drug is poisonous.

Employed as antipyretic, antispasmodic in typhoid fever, encephalitis, meningitis. Dose, 1–3 gm. as powder, 5–7 gm. in decoction.

精 黃

POLYGONATUM CIRRHIFOLIUM Royle

(Liliaceae)

A perennial herb with thick, branching rootstocks. Stem supple, undulate, 6–12 cm. tall. Leaves alternate, sessile, membranous, oblong, acuminate, 7.5–12.0 cm. long. Flowers axillary, grouped in twos or fours; perianth nearly cylindrical, white, greenish or purple; limb in 6 lobes; ovary 3-celled. Fruit a globular berry of variable size. Northern China, Himalayas. (Syn. *P. chinense* Kunth., *P. sibiricum* Baker., *Convallaria cirrhifolia* Wall)

"The root is soft, of a yellow color, its lower part red. It has some resemblance to young ginger root, is very sweet and of a pleasant taste. It is dug up in the second month, boiled, and dried in the sun."[142]

The root is used as tonic. Dose, 7–10 gm.

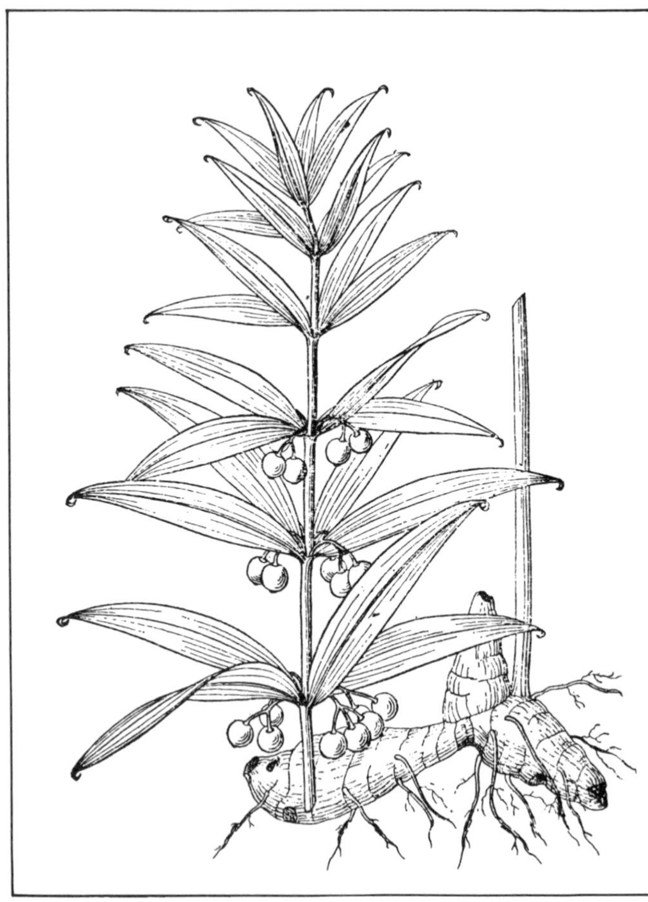

Polygonatum cirrhifolium

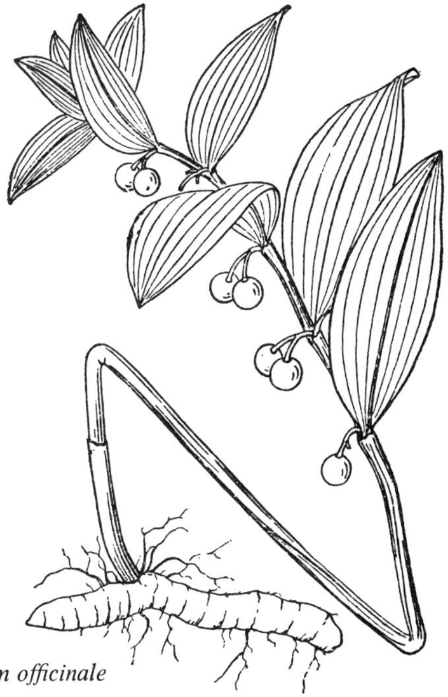

Polygonatum officinale

蕤 萎

POLYGONATUM OFFICINALE All.

(Liliaceae)

Solomon's seal. A perennial herb, the stem simple, erect, angular, 25–50 cm. tall. Leaves alternate, nearly sessile, oval or oblong. Flowers greenish white, odoriferous, in clusters hanging from short peduncles; April–May. Perianth with cylindrical tube and limb in 6 lobes, 2 cm. long by 5–8 mm. across, attenuate at the base; ovary 3-celled. Fruit a globular berry; seeds few. Northwestern China, Asia, Europe. (Syn. *P. vulgare* Desf., *Convallaria polygonatum* L.)

The rhizomes occur as pieces 14–15 cm. long by 15 cm.

wide, pale yellow, translucid, articulate, fleshy. The taste is sweetish. The drug contains the glycosides convallarin ($C_{34}H_{62}O_{11}$; yellowish white amorphous powder; taste acrid; soluble in alcohol, insoluble in water) and convallamarin ($C_{23}H_{44}O_{12}$; yellowish amorphous powder; taste bitter; soluble in water and dilute alcohol), and a large amount of mucilage.[140] The cardiac action of convallamarin is analogous to that of digitalis; it stimulates the appetite without impairing digestion, increases peristalsis without producing catharsis, slows the heart and raises the arterial tension, slows and deepens respiration; convallarin is a drastic purgative in 3-grain doses.[150]

Prescribed as tonic. Dose, 5–10 gm.

山慈姑

TULIPA EDULIS Bak.

(Liliaceae)

Edible tulip. A perennial herb, the bulb tunicate, oval, 1.5 cm. long. Leaves basal, linear, acute, attaining 30 cm. Scape erect, with 2 or 3 verticillate bracts. Flowers solitary, terminal, erect, 2.5 cm. in diameter; March–April. Perianth in 6 segments, extended, white striate with purple, lanceolate, acute; stamens 6, shorter than the perianth; ovary oblong; stigmas 3, short, thick. Fruit an oblong capsule; seeds numerous. Northern China, Japan. (Syn. *T. graminifolia* Bak., *Orithia oxypetala* Gray)

The bulbs occur 2–3 cm. in diameter. They contain the alkaloid tulipine.[140] Tulipine is closely related to solanine and colchicine.[152] The white interior portion of the bulb is employed in Chinese medicine.

Used as antipyretic and antidote in the treatment of ulcers, abscesses, boils, scrofula, insect bites. Dose, 3–6 gm.

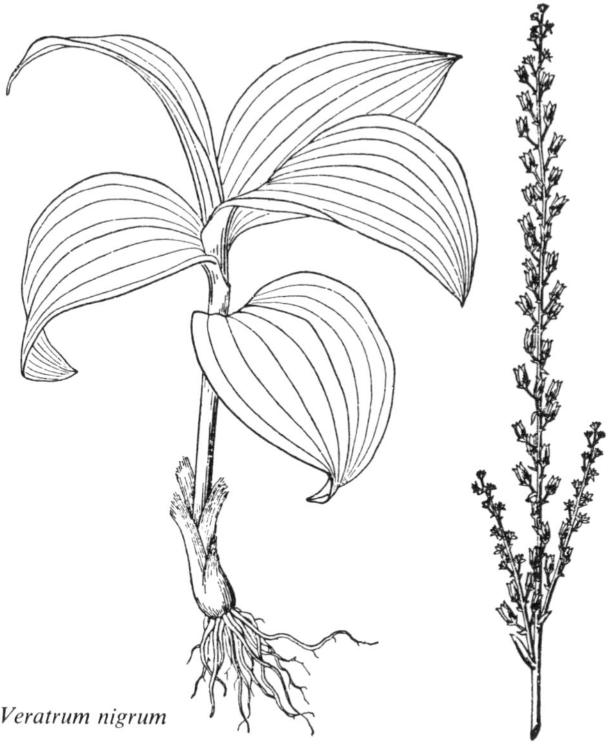

Veratrum nigrum

蘆 藜

VERATRUM NIGRUM L.

(Liliaceae)

A rhizomatous perennial herb, pubescent, 1 m. high. Pseudo-stem consisting of tubular sheaths of the leaves applied one upon the other. Leaves large, plicate, glabrous, the inferior leaves oval or oblong-elliptical, attenuate; petiole short, clasping. Bracts lanceolate-linear, shorter than the pedicel. Flowers blackish purple, pedicellate, in loose clusters, tomentose, forming a long narrow panicle; July–August. Perianth in regular divisions, elliptical, entire, nearly equalling the pedicel. Ovary slightly depressed in the floral axis, 3-celled. Alpine northeastern China, northern China, Europe. (Syn. *Melanthium nigrum* Thunb.)

The root, which is poisonous, contains the alkaloids jervine ($C_{27}H_{39}NO_3$; needles), pseudojervine ($C_{29}H_{43}NO_7$; colorless hexagonal plates; m.p. 304°; soluble in alcohol; nearly insoluble in water, ether), and rubijervine ($C_{26}H_{43}NO_2 \cdot H_2O$; crystals; m.p. 240–246°; soluble in alcohol, chloroform; insoluble in water).[151] Jervine slows the heart rate, then increases it, lowers the blood pressure progressively, presumably by depression of the cardiac muscle and vasomotor center, respiration failing simultaneously; rubijervine acts mainly on the respiratory center, with some cardiac depression, it is emeto-cathartic; pseudojervine is inactive physiologically.[152] The drug is a powerful sternutament.[140]

Used as emetic, and in apoplexy. Dose, 2–4 gm.

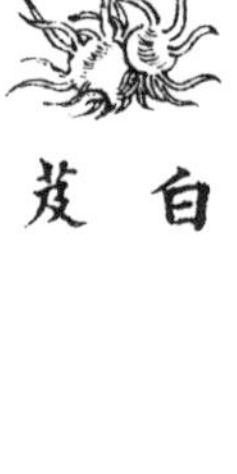

芨 白

BLETILLA HYACINTHINA R. Br.

(Orchidaceae)

A perennial orchid 20–30 cm. tall. Stem thickened at the base into a flat tubercle consisting of several internodes. Leaves 3–4, 9–18 cm. long by 1–2 cm. wide, plicate, linear or lanceolate, without evident petiole. Inflorescence a terminal cluster with 3–6 flowers; April–May. Flowers violet-pink, sepals and petals nearly similar, erect, showy. Labium deeply trilobate, the middle lobe more purplish, with 5–7 undulating crests. Column slender, white at the base, purplish at the tip; anther convex, operculate. China, Indochina. (Syn. *B. striata* Reichb., *Limodorum striatum* Thunb., *Epidendrum tuberosum* Lour., *E. striatum* Thunb., *Cymbidium hyacinthinum* Sm., *C. striatum* Sw., *Gyas humilis* Salib.)

The pseudobulbs are oblong, flat, hard, yellow, 5–6 cm. long, carrying traces of the stem in the form of an umbilicus consisting of several concentric circles. The taste is bitter. The drug contains mucilage, essential oil, glycogen.[140]

The pseudobulbs are powdered and mixed with sesame oil, and used externally as emollient for burns and skin disorders.

斛 石

DENDROBIUM NOBILE Lindl.

(Orchidaceae)

A perennial alpine epiphyte. Stem erect, compressed, yellowish, rather deeply furrowed, 30–60 cm. high. Leaves oblong, 7–10 cm. long, coriaceous, persistent 2 years. Inflorescence a cluster of 2–4 flowers, white or purple; sepals oblong-linear; petals much larger; labium broadly oval, oblong, pubescent; anther truncate in front, 4 pollen sacs in compressed pairs. Northwestern China, Himalayas, Laos. (Syn. *Epidendrum monile* Thunb).

The stem contains dendrobine ($C_{16}H_{25}NO_2$; colorless crystals; m.p. 134°; soluble in ether, acetone, alcohol, chloroform; insoluble in water).[151] The analgesic action of dendrobine upon frogs is slight but definite; it induces faint hyperglycemia and lowers the blood pressure; it augments salivary secretion.[14 51]

Prescribed as secretagogue and salivant in fever and dehydration, as sedative in arthritis. Dose, 5–10 gm.

天麻

GASTRODIA ELATA Blume.

(Orchidaceae)

An alpine perennial herb with tuberous root. Stem simple, erect, 9–12 cm. high, bluish red, provided on its upper part with sheathing scales, the interior hollow. Inflorescence a terminal cluster; flowers numerous, yellowish red, small, the pedicel short. Bracts longer than the flowers, acuminate; sepals nearly regular, acute; lobes lateral, rounded; column erect with 2 teeth at its extremity. Western China, Tibet, Korea, Japan.

"The root is dug up in the 5th month and dried in the sun; the principal root is connected with 12 secondary tubers of various sizes."[139] The taste is acrid.

The tubercles are prescribed as tonic in vertigo, headache, myoneuralgia, rheumatism. Dose, 5–10 gm.

檳榔

ARECA CATECHU L.

(Palmae)

Betel palm. A graceful, slender tree 10–30 m. high with 10–12 leaves forming the head. Leaves 1.0–1.8 m. long, pinnate, the upper segments joined, petiole sheathed, sheaths encircling the tip of the stipule. Inflorescence paniculate, axillary, monoecious. Female flowers not numerous, growing from the axis of the spadix or a few at the base; male flowers very numerous, very small, located at the tips of the branches. Sepals 3; petals 3; stamens 6 in the male; ovary 1-celled in the female; style short, terminated with 3 stigmas. Fruit a monospermous berry, fibrous, ovoid, the shape and color variable; seed with corneous albumen, hard, the interior marbled with brown and white. Laos, northern and southern Vietnam, Malaysia. (Syn *A. hortensis* Lour.)

The seeds, known as betel nuts, are more or less globular, flattened at the base, light brown, reticulate. The taste is astringent and slightly bitter. They contain 14% fixed oil (palmitic, oleic, stearic, caproic, caprylic, lauric, myristic acids), mannosan and galactans, 15% red tannin, choline, and the alkaloids arecoline 0.1% ($C_8H_{13}NO_2$; oily liquid, colorless, odorless, very alkaline, volatile in water vapor; very soluble in water, alcohol, ether, chloroform; b.p. 209°), its isomer arecolidine ($C_8H_{13}NO_2$; colorless crystals; m.p. 105°; freely soluble in water, alcohol, ether, acetone), arecaidine (or arecaine; $C_7H_{11}NO_2 \cdot H_2O$; colorless plates; decomposing at 232°; freely soluble in water; insoluble in absolute alcohol, chloroform, ether, benzene), guvacoline ($C_7H_{11}NO_2$; colorless alkaline liquid; b.p. 114°; soluble in alcohol, chloroform), guvacine ($C_6H_9NO_2$; colorless prisms; decomposing at 295°; soluble in water; almost insoluble in absolute alcohol, ether, chloroform, benzene).[151] Arecoline is closely related to pilocarpine in its action; it stimulates peristalsis and produces marked bronchial constriction by peripheral action, which is overcome by atropine or epinephrine.[152] It is vermicidal, and is now used as such only in veterinary medicine in the U.S., because of its toxic effects and unreliability.

Used in Chinese medicine as taeniafuge. Dose, 30 gm. areca powder in 200 cc. water, simmered 1 hour, taken before breakfast; if expulsion does not take place within 9 hours, 50 cc. of 50% magnesium sulfate solution may be taken; side effects include mild dyspnea, diaphoresis, vertigo, and nausea.

DAEMONOROPS DRACO Blume.

(Palmae)

Dragon's blood palm. A climbing rattan palm. Stem several hundred feet long, climbing about other trees, 6 cm. thick, thorny. Leaves compound pinnate. Flowers yellowish white, corollate. Fruit spherical, coarse, covered with yellowish brown scales. Malaysia.

竭 血

The resinous secretion which is found on the fruits is used medicinally. It appears in the pharmacies as red sticks, pieces, or cakes, fracture vitreous, odorless and almost tasteless, m.p. about 120°, soluble in alcohol, insoluble in water. It makes a bright crimson powder which is easily ignited. It contains about 12–15% of the bright yellow, amorphous dracoresene, 2–3% white amorphous dracoalban;[148] benzoic and cinnamic acids.[140] The resin is astringent.

Used as internal hemostatic. Dose, 1–3 gm., powdered and taken in wine.

櫚 棕

TRACHYCARPUS FORTUNEI H. Wendl.

(Palmae)

Hemp or windmill palm. Growing to 15 m., the trunk covered with the remains of the old leaf sheaths. Leaves numerous, roundish, 40–80 cm. long by 0.6–1.2 m. wide, deeply divided into narrow, pointed segments 3 cm. wide, the leafstalk rough. Flowers in large hanging panicles among the crown of leaves, dioecious, yellowish; sepals and petals free; stamens 6; carpels 3. Fruit drupe-like, bluish, pea-sized, pericarp fleshy. Southern China, Burma, Japan. (Syn. *T. excelsa* Wendl., *Chamaerops excelsa* Thunb.)

The seeds are officinal and occur 1 cm. long by 6 mm. in diameter, reniform, greenish yellow, leathery. They contain mannosan, galactan, saccharose, and a large amount of tannin.[47]

Used as astringent hemostatic, both internally and externally. Dose, 7–15 gm.

百部

STEMONA TUBEROSA Lour.

(Stemonaceae)

An herbaceous volubilate plant, attaining 10 m. in height. Roots tuberous, fusiform. Leaves opposite, triangular-oval, barely cordate at the base, rather truncate, acuminate, 9–15 cm. long by 6–12 cm. wide. Inflorescence axillary; March–June; perianth in 4 segments, reddish yellow, 4 cm. in diameter; stamens 4; ovary 1-celled, conical. Fruit an oblong capsule, 35 mm. long. Central China, Indochina, Taiwan, India. (Syn. *Roxburghia gloriosoides* Roxb., *R. viridiflora* Smith, *R. stemona* Steud.)

The drug occurs as yellowish white, cylindrical tubers, the interior hollow and dark brown. The taste is bittersweet. The tubers contain stemonine ($C_{22}H_{33}NO_4$; white needles, odorless, slightly bitter; soluble in alcohol, ether, acetone, toluene, benzene, chloroform; m.p. 160°),[151] which is mildly toxic. Stemonine calms the respiratory center; it is strongly effective against *Pediculus capitus, P. corporis,* and *Phthirus pubis* without irritation or toxicity.[151]

Used internally as antitussive. Dose, 5–10 gm. Externally, as pediculicide.

蒲黃

TYPHA LATIFOLIA L.

(Typhaceae)

Cattail. A reed-like plant growing in dense stands. Rootstock thick. Leaves stiff, 1.5–2.7 m. long, scarcely 19 mm. wide. Floral spike terminal, cylindrical, brownish, 15–20 cm. long. Flowers extremely minute, numerous, being crowded in the dense spike, monoecious. Staminate flowers at upper end of the spike, evanescent; no perianth; stamens 2–7 united at the base to a common short filament; usually accompanied by numerous bristly hairs. Pistillate flowers consisting of a single, simple pistil on a short stalk; style long, slender; stigma flattened; ovary 1-celled. Cosmopolitan.

The yellow pollen is collected for medicinal use. It contains iso-rhamnetin ($C_{16}H_{12}O_7$), fatty oil, and a sitosterol.[140]

Used internally as hemostatic and diuretic. Dose, 5–10 gm. Externally, as astringent and dessicant vulnerary.

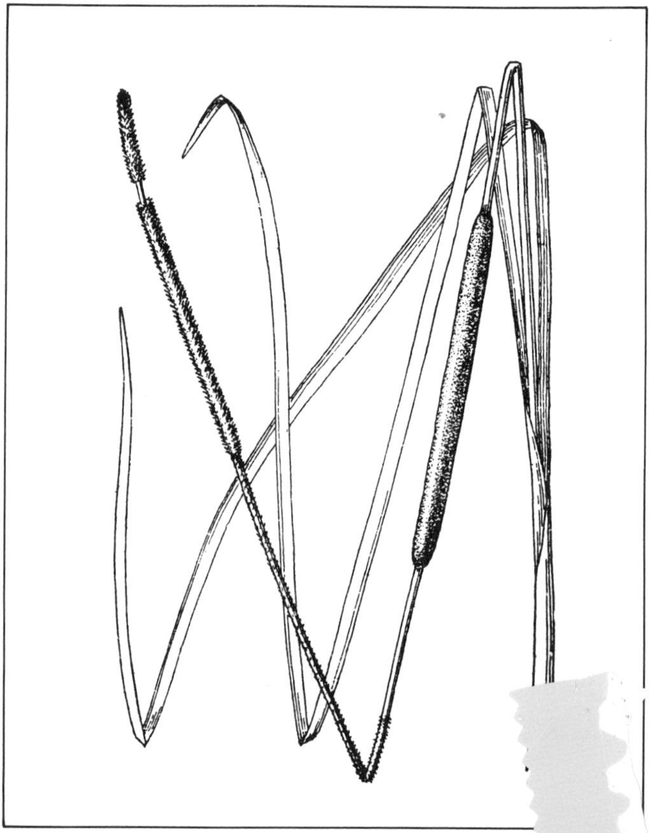

Typh

薑 良

ALPINIA OFFICINARUM Hance.

(Zingiberaceae)

Galanga. A ginger-like, perennial, leafy-stemmed herb, 0.7–1.2 m. tall. Rhizome creeping, 12–18 mm. in diameter, reddish brown, glabrous, covered with fibrous scales which leave irregular rings. Leaves cartilaginous, glabrous, lanceolate, 29–40 cm. long by 24 mm. wide; sheath scariose. Inflorescence paniculate, enclosed in the superior sheaths before anthesis. Bracts very small, caducous. Calyx tubular, with 3 short teeth; corolla longer than the calyx, lobes 15–20 mm. long by 4–5 mm. wide; stamens awl-shaped, short; labium white streaked with red, entire, 20 mm. long, 15–18 mm. wide; ovary 3-celled. Fruit a 3-valved capsule. Southern China, Hainan, northern Vietnam.

The rhizome occurs pharmaceutically as long transverse pieces 11.5 cm. long by 2 cm. in diameter, ramificate, dark reddish or cinnamon brown, texture fibrous, surface annulate with yellowish, wavy leaf bases. The odor is aromatic, the taste aromatic and pungent. The drug contains the oily, acrid resin galangol ($C_{15}H_{10}O_5 \cdot H_2O$; yellow needles; m.p. 217°; very soluble in alcohol; slightly soluble in ether, chloroform; insoluble in water), 0.5–5.0% essential oil (comprising cineol, eugenol, pinene, cadinene, methyl cinnamate), a sesquiterpene, and dioxyflavonol.[151] The action of galangol and the essential oil is that of an aromatic stimulant, with effects similar to those of ginger.[144]

Prescribed as stomachic in dyspepsia, gastralgia, chronic enteritis. Dose, 1–3 gm.

(In Japan, *A. kumatake* Mak. is employed.)

白荳蔻

AMOMUM CARDAMOMUM L.

(Zingiberaceae)

Round or cluster cardamom. An herbaceous perennial, the stem leafy, fleshy, about 1.8 m. tall. Leaves narrowly lanceolate, 20–30 cm. long, margin entire. Floral stalk growing directly from the creeping rootstock, much shorter than the stem. Flowers in dense spicate clusters, brownish yellow, tubular, 2.5 cm. long, with a distinct lip. Fruit a capsule, growing in clusters, green when immature, white when ripe, with 3 blunt angles, 3-celled, containing 9–12 seeds. East Indies.

The fruits occur as golden capsules, globular, villous, glabrous, 16 mm. in diameter, 3-celled. The seeds contain an essential oil comprising cineol, camphor, d-borneol, terpineol.[140] The taste is pungent and slightly bitter, the odor aromatic.

The seeds are used as an aromatic stomachic with anti-emetic action. Dose, 2–4 gm.

草果

AMOMUM GLOBOSUM Lour.

(Zingiberaceae)

A perennial herb 1–2 m. high. Leaves glabrous, oval or oblong, base attenuate, tip acuminate, margin dentate-ciliate, 60 cm. long by 12 cm. wide. Inflorescence terminal, enclosed within the superior sheaths before anthesis. Spathe coriaceous, 20 cm. long, the tip hooded with a point 2 cm. long; bracts very small, being reduced to scales. Flowers 30–35 mm. wide; calyx cylindrical, with 3 teeth; corolla tube nearly equalling the calyx; labium elliptical, slightly narrow at the base, slightly emarginate at the top, white streaked with purple, 12 mm. long by 10 mm. wide; stamens awl-shaped, adnate with the posterior lobe of the corolla; ovary globular. Fruit a globular berry, 7–10 mm. in diameter, whitish; seeds

5–7, trigonal-compressed, slightly emarginate at the tip. Northern Vietnam. (Syn. *Alpinia globosa* Horan., *Languas globosa* Burkill.)

The capsules occur mostly pedicellate, nearly spherical, 12–14 mm. in diameter, lightly striate axially, the shell thin and light, easily torn, yellowish outside, white inside; the seeds form a globular mass, coherent, cuneiform, ash gray, on the surface a bifurcated furrow forming the letter Y. The odor and taste are strongly aromatic. The seeds contain an essential oil.[140]

Used as aromatic stomachic and digestive. Dose, 2–5 gm.

金 鬱

CURCUMA LONGA L.

(Zingiberaceae)

Turmeric. An aromatic, perennial herb 0.6–1.0 m. tall. Rhizome stout, the tubercles sessile, ellipsoid or cylindrical, golden yellow inside, some terminating with filiform roots. Leaves oblong or elliptical, shortly acuminate, base narrow, both faces glabrous, to 45 cm. in length by 18 cm. wide. Scape 12–20 cm., rising from the center of the leaves. Inflorescence cylindrical or lengthily ovoid, 12–15 cm. long by 4–6 cm. wide; bracts membranous, lanceolate-obtuse, very pale white or greenish, 3–5 cm. long, the superior bracts sterile, narrower. Flowers pale yellow; calyx tubular; corolla 2–3 times longer, tubular, lobes 10 mm. long; stamens lateral, petaloid, widely elliptical, longer than the anther; labium nearly orbiculate, vaguely trilobate, the hooded tip entire, longer and wider than the stamens; ovary villous, style glabrous, stigmas barely ciliate. India, Madagascar, Antilles, Oceania, Cambodia, Laos, Vietnam, Taiwan. (Syn. *Amomum curcuma* Jacq.)

The rhizomes occur cylindrical, bluntly attenuate, yellowish gray, the surface powdery, 3–5 cm. long by 1–2 cm. in diameter. They contain about 5% essential oil (comprising turmerol, curcumon, phellandrene, valeric and caproic acids), and the coloring matter curcumin ($C_{21}H_{20}O_6$; orange-yellow crystalline powder; m.p. 183°; soluble in alcohol; insoluble in water, ether).[151] Turmeric root is said to cause marked choleresis by irritation of the hepatic cells; large doses cause fatty degeneration of the liver; it also stimulates the gallbladder.[152]

Used as aromatic stomachic, cholagogue, hemostatic. Dose, 4–7 gm.

子智益

ELETTARIA CARDAMOMUM Maton.

(Zingiberaceae)

True cardamom. A stout, perennial herb 1.5–2.7 m. high. Leaves large, the underside hairy. Floral stalk rising from the rootstock; flowers in loose spikes or racemes, very irregular. Fruit a capsule. India, Malaysia.

Cardamom seeds occur as entire, albuminous seeds 5 mm. long by 3 mm. in diameter, 3–4 sided, irregular, gray to yellow to brown, deeply grooved on one side, the remaining part irregularly furrowed and tuberculated, the base of the seed with a circular, depressed scar. The taste is pungent, the odor aromatic. The seeds contain 2–8% of a volatile oil comprising limonene, terpinene, dipentene.[148] The oil is an aromatic, carminative stomachic.[144]

Prescribed as stomachic and tonic in gastralgia, enuresis, spermatorrhea. Dose, 3–5 gm.

山柰

KAEMPFERIA GALANGA L.

(Zingiberaceae)

A perennial, acaulescent herb. Leaves 2–3, resting on the ground, roundish, abruptly acuminate, base attenuate, margin thin, reddish, 8–10 cm. long by 6–7 cm. wide. Inflorescence sessile, included within the leaf sheaths; bracts lanceolate-acute, 2.5–4.5 cm. long. Flowers 6–12 in an extended rosette, white with violet patch in the center; calyx matching the bracts; corolla tube 2.0–2.5 cm. long; anther nearly sessile; stamens oboval-cuneiform; labium deeply divided into 2 obovoid lobes. Southern China, Indochina, Malaysia, India.

The rhizomes occur in slices 2.5 cm. in diameter, the epidermis reddish, the interior white. The odor is aromatic, the taste pungent. The drug contains an essential oil comprising borneol, camphor, cineol, and ethyl alcohol.[81]

Prescribed as stomachic, carminative, stimulant. Dose, 3–5 gm. Also used in odontalgia.

生薑

ZINGIBER OFFICINALE Rosc.

(Zingiberaceae)

Ginger. Stem 0.9–1.2 m. high, stout, cane-like. Leaves with sheathing base, narrowly lanceolate, tip acute, 20–30 cm. long. Inflorescence a terminal spike; bracts persistent. Flowers irregular, yellowish green, small, labium purple with yellow spots; summer. Fruit a capsule. Cultivated in all tropical countries. (Syn. *Amomum zingiber* L.)

The rhizomes of Chinese ginger occur as irregular, ramose, entire or as broken pieces, to 6.7 cm. long by 12 mm. in diameter, the flat surfaces peeled, fibrous, light gray or yellowish brown. The odor is aromatic, the taste strongly aromatic and pungent. The rhizomes contain 1–3% of a volatile oil comprising zingerone ($C_{11}H_{14}O_3$; colorless crystals; m.p. 40–41°; soluble in ether; sparingly soluble in water, petroleum ether), phellandrene, camphene, cineol, borneol, and citral; a non-volatile oily substance, gingerol (yellow syrupy mass; bitter, sharp taste; b.p. 235–240°; soluble in alcohol, petroleum ether; slightly soluble in water); and an acrid resin.[148] Ginger is sialogogue when chewed, sternuatory when inhaled, and externally a rubefacient; internally it is stimulant and carminative, producing a sensation of warmth at the epigastrium; it is employed in colic, in relaxed conditions of the throat, in atonic dyspepsia, and as an adjunct to purgatives to correct their griping properties.[150]

Used as stomachic, stimulant, antiemetic. Dose, 3–5 gm.

ANGIOSPERMAE: Dicotyledonae

Archichlamydeae

牛膝

ACHYRANTHES BIDENTATA Blume.

(Amaranthaceae)

A slender, perennial herb. Leaves opposite, petiolate, elliptical or linear, base attenuate, acuminate, glabrous, 5–12 cm. long by 4 cm. wide. Inflorescence a terminal or axillary spike, 2–5 cm. long, pedunculate; August–October. Bractlets often reduced to spines. Perianth in 5 acute segments; stamens 5; staminodes 5, truncate, finely denticulate; ovary superior, obovoid. Fruit an achene. China, Vietnam, Laos, Japan, India, Sri Lanka, Malaysia, Indonesia.

The drug occurs as straight or irregular roots, flexible, streaked lengthwise, brownish yellow, often with traces of fibrous rootlets. The taste is slightly bitter. The root contains saponins.[151]

Used as diuretic, emmenagogue, tonic. Dose, 5–10 gm.

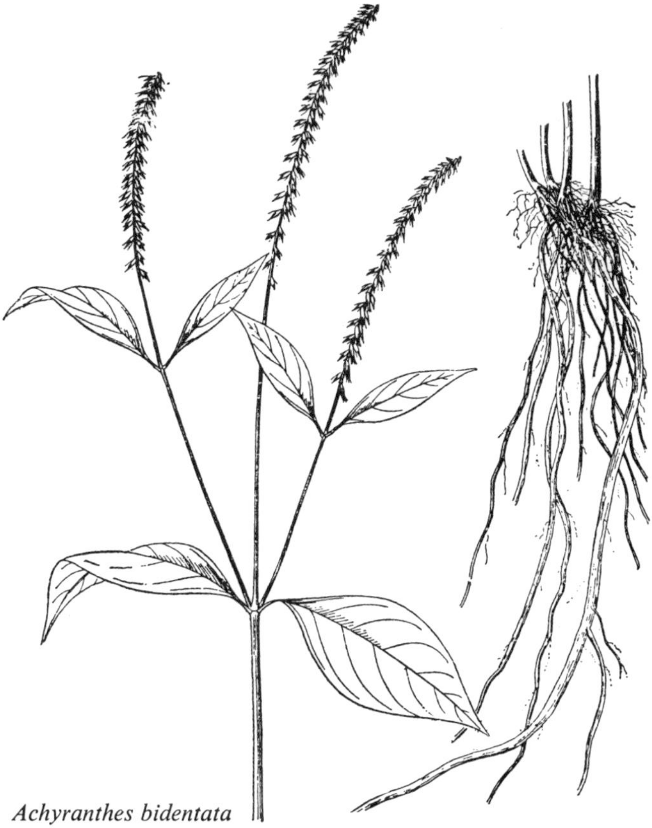

Achyranthes bidentata

CELOSIA ARGENTEA L.

(Amaranthaceae)

A tropical annual herb, erect, glabrous, more or less branching, 0.3–1.0 m. tall. Leaves linear or lanceolate, attenuate with the petiole, tip acuminate, 8–10 cm. long by 2–4 cm. wide; petiole 15–40 mm. long. Inflorescence a white or pink spike, acuminate, 3–10 cm. long, accrete, at first very com-

明決草

pact; August–September. Flowers contiguous, sessile, provided with an aristate bract below the bifid tip, shorter than the calyx; calyx scariose, 7 mm. long; sepals 5, estivation quincuncial, oval or linear, acuminate; stamens 5; filaments acuminate, united at the enlarged base into a cupula enclosing the ovary; ovary ovoid; ovules about 7. Fruit a pyxis; seeds black, reniform. Southern China, India, Sri Lanka, Africa, America (Syn. *C. margaritacea* L.)

The seeds are used medicinally. They occur as black, shining, flat, small. The taste is bitter.

Employed as ophthalmic antiphlogistic and astringent in conjunctivitis, retinal hemorrhage.

Celosia argentea

C. argentea var. *cristata*

雞冠花

CELOSIA ARGENTEA var. CRISTATA Bth.

(Amaranthaceae)

Cockscomb. A deformation of *C. argentea* L. due to cultivation. The spikes are flattened, truncate, often 15 cm. wide and irregularly laciniate at the top, so resembling a rooster's crest. Color varieties such as yellow, whitish, and bright purple exist.

The flowers are officinal.

Used as astringent, hemostatic, antidiarrheic in dysentery, enterorrhagia, metrorrhagia, epistaxis. Dose, 5–10 gm.

乳香

PISTACIA LENTISCUS L.

(Anacardiaceae)

A small tree 1–3 m. high, the branches tortuous. Leaves persistent, paripinnate; leaflets 4–10, elliptical, obtuse, coriaceous, surface glossy, underside pale; petiole narrowly winged. Flowers in spiciform clusters, axillary, compact, 1–2 clusters in each leaf axil, no longer than the leaflets, dioecious. Calyx 5-lobed in the male, 3- or 4-lobed in the female; petals none; stamens 5. Fruit a small, nearly globular drupe, red becoming black at maturity. Mediterranean.

The drug consists of the concrete resinous exudation of the tree; it is known as mastic. It occurs as globular, elongate, or pear-shaped tears, pale yellow or greenish yellow, 2 cm. long by 12 mm. wide at the most, texture vitreous, surface transparent, smooth and shiny, fracture even. The odor is slightly balsamic, the taste slightly pungent and terebinthine. The drug is insoluble in water, nearly soluble in alcohol. It contains about 2% volatile oil, masticinic acid, masticonic acid, masticoresene.[148]

Mastic is employed as analgesic and sedative in gastralgia, cardiodynia, mastitis, peptic ulcer, boils, carbuncles; also as antitussive and expectorant. Dose, 2–5 gm.

五倍子

RHUS SEMIALATA Murr.

(Anacardiaceae)

Chinese sumac. A tree growing to 8 m. Leaves alternate, pinnate with an odd leaflet at the tip; leaflets 5–13, nearly sessile, oval or oval-oblong, 6–12 cm. long, acute or briefly acuminate, crenelate-dentate, the rachis and petiole winged. Inflorescence a panicle 15–25 cm. long; August–September. Flowers polygamous; sepals 5; petals 5, creamy white, longer than the sepals; stamens 5, inserted below the disk; ovary superior, sessile, 1-celled. Fruit a nearly globular drupe, reddish orange, pubescent; October. China. (Syn. *R. javanica* L., *R. osbeckii* Decne.)

The drug consists of the nutgalls which form on the leaves or leafstalks as the result of the puncture and deposited ova of the aphid *Schlechendaria sinensis.* The subsequent response of the plant to the stimulating action of a secretion of the insect larva is the cause of the excrescence.[144] The nutgalls occur as hard, globular bodies of a blackish gray color, having a central cavity. The taste is sour and intensely astringent. They contain about 70% tannin.[148]

Used as astringent and styptic; internally in diarrhea, hemorrhage, spermatorrhea. Dose, 1–3 gm.

RHUS VERNICIFERA DC.

(Anacardiaceae)

Japanese lacquer tree, 8–20 m. high. Leaves pinnate with an odd leaflet at the tip; leaflets 5–13, oval or oblong-oval, 7–20 cm. long by 3–7 cm. wide, tip acuminate, base rounded or nearly cuneate, entire, pubescent when young. Inflorescence a drooping panicle 15–25 cm. long; June. Flowers yellowish white, small, polygamous; calyx in 5 segments; petals 5, longer than the sepals; stamens 5; ovary sessile, 1-celled.

漆 乾

Fruit a nearly globular drupe, 6–8 mm. in diameter, yellow; September. China, Japan.

The drug consists of the hardened exudation of the bark. It occurs as irregular, blackish pieces. The fresh exudation is toxic, the main constituent being the resinous oil urushiol, which is a mixture of closely related catechol derivatives having unsaturated C_{15} side chains (pale yellow liquid; b.p. 200–210°; soluble in alcohol, ether, benzene; moderately soluble in petroleum ether).[73] Upon exposure to the air, the oil becomes inactivated by oxidation through laccase, a polyphenolase also occurring in the exudation.[103] The toxicity of the hardened Chinese drug is not determinate, and the native descriptions disagree. Internally, urushiol produces gastric and intestinal irritation, proctitis, vulvitis, and nephritis, but the systemic toxicity is relatively low.[152] The degree to which the Chinese drug may produce these effects is not known.

Prescribed as hemolytic, emmenagogue, vermifuge. Dose, 3–5 gm. Incompatibles: *Xanthoxylum piperitum, Perilla frutescens*, eggs, crabmeat.

皮加五

ACANTHOPANAX SPINOSUM Miq.

(Anacardiaceae)

A deciduous shrub with prickly branches. Leaves alternate, compound pinnate; leaflets 5, nearly sessile, the main leafstalk about 10 cm. long. Inflorescence an axillary, umbelliferous cluster, lengthily pedunculate; summer. Flowers greenish white, small, dioecious. Fruit a spherical berry, black when mature. China, Japan.

The root epidermis is employed medicinally. It occurs as pieces of varying dimensions, more or less rolled or contortive, brown, mixed with root and stem fragments. The taste is pungent. It contains an essential oil, a large amount of resin, starch, and a high concentration of vitamin A.[140]

Prescribed as tonic and analgesic in rheumatic pain, colic, gastralgia, impotence. Dose, 5–10 gm. A highly alcoholic wine prepared from the drug is much respected as antirheumatic and general tonic for restoring vigor and sexual potency.

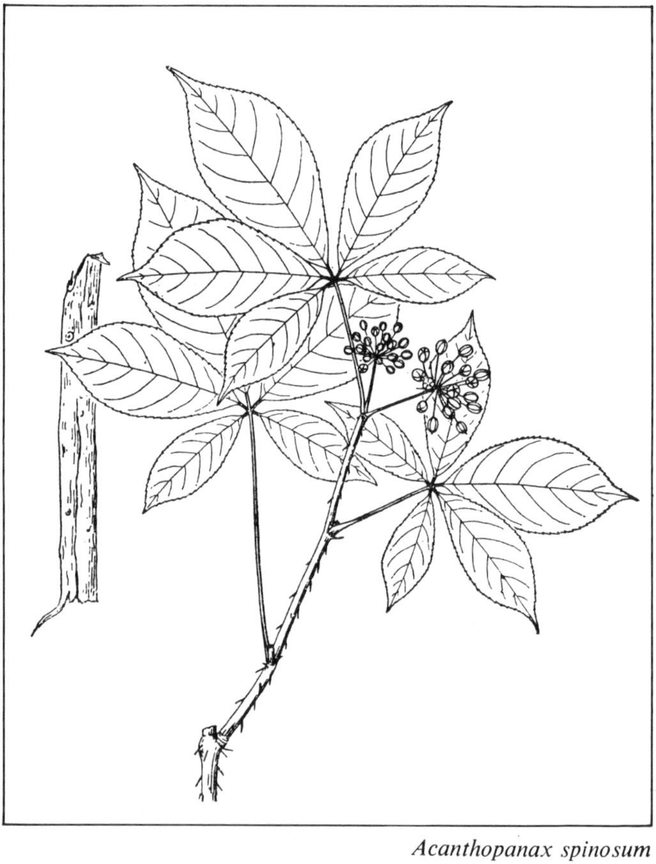

Acanthopanax spinosum

人參

PANAX GINSENG C. A. Mey.

(Araliaceae)

Ginseng. A perennial herb 60–80 cm. tall. Root fleshy, often bifurcate, aromatic. Stem erect, simple, not branching, deep red. Leaves verticillate, compound, digitate, oval-oblong, thin; leaflets 5, the 3 terminal leaflets larger than the lateral ones, finely bidentate, tip gradually acuminate, base rounded or nearly cordate. Inflorescence a small, terminal umbel, hemispherical; August. Flowers polygamous, pink; calyx vaguely 5-toothed; petals 5; stamens 5. Fruit a small berry, nearly drupaceous, red. North Korea, northeastern China. (Syn. *P. schinseng* Nees.)

Ginseng occurs as bifurcate roots 5–6 cm. long, grayish white to amber yellow, the surface wrinkled and furrowed. The taste is sweetish at first, with a somewhat bitter aftertaste. True ginseng root is rare, and is regarded by the Chinese as a valuable panacea because of the resemblance of the root to the human form. The drug is costly and is often adulterated with roots of *Adenophora*, *Platycodon*, *Campanula*, *Angelica*, and *Rehmannia*. Much of the American ginseng, *P. quinquefolia* L., has been exported to China, as well as used by the Chinese in America.

Korean ginseng root has been analyzed as containing a glycoside panaquilon (yellow, amorphous powder; soluble in water, alcohol; insoluble in ether), a saponin panaxin $C_{38}H_{66}O_{12}$, 0.05% volatile oil, phytosterols, vitamins B_1 and B_2, a hormone, resin, mucilage, and starch.[148] Injected into the thoracic duct of frogs, panaquilon induces cardiac paralysis; in warm-blooded animals the pulse is slowed, the arterial pressure lowered; small doses appear to stimulate the function of the heart by an essentially vasoconstrictive effect.[34] Large doses of an ether extract of ginseng induce cerebral sedation and anesthesia in animals; smaller doses appear to stimulate the nerve centers of the medulla oblongata; subcutaneous injections in young mice induce follicule arrector muscle stimulation, the action being similar to that of yohimbine, stimulating the sympathetic nervous system, increasing adrenal response, and elevating body temperature.[93] Ginseng appears to have a close relationship with carbohydrate metabolism in animals; oral and intravenous administration lowers blood sugar in various hyperglycemias.[2] Without excluding the secondary effects possible upon the craniosacral and orthosympathetic systems, the fundamental action of the active principles in ginseng root appears to be that which affects smooth muscle fiber.[151] Repeated experiments by U.S. scientists have failed to confirm any important medicinal virtues; the drug is stated to be of merit as a demulcent alone. The Chinese pharmacologist states that ginseng has positive action as a nerve and cardiac stimulant, increasing metabolism, retarding impotence, regulating blood pressure and blood sugar; large dosages are reputed to have resulted in insomnia, depression, and nervous disorder.

Prescribed as tonic, stimulant, aphrodisiac; indicated in neurasthenia, dyspepsia, palpitation, impotence, asthma. Dose, 5–10 gm. in decoction before breakfast. Abstinence from tea is essential during ginseng therapy; iron is also regarded as incompatible.

TETRAPANAX PAPYRIFERA C. Koch
(Araliaceae)

Rice-paper tree. A small tree or shrub without spines, the young foliage felty-hairy, the stem containing much pith. Leaves alternate, large, cordate or ovalish, deeply palmate, underside tomentose; lobes 5–7, acuminate, dentate, the lateral lobes bilobate, the terminal trilobate. Inflorescence consisting of numerous umbels arranged in a large, woolly panicle, terminal, somewhat villous. Flowers greenish; sepals 4; petals 4; receptacle obconical, completely enclosing the ovary; ovary 2-celled; styles 2, diverging. Fruit small, bacciform, blackish, striate. China, Taiwan. (Syn. *Fatsia papyrifera* Benth., *Aralia papyrifera* Hook.)

The pith is cut into thin slices, dried, and used medicinally. It contains akebin $C_{35}H_{56}O_{20}$ and inositol.[140 151]

Prescribed as diuretic and galactagogue. Dose, 3–5 gm. The pith is also used like cotton as a dressing.

馬兜鈴

ARISTOLOCHIA DEBILIS Sieb. et Zucc.

(Aristolochiaceae)

A perennial creeping herb. Stem supple, erect. Leaves alternate, petiolate, auriculate, deltoid; lobes rounded. Peduncles solitary, without bracts. Flowers irregular; July–September; perianth simple; tube globular, inflated at the base, narrow, cylindrical at the top; limb oblique, descending, oval-lanceolate, acuminate, nearly as long as the tube; stamens 6; ovary inferior. Fruit a rounded capsule, 6-valved; September–October; seeds very numerous, compressed. Northern China, Japan. (Syn. *A. longa* Thunb., *A. recurvilabra* Hance.)

The fruit is used in Chinese medicine. Because of the resemblance of the opened fruit to the human lung, the drug has long been employed in pulmonary disorders. It contains the poisonous alkaloid aristolochine ($C_{32}H_{22}N_2O_{13}$; white to yellow crystalline needles; m.p. about 215°; soluble in alcohol, chloroform, ether, acetone, acetic acid; slightly soluble in water; insoluble in benzene, carbon disulfide).[140] Toxic doses of the alkaloid cause cardiac and respiratory arrest in experimental animals.[148]

Prescribed as antitussive and expectorant in asthma and bronchitis. Dose, 3–7 gm.

(*A. kaempferi* Willd. and *A. contorta* Bunge. are probably also used.)

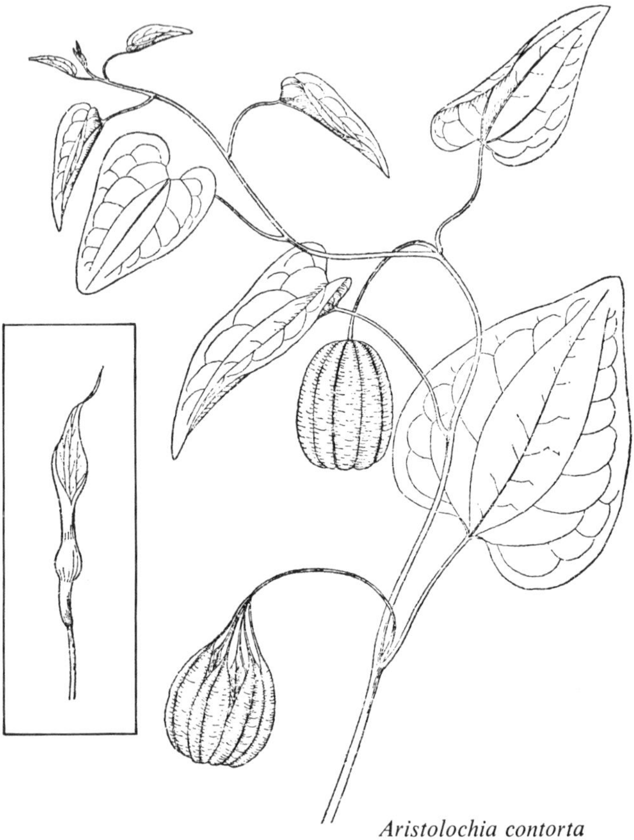

Aristolochia contorta

ASARUM SIEBOLDI Miq.
(Aristolochiaceae)

A perennial herb, the rhizome fleshy, nodose, emitting very fine rootlets. Petiole 5–8 cm., violet. Leaves simple, oval, tip acuminate, base deeply cordate, membranous, pubescent. Flowers solitary, axillary; calyx a globular tube, somewhat

辛 細

membranous, reddish, 10–15 mm. in diameter; corolla none; stamens 12; ovary adnate with the calyx tube. Fruit an angular capsule, irregularly dehiscent. Northern China, Japan. (Syn. *A. heterotropoides* F. Schmidt)

The drug consists of the tender, fibrous roots. The taste is very pungent. The root contains about 3% essential oil comprising methyl eugenol, phenol, safrol, pinene, eucarvone, and asarinine $C_{20}H_{18}O_6$.[151] Administration of the essential oil to frogs, mice, and rabbits induces at first extreme stimulation and irritability, followed by a decrease in voluntary and respiratory movement, hyporeflexia, total paralysis, asphyxia; cardiac function is noted following respiratory cessation.[46] The root of the related *A. canadense* has been used as carminative and aromatic.[144]

Prescribed as analgesic, sedative, expectorant in headache, cough, pharyngitis, chronic gastritis, arthritis. Dose, 2–5 gm. Incompatibles: *Astragalus hoantchy*, *Cornus officinalis*, potassium nitrate, magnesium silicate.

EPIMEDIUM MACRANTHUM Moore et Decne.

(Berberidaceae)

藿羊淫

A woody, perennial herb. Rhizome creeping, very slender, covered with long filiform rootlets. Stem erect, striate, glabrous, very slender. Leaves alternate, compound pinnate; leaflets 3, oval, oblong, acuminate, base cordate, dentate. Inflorescence a terminal cluster on a long peduncle; calyx in 8 segments in 2 whorls, the interior 4 violet, the outer 4 red, oblong-navicular; petals 4, white, the base spurred; stamens 4; ovary 1-celled. Fruit a dehiscent capsule, 2-valved; seeds few. China, Japan. (Syn. *Aceranthus sagittatum* Sieb. et Zucc.)

The leaves are used medicinally. They have been analyzed as containing a glycoside (icariin $C_{33}H_{42}O_{16}$ or epimedin), and an alkaloid; oral administration of an extract of the leaves increases the frequency of copulation in animals, presumably through spermatopoeia; intravenous injections of the glycoside increase seminal secretion in dogs.[140]

Used as aphrodisiac. Dose, 3–8 gm.

南燭

NANDINA DOMESTICA Thunb.

(Berberidaceae)

An evergreen shrub 1.8–2.4 m. high. Leaves alternate, petiolate, bipinnate or tripinnate, 30–50 cm. long, grouped in rosettes toward the extremities of the branches; leaflets oval, lanceolate, 3–10 mm. long, tip acuminate, base cuneiform, coriaceous. Inflorescence a terminal panicle; July. Flowers white; sepals numerous, in series of 3, the outermost bractiform gradually becoming larger and more petaloid toward the center; stamens 6; ovary superior. Fruit a globular berry, red, 8 mm. in diameter; seeds 2. Southern China, Japan.

The fruit, bark, and leaves are all officinal. The bark contains the alkaloids domesticine ($C_{19}H_{19}NO_4$; solvated crystals from alcohol; m.p. 115–117°; very soluble in chloroform; soluble in hot alcohol, ethyl acetate, acetic acid; slightly soluble in ether; insoluble in water), nandinine ($C_{19}H_{19}NO_4$; white powder or leaflets; m.p. 145–146°; soluble in alcohol, benzene, chloroform, ether, dilute acids; slightly soluble in water), nandazurine ($C_{28}H_{18}N_2O_6$; dark blue crystals; m.p. 350°), and berberine; the fruits contain domesticine and its methyl ether nantenine (or domestine; m.p. 139°); the leaves contain cyanic acid.[56] The toxic effects of nandinine appear to be similar to those of strychnine, producing intense convulsions and sensory nerve paralysis.[140]

Prescribed as antitussive. Dose, 5–10 gm.

橄欖

CANARIUM ALBUM Raeusch.

(Burseraceae)

A tree 20–25 m. high. Leaves alternate, 40–50 cm. long; leaflets 11–15, 6–10 cm. long by 2.5 cm., opposite, oblong-lanceolate, acuminate, base cuneiform, membranous, rigid, surface pale green, underside silvery green, entire. Inflorescence terminal; May. Flowers globular, somewhat compact, in groups of 2–3, nearly sessile, hermaphrodite or polygamous; calyx cupuliform, segments 3, rarely 5; petals 3–5; stamens 6; ovary 2- or 3-celled, often all fertile. Southeastern China, Indochina. (Syn. *C. sinense* Rumph., *Pimela alba* Lour.)

The seeds are powdered and used medicinally.

Used as antiphlogistic and astringent in pharyngitis. Dose, 5–10 gm.

瞿麥

DIANTHUS SUPERBUS L.

(Caryophyllaceae)

A perennial, glabrous herb. Stem 30–80 cm. Leaves opposite, lanceolate-linear, acute; the inferior leaves nearly obtuse, 3-veined. Inflorescence a panicle; July–September. Flowers pink or lilac, large, odoriferous; calycle consisting of broadly oval scales with an awn one-fourth the size of the calyx; calyx somewhat attenuate at the top, striate the length, teeth 5; petals 5, lengthily unguiculate, with a deep capillary fringe, oblong; stamens 10; ovary 1-celled; styles 2. Fruit a 4-valved capsule, cylindrical. China, Japan, Europe. (Syn. *D. oreadum* Hance.)

The entire plant is officinal. The taste is bitter.

Used as diuretic and emmenagogue. Dose, 5–10 gm.

Saponaria vaccaria

SAPONARIA VACCARIA L.

(Caryophyllaceae)

Cowherd. Annual herb 30–60 cm. tall, the stem erect. Leaves opposite, sessile, oblong-lanceolate, smooth. Inflorescence a loose, dichotomous cyme; April–May; pink. Calyx a long cylindrical tube, 5-lobed; petals 5, unguiculate; stamens 10;

行留不王

ovary superior. Fruit a 1-celled capsule, ovoid, enclosed, dehiscent at the top. Western Asia, southern Europe.

The seeds are used medicinally. They occur as reddish brown, rounded, resembling mustard seeds. The taste is bitter. They contain the glycoside saponin.[151] Saponin alters the permeability of the protoplasmic surface of cells and is generally a protoplasmic poison; it lakes blood even in isotonic media, the phenomenon depending on the affinity for the lipoids of the cell envelope and stroma, and being prevented by the addition of cholesterol; toxicity is low in higher animals because of poor absorption, and the main action is that of local irritation to mucous membrane, provoking salivation, nausea, vomiting, and diarrhea; the expectorant action is useful in chronic cough.[152]

Used as vulnerary for abscesses, furuncles, ulcers, scabies, mastitis, lymphangitis; also as emmenagogue and galactagogue. Dose, 5–7 gm. Contraindicated in pregnancy.

矛 衛

EVONYMUS ALATUS Regel

(Celastraceae)

Winged spindle-tree. A stiff, spreading shrub 2–3 m. high, the twigs corky-winged. Leaves opposite, simple, elliptical or obovate, 3–5 cm. long by 2 cm. wide, acuminate, base wedge-shaped, finely dentate. Inflorescence an axillary cyme, yellowish, April–June. Flowers 6 mm. in diameter, generally in groups of 3; peduncle short; calyx in 4 segments; petals 4; stamens 4; ovary embedded in the disk. Fruit a purplish capsule, 6–8 mm. long; September–October. Northern China, Manchuria, Japan. (Syn. *E. thunbergianus* Blume., *E. subtriflorus* Blume., *Celastrus alatus* Thunb., *C. striatus* Thunb., *Melanocarya alata* Turcz.)

The winged twigs are officinal. The taste is bitter, sour, and astringent.

Used as analgesic, emmenagogue, and purgative in female disorders. Dose, 5–10 gm.

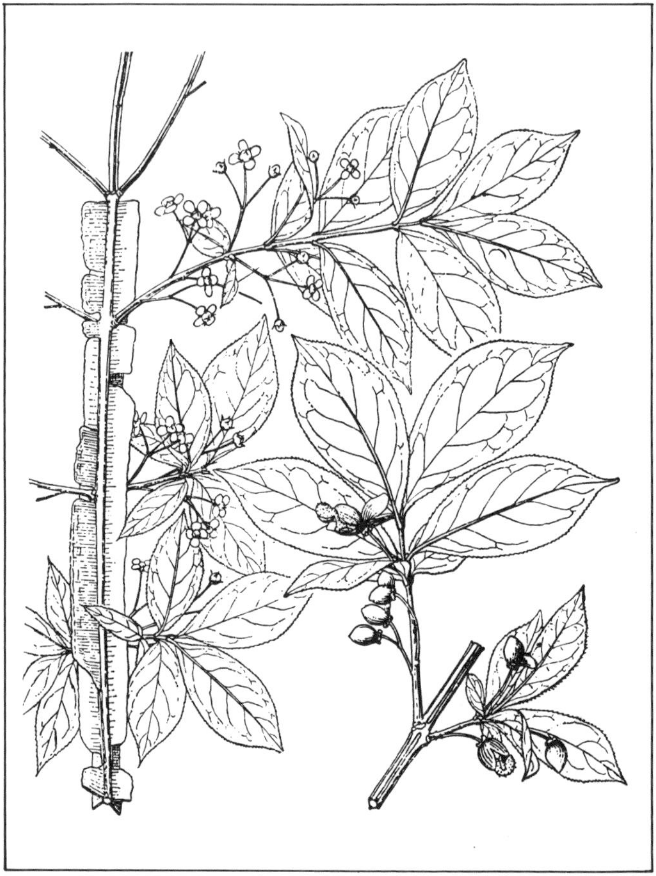

Evonymus alatus

KOCHIA SCOPARIA Schrad.

(Chenopodiaceae)

Belvedere cypress. An annual herb 0.4–1.5 m. high, much branched, finely pilose. Stems and branches rigid, erect, often turning reddish in autumn. Leaves alternate, nearly ses-

地膚子

sile, lanceolate or lanceolate-linear, 3–8 cm. long by 4–12 mm. wide, ciliate, 3-veined, entire, red or green or yellow, turning purplish red in autumn. Flowers August–October, greenish, axillary, sessile, very small; calyx in 5 segments; petals none; stamens 5. Fruit an utricle enclosed within the perianth tube. Eurasia. (Syn. *Chenopodium scoparia* L.)

The seeds are officinal. They are green, small, rounded. The taste is bitter. They contain saponin.[140]

Used as diuretic, astringent, and antiphlogistic in disorders of the urinary tract. Dose, 5–10 gm.

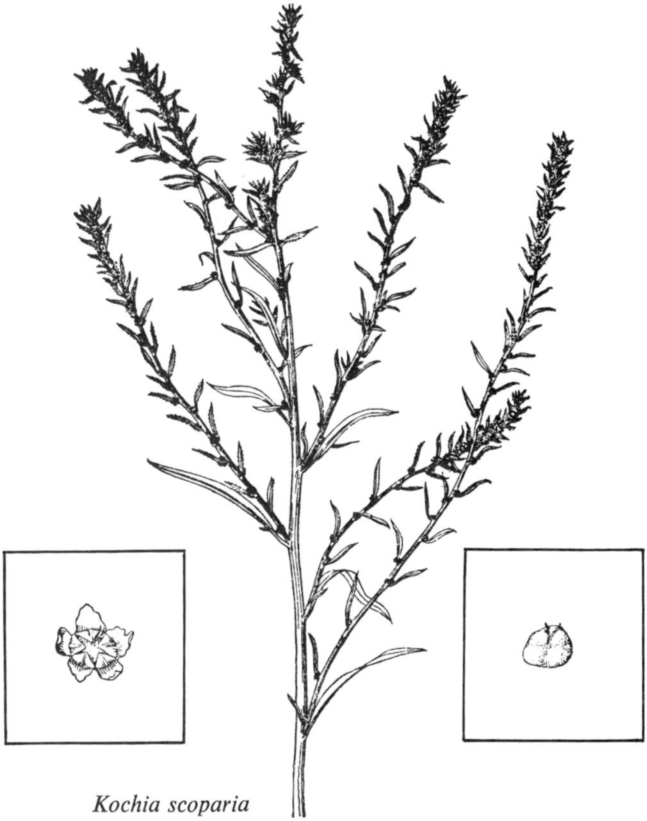

Kochia scoparia

使君子

QUISQUALIS INDICA L.

(Combretaceae)

Rangoon creeper. A woody vine. Leaves opposite, petiolate, oval, base rounded or nearly cordate, tip briefly acuminate, membranous, 7–9 cm. long by 4–5 cm. wide. Inflorescence a terminal spike, compact, 4–10 cm. long; summer. Calyx a 5-lobed tube, green; petals 5, white changing to pink; stamens 10; ovary cylindrical-fusiform, 5-angled, villous, glandular. Fruit a dry capsule, 5-sided, chestnut brown, leathery, monospermous, tardily dehiscent. Northwestern China, India, Malaysia, Vietnam, Laos, Philippines. (Syn. *Q. sinensis* Lindl., *Q. grandiflora* Miq., *Q. longifolia* Presl., *Q. loureiri* G. Don., *Q. pubescens* Burm.)

The fruits occur as oval or oblong, pointed at the ends, with a pentagonal cross-section; the oily seed is enclosed in a thin, brittle, mahogany pericarp.[153] The seeds contain 25% fatty oil comprising oleic, myristic, palmitic, stearic, and linoleic acids; gum and resin.[151] The drug was formerly considered as containing an active principle similar to santonin,[25] but any santonin-like anthelmintic action has been disproved.[15] Side effects of anthelmintic therapy include hiccough, vertigo, nausea, emesis, and diarrhea.[140]

The fruits are used as vermifuge. Dose, 10–35 gm. (8–10 fruits) in decoction. A small dose of castor oil taken 6 hours later will aid expulsion.

TERMINALIA CHEBULA Retz.

(Combretaceae)

A tropical shade tree 15–20 m. high. Leaves opposite, oval-rounded, base somewhat attenuate, tip obtuse, 12–25 cm. long by 7–15 cm. wide, coriaceous, both sides softly villous, becoming glabrous. Inflorescence an axillary or terminal

勒黎訶

panicle. Flowers yellowish white, odoriferous; calyx cupuliform, the lobes triangular and shorter than the tube; stamens 10; ovary inferior, 1-celled; disk consisting of 5 pilose glands surrounding the base of the style. Fruit a dry drupe, ovoid-oblong, 3–4 cm. long by 22–25 mm. in diameter, angled, pericarp coriaceous, brownish yellow. India, Burma, Cambodia, Thailand, Laos, Vietnam, Malaysia.

The fruits, known as myrobalans, contain 3.5% chebulic acid ($C_{28}H_{24}O_{10} \cdot H_2O$; colorless rhombic crystals; odorless, sweetish; m.p. 234°; very soluble in alcohol, acetic ether; poorly soluble in cold water, ether),[151] 37% fatty oil, 27–39% tannin, and ellagic acid.[31] The drug is highly astringent, more intensely so in the large intestine than in the small intestine or stomach.[140]

Prescribed as astringent in diarrhea, enterorrhagia, metrorrhagia, metritis, leukorrhea. Dose, 3–5 gm.

草何葉昨

COTYLEDON FIMBRIATUM Turcz.

(Crassulaceae)

A succulent plant occurring on old tile roofs and rocks. Basal leaves in rosettes, spatulate, terminated with a fimbriate appendage, cartilaginous; cauline leaves linear, the tip mucronate. Inflorescence a terminal, dense raceme, cylindrical or nearly pyramidal, the pedicels often elongate, flowers 1–3; September–October. Calyx 5-parted; corolla much longer than the calyx; stamens 10; carpels 5, free. Northern China. (Syn. *Sedum fimbriatum* Franch., *Umbilicus fimbriatus* Turcz.)

The young plants are dried and used medicinally. The taste is sour. An alcoholic extract of the herb increases the tonus of the intestinal wall of animals.[140]

Used as laxative and intestinal astringent. Dose, 4–7 gm.

Also used, *Cotyledon malacophylla* Pall. (Syn. *Umbilicus malacophyllus* DC., *Sedum malacophyllum* Franch.)

Cotyledon fimbriatum

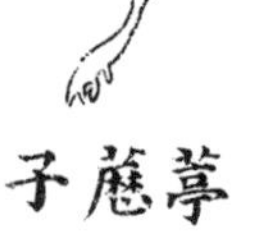

子藶葶

DRABA NEMOROSA L.

(Crucifereae)

An annual plant 10–30 cm. tall. Leaves simple, oval or oblong, entire or dentate; the basal leaves in rosettes; the cauline leaves sessile, not auriculate. Inflorescence a loose, elongate cluster; March–April. Flowers yellow, small; petals 4, indented at the tips; stamens 6; ovary sessile; style nearly wanting. Fruit a small silicle, oblong; April–May; seeds small, yellow, slightly oblong, flattened. Northwestern China, northern Asia, Europe, North America.

The seeds are used medicinally. The taste is bitter.

Prescribed as expectorant and diuretic in chronic trachitis, asthma, pleurisy, hydrothorax, edematous beriberi. Dose, 3–7 gm.

萊菔

RAPHANUS SATIVUS L.

(Crucifereae)

Radish. An annual or biannual herb with a fleshy-inflated root. Stem 50–80 cm., covered with rigid hairs. Inferior leaves lyrate, superior leaves lanceolate, dentate, or incised. Inflorescence an auriculate, terminal raceme. Flowers white or purplish; May–June; not produced in ordinary harvested plants; sepals 4, erect; petals 4, longer than the sepals, with an expanded limb; stamens 6; ovary sessile. Fruit an erect silicle, oblong-lanceolate; June. Cosmopolitan.

The roots, leaves, and seeds are all officinal. The fresh root contains glucose, pentosan, adenine, arginine, histidine, choline, trigonelline, diastase, glucosidase, oxydase, catalase, vitamins A, B, C;[137] also allyl isothiocyanate, oxalic acid.[154] The leaves or tops contain an essential oil and appreciable amounts of vitamins A and C.[140] The seeds contain 30–40% fatty oil,[137] as well as raphanin ($C_{17}H_{26}N_3O_3S_5$ or $C_{17}H_{26}N_3O_4S_5$; syrup of neutral reaction; freely soluble in water, alcohol, and chloroform).[148] Raphanin is an antibiotic principle active, in vitro, against several species of bacteria.[144]

The fresh root is considered digestant, diuretic, and antiscorbutic; the dried root, diuretic. The seeds are employed as stomachic and expectorant. A decoction of the leaves is used as antiphlogistic, being applied to the temples in cephalalgia.

白芥子

SINAPIS ALBA L.

(Cruciferae)

White mustard. A stout, branching annual 30–80 cm. high, the foliage villous-prickly. Leaves petiolate, lyrate-pinnatifid with a large terminal lobe, the segments sinuate-dentate. Inflorescence a terminal raceme, the pedicels erect, expanded, and as long as the valves. Flowers yellow, 8–12 mm. wide; petals 4, unguiculate; stamens 6; ovary sessile. Fruit a cylindrical, embossed silique covered with white hairs, constricted between the seeds; valves with 3 prominent veins; beak compressed, tip attenuate, longer than the valves. Seeds 2–3 in each cell, yellow, globular, 1–2 mm. in diameter. Europe, Asia, North America. (Syn. *Brassica alba* [L.] Boiss.)

The seeds are officinal. They occur as entire, globular seeds, the color varying from light to dark yellow, one of the curved surfaces having a ridge and 2 grooves parallel to the length, the opposite curved edge without groove or ridge. The odor is aromatic, the taste very pungent. The seeds contain 22–30% fixed oil (arachic, lignoceric, erucic, linolenic acids), 25% mucilage, the glycoside sinalbin, and the enzyme myrosin.[9] Sinalbin ($C_{30}H_{42}N_2O_{15}S_2 \cdot 5H_2O$; levorotatory bitter crystals; m.p. 83–84°, 139° when anhydrous, loses all water at 100°; soluble in water, alcohol; insoluble in ether), upon enzymatic hydrolysis with myrosin, yields glucose, choline, sinapinic acid, and parahydroxybenzylisothiocyanate (acrinyl isothiocyanate).[144] The latter substance, known as "white mustard oil," is a yellowish oily liquid, of pungent odor and unpleasant hot taste, with the formula C_7H_7ONCS;[149] externally it is vesicatory and rubefacient similar to black mustard. White mustard seeds have a cathartic action, due to the liberation of H_2S on contact with water; large doses may produce sulfide poisoning, with cyanosis, etc.; it may be used as emetic as black mustard.[152]

Used internally as expectorant and diaphoretic. Dose, 3–6 gm. As emetic, 10 gm. Externally as rubefacient in various neuralgias.

DRYOBALANOPS AROMATICA Gaertn.

(Dypterocarpaceae)

龍腦香

Borneo camphor tree. A tall tree reaching 50–60 m. Leaves alternate, coriaceous, glabrous, elliptical, acuminate; stipules small, caducous. Inflorescence a terminal panicle, poorly branching. Flowers white, bibracteolate; calyx obconical, segments 5; petals 5; stamens numerous; ovary somewhat inferior. Fruit dehiscent, 3-valved, the base sunk into the cupuliform calyx, ligneous, ovoid, fibrous, finely striate. Malaysia. (Syn. *D. camphora* Colebr.)

Borneo camphor occurs as concrete masses in fissures of the above tree. The taste is bitter, pungent, and astringent; the odor is aromatic. The drug consists chiefly of d-borneol (camphol, $C_{10}H_{18}O$; hexagonal plates; peculiar peppery odor and burning taste; less volatile than camphor; m.p. 208°, b.p. 212°; soluble in alcohol, ether; slightly soluble in water), with traces of camphene and sesquiterpenes.[151] The action of borneol is similar to that of camphor.[152]

Used internally as sedative and antispasmodic. Dose, 175–350 mg. Externally it is employed as antiphlogistic in stomatitis, nasal mucositis, conjunctivitis.

EUCOMMIA ULMOIDES Oliv.

(Eucommiaceae)

杜仲

An elm-like tree attaining 20 m. in height, but generally only 5 m. Leaves alternate, petiolate, oval-lanceolate, acuminate, the base wedge-shaped, 12 cm. long by 6 cm. wide, dentate. Flowers dioecious, appearing in April before the leaves unfold, no perianth. Male flowers solitary, stamens 4–10, anthers red; female flowers solitary, ovary 1-celled. Fruit a stalked, oblong samara, 3–4 cm. long by 6–12 mm. wide, winged; September–October; seed 1, oblong, compressed. Cultivated. Southern China.

The bark is officinal. When broken, it reveals silvery, extensible filaments. The taste is sweet, slightly pungent. The bark contains the latex gutta-percha (essentially a polymerized hydrocarbon of the general formula $[C_5H_8]_n$ with other resinous substances;[144] m.p. 100° with partial decomposition, soluble in chloroform, petroleum ether, partially soluble in hot alcohol, insoluble in water.)[148, 151] Gutta-percha has neither physiological nor therapeutic action, being used for its physical qualities alone.[150] "An injection of the decoction lowers the blood pressure of cats, the action being less apparent with excision of the tenth cranial nerve."[140]

Prescribed as tonic and hypotensor with sedative and analgesic properties. Dose, 5–10 gm., or 30 cc. of a 20% tincture 3 times a day.

巴豆

CROTON TIGLIUM L.

(Euphorbiaceae)

A small evergreen tree 5–6 m. tall. Leaves alternate, lengthily petiolate, stipulate, oboval, entire, acuminate, base-rounded, 9–16 cm. long by 4–7 cm. wide; stipules narrow. Inflorescence axillary; January–May. Flowers dioecious, small. Male flowers with glandular calyx, sepals 5; petals 5, white; stamens 15–30, free. Female flowers with 5 glandular sepals; petals 5, free, tongue-shaped; ovary 3-celled; styles 3, 2-branched. Fruit a dehiscent capsule with 3 bivalvular hulls. Southwestern China, Burma, Laos, Vietnam, Malaysia.

The seeds are used medicinally. They occur 12 mm. long by 8 mm. wide, oblong, rounded at the two extremities, with 2 faces, the dorsal face more convex than the ventral, the latter being marked with an awn, epidermis brownish, albumen oleaginous and voluminous, cotyledons foliaceous. The taste is oily, at first sweet and then burning. The seeds contain 35–55% fixed oil (croton oil; pale yellow or brownish yellow, viscid liquid; slight disagreeable odor; poisonous; freely soluble in chloroform, ether; slightly soluble in alcohol).[151] The oil comprises about 10% of a powerfully vesicant resin; the glyceride of tiglic acid ($C_5H_8O_2$; isometric with angelic acid; triclinic plates, rods; odor spicy; vesicant; m.p. 64°; freely soluble in hot water; poorly soluble in cold water); and the protoplasmic poison crotin (a mixture of toxic albuminoids; white or yellowish powder; soluble in NaCl solution); the phenol phorbol has been isolated from the resin.[11 144 152] Croton oil is the most violent of all cathartics, $\frac{1}{2}$ to 1 drop producing burning in the mouth and stomach, often emesis, several extensive fluid evacuations, much colic and tenesmus; toxic doses produce gastroenteritis and collapse.[10] Applied externally, croton oil produces irritation, proceeding to pustulation and even sloughing; when diluted with 2 to 10 parts of olive oil it may be used as a counter-irritant, but is dangerous.[152]

Employed as violent purgative in lead colic, etc. Dose of the seeds, 40–100 mg.

戟 大

EUPHORBIA PEKINENSIS Rupr.

(Euphorbiaceae)

A perennial herb with cespitose rhizome. Stem 60 cm. tall, terminated with a 5-branched umbel. Leaves alternate, oblong-elliptical, oval, acute, dentate, glabrous, the underside glaucous, 2–5 cm. long by 6–9 mm. wide. Involucre campanulate, the interior hairy; flowers monoecious, without true perianth, growing within the cupuliform involucre. Male flowers reduced to 1 stamen; female flowers in the center of the involucre, ovary 3-celled. Fruit a globular, depressed capsule, warty; seeds oval. China, Korea, Japan. (Syn. *E. coraroides* Thunb., *E. lasiocaula* Boiss., *E. sampsoni* Hance.)

The root is officinal, occurring as yellowish brown pieces 4–6 cm. long by 1 cm. in diameter. The taste is bitter. The plant contains the latex euphorbium.[140] The active constituent of euphorbium is the resinous euphorbon, which resembles the active resin of croton oil.[10] The plant also contains alkaloids, and the 3 coloring matters *Euphorbia* A ($C_{16}H_{11}O_5$; golden yellow needles; m.p. 217°), *Euphorbia* B ($C_{15}H_8O_5$; brilliant reddish orange scales; m.p. 224°), and *Euphorbia* C (fine red needles; m.p. 283°).[151]

Employed as purgative and diuretic. Dose, 2–4 gm.

(Other species of *Euphorbia* used for this purpose include *E. helioscopia* L., *E. lathyris* L., and *E. sieboldiana* Moore et Decne.)

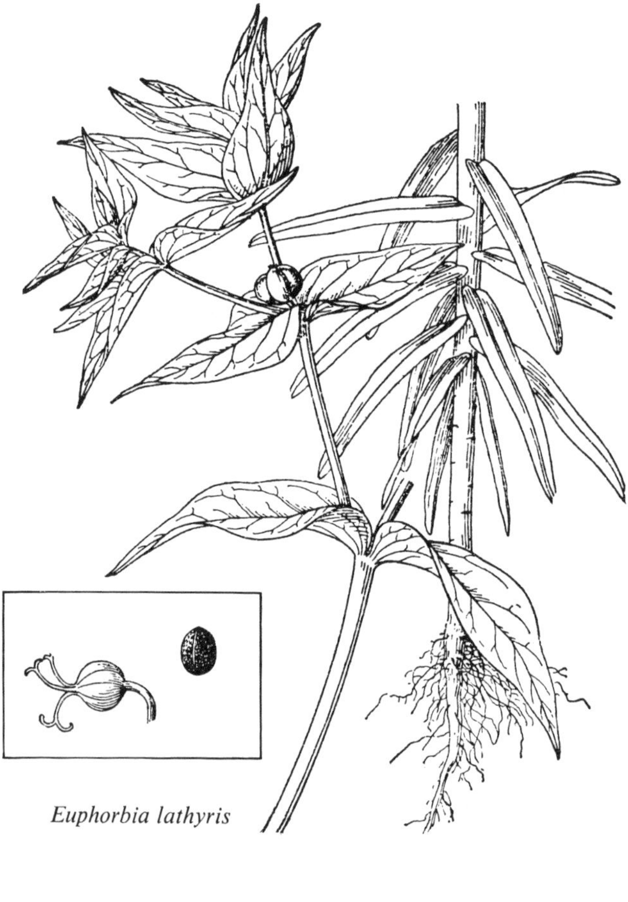

Euphorbia lathyris

蓖麻子

RICINUS COMMUNIS L.

(Euphorbiaceae)

Castor-oil plant. An annual herb occurring as a small shrub to a tree 15 m. high in some tropical regions. Leaves alternate, petiolate, peltate, palmate; lobes 5–11, dentate. Inflorescence a dense, terminal panicle often 30–60 cm. high; July–August. Flowers monoecious, apetalous; male flowers at the base of the panicle, stamens numerous; female flowers on the superior portion of the same panicle, sepals 5, caducous, ovary superior. Fruit an echinate capsule divided into 3 bivalvular hulls; October; seeds smooth, somewhat compressed, marbled. Cultivated.

The seeds of *R. communis* are the source of 50–55% of castor oil. The oil consists mainly of ricinolein, which is the triglyceride of the unsaturated ricinoleic acid; the neutral fat is not active, but becomes so upon saponification in the intestine, where it yields glycerin and ricinoleic acid ($C_{18}H_{34}O_3$; liquid; soluble in alcohol, acetone, ether, chloroform); the cathartic effect is due mainly to motor stimulation of the small intestine.[152] The seeds also contain 2 substances which do not pass into the oil, the highly toxic albumin ricin (white powder; soluble in 10% sodium chloride solution) and a toxic alkaloid ricinine (ricidine; $C_8H_8N_2O_2$; brilliant needles or prisms; m.p. 201.5°; sparingly soluble in water, alcohol, chloroform, ether).[148] Ingestion of the seeds may cause violent gastro-enteritis with nausea, headache, persistent vomiting, colic, thirst, emaciation, and great debility; more severe intoxication includes small, frequent pulse, cold sweat, icterus, and convulsions; low fatality is due to the destruction of the poison in the alimentary canal.[152] Ricin hemolyzes and agglutinates the corpuscles of warm-blooded animals; the agglutinating action is powerful.[104]

The oil is used as purgative. Dose, 4–16 cc. The seeds are powdered and applied externally to abscesses, carbuncles, etc.

大風子

HYDNOCARPUS ANTHELMINTICA Pierre.

(Flacourtiaceae)

Chaulmoogra tree. 25–30 m. tall. Leaves coriaceous, entire, 10–30 cm. long by 3–7 cm. wide, oboval-elliptical, base obtuse, tip attenuate, surface dull, underside yellowish. Inflorescence axillary, consisting of 2–3 few-flowered clusters, unilateral, 5–7 mm. long, pedunculate. Flowers polygamous or monoecious, greenish; sepals 5; scales (staminodia) linear, united at the base with the petals and opposite them; stamens 5; ovary free, sessile, 1-celled. Fruit globular, superiorly attenuate, as large as the human fist; seeds 30–40, polygonal, 2 cm. long by 1 cm. wide. Thailand, Burma, India.

The seeds are used medicinally. They occur the size of an almond, ovoid, grayish. They contain about 16% chaulmoogra oil, which differs little from that expressed from the true chaulmoogra, *Taraktogenos kurzii.* Chaulmoogra oil (yellow or brownish yellow oil; below 25° a soft solid; characteristic odor; soluble in benzene, ether, chloroform; slightly soluble in cold alcohol, nearly soluble in hot alcohol) consists of the glyceryl esters of a unique series of cyclic fatty acids which contain a closed 5-carbon ring, are optically active, and have not been found in any other oils; the most abundant of these acids are chaulmoogric acid ($C_{18}H_{32}O_2$; shiny leaflets; m.p. 68.5°; freely soluble in ether, chloroform) and hydnocarpic acid ($C_{15}H_{27}COOH$).[84] These acids possess a specific toxicity for acid-fast bacteria; it has been reported that the administration of these acids and their esters appears to stay the progress of clinical leprosy, producing recession of the nodular, macular, and anesthetic lesions, and the degeneration and disappearance of the bacilli; clinical treatment is successful in only part of the patients, the response of early cases requiring three months of energetic treatment, while older cases do not respond; relapses tend to occur when treatment is stopped.[97] The nauseating taste of chaulmoogra oil and the resulting gastrointestinal irritation render intensive medication by mouth difficult; the emetic action is reflex and may decrease on continued administration; overdosage may cause dyspnea, laryngeal spasm, renal irritation, weakness, and intensification of the lepra lesions.[89] Better tolerated is ethyl chaulmoograte, which is essentially a mixture of the ethyl esters of the fatty acids (pale yellow, clear liquid; slight fruity odor; not unpleasant taste; miscible with alcohol, chloroform; insoluble in water). Intramuscular injection of chaulmoogra oil produces severe local irritation; subcutaneous and intravenous administration of the sodium salt gives good response, but often leads to obliteration of the vein; intramuscular injection of the esters is best, producing some pain and irritation, and sometimes necrosis, but much less than the oil; intravenous injection of the esters is dangerous, resulting in pulmonary embolism.[152]

The powdered seeds are employed in the Chinese pharmacopoeia as disinfectant in leprosy, elephantiasis, syphilis, and various skin diseases. Dose, 3–5 gm.

CORYDALIS AMBIGUA Cham. et Schlecht.

(Fumariaceae)

延胡索

An herbaceous perennial, the stem erect, tender, 20 cm. high. Leaves alternate, compound, the last leaflet larger than the others and tridentate at the tip. Inflorescence a multifloral cluster; April–May. Sepals 2; corolla irregular, with 4 erect, connivent petals, one of which is spurred, greenish violet; stamens 6; ovary 2-celled. Fruit an oblong, linear capsule. Siberia, Manchuria, Japan.

The root is officinal. It occurs as a small, flat tuber 17 cm. thick by 20 mm. in diameter, hard, ochre-yellow, the exterior covered with a thin, wrinkled cuticle, the interior light yellow, semi-transparent, cirrose. The taste is bitter. A large number of alkaloids have been isolated from the tuber, including corydaline ($C_{22}H_{27}NO_4$; prisms; m.p. 135°; freely soluble in chloroform, ether, benzene; slightly soluble in alcohol; insoluble in water; oxidizes to the yellow dehydrocorydaline $C_{22}H_{23}NO_4$), corybulbine (corydalis-G; $C_{21}H_{25}NO_4$; needles; m.p. 238°; soluble in chloroform, hot benzene, acetone; sparingly soluble in water, alcohol, ether), isocorybulbine ($C_{21}H_{25}NO_4$; leaflets; m.p. 179–180°; soluble in alcohol, dilute acids), corycavidine ($C_{22}H_{25}NO_5$; crystals; m.p. 212°), corycavamine ($C_{21}H_{21}NO_5$; rhombic columns; m.p. 149°; soluble in alcohol and chloroform; at melting point converted to corycavine), corydine ($C_{20}H_{23}NO_4$; tetragonal prisms; m.p. 149°; freely soluble in chloroform, alcohol, ethyl acetate; moderately soluble in ether), bulbocapnine ($C_{19}H_{19}NO_4$; rhombic needles; m.p. 199°; soluble in alcohol, chloroform; insoluble in water), protopine (fumarine; $C_{20}H_{19}NO_5$; monoclinic prisms; m.p. 208°; soluble in chloroform, alcohol, ether; slightly soluble in ethyl acetate, benzene, petroleum ether, carbon disulfide; practically insoluble in water), d-tetrahydropalmatine ($C_{21}H_{25}NO_4$; crystals; m.p. 141–142°).[140] Ten additional corydaline alkaloids have been isolated, corydaline B ($C_{20}H_{23}NO_4$; m.p. 148–149°), corydaline D ($C_{19}H_{16}NO_4$; m.p. 204°), corydaline E (silky needles; m.p. 219°), corydaline F ($C_{20}H_{23}NO_4$; m.p. 237°), corydaline H (yellow prisms; m.p. 235°), corydaline I (m.p. 104°), corydaline J ($C_{30}H_{30}N_2O_5$; prismatic needles; m.p. 118°), corydaline K ($C_{21}H_{25}NO_4$; m.p. 225°), corydaline L ($C_{13}H_{21}NO_4$; m.p. 236°), corydaline M ($C_{21}H_{24}NO_5$; m.p. 161°).[20] Bulbocapnine induces catatonic rigidity of the skeletal muscle by peculiar narcotic and stimulant actions, a "perturbation of the cortico-diencephalic automatism"; the phosphate and hydrochloride have been used in certain diseases of the nervous system such as paralysis agitans, chorea, and ataxic conditions.[144] The action of isocorydine resembles closely that of bulbocapnine.[115] Curare and muscular actions have been described for protopine.[152]

Prescribed as sedative, antispasmodic, analgesic in headache, gastralgia, menstrual colic. Dose, 3–5 gm.

脂香楓

LIQUIDAMBAR FORMOSANA Hance.

(Hamamelidaceae)

Formosa sweet gum. A tree 40 m. tall. Leaves alternate, palmate; lobes 3–5, acuminate, base cordate or truncate, 8–13 cm. wide; petiole lengthy. Inflorescence monoecious; March. Male capitula grouped in terminal panicles, no calyx, stamens numerous; female flowers solitary, hanging, the calyx barely distinct, staminodia 4–10, ovary inferior. Fruit spherical, 3 cm. in diameter, hispid; August–September. Southern China, Vietnam, Laos, Japan, Taiwan. (Syn. *L. acerifolia* Max., *L. maximowiczii* Miq.)

The tree yields a balsam which is analogous to that of *L. orientalis* Mill.[109]

The balsam is used externally as antiphlogistic and astringent in various skin disorders.

桃 胡

JUGLANS REGIA L.

(Juglandiaceae)

English or Persian walnut. A tree 10–20 m. tall, the bark silvery gray. Leaves alternate, petiolate, to 25 cm. long; leaflets 5–9, rarely 11, nearly sessile, oblong or elliptical-oblong, acute, entire, coriaceous, 6–12 cm. long, aromatic. Flowers monoecious, blooming before the leaves; April. Male catkins terminal or lateral, cylindrical; stamens 14–36, with short filaments and bilobed anthers. Female flowers 1–4 in erect racemes with caducous scales; ovary adherent to the calyx tube. Fruit a globular drupe; exocarp fleshy, green, indehiscent; endocarp with 2 ligneous, elevated valves; seed with 4 sinuate lobes. Northwestern China, Tibet, Iran, Asia Minor, Europe.

The kernel contains juglone ($C_{10}H_6O_3$; yellow needles; m.p. 155°; volatile with steam; freely soluble in alcohol, ether; slightly soluble in hot water), isojuglone ($C_{10}H_8O_5$;

colorless crystalline spangles; m.p. 168–170°; freely soluble in alcohol, ether; insoluble in water, chloroform), 0.03% essential oil, 0.37% inositol, phytin, phytosterols, oxidase, vitamins A, B, C, and E, and ellagic, lauric, myristic, arachic, linoleic, linolenic, isolinolenic, and oleic acids.[151] An antifungal activity is claimed for juglone.[144] The hull (endocarp) as well as the leaves is highly astringent owing to the contained tannin, but especially to the bitter substance, juglandin.[146]

The oil of the kernel is used as a mild laxative and anthelmintic. The leaves and powdered hull are used as astringent, and as "blood purifier" in syphilis; a decoction is used externally in phlyctenular conjunctivitis.

通木

AKEBIA QUINATA Decne.

(Lardizabalaceae)

A creeping, woody vine. Leaves digitate; leaflets 5, oval or oval-oblong, entire, emarginate, deep green, 2–3 cm. long by 12–18 mm. wide. Inflorescence an axillary, loose cluster. Flowers monoecious; April–May; odoriferous; perianth petaloid, purplish brown. Male flowers with varying amount of stamens, most often 6; female flowers with sterile stamens, ovary consisting of several free carpels, 3–12, ovules numerous. Fruit a fleshy follicle, bacciform, dehiscent lengthwise; September–October; seeds black. Eastern China, Japan. (Syn. *Rajania quinata* Thunb.)

The stem is used medicinally, occurring as thin-sliced, transverse sections of the ligneous stem, 1 cm. in diameter, the marrow showing small black holes like a sieve. The taste is pungent. The plant contains the crystalline glycoside akebin, which hydrolyzes to yield hederagenin, rhamnose, and oleanolic acid; and 30% potassium salts.[140] The diuretic action of the drug is evidently due to the potassium salt content.

Prescribed as diuretic and antiphlogistic. Dose, 4–7 gm.

枝 桂

CINNAMOMUM CASSIA Blume.

(Lauraceae)

Cassia, Chinese cinnamon. A tree 10 m. high. Leaves alternate, petiolate, elliptical-oval, 8–15 cm. long by 3–4 cm. wide, tip acuminate, base rounded, entire, coriaceous, underside lightly pubescent; petiole 10 mm. long, lightly pubescent. Inflorescence a densely hairy panicle as long as the leaves; May. Flowers yellowish white, small, in cymes of 2–5; perianth 6-lobed, no petals; stamens 6, pubescent; ovary free, 1-celled. Fruit a globular drupe, 8 mm. long, red. Southern China, Laos, Vietnam, Sumatra. (Syn. *C. aromaticum* Nees.)

The dried bark is officinal. It occurs as rolled tubes, the exterior surface a deep fawn color, often a little reddish; the interior surface brown, finely granular; the break is clean, not fibrous; the taste is warm and piquant, the odor strongly aromatic. The bark yields an essential oil comprising 80% cinnamic aldehyde ($C_6H_5CH{=}CHCHO$; yellowish oily liquid, strong cinnamon odor; b.p. 246°, oxidizing rapidly and forming cinnamic acid; soluble in 700 parts water, 7 volumes of 60% alcohol; miscible with ether, chloroform, oils), eugenol, phellandrene, orthomethylcoumaric aldehyde, cinnamyl acetate, phenylpropyl alcohol, cinnamic alcohol, and traces of coumarin.[151] Cassia bark is an agreeable carminative, somewhat astringent and stimulant, also highly aromatic and antiseptic; the oil is not astringent, but is a general stimulant to the nervous and vascular systems, also checking nausea and vomiting; the bark is useful in checking diarrhea.[150]

Prescribed as aromatic stomachic, astringent, tonic, analgesic, and stimulant. Dose, 1–5 gm.

烏藥

LINDERA STRYCHNIFOLIA Vill.

(Lauraceae)

An aromatic shrub 5 m. high. Leaves alternate, petiolate, oval-elliptical, often orbicular, 4–5 cm. long by 1.5–5.0 cm. wide, abruptly acuminate, coriaceous, 3-veined. Flowers dioecious or polygamous; perianth a very short tube, 6-lobed; male flowers with 9 stamens; female with staminodia, the ovary superior. Fruit a black drupe. Central China, Taiwan. (Syn. *Benzoin strychnifolium* Kuntze., *Daphnidium strychnifolius* Sieb. et Zucc., *D. myrrha* Sieb. et Zucc.)

The root is used medicinally. The taste is pungent. The drug contains an essential oil comprising linderene, linderol, and linderane, the latter being identical to l-borneol.[64] Used as aromatic stomachic. Dose, 6–8 gm.

合歡皮

ALBIZZIA JULIBRISSIN Duraz.

(Leguminosae)

Silk tree. A tree about 12 m. high, with a broad, spreading crown. Leaves bipinnate; leaflets 8–24, each subdivided into 40–60 very oblique leaflets which are sessile, lanceolate, cuspidate, 6 mm. long by 3 mm. wide. Inflorescence a nearly globular head, grouped in panicles at the tips of branches; June. Flowers small, sessile, pink; calyx infundibular, with short teeth, 3–4 mm. long; corolla 3 times longer than the calyx, petals 5; stamens numerous, lengthily exserted; filaments pink, 2.5 cm. long. Fruit a glabrous pod, flat, membranous, gray or light brown, indehiscent, 13–15 cm. long by 18–25 mm. wide; September–November; seeds 8–12. China, Japan, India, Iran, Ethiopia. (Syn. *Acacia nemu* Willd., *Mimosa arborea* Thunb.)

The bark is officinal, and occurs brownish and smooth.

The taste is bitter and astringent. The drug contains tannin and saponins.[107]

Used as tonic, stimulant, and anthelmintic. Dose, 5–10 gm. An extract of the bark is used externally as vulnerary.

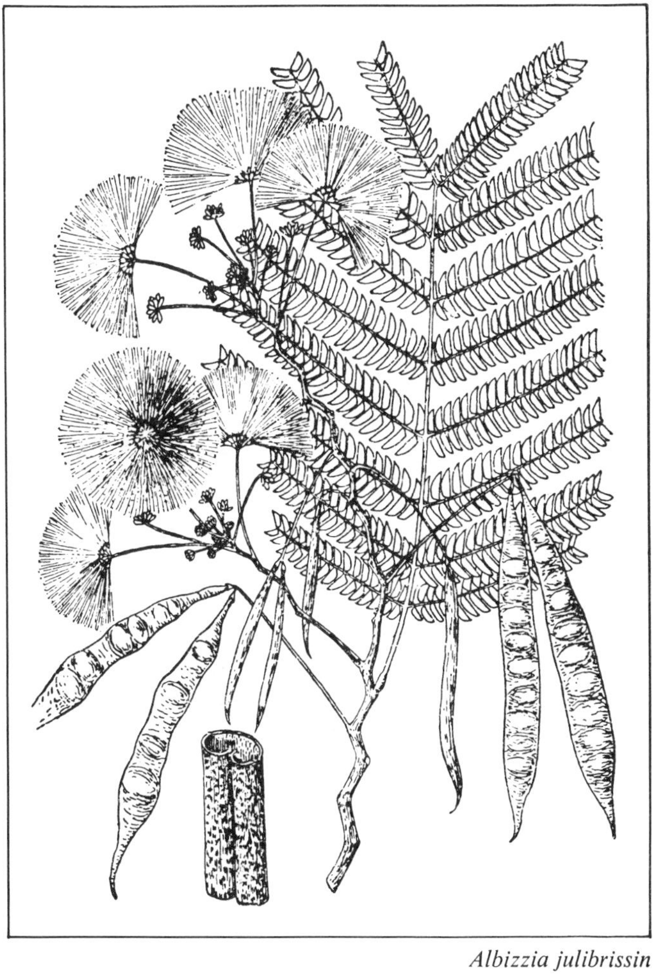

Albizzia julibrissin

耆 黃

ASTRAGALUS HOANTCHY Franch.

(Leguminosae)

A vetch-like herb, the stem 1 m. tall, angular, glabrous. Stipules membranous, white, often free beyond the petiole, broad, triangular, acuminate. Petiole rigid, nearly foliaceous at the base. Leaflets 8–12 pair, the terminal leaflet rapidly caducous, glandular, glabrous, broadly oval, the apex emarginate and finely mucronate, 1.0–1.5 cm. long. Peduncles longer than the leaves, ordinarily 30 cm. Flower clusters sparse, flowers 12–15; calyx swelling at the base, tubular, thin, and membranous, with several black hairs, teeth irregular; petals lengthily unguiculate; carina regular, winged; stamens 10, diadelphous. Fruit a lengthily stipitate pod, compressed, oblong, tip acuminate, valves rigid, coriaceous, 5–6 cm. long; seeds usually 12, black, oblong-reniform, 5–6 mm. long. Northern China, Mongolia, Manchuria. (Syn. *A. reflexistipulus* Franch.)

The root is officinal, occurring as pieces 20 cm. long by 15 mm. in diameter, the epidermis whitish. The taste is sweetish. The drug has not been found to contain any diuretic principle.[98]

Used as diuretic, tonic, and antipyretic. Dose, 4–18 gm. (*A. henyri* Oliv. is also employed.)

木 蘇

CAESALPINIA SAPPAN L.

(Leguminosae)

Sappan-wood. A tree 7–10 m. tall, the trunk 15–25 cm. in diameter, covered with short, conical thorns. Leaves bipinnate; leaflets 12 pair or more, contiguous, membranous, oblong, base truncate, tip rounded, 15–20 mm. long by 6–7 mm. wide. Inflorescence a broad, terminal panicle consisting of axillary and terminal clusters; May. Calyx a short tube, 5-lobed; petals 5, 4 orbiculate, shortly unguiculate,

6–8 mm. wide, the interior petal with an orbiculate limb 5 mm. in diameter; stamens 10, free; pistil entirely villous; ovary sessile. Fruit oblong, 75 mm. long by 35 mm. wide, the interior third attenuate, base obtuse, ligneous, the tip with a horn of 15 mm.; seeds 4, ellipsoid-compressed, 18–20 mm. long by 10–12 mm. wide by 7–9 mm. thick, dirty brown, valves 2 mm. thick, the interior tomentose, russet. Southern China, Indochina, India, Malaysia.

The wood is used medicinally, being cut into sticks 2–5 mm. in diameter, the color orangish red. The taste is sweetish-saline. The drug contains the coloring matter brazilin ($C_{16}H_{14}O_5$; amber-yellow crystals turning orange on exposure to air and light; decomposes above 130°; soluble in water, alcohol, ether), and sappanin ($C_{12}H_{12}O_4$).[100]

Used as hemostatic and astringent in metrorrhagia, dysentery, enterorrhagia. Dose, 4–11 gm. Employed externally for bruises, orchitis.

CASSIA ANGUSTIFOLIA Vahl.

(Leguminosae)

Tinnevelly senna. A shrub with leaves paripinnate; leaflets 7 pair, lanceolate, entire, tip acute, base attenuate, 3–6 cm. long by 7–8 mm. wide, surface yellowish green, underside darker and with several fine short hairs. Inflorescence an axillary cluster; calyx with 5 nearly regular teeth; petals 5, nearly regular; stamens 10. Fruit an indehiscent pod. India, Arabia, Africa.

The leaflets, known as senna, are officinal. They occur as a mixture of entire and broken leaves, the texture subcoriaceous. The odor is slight, the taste bitter and mucilaginous. The drug has been reported to contain the anthraquinone derivatives, either free or in glycosidal combination, rhein ($C_{15}H_8O_6$; yellow needles; m.p. 321–322°; soluble in alkalies, pyridine; slightly soluble in alcohol, benzene, chloroform, ether; insoluble in water) and aloe-emodin ($C_{15}H_{10}O_5$;

orange needles; m.p. 223–224°; freely soluble in hot alcohol, in ether, benzene); sennanigrin, which yields chrysophanol and emodin, has also been isolated; more recently the glycosides sennoside A and sennoside B have been found and are claimed to be the laxative principles; other substances which have been found, but which probably are not connected with the purgative action, are sennacrol, sennapicrin, sennarhamnetin, kaempferol and its glycoside kaempferin, and a small amount of volatile oil.[144] Senna is the most active of the anthraquinone cathartics, generally causing griping and semiliquid stools; the griping may be corrected by carminatives, or by the previous extraction of the resins with alcohol.[152] The drug is contraindicated in spastic colitis; is incompatible with mineral acids, carbonates, cinchona, and tartar emetic.[148]

As laxative, 0.5–1.0 gm. As mild cathartic, 1–3 gm. As drastic purgative, 4–8 gm.

決明子

CASSIA TORA L.

(Leguminosae)

Sickle senna. An annual herb 30–90 cm. high. Leaves 8–12 cm. long; leaflets 6, oboval, obtuse, base attenuate, 3–5 cm. long by 15–25 mm. wide. Flowers grouped 1–3 in the leaf axils; August; sepals 5, slightly irregular; corolla nearly regular, petals 5, oboval; stamens 7. Fruit a linear pod 12–14 cm. long by 4 mm. wide; October; seeds about 25, pointed at one extremity, rounded or truncate at the other, deep brown. Southern China, Indochina, India, Japan, Philippines, Java.

The seeds are used medicinally, and occur oblong, rounded at the base, 5 mm. long by 2 mm. in diameter, brown, smooth, and glossy. The taste is mucilaginous and somewhat bitter. The seeds contain emodin, a glycoside, and a phytosterol.[151] A reddish brown substance soluble in water and insoluble in ether, and which upon hydrolysis yields trihydromethylanthraquinone, has been found.[29]

Prescribed in various eye and hepatic disorders. Dose, 5–8 gm.

Cassia tora

海桐皮

ERYTHRINA INDICA Lam.

(Leguminosae)

India coral tree. A tree 10 m. tall, covered with short, conical spines. Leaves alternate, trifoliate, stipulate, 20–30 cm. long. Inflorescence a dense cluster, 10–15 cm. long, bracteate. Flowers grouped 1–3 in the bracteal axils; calyx 25–30 mm., glabrous, spathaceous, divided to the base, teeth 5 or often 1–3; petals irregular, bright red; vexillum 15–25 mm. wide, 5–6 cm. long; wings and keel free; stamens 10, monadelphous. Fruit 15–30 cm. long, black, glabrous, finely veined, tardily dehiscent; seeds 6–8, nearly reniform, 15 mm. long by 10 mm. wide, brown; hilum large, oval, blackish gray with a pale margin. Southern China, Laos, southern Vietnam, India, Malaysia.

The bark is used medicinally. The taste is bitter. The drug contains several alkaloids, notably the betaine of tryptophane, hypaphorine ($C_{14}H_{18}N_2O_2$; colorless crystals, decomposing at 237°; soluble in water; slightly soluble in alcohol).[74] The Erythrina alkaloids produce curare-like effects of short duration;[95] they produce strong parasympathetic stimulation perhaps analogous to that of nicotine.[69]

Used as analgesic in arthritis, rheumatism, neuralgia. Dose, 4–7 gm.

皂莢

GLEDITSCHIA SINENSIS Lam.

(Leguminosae)

A tree 15–20 m. tall, the trunk and branches covered with ramified thorns. Leaves pinnate, 12–18 cm. long; leaflets 1–14 pair, oval, 3–8 cm. long, obtuse, mucronate. Flowers polygamous; May; calyx campanulate; petals 3–5; stamens 10, inserted with the petals into the disk; ovary nearly sessile. Fruit a flat pod, nearly straight, 14–20 cm. long by 2–3 cm. wide; September–October. China, Japan. (Syn. *G. horrida*

Willd., *G. xylocarpa* Hance., *Gymnocladus williamsii* Hance.)

The pods are officinal. The taste is pungent and saline. The pods contain saponins.[106]

Used as stimulant expectorant. Dose, 5–8 gm.

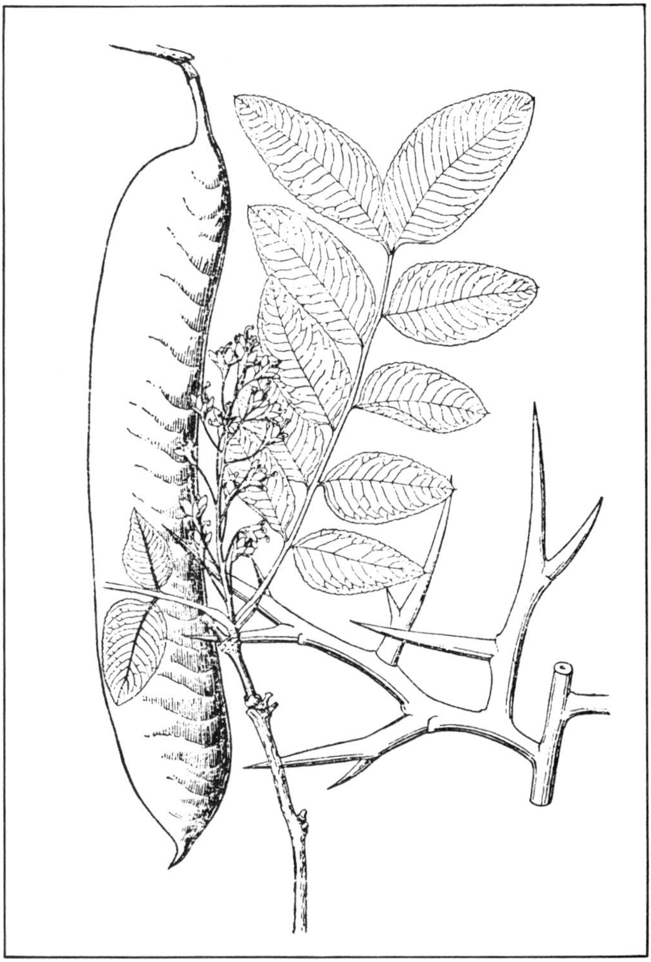

Gleditschia sinensis

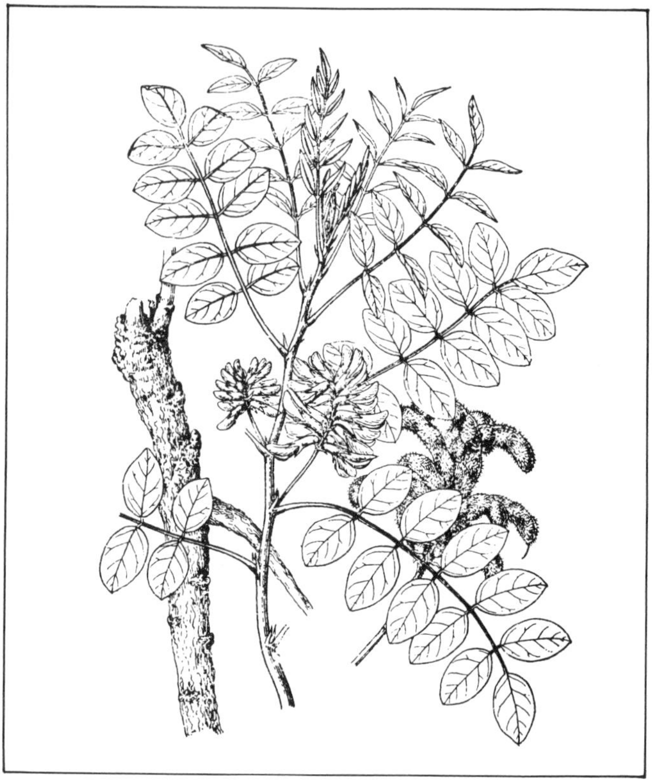

Glycyrrhiza uralensis

GLYCYRRHIZA URALENSIS Fisch.

(Leguminosae)

Chinese licorice. A perennial herb, the stem erect, pubescent. Leaves alternate, pinnate; leaflets oboval, obtuse, nearly glabrous; stipules lanceolate. Inflorescence an axillary cluster. Flowers purplish, papilionaceous; calyx villous. Fruit a flat pod. Northern China, Mongolia, Siberia.

The root is officinal. It occurs as cylindrical, fibrous pieces, flexible, 20–22 cm. long by 15 mm. in diameter, with

草 甘

or without epidermis; epidermis reddish, furrowed, interior light yellow. The taste is sweet. The drug contains salts of the glycoside glycyrrhizic acid (glycyrrhizin; $C_{42}H_{62}O_{16}$; platelets, prisms; intensely sweet; decomposes at 220°; freely soluble in hot water; insoluble in absolute alcohol, ether), asparagin, sugars, resin, urease.[140] Glycyrrhizic acid upon hydrolysis yields 2 molecules of glucuronic acid and one of glycyrrhetinic acid; both glycyrrhizic acid and glycyrrhetinic acid appear to have certain of the physiological actions of desoxycorticosterone, with increase in retention of sodium ions and water, and potassium ion excretion.[144] Licorice is demulcent, increasing the flow of saliva and mucus, the increased secretion acting as emollient to the throat; in sufficient doses it is mildly laxative.[150]

Used as demulcent and expectorant in pharyngeal irritation, cough, and as emollient in peptic ulcer. Dose, 3–10 gm. Incompatibles: *Polygala tenuifolia, Euphorbia pekinensis, E. sieboldiana, Daphne genkwa.*

紙故破

PSORALEA CORYLIFOLIA L.

(Leguminosae)

An annual plant 90 cm. high, with blackish glands. Leaves petiolate, roundish-oval, dentate, 2.5–7.5 cm. long, both surfaces spotted with black. Inflorescence an axillary, pedunculate head. Calyx cupuliform, teeth 5; corolla yellow; stamens 10; ovary sessile. Fruit an oval pod, short, dry, indehiscent, black, glabrous, surrounded with the persistent calyx. India, Iran.

The seeds are used medicinally, occurring oval or reniform, compressed, blackish yellow, 4 mm. long by 3 mm. in diameter. The taste is pungent and bittersweet. The drug contains a fatty oil, an alkaloid, and the substance psoralein or poraline ($C_{11}H_6O_3$).[140 151]

Prescribed as tonic and stimulant in impotence, spermatorrhea, leukorrhea. Dose, 4–10 gm. Used externally in skin disorders such as vitiligo, callosity.

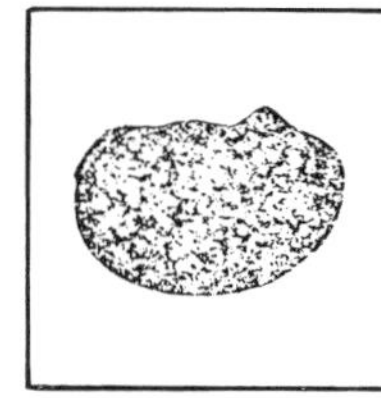

Psoralea corylifolia

PUERARIA THUNBERGIANA Benth.

(Leguminosae)

Kudzu vine. A somewhat woody, hairy-stemmed vine, volubilate, the root tuberous. Leaves pinnate-trifoliate; leaflets entire or slightly lobate, the central leaflet 14–18 cm. long, the lateral leaflets smaller, pubescent; petiole 10–20 cm. long. Inflorescence an axillary or terminal raceme, dense,

根 葛

erect, nearly 25 cm. long. Flowers purple, 1.5 cm. long; July–September; calyx 5-toothed; petals 5, nearly regular; stamens 10, monadelphous. Fruit a linear pod, straight, compressed, 4–9 cm. long by 6–15 mm. wide, hirsute, yellowish brown; October. China, Japan. (Syn. *Pachyrhizus thunbergianus* Sieb. et Zucc.)

The root is officinal. The taste is sweet and pungent. The root contains a large amount of starch; the leaves of the plant contain glutamic and butyric acids, asparagin, and adenine.[130]

The root is used as antipyretic, refrigerant. Dose, 4–11 gm.

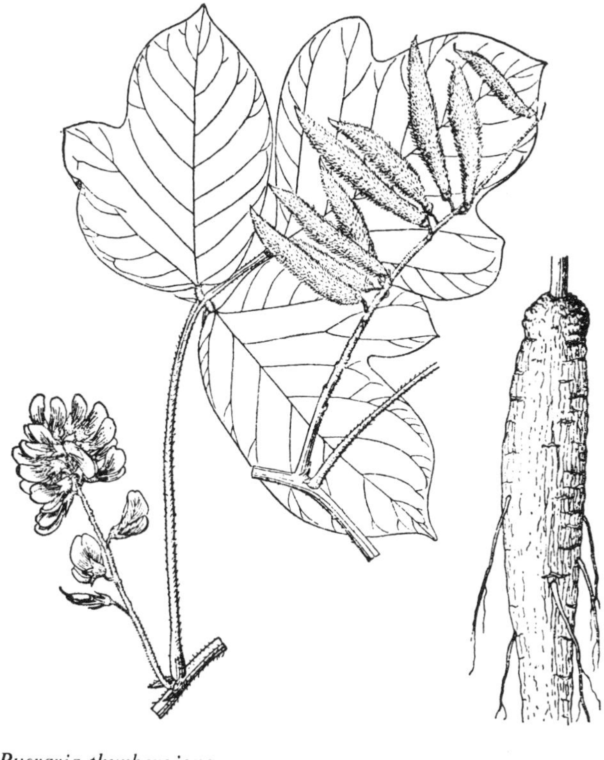

Pueraria thunbergiana

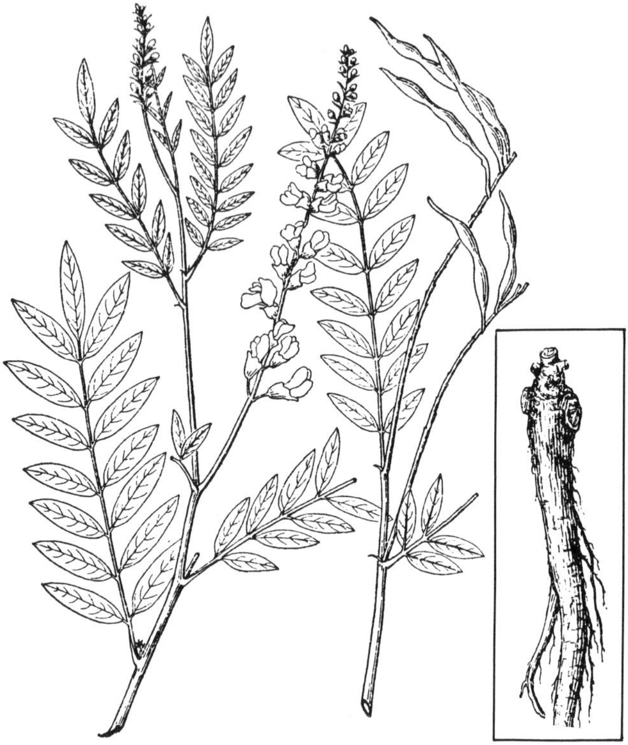

Sophora flavescens

參 苦

SOPHORA FLAVESCENS Ait.

(Leguminosae)

A shrub 2 m. tall. Leaves alternate, pinnate; leaflets 5–6, oblong, acute or obtuse, 3–5 cm. long by 1.5 cm. wide, the surface glabrous, underside tomentose. Inflorescence an axillary or terminal cluster. Flowers yellowish; May–July; calyx campanulate, teeth 5; petals 5, unguiculate; stamens 10, free; ovary tomentose. Fruit a pod, constricted between the seeds, 10–13 cm. long; August–September. China. (Syn.

S. angustifolia Sieb. et Zucc., *S. galegoides* Pall., *S. kronei* Hance., *S. sororia* Hance.)

The root is used medicinally. It occurs as transverse slices, oval, 2–3 mm. thick. The taste is very bitter. The root contains the alkaloid matrine, which has been obtained in 4 forms ($C_{15}H_{24}N_2O$; as needles or flat crystals, m.p. 76°; as orthorhombic prisms, m.p. 87°; as a liquid; as prisms, m.p. 84°; soluble in water, ether, chloroform, benzene; slightly soluble in petroleum ether).[59] Subcutaneous injection of matrine in rabbits produces CNS inhibition, intense convulsions, and respiratory paralysis.[140]

Used as bitter stomachic, and astringent in dysentery, enterorrhagia. Dose, 4–7 gm. Incompatibles: *Fritillaria verticillata, Cuscuta japonica, Echinops dahuricus, Veratrum nigrum.*

SOPHORA JAPONICA L.

(Leguminosae)

Pagoda tree. A spreading, round-headed tree 7–15 m. high. Leaves alternate, pinnate, 15–25 cm. long; leaflets 7–17, stalked, opposite, oblong, 2.5–5.0 cm. long by 1–2 cm. wide, tip acute, base rounded. Inflorescence a loose, terminal panicle, 15–30 cm. long. Flowers white, 1.0–1.5 cm. long; June–July; calyx campanulate; petals shortly unguiculate; stamens 10, free. Fruit a cylindrical pod, 5–8 cm. long, glabrous; October; seeds 4–6, ellipsoid, compressed, 9 mm. long by 4–5 mm. wide. China, Korea, northern Vietnam. (Syn. *Styphnolobium japonicum* Scott)

The seeds and flowers are used medicinally. The fruits contain rutin, sophoretin (quercetin), rhamnose, sophoricoside ($C_{21}H_{20}O_{10}$; crystals; m.p. 298°; soluble in pyridine, dilute alkalies; sparingly soluble in hot alcohol, water; insoluble in acetone, ethyl acetate), sophorabioside ($C_{27}H_{30}O_{14} \cdot 3H_2O$; needles; m.p. 156–160°, anhydrous m.p. 248°; freely soluble in pyridine; soluble in hot alcohol; slightly soluble in boiling water); the floral buds contain rutin.[151] Injection of the extract of the fruit induces hyperglycemia from diminution of red corpuscles and impaired hematosis; this hyperglycemia is of short duration; the total extract of the fruit is very toxic.[151]

The seeds and flowers are used as hemostatic. Dose, 5–10 gm.

Sophora japonica

巴盧胡

TRIGONELLA FOENUM-GRAECUM L.

(Leguminosae)

Fenugreek. An annual herb 10–40 cm. high, the stems not branched. Leaves petiolate, trifoliate; leaflets oboval or oblong, the upper part denticulate; stipules entire. Flowers whitish, solitary or geminate, sessile in the leaf axils, 12–15 mm. long; calyx a campanulate tube, teeth 5, covered with soft hairs; vexillum longer than the wings and the obtuse keel. Fruit an erect pod, 7–9 cm. long, linear, barely arched, glabrous, with fine longitudinal veins, terminated with a beak 2–3 cm. long; seeds nearly smooth, brown or russet, resembling a parallelepipedon with rounded corners, 2–3 mm. wide by 3–5 mm. long. India, southern Europe, northern Africa, southern China.

The seeds are officinal. They contain 28% mucilage, fatty oil, saponins, choline, lecithin, phytosterols, and the alkaloid trigonelline ($C_7H_7NO_2$; prisms; anhydrous at 100°, m.p. 218°; very soluble in water, soluble in alcohol; almost insoluble in ether, chloroform).[140]

Used as stimulant and carminative, and in renal disorders (apparently because of the shape and color of the seeds). Dose, 4–11 gm.

生寄桑

LORANTHUS YADORIKI Sieb. et Zucc.

(Loranthaceae)

A parasitic shrub growing on the branches of *Morus alba.* Leaves opposite, rounded, elliptical or elliptical-lanceolate, tip obtuse, base acuminate or rounded, entire, thick, pliable, surface glabrous, glossy green, underside pubescent, 4–7 cm. long by 2.0–3.5 cm. wide. Flowers in groups of 2–5, pedicel short; calycle campanulate, 2–4 mm. long, pubescent; calyx 1.5–2.5 cm. long, tomentose; petals reflected;

ovary inferior, 1-celled. Fruit an ovoid berry, light yellow, tomentose. Central China, Japan.

The entire plant is used medicinally, and occurs as withered branches and leaves, the color yellowish. The taste is bitter.

Prescribed as tonic, antiphlogistic, and hypotensor. Dose, 7 gm.

槲寄生

VISCUM ALBUM L.

(Loranthaceae)

European mistletoe. A parasitic shrub 20–50 cm. high, growing chiefly on deciduous trees. Stem articulate, yellowish green, glabrous. Leaves oblong, obtuse, base attenuate, thick, coriaceous. Flowers yellowish, grouped at the tips of the branches in the leaf axils, monoecious or dioecious; March–May. Male flowers with perianth tubular, short, limb in 4 segments; anthers 4, sessile; female flowers with perianth scaly, 4-lobed, fleshy, ovary inferior, stigma sessile. Fruit a sessile berry, globular, white, the pulp very viscous; October. Central China, Japan, Europe, Iran.

The stems are used medicinally. They contain viscine (oily liquid, yellowish; very soluble in alcohol, ether, chloroform; poorly soluble in water), ursolic acid, tannin, inositol, oxydase, acetylcholine, caoutchouc, myristic and arachic acids, cerylic alcohol, galactan, and a glycoside; inositol is widely distributed in plants, but is particularly abundant in *V. album;* the presence of saponins in this plant has been disputed.[151] Injection of extracts of the plant produces fall of blood pressure by vasodilation which has been attributed to excitation of the afferent depressant nerves of the heart; the heart is first slowed by increased vagal tone and then becomes rapid and arrhythmic by heterotopic stimuli.[45] Bradycardia has been attributed to reflexes from cardiac receptors, stimulating the vagus and inhibiting the accelerator centers.[90] These actions are not characteristic of tyra-

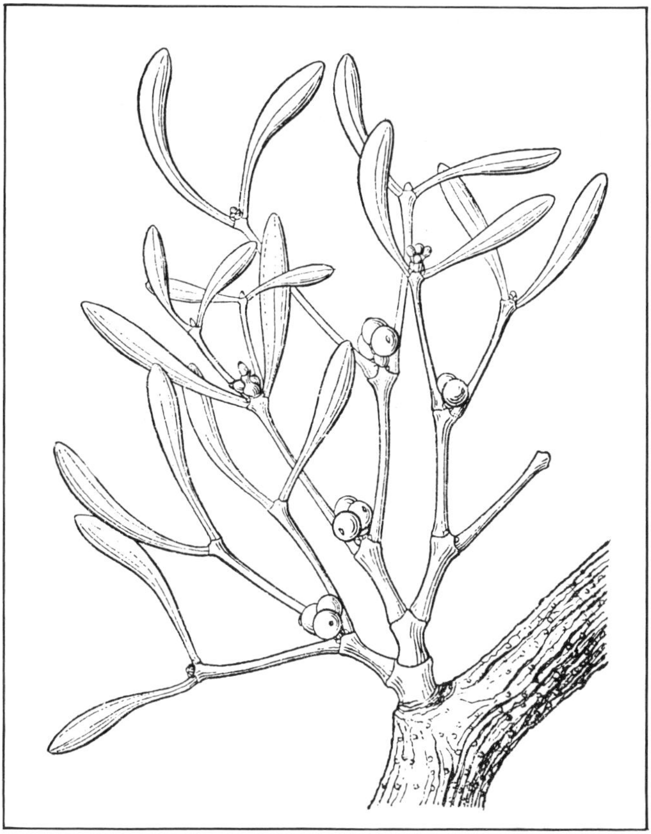

Viscum album

mine ($C_8H_{11}NO$; crystals; m.p. 164–165°), which the plant is said to contain; a saponin has been suggested.[42] The berries of mistletoe have produced emeto-catharsis with great thirst, tenesmus, bloody stools, convulsions, and even death in young children; the leaves and twigs have been used in epilepsy, hysteria, chorea, asthma, and other nervous affections.[150]

Prescribed as hypotensor, lactagogue.

厚朴

MAGNOLIA OFFICINALIS Reh. et Wils.

(Magnoliaceae)

A tree 6–15 m. tall, the bark dark gray and aromatic. Leaves large, oblong-spatulate, 35–45 cm. long by 12–20 cm. wide, surface glabrous, tomentose when young. Flowers odoriferous, white, 15–20 cm. in diameter; sepals and petals 9–12, nearly regular, obovoid; stamens numerous; filament expanded, scarlet; anthers introrse, mucronate; gynoecium and staminiferous section 3.5 cm. long, red; carpels numerous. Fruit oblong-ovoid, tip truncate, base rounded. Central China, cultivated; the tree dies when stripped of its bark. (Syn. *M. hypoleuca* Diels. non Sieb. et Zucc.)

The bark is used medicinally. The taste is bitter. The drug contains an essential oil and ho-curare, a substance whose muscle-paralyzant action is similar to that of South American curare.[44]

Used as antispasmodic and stomachic in spastic gastritis, peptic ulcer, diarrhea, emesis; and as antiseptic in typhoid fever, malaria. Dose, 6–10 gm. Incompatibles: *Euphorbia helioscopia*, potassium nitrate.

辛夷

MAGNOLIA LILIFLORA Desr.

(Magnoliaceae)

A deciduous tree-like shrub, the branchlets smooth except at the tips. Leaves alternate, somewhat oval, light green, 7–17 cm. long, the underside softly tomentose when young. Flowers solitary, lily-shaped, odoriferous, white inside, purple outside, 20 cm. wide; May–June; pedicel short, stout; sepals 3, shorter than the petals, soon falling; petals 6, 7–10 cm. long. Fruit oblong, brown. China, Japan. (Syn. *M. discolor* Vent., *M. purpurea* Curt.)

The unopened floral buds are officinal. The taste is pungent. They contain an essential oil comprising citral, safrole, anethole, estragole, cineol, eugenol.[140]

Prescribed as tonic and analgesic in sinusitis, rhinitis, coryza, headache, vertigo. Dose, 5–8 gm. Incompatibles: *Acorus gramineus*, *Astragalus hoantchy*.

五味子

SCHIZANDRA CHINENSIS Baill.

(Magnoliaceae)

An aromatic, woody vine. Leaves alternate, petiolate, oblong-obovoid, 5.0–7.5 cm. long by 2.5–5.0 cm. wide. Inflorescence a few-flowered, axillary cluster, monoecious or dioecious; May–June. Flowers pink or white, odoriferous, 1 cm. wide; sepals and petals alike, totaling 7–12; stamens 5–15; in the female flowers ovaries numerous, compact, 1-celled, the style short. Fruit a collection of berry-like, ripened carpels in a short, spike-like, drooping head, fleshy, indehiscent. Manchuria, northeastern China, Japan. (Syn. *Maximowicza chinensis* Rup., *Sphaerostema japonica* Sieb. et Zucc., *Sp. japonica* Hance.)

The dried berries are used medicinally. They occur blackish, with a transparent aril through which the 2 kidney-shaped seeds can be seen. The taste is sour. The drug contains an essential oil, a fatty oil, and mucilage; intravenous injection of an extract of the fruits in rabbits produces marked deepening of respiratory movement.[151]

Prescribed as tonic, stimulant, antitussive. Dose, 2–5 gm.

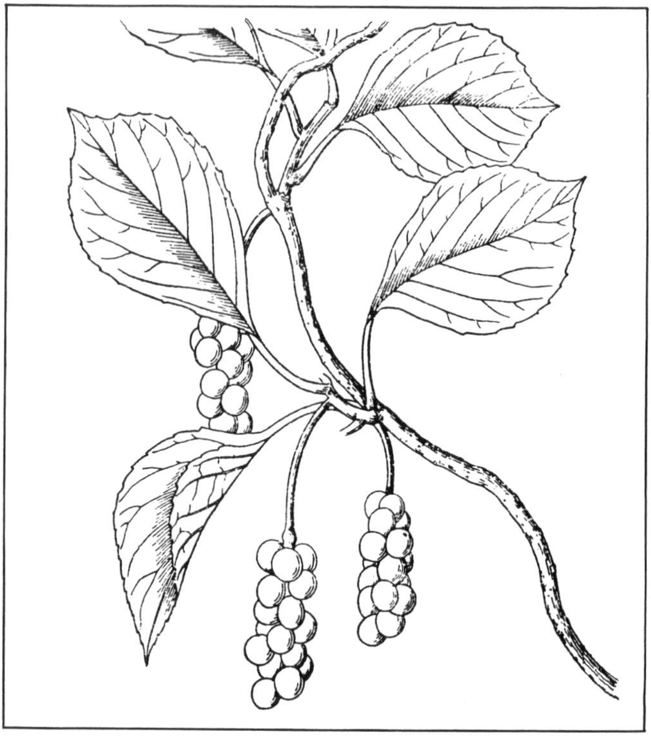

Schizandra chinensis

槿 木

HIBISCUS SYRIACUS L.

(Malvaceae)

Rose-of-Sharon. A shrub 3–5 m. tall. Leaves cuneate-oval, 8 cm. long by 6 cm. wide, trilobate, irregularly crenelate and dentate toward the tip; lateral lobes short, rounded; terminal lobe elongate, pointed. Peduncles axillary, solitary, uniflorous, as long as the petioles; bracts 6 or 7, linear, acute, longer than the sepals. Petals 5, oboval, white or pink or purplish; stamens numerous, united in a column; ovary 5-celled, styles 5; September–October. Fruit a 5-valved capsule, yellowish, globular, 2.5 cm. long. China, Japan, Taiwan. (Syn. *H. chinensis* DC., *H. rhombifolius* Cav.)

The root epidermis is officinal. The taste is bitter, pungent, and intensely astringent.

Used as emollient and antiphlogistic in intestinal affections, especially amebic colitis. Dose, 5–10 gm. A decoction is used externally as lotion in hemorrhoids.

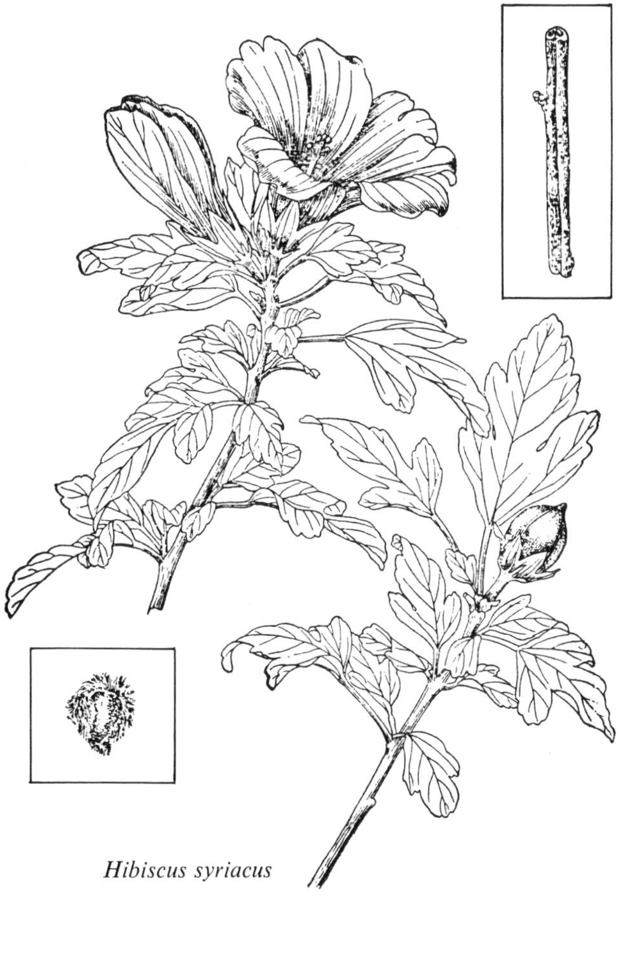

Hibiscus syriacus

皮白根樗

CEDRELA SINENSIS Juss.

(Meliaceae)

A hardy tree 25 m. tall. Leaves lengthily petiolate, alternate, paripinnate, 25–60 cm. long; leaflets 10–20, oblong or oval, 8–15 cm. long, acuminate, entire. Inflorescence a panicle 30 cm. long; June. Flowers odoriferous, white, campanulate, 5 mm. long; calyx tubular, 5-toothed; petals 5; stamens 5; staminodia 5, alternating with the stamens; disk columnar, supporting the ovary. Fruit a ligneous capsule, obovoid, 2.5 cm. long; September; seeds winged. China, Japan. (Syn. *Ailanthus flavescens* Carr., *Toona sinensis* Roem.)

The root epidermis is officinal. The taste is bitter. The epidermis contains tannin, quassin, cetylalcohol, stearin, olein, palmitin.[140] The leaves of the tree contain a toxin which in mice induces violent convulsions and death.[101]

The root epidermis is used as bitter stomachic and astringent in dysentery, enteritis, metrorrhagia. Dose, 2–5 gm.

子楝苦

MELIA AZEDARACH L.

(Meliaceae)

Chinaberry tree. A tree 20 m. tall, the leaves alternate, pinnate, 25–80 cm. long. Leaflets opposite, 2–6 cm. long by 20–25 mm. wide, glabrous when mature, oval-lanceolate, acuminate, margin irregularly dentate. Inflorescence an axillary panicle, compound, divaricate, shorter than the leaves. Flowers odoriferous, elongate, purple, 1 cm. long; April–May; calyx with 5–6 segments; petals 5–6; stamens 10, united into a tube somewhat shorter than the petals; disk very short; ovary 5-celled. Fruit a glabrous drupe, 1–3 cm. long; September–October; pericarp fleshy; endocarp ligneous, angular; seeds black, elliptical, tegument coriaceous. China, Indochina, India, Iran, Syria, Madagascar, Guiana,

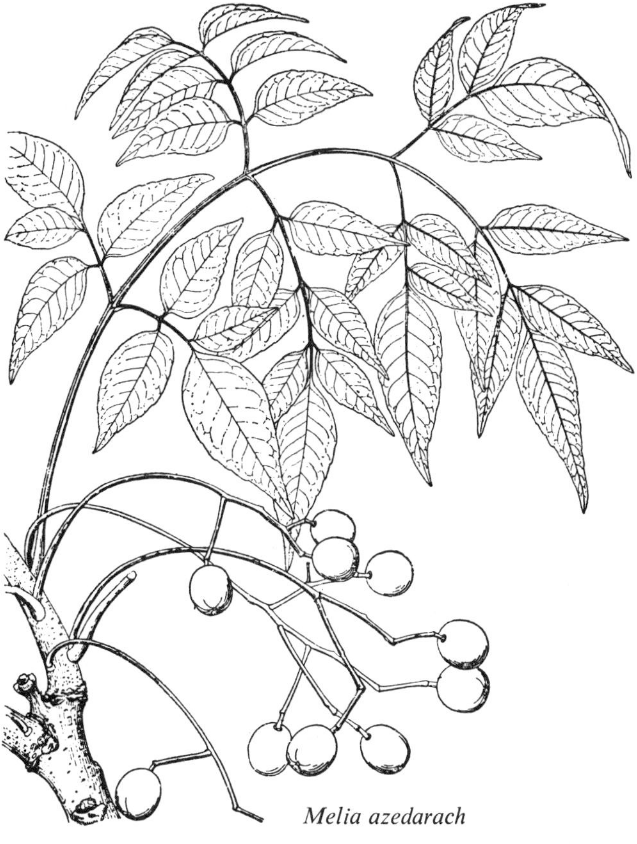

Melia azedarach

Antilles. (Syn. *M. japonica* G. Don., *M. toosendan* Sieb. et Zucc.)

The root epidermis and fruit are officinal. The taste is bitter. The drug is mildly poisonous. The bark of the tree contains tannin and the alkaloid margosine (crystalline, m.p. 175°);[140] the seeds yield 60% of a fatty oil comprising stearic, palmitic, lauric, valerianic, and butyric acids, and traces of a sulfurated essential oil.[151] The drug is known to produce symptoms of narcotic poisoning as giddiness, dimness of sight, mental confusion, stertorous breathing, dilated pupils, and stupor; large doses are necessary to cause these effects, and the occurrence of such symptoms has been questioned; the drug is, however, a gastrointestinal irritant, producing vomiting and purging, and is anthelmintic against *Ascaris*.[150]

Used as anthelmintic. Dose, 15–20 gm. in decoction every 2 hours; or 0.5 gm. powdered 3 times a day.

MENISPERMACEAE (fam.)

己防

The drug *fang chi* has been studied by a number of Chinese and Japanese chemists. Unfortunately, the botanical determination remains uncertain, the name *fang chi* being applied to several plants of the family Menispermaceae, including *Cocculus diversifolius* Miq. (Syn. *Sinomenium diversifolium* Diels., *S. acutum* Rehd. et Wils.), *C. trilobus* DC., *C. sarmentosus, C. laurifolius* DC., *C. thunbergii* DC., *Stephania tetrandra* S. Moore. China, Japan, Himalayas.

Numerous alkaloids have been isolated from the roots of the various above-mentioned plants. From *C. diversifolius,* cocculine (kokuline, kukoline; $C_{16}H_{20}NO_3 \cdot 3H_2O$; crystals; m.p. 162°; soluble in alcohol, chloroform; insoluble in water);[77] sinomenine (coculine; $C_{19}H_{23}NO_4$; clusters of needles; m.p. 161°, after melting once, m.p. 182°; soluble in alcohol, chloroform acetone; slightly soluble in water, ether, benzene);[63] diversine ($C_{20}H_{27}NO_5$; brownish gray, amorphous powder; m.p. 80–93°; soluble in alcohol; insoluble in water).[60] From *C. trilobus,* trilobine ($C_{36}H_{36}N_2O_5$; crystals; m.p. 235°; soluble in chloroform; sparingly soluble in alcohol, acetone, ether; insoluble in water).[62] From *C. sarmentosus,* menisarine ($C_{36}H_{34}N_2O_6$; tablets, scales; m.p. 203°; soluble in usual organic solvents except petroleum ether); from *C. laurifolius,* coclaurine ($C_{17}H_{19}NO_3$; plates, tablets; m.p. 221°; freely soluble in hot alcohol, hot acetone; slightly soluble in water, alcohol, chloroform, ether, acetone; insoluble in benzene, petroleum ether); from *Stephania tetrandra,* tetrandrine ($C_{38}H_{42}N_2O_6$; needles; m.p. 217–218°; soluble in ether; insoluble in water, petroleum ether).[61] Tuduranine ($C_{18}H_{19}NO_3$; minute needles difficult to crystallize; m.p. about 125°; freely soluble in usual organic solvents) has been isolated from sinomenine mother liquors.[37] From the drug *han fang chi* has been isolated fangchinoline ($C_{37}H_{45}N_2O_6$);[121] from the drug *mu fang chi,* thunbergine.[129] The alkaloid sinomenine has a morphine-like structure but not the sedative or analgesic properties of morphine; it is a convulsive poison.[144]

The roots are used as antipyretic, diuretic, analgesic, being prescribed especially in arthritis, lumbago, myalgia. Dose, 3–7 gm. Incompatible: *Asarum sieboldii.*

仁麻大

CANNABIS SATIVA L.

(Moraceae)

Hemp. A strong-smelling, annual herb. Stem erect, woody, rough, 1–3 m. tall. Leaves opposite, sometimes alternate at the top of the plant, compound palmate; leaflets 3–7, acute, dentate, provided with persistent stipules. Flowers green, small, inconspicuous, dioecious; May. Male flowers in short, drooping panicles; calyx with 5 regular sepals; stamens 5; filaments short and straight; anthers introrse, bilocular, dehiscence longitudinal. Female flowers solitary, entirely enveloped in a mother bract; calyx gamosepalous, urceolate; gynoecium consisting of 2 carpels; ovary 1-celled; style none; stigmas 2, elongate, pubescent. Fruit a bivalvular achene, glossy, greenish, enclosed in the persistent perianth; seeds nearly devoid of albumen. China, India, Indochina, Afghanistan, Iran, northern Africa. (Syn. *C. chinensis* Del.)

The seeds are used medicinally. They occur ovoid, 5 mm. long by 3 mm. in diameter, beige, glossy. The taste is sweet, the odor aromatic. The seeds contain 19% protein, 31%

lipids, choline, trigonelline, xylose, inositol, phytin, enzymes (lipase, maltase, emulsin, linamarase, amylase, urease, nuclease, erepsin, tryptase, catalase).[151] The seeds do not have any marihuana activity, which action is confined to the resinous exudate of the female flowers.

Prescribed as tonic and emollient. Dose, 11 gm.

MORUS ALBA L.

(Moraceae)

White mulberry. A tree 3–15 m. tall, the sap milky. Leaves alternate, broadly oval, 6–18 cm. long by 2.0–4.5 cm. wide, base rounded or cordate, acuminate, irregularly dentate or incised-lobate, glabrous except on the veins, soft green. Flowers monoecious or dioecious, greenish, grouped in stalked, hanging catkins; May; calyx in 4 segments; no petals; female catkins 5–10 mm. long, the male catkins twice longer. Fruit aggregate, consisting of all the ovaries of the catkin having become a crustaceous achene, compressed, covered with the fleshy sepals of several flowers, black; July–August. China, Indochina, Japan, Philippines. (Syn. *M. constantinopolitana* Poir., *M. indica* L.)

The root epidermis, leaves, and fruit are officinal. The leaves contain carotene, succinic acid, adenine, choline, amylase; the fruit contains 27% saccharides, 3% citric acid, vitamin C; the seeds contain urease.[151]

The root epidermis is used as antitussive and expectorant in asthma, bronchitis, cough. Dose, 5–10 gm. The fruit is considered tonic in neurasthenia, insomnia, hypertension. Dose, 20 gm. The leaves are used as antipyretic. Dose, 5–10 gm.

Morus alba

荳蔻肉

MYRISTICA FRAGRANS Houtt.

(Myristicaceae)

Nutmeg. A tree 10–15 m. tall. Leaves alternate, glabrous, nearly coriaceous, oval, elliptical or lanceolate, base acute or more or less rounded, tip acuminate, 5–15 cm. long by 3–7 cm. wide. Inflorescence axillary. Flowers dioecious; perianth in 3 segments; male flower with 9–12 stamens; female flowers with ovary 1-celled, ovoid, the style very short. Fruit oblong, with a fleshy, crustaceous pericarp, dehiscent; seed ovoid, 2.5–3.5 cm. long by 1.5–2.0 cm. in diameter, surface furrowed lengthwise, testa hard. Moluccas, cultivated in India, Indochina. (Syn. *M. moschata* Thunb.)

The seeds are used medicinally. They occur as entire seeds, globular-oval-ellipsoidal, 26–30 mm. long by 21–24 mm. wide, surface furrowed and deeply grooved along one side, cross section with mottled surface. The odor is aromatic, the taste strongly pungent. The seeds contain 3.6% of a volatile oil comprising 60–80% d-camphene, 8% d-pinene, 8% dipentene, 6% d-linalol, 0.6% safrole, 0.2% eugenol, iso-eugenol, d-borneol, l-terpineol, geraniol, and 4% myristicin ($C_{11}H_{12}O_3$).[86] Severe symptoms have occurred in man from 1 to $1\frac{1}{2}$ nutmegs or 1 teaspoonful powdered mace, the effects appearing in 1 to 6 hours, being mainly narcotic varied by excitement and delirium with some motor stimulation and local irritation, ending in recovery in 24 hours; nutmeg is also ecbolic; hepatic necrosis has been demonstrated in cats; the narcotic effect has been shown to be produced by myristicin.[152] In small doses nutmeg stimulates production of gastric juice, promoting digestion, increasing appetite, relieving intestinal spasm and flatulence.[150]

Used as aromatic stomachic and carminative. Dose, 2–5 gm.

丁香

EUGENIA CARYOPHYLLATA Thunb.

(Myrtaceae)

Clove tree. A tree 10–12 m. tall. Leaves opposite, lengthily petiolate, simple, persistent, coriaceous. Flowers pink, in terminal cymes; calyx in 4 segments; petals 4, reddish pink, united at their tips forming a sort of hood; stamens very numerous, in several rows; ovary inferior, 2-celled. Fruit a somewhat elongate berry, crowned with the remnants of the calyx. Moluccas, Celebes, India, Malaysia, Madagascar,

Réunion, Antilles, Brazil. (Syn. *E. aromatica* Baill., *Caryophyllum aromaticum* L.)

The floral buds, or cloves, are used medicinally. They contain 15–19% volatile oil comprising 82–87% eugenol which includes about 10% acetyl-eugenol, caryophyllene, and traces of furfural, vanillin, and methylamylketone.[148] Oil of cloves is antiseptic, locally anesthetic, antispasmodic, stomachic, and carminative; internally it increases circulation and is generally stimulating.[150]

Used as stimulant, carminative, antiemetic. Dose, 2–4 gm. Incompatibles: *Curcuma longa,* iron and silver compounds, zinc sulfate.

實 芡

EURYALE FEROX Salisb.

(Nymphaceae)

A large aquatic plant, the rhizomes provided with long fleshy fibers. Leaves large, floating, spiny, orbiculate, surface a dull green, underside purplish. Peduncle spiny, terminated with a large purple flower; August–September; calyx in 4 segments, exterior prickly; receptacle also prickly; petals and stamens numerous; ovary inferior. Fruit bacciform, crowned with the calyx, covered with spongy prickles; October–November; seeds 7–8, enclosed in a pulpy sac, pink. Manchuria, southern China, Japan, India.

The seeds are used medicinally. They occur ovoid, 1 cm. in diameter, soft white. The taste is sweetish and astringent. The seeds contain 8–11% protein, and a large amount of starch.

Used as tonic and astringent in spermatorrhea, chronic diarrhea; as analgesic in neuralgia, arthralgia. Dose, 10–20 gm.

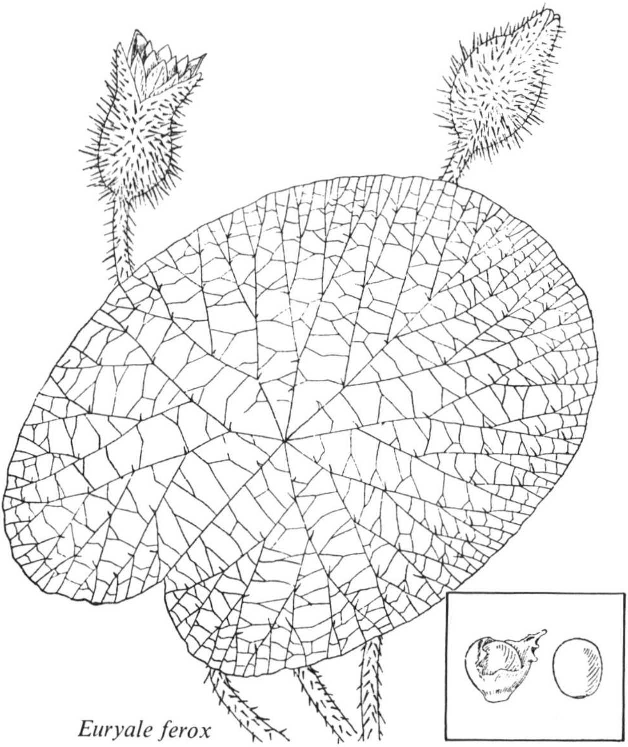

Euryale ferox

蓮

NELUMBIUM NELUMBO Druce.
(Nymphaceae)

Lotus. A perennial aquatic plant, the rhizome thick and scaly. Leaves lengthily petiolate, peltate, entire, glaucous, 30–50 cm. in diameter. Scape elongate. Flowers pink or white; June–August; sepals 4–5; petals and stamens numerous; gynoecium consisting of separate carpels sunk into the cavities of the fleshy obconic floral axis. Fruit consisting of the withered floral axis and carpels, which have become globular, prominent achenes; September–October; seeds black.

Cultivated, tropical Asia to Australia. (Syn. *N. speciosum* Willd., *N. nuciferum* Gaertn.)

The entire plant is used medicinally. It contains a large amount of starch, vitamin C, asparagin, and nelumbine (colorless, transparent mass or white powder; soluble in alcohol, ether, chloroform; slightly soluble in petroleum ether, carbon disulfide).[38]

The seeds are employed as tonic in chronic enteritis, diarrhea, spermatorrhea, insomnia, neurasthenia. The rhizomes, leaves, peduncle, and stamens are used as astringent and hemostatic. The plant is also prescribed as antidote in mushroom and alcoholic poisoning. Dose, 10–15 gm.

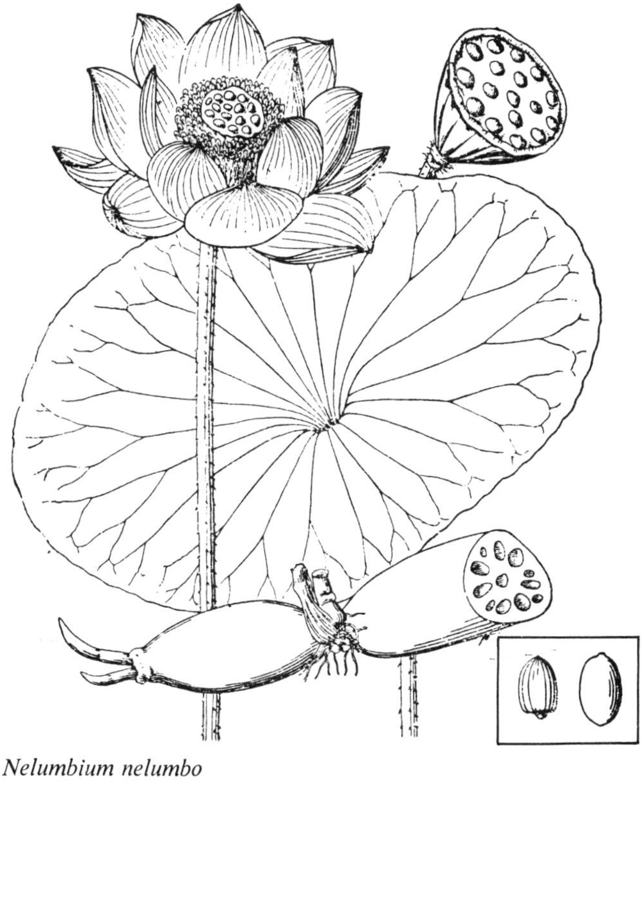

Nelumbium nelumbo

御米殼

PAPAVER SOMNIFERUM L.

(Papaveraceae)

Opium poppy. A strong-smelling, annual plant. Stem 0.4–1.0 m. tall, hollow, not branching. Leaves oblong, base cordate; the inferior leaves nearly petiolate, grayish green, coarsely lobed and toothed; cauline leaves clasping. Flowers white, pink, red, or purple, solitary, lengthily pedunculate; April–May; sepals 2; petals 4; stamens numerous; filaments white. Fruit a globular capsule, glabrous, 6–7 cm. long; August; seeds numerous, very small. Cultivated. Mediterranean, India, China.

The dried, empty capsules are used medicinally in the Chinese pharmacopoeia. Opium, the milky exudation of the unripe capsule, is well known to Occidental medicine. This latex has been found to contain about two dozen alkaloids; their narcotic, antispasmodic, sedative, hypnotic, and analgesic properties have been fully described. It may be noted that the seeds do not contain opium. The Chinese drug here indicated refers to the dried capsules from which the latex has been extracted; the alkaloid content remaining is not determinate.

Employed as antitussive, antispasmodic, analgesic, astringent, narcotic; prescribed in chronic enteritis, diarrhea, enterorrhagia, headache, toothache, asthma.

商陸

PHYTOLACCA ACINOSA Roxb.

(Phytolaccaceae)

A perennial herb, the stem erect, slightly ligneous at the base, 1.0–1.5 m. tall. Leaves simple, entire, oval-elliptical or lanceolate, tip acuminate, narrowing toward the petiole. Inflorescence a briefly pedunculate raceme; May–July. Perianth greenish white; calyx with 5 nearly regular lobes, corolla-like; petals none; stamens 7–8; ovary nearly globular, consisting of 5–7 united carpels. Fruit a berry, blackish blue, pericarp fleshy; July–September. China, Taiwan, Japan, India. (Syn. *P. kaempferi* A. Gray, *P. octandra* Bge., *P. pekinensis* Hance.)

The root is officinal. The taste is bitter-sour and pungent. The root contains saponins and 4–5% phytolaccatoxin ($C_{24}H_{30}O_8$; freely soluble in alcohol; poorly soluble in water).[140] The action of the drug appears to be similar to that of *P. decandra,* being emeto-cathartic with persistence and great nausea, lowering the rate of respiration and of cardiac action, and acting as a motor depressant.[137] *P. decandra* has been used in Occidental medicine to promote absorption of adipose tissue.[150]

Prescribed as diuretic in hydrops. Dose, 3–5 gm.

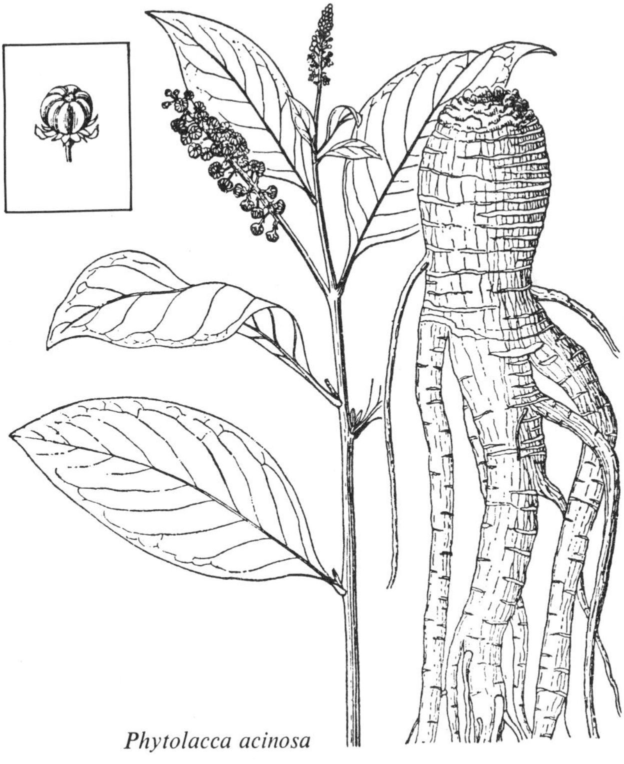

Phytolacca acinosa

茄澄畢

PIPER CUBEBA L.

(Piperaceae)

A woody vine, ultimately tree-like. Leaves alternate, elliptical or oval, tip acute, base irregularly cordate. Flowers simple, minute, white, in catkin-like spikes; no sepals or petals. Fruit a small berry, brownish. East Indies, Sri Lanka.

The dried, unripe fruits, known as cubebs, are used medicinally. They occur as drupes, the upper portion globular, acute, pointed, the lower portion tapering into a thecaphore, 2 cm. long by 7 mm. wide, thecaphore 14 mm. long, brownish to bluish grayish black, surface of the globular portion reticulate, of the thecaphore wrinkled, epicarp thin, mesocarp greenish brown and oily, endocarp hard and smooth on the inner surface, seed reddish brown and smooth. The taste is strongly pungent, the odor aromatic. The fruits contain cubebin ($C_{20}H_{20}O_6$; bitter levorotatory crystals; m.p. 131–132°; soluble in alcohol, chloroform, ether; almost insoluble in water), 1% cubebic acid, and 10–18% volatile oil (comprising dipentene, cadinene, cineol, carene, camphene, pinene, sabinene, azulene, terpineol).[148 151] An oleoresin of cubeb was formerly administered in Occidental medicine as urinary antiseptic in subacute and chronic urethritis, to diminish the pain and discharge and to hasten healing, but was not curative; it was also employed in bronchitis.

Used as urinary antiseptic, stomachic, carminative. Dose, 1–3 gm.

PIPER LONGUM L.

(Piperaceae)

Long pepper. A woody shrub, creeping at the base. Leaves alternate; inferior leaves lengthily petiolate, oval, base cordate, lobes regular, acuminate, 5–8 cm. long, veins 7; superior leaves sessile, clasping, oblong, base cordate, lobes often

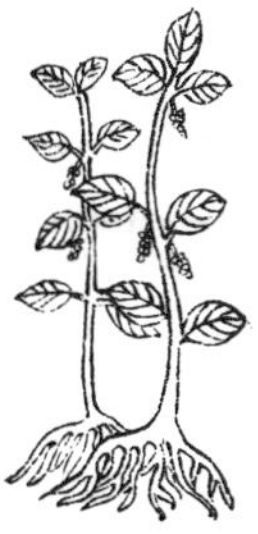

茇 蓽

irregular. No perianth; male spikes 3–8 cm. long, stamens 2; female spikes 15 mm. long, ovary sessile and 1-celled. Fruit consisting of a large number of very compact ovaries in a spike 4 cm. long, dry and hard. India, Malaysia. (Syn. *Chavica roxburghii*, Miq.)

The fruits are used medicinally. They contain 0.9 % of a volatile oil nearly identical to that of *P. nigrum*, and 0.19 % of the alkaloid piperine ($C_{17}H_{19}NO_3$; monoclinic prisms; m.p. 130°; tasteless at first, with burning aftertaste; soluble in benzene, acetic acid; somewhat soluble in alcohol, chloroform, ether; almost insoluble in water, petroleum ether).[116] Piperine has been employed as an antipyretic and carminative in Occidental medicine.[152]

Used as aromatic stomachic, analgesic in gastralgia, flatulence, headache. Dose, 1–3 gm.

椒 胡

PIPER NIGRUM L.

(Piperaceae)

Black pepper. A woody vine with aerial roots. Stem ligneous at the base, branches herbaceous. Leaves alternate, petiolate, elliptical, acuminate, base cordate or rounded, 13–18 cm. long by 5–14 cm. wide, coriaceous, veins 5–9. Spike somewhat shorter than or barely as long as the leaf blade; bracts oblong-linear; no perianth; stamens 2; ovary sessile, 1-celled. Fruit a spherical berry without style, 3–4 mm. in diameter. Tropical Asia.

The dried unripe fruits are officinal. They occur as entire drupes, nearly globular, 6 mm. in diameter, grayish to black, surface coarsely reticulate and dull, epicarp thin and dark, mesocarp thin, endocarp light; the seed adheres to the endocarp, yellowish green in the outer layers, yellow or gray around the cavity. The taste is strongly pungent, the odor aromatic. The fruit contains 5–9 % piperine, piperidine (C_5

$H_{11}N$; liquid; soluble in alcohol, benzene, chloroform; miscible with water), chavicine ($C_{17}H_{19}NO_3$; yellowish oily mass, sharp peppery taste; soluble in alcohol, ether, petroleum ether), and a volatile oil comprising chiefly l-phellandrene and caryophyllene.[148 149] *P. nigrum* is stimulant to gastric mucosa, and is less an irritant than capiscum.[152]

Used as stomachic and carminative. Dose, 0.5–1.0 gm.

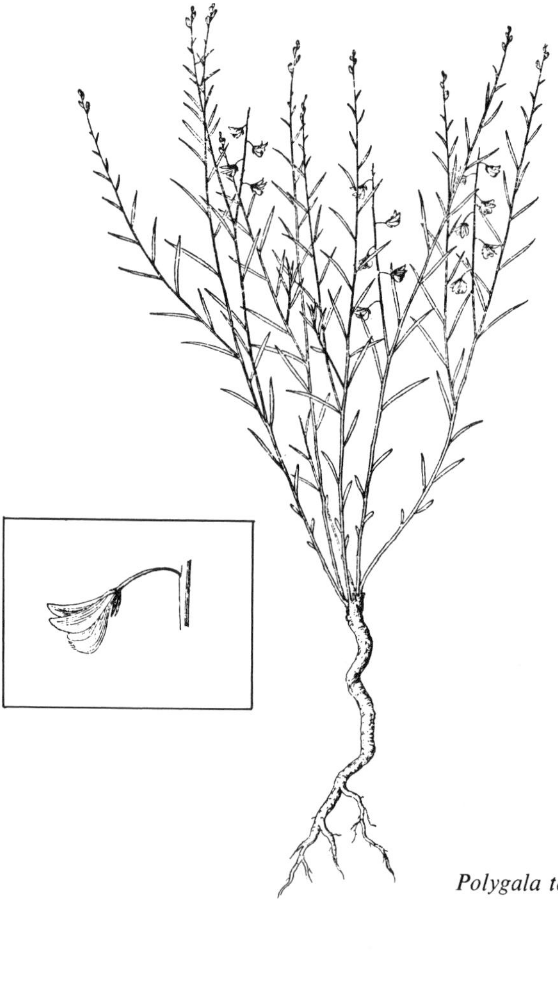

Polygala tenuifolia

遠志

POLYGALA TENUIFOLIA Willd.

(Polygalaceae)

A sub-shrub, the stem slender, 25 cm. high. Leaves alternate, nearly sessile, entire, linear, acuminate, 2.5–3.5 cm. long by 2 mm. wide. Flowers in terminal spikes, generally without bracts; April–May; sepals 5; petals 3, the inferior petal carinate, purple; stamens 8; ovary 2-celled. Fruit a membranous capsule, compressed. Northern China, Mongolia.

The root is used medicinally. It occurs in pieces 5–6 cm. long by 7 mm. in diameter, nodose, tortuous, striate transversally, purplish yellow, the fracture clean, the pith extracted. The taste is acrid and bitter. The root contains the two glycosidal saponins senegin (yellowish white powder; m.p. 240°; soluble in water) and polygalic acid.[140] With an action similar to *P. senega* and other drugs containing saponins, the root of *P. tenuifolia* is irritant to pharyngeal mucosa, inducing hypersecretion and expectoration.

Prescribed as expectorant, cardiotonic, renal tonic. Dose, 4–7 gm.

萹蓄

POLYGONUM AVICULARE L.

(Polygonaceae)

Knotweed. An annual herb, glabrous, sometimes erect, sometimes diffuse or decumbent. Stem generally much branching. Leaves briefly petiolate, lanceolate or elliptical, obtuse, margin rough; ocrea striate, diaphanous, silvery-white, segments oval-lanceolate, acuminate. Flowers axillary, nearly sessile, very small; May–November; perianth greenish, pink-margined; ovary free. Fruit a trigonal achene. Cosmopolitan. (Syn. *P. debeauxii* Legrand, *P. gymnopus* Franch. et Sav., *P. meyenii* C. Koch)

Polygonum aviculare

The leaves and stems are officinal. The taste is bitter. The plant contains tannin, anthraquinone derivatives, an essential oil, a volatile alkaloid, avicularin, quercite, rutin.[24 78]

Used as diuretic, anthelmintic, antidiarrheic. Dose, 5–10 gm. Employed externally as emollient and astringent for hemorrhoids, pruritis, chancroid.

POLYGONUM MULTIFLORUM Thunb.

(Polygonaceae)

烏首何

A perennial, volubilate herb, 7–10 m. tall. Rhizome tuberiferous. Leaves petiolate, 5–7 cm. long by 3–5 cm. wide, tip acuminate, base cordate; ocrea membranous, short, cylindrical, devoid of hairs. Inflorescence a terminal or axillary panicle, much longer than the leaves, consisting of slender branches, more or less flexuous. Flowers solitary in the axil of the short bracts; September–October; perianth white, gradually narrowing toward the base; stamens 8; ovary free.

Polygonum multiflorum

Fruit trigonal, smooth, glossy, enclosed in the perianth whose 3 external parts have developed into large, membranous wings; October–November. Southwestern China, Japan, Taiwan, Vietnam. (Syn. *P. chinense* Houtt., *Pleuropterus cordatus* Turcz., *Pl. convolvulus* Thunb.)

The root, stem, and leaves are officinal. The root occurs as polyhedral or irregular tubers, ligneous, reddish brown. The taste is bitter and astringent. The tubers contain 45% starch, 3.7% lecithin, chrysophanol.[140]

Used as tonic, hematogenic. Dose, 7–15 gm. Incompatibles: *Allium* gen., iron compounds.

黄 大

RHEUM OFFICINALE Baill.

(Polygonaceae)

Medicinal rhubarb. A perennial, suffruticose herb, the stem 1.0–2.5 m. high. Leaves alternate, petiolate, oval, orbiculate, 30–90 cm. in diameter, lobes 3–7, palmately veined, irregularly incised. Floral stalks 1.5 m. high; thick, erect, pubescent. Inflorescence a dense, spiciform cluster; June. Flowers greenish; perianth with 6 segments arranged in 2 verticils; stamens 9, as long as the perianth; disk with 3 glandular nipples; ovary ovoid, trigonal, 1-celled. Fruit a trigonal achene of 1 cm., winged, bright red. Western China, Tibet.

The rhizomes are officinal. They occur as long, transverse or oblique pieces, or as cubes or rectangular pieces of the peeled roots, leaf scars present, 15 cm. long by 15 cm. wide, texture fibrous and resinous, color yellowish to reddish brown, surface smooth, longitudinally wrinkled, frequently with an irregular perforation through which a string was inserted when the drug was dried; cortex thin, wood mottled irregularly. The taste is bitter and astringent, the odor aromatic. The rhizomes contain chrysophanic acid ($C_{15}H_{10}O_4$; hexagonal or monoclinic prisms; m.p. 196°; freely soluble in boiling alcohol; soluble in benzene, chloroform, ether, acetone; slightly soluble in cold alcohol; almost insoluble in water), chrysophanein ($C_{21}H_{20}O_9$; yellow tasteless needles; m.p. about 245°; soluble in pyridine; slightly soluble in hot water; insoluble in cold water, ether, chloroform), rhein ($C_{15}H_8O_6$; yellow needles; m.p. 321–322°; soluble in pyridine, alkalies; slightly soluble in alcohol, benzene, ether, chloroform; insoluble in water), emodin ($C_{15}H_{10}O_5$; orange needles; m.p. 256–257°; soluble in alcohol, alkalies; slightly soluble in ether, chloroform, benzene; practically insoluble in water), aloe emodin ($C_{15}H_{10}O_5$; orange needles; m.p. 223–224°; freely soluble in hot alcohol, ether, benzene), rheochrysin ($C_{22}H_{22}O_{10}$; yellow tasteless needles; m.p. 211°; slightly soluble in cold water; sparingly soluble in hot water), alizarin ($C_{14}H_8O_4$; orange orthorhombic needles; m.p. 290°; freely soluble in hot methanol, ether; moderately soluble in alcohol, benzene, pyridine; slightly soluble in water), glucogallin ($C_{13}H_{16}O_{10}$; white to yellowish crystals; m.p. about 220°; soluble in water, alcohol, pyridine, alkalies; slightly soluble in benzene, ether; insoluble in chloroform, petroleum ether), tetrarin ($C_{32}H_{32}O_{12}$; small plates; m.p. 204–205° with decomposition; freely soluble in alcohol, methanol, acetone; insoluble in water, benzene, chloroform, ether), catechin ($C_{15}H_{14}O_6 \cdot 4H_2O$; white needles; becoming anhydrous at 100°, m.p. 96°, when anhydrous 177°; freely soluble in hot water, alcohol, acetone; slightly soluble in cold water, ether; almost insoluble in benzene, chloroform, petroleum ether).[116] The cathartic principle of *R. officinale* is a non-glycosidal resin which upon hydrolysis yields the various anthraquinone derivatives, which also exist partly free; the astringent properties are glycosidal compounds of tannin; there is also a large amount of calcium oxalate.[110] An astringent action predominates with smaller doses of 50–300 mg., used as stomachic in gastric catarrh and in diarrhea; larger doses of 1–5 gm. are laxative with little colic; the drug may cause skin eruptions.[152]

As bitter stomachic, 0.5 gm. As purgative, 2–3 gm. Incompatibles: mineral acids, iron and zinc salts, catechu, cinchona, nutgall, tannic acid.

Portulaca oleracea

莧齒馬

PORTULACA OLERACEA L.

(Portulacaceae)

Purslane. An annual, trailing herb. Stem fleshy, reddish, 10–30 cm. long, the joints of which produce roots when in contact with the soil. Leaves opposite or alternate, obovate-oblong, sessile, thick, fleshy, glossy, 2 cm. long by 8–14 mm. wide, the superior leaves often forming a kind of involucre around the stems. Flowers terminal, small, sessile, bright yellow; June–September; sepals 2, irregular; petals 4–6, free or somewhat united at the base, very caducous;

stamens 6–12; ovary adherent at the base. Fruit a globular, membranous capsule, dehiscent transversely; seeds numerous, black, glossy. Wastelands, China, Europe, North America.

The leaves are used medicinally. The taste is bitter and sour. The plant contains tannin, phosphates, urea, and various minerals with a large amount of magnesium.[151] The Chinese believed that the drug contained a "vegetable mercury."[153]

Used as antiphlogistic and bactericide in bacillary dysentery, diarrhea, hemorrhoids, enterorrhagia. Dose, 7–10 gm.

石榴皮

PUNICA GRANATUM L.

(Punicaceae)

Pomegranate. A deciduous shrub 3–5 m. high, the branches spiny-tipped. Leaves opposite or fasciculate, simple, oval or oblong, 2–8 cm. long by 1.8 cm. wide, obtuse, glabrous, coriaceous. Flowers in terminal clusters of 1–5, at the ends of short axillary shoots; May–June; calyx fleshy, partly tubular, lobes 5–7, red; petals 5–7, separate, wrinkled, orange red or white; stamens very numerous; ovary inferior. Fruit a large fleshy berry crowned with the persistent calyx, brownish yellow or red, several chambers, partitions coriaceous; September–October; seeds with a fleshy-pulpy external testa, the interior testa corneous. Cultivated in Old and New World.

The bark and root epidermis are officinal. They occur as broken pieces 14 cm. long by 4.5 cm. wide, 5 mm. thick, surface of stem bark with shallow fissures, the root bark rough and often with scars where a portion of the cork has become detached, yellowish, fracture brittle and even. The taste is sour and astringent. The drug contains about 20% tannin, and 0.5–1.0% alkaloids consisting of pelletierine ($C_8H_{15}NO$; syrupy liquid, very unstable; b.p. 195°; soluble in water, alcohol, chloroform, benzene, ether), methylpelletierine ($C_8H_{14}NO \cdot CH_3$; colorless oily liquid; soluble in water, alcohol, chloroform, ether), pseudopelletierine ($C_9H_{15}NO$; orthorhombic prisms; m.p. 54°, b.p. 246°; freely soluble in alcohol, chloroform; sparingly soluble in petroleum ether; slightly soluble in water, ether), isopelletierine ($C_8H_{15}NO$; oily liquid; soluble in alcohol, chloroform, dilute acids), methylisopelletierine($C_9H_{17}NO$; colorless oily liquid; soluble in water, petroleum ether).[148] The bark of *P. granatum* and its contained alkaloids act more powerfully on *Taenia* than on *Ascaris;* but because the large amount of tannin often causes vomiting, the alkaloids alone, in the form of tannates, are preferred; ordinary doses often cause mild toxic symptoms of vertigo, dimmed vision, great weakness and cramps in the legs, formication, convulsive trembling, etc.; toxic doses promptly produce mydriasis, partial blindness, violent headache, vertigo, vomiting and diarrhea, profound prostration, sometimes convulsions.[152]

Prescribed as intestinal astringent, anthelmintic. Dose, 7 gm. in decoction.

ACONITUM (gen.)
(Ranunculaceae)

The drug aconite found in Chinese pharmacies represents the roots of several species of *Aconitum*, including *A. fischeri* Reichb., *A. chasmanthum* Stapf., *A. laciniatum* Stapf., *A. balfouri* Stapf., *A. deinorrhizum* Stapf., and others. The taste of the drug is acrid; it is very poisonous. It contains aconitine ($C_{34}H_{47}NO_{11}$; hexagonal plates; m.p. 204°; one gram dissolves in 2 ml. chloroform, 7 ml. benzene, 28 ml. absolute alcohol, 50 ml. ether, 3,300 ml. water), and related alkaloids; the fresh herb is extremely toxic, but in the dried root much of the aconitine has decomposed to picroaconitine and aconine, which are less toxic.[140] The drug presents the same effects as those of *A. napellus* L.; the tincture is used in China as a local anesthetic.[21]

Used internally as stimulant, cardiotonic, analgesic.

翁頭白

ANEMONE CERNUA Thunb.

(Ranunculaceae)

Nodding anemone. An alpine, perennial herb covered with white hairs. Rhizomes ligneous, erect. Basal leaves oval, divided feather-fashion, petiole 5–10 cm; leaflets opposite, 2.5 cm. long, incised-lobate, coarsely dentate. Cauline leaves sessile, pinnatifid, leaflets 3, linear, division very wide, the terminal leaflet tripartite. Flowers large, solitary, hanging, 2.5–5.0 cm. in diameter; February–April; sepals 6, pale purple; no petals; stamens very numerous; styles accrete, plumose. Fruit a dense head of achenes, the styles long, slender, united at the oblong carpels, villous, with a long, plumose awn. Northern China, Korea, Japan. (Syn. *A. pulsatilla* var. *chinensis* Bunge.)

The root is used medicinally. The taste is bitter. The plant contains saponins and protoanemonin ($C_5H_4O_2$; pale yellow oil, volatile; soluble in ethylene dichloride, chloroform; 1% solution in water); protoanemonin rapidly polymerizes to yield anemonin ($C_{10}H_8O_4$; crystals; m.p. 157–158°; soluble in hot alcohol, chloroform; slightly soluble in cold water; insoluble in ether).[5] The fresh herb produces severe local irritation, vesicating the skin, and internally inducing gastroenteritis accompanied by emesis; it is a cardiac and nervous sedative, producing a hypnotic state with diminution of senses, followed by a paralyzing action.[39] Anemonin has been used as antispasmodic, sedative, anodyne in asthma and pulmonary affections.[144] *A. pulsatilla* has been used in doses of 100–400 mg. in hemicrania.[152] The active principle of *A. cernua* appears to be largely destroyed upon desiccation of the root.[151]

Prescribed in the Chinese pharmacopoeia as antidiarrheic. Dose, 5–10 gm. in alcoholic decoction.

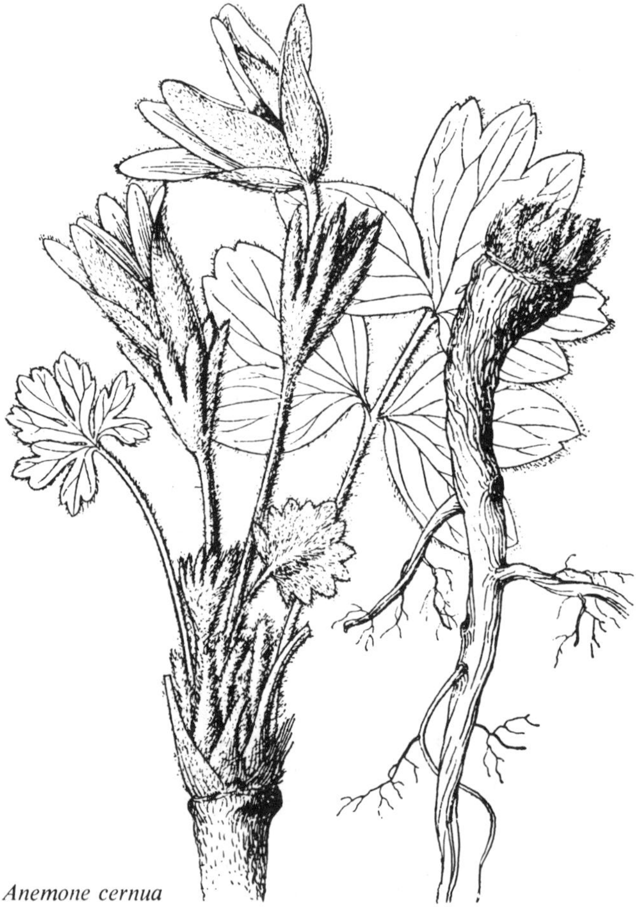

Anemone cernua

CIMICIFUGA FOETIDA L.

(Ranunculaceae)

升麻

A tall perennial herb. Leaves thrice-compound, the ultimate leaflets elliptical, acute, serrate. Inflorescence a dense, terminal raceme, spicate; autumn. Flowers small, white; stamens numerous. Fruit a collection of small follicles, black. China, Siberia, Europe.

The root is used medicinally. The taste is bittersweet. The drug contains tannin and the resin cimicifugin (macrotin; yellowish brown, hygroscopic powder; soluble in alcohol).[140] The related plant *C. racemosa,* which contains 15–20 % cimicifugin, has been employed as stomachic, against chorea, and as "uterine tonic."[152] Extensive pharmacologic study has failed to reveal any distinctive effects except some depression of excised intestine and uterus.[72]

Used as antipyretic, sedative, analgesic. Dose, 5–8 gm. A decoction is used as gargle in tonsillitis, pharyngitis, stomatitis.

CLEMATIS CHINENSIS Retz.

(Ranunculaceae)

威靈仙

A climbing vine, the stem striate, pubescent. Leaves opposite, lengthily petiolate, pinnate; leaflets 3–5, oval or lanceolate, entire, tip acuminate, base rounded or truncate, 3–5 cm. long by 1.0–4.5 cm. wide; petiole volubilate, acting as a tendril. Flowers grouped in ramified cymes; May–June; sepals 4, petaloid; no petals; stamens numerous; carpels free, numerous. Fruit an achene surmounted with a persistent, villous style 3 cm. long, 1-seeded; September–October. China, Taiwan, Vietnam. (Syn. *C. minor* Lour., *C. sinensis* Lour., *C. terniflora* DC.)

The root is officinal. It occurs cut into rounds 2.5 cm. in diameter by 2 cm. thick, epidermis brown, interior whitish. The taste is bitter. The drug contains anemonin.[140]

Prescribed as analgesic in rheumatism, as antipyretic and diuretic. Dose, 5–10 gm. Incompatible: tea.

連 黄

COPTIS TEETA Wall.

(Ranunculaceae)

A perennial herb. Leaves basal, lengthily petiolate, glabrous, pinnate; leaflets 12–15 mm. long, oval-lanceolate, incised, the terminal leaflet longer than the others. Peduncle as long or longer than the leaves; bracts resembling leaves. Flowers yellowish white; sepals linear, lanceolate; petals to 10, margin undulate, two-thirds as long as the sepals; carpels to 14. Fruit a pod; seeds cylindrical, inflated at the middle, surface striate lengthwise, chestnut brown. Southern China, northern India.

The rhizome is officinal. It occurs in pieces 5–6 cm. long, often covered with rootlets, the color brownish yellow, interior yellow-orange, the central pith deeper in color. The taste is bitter. The root of the related *C. japonica* Makino, indigenous to Japan and which commonly adulterates the Chinese market, contains the alkaloids coptisine ($C_{19}H_{15}NO_5$; yellowish needles; m.p. 218°; soluble in alkalies; sparingly soluble in alcohol; very slightly soluble in water), worenine ($C_{20}H_{17}NO_5$; yellow crystalline powder; soluble in hot dilute alcohol), and berberine.[57]

Used as bitter stomachic and digestive, and antidysenteric. Dose, 3–7 gm.

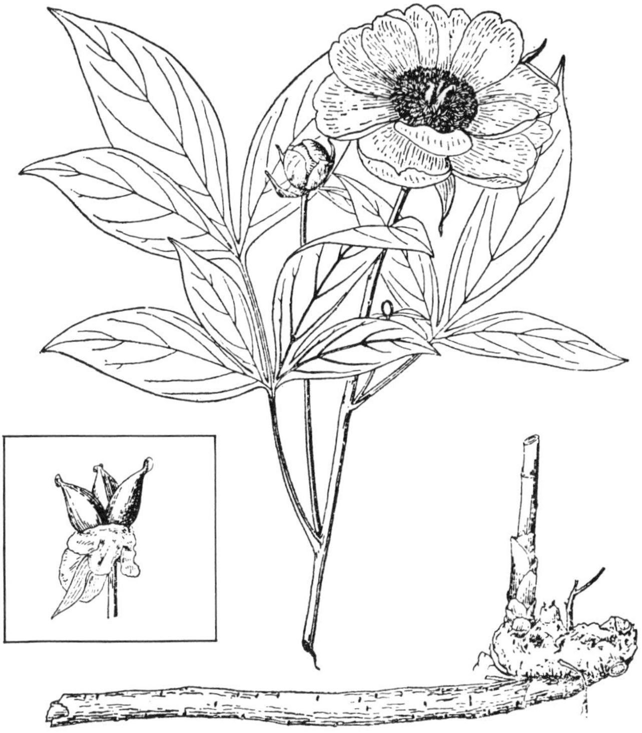

Paeonia albiflora

PAEONIA ALBIFLORA Pall.

(Ranunculaceae)

Chinese peony. A perennial herb, the stem simple, erect, glabrous, 60–90 cm. tall. Root a collection of narrow tubers. Leaves alternate, twice-compound, the ultimate segments red-veined, oblong-elliptical. Peduncle long, stout, often bracteate. Flowers terminal, solitary, large, white or pink;

藥芍白

May; calyx briefly cupulate; petals 5–10, large, wide; stamens numerous, golden yellow; gynoecium surrounded with a disk at the base. Fruit a dehiscent follicle, generally glabrous; seeds numerous. China, Manchuria, Siberia, Japan. (Syn. *P. edulis* Salisb., *P. lactiflora* Pall., *P. officinalis* Thunb.)

The root is used medicinally. It occurs in pieces 20 cm. long by 12 mm. in diameter, surface reddish brown, interior pink. The taste is bitter. The root contains asparagin and 5% benzoic acid.[140] It has been claimed that this drug contains an alkaloid that stimulates uterine contraction, constricts blood vessels, and increases blood coagulation; this has not been confirmed.[152]

Used in gastric disorders, as intestinal antiseptic, expectorant, emmenagogue. Dose, 5–10 gm.

皮丹牡

PAEONIA MOUTAN Sims.

(Ranunculaceae)

Tree peony. A much-branched perennial shrub, 1 m. tall. Leaves alternate, lengthily petiolate, 10–25 cm. long, bipinnate, the ultimate segments oval-oblong, acuminate, 3- to 5-lobed, pale beneath. Flowers solitary, 10–30 cm. in diameter, pink or red; July–August; sepals 5; petals 8–10, obovate; stamens numerous, nearly as long as the calyx. Fruit a densely pubescent follicle. Northern China. Cultivated. (Syn. *P. suffruticosa* Andr., *P. arborea* Donn.)

The root is used medicinally. It occurs as cylindrical fragments, 10–12 cm. long by 5–10 mm. thick, epidermis brown, the cross section revealing a very thick cortical parenchyma. The taste is at first sweetish, becoming somewhat bitter. The root contains the ketone paeonol ($C_9H_{10}O_3$; white crystalline powder, very aromatic; m.p. 49°; soluble in alcohol, ether, chloroform), glycosides, and benzoic acid.[118] Paeonol has been considered to be the monomethyl ether of resacetophenone.[75] Melted with KOH, paeonol decomposes to yield resacetophenone, resorcylic acid, and resorcinol.[126]

Prescribed as antipyretic, emmenagogue, for infections of the digestive tract. Dose, 5–10 gm. Incompatibles: *Fritillaria verticillata, Cuscuta japonica, Rheum officinale.*

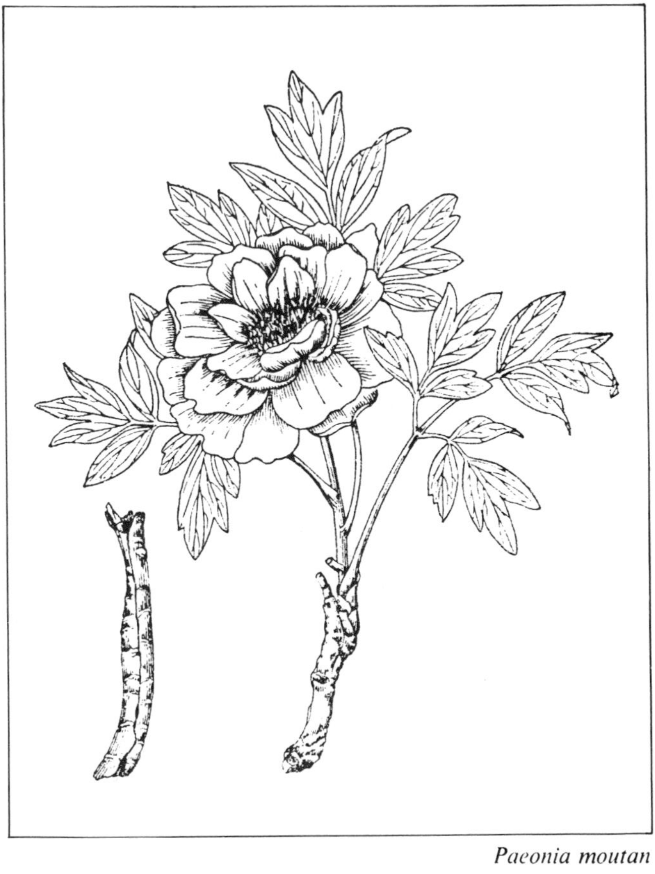

Paeonia moutan

子椇枳

HOVENIA DULCIS Thunb.

(Rhamnaceae)

Japanese raisin tree. A tree 20 m. tall. Leaves alternate, lengthily petiolate, broadly oval, acute, dentate, 10–15 cm. long by 5–9 cm. wide, glabrous, 3-veined at the base, the veins pubescent. Inflorescence an axillary or terminal cyme, pedunculate. Flowers 7 mm. wide, greenish white, July; calyx in 5 segments; petals 5; stamens 5; disk fleshy, lining the calyx tube, clinging to the ovary, very lanate; ovary 3-celled; styles 3. Fruit a nearly dry drupe on the dilated pedicel, fleshy, sweet, reddish; October. China, Japan, India. Cultivated.

The fruit and pedicel are officinal. They contain potassium malate and a large amount of dextrose.[140]

Employed as refrigerant diuretic in inebriety. Dose, 5–10 gm.

仁棗酸

ZIZYPHUS JUJUBA Mill.

(Rhamnaceae)

Chinese jujube. A spiny, deciduous shrub 10 m. high; spines in groups of 2, one spine of each group curved. Leaves alternate, petiolate, oval-lanceolate, 2–6 cm. long, obtuse, crenelate, glabrous, 3-veined. Inflorescence an axillary cyme; April–May. Flowers perfect; calyx with cupuliform tube and 5 segments; petals 5, yellow; disk lining the calyx tube; stamens 5; ovary depressed into the disk. Fruit a fleshy drupe, ovoid or oblong, 1.5–2.5 cm. long, dark reddish brown when mature; September–October. China, Japan, India, Afghanistan, Malaysia, Australia, tropical Africa. (Syn. *Z. vulgaris* Lam., *Z. zizyphus* Kaist., *Z. sativa* Caertn., *Rhamnus ziziphus* L.)

The fruit is used medicinally. It contains mucilage, sugar, fat, and zizyphic acid.[140]

Prescribed as nutrient tonic and sedative in insomnia, neurasthenia. Dose, 3–5 fruits. The kernel of the stone is also employed. Dose, 5–10 gm., powdered. Incompatible: Menispermaceae fam.

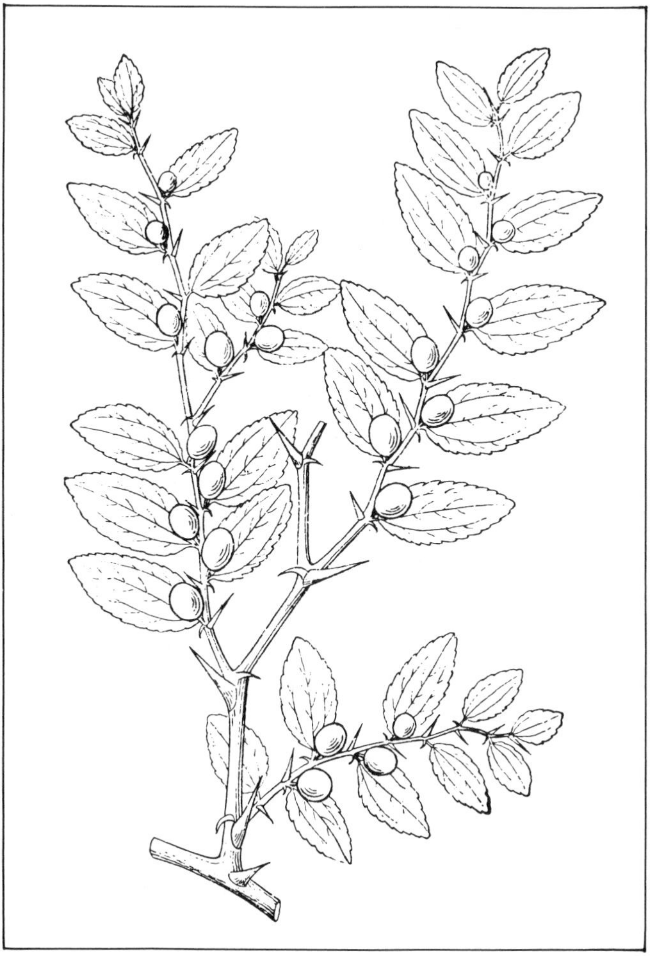

Zizyphus jujuba

龍芽草

AGRIMONIA EUPATORIA L.

(Rosaceae)

Agrimony. A perennial herb, the stem 30–60 cm. high, villous, reddish. Leaves alternate, pinnatifid; segments oval-lanceolate, deeply dentate, irregular, underside villous white and without glands; stipules purplish, clasping, incised-dentate. Inflorescence an elongate raceme, terminal; September–October. Flowers small, yellow; receptacle concave, with a narrow opening; calyx tube furrowed and provided

Agrimonia eupatoria

at the tip with curved spurs, lobes 5; petals 5, small, imbricate; stamens 5–15, slender; ordinarily a single carpel at maturity. Fruit an achene surrounded with the withered receptacle and crowned with the persistent calyx. China, Japan, Korea, Taiwan, Europe. (Syn. *A. pilosa* Ledeb., *A. viscidula* Bunge.)

The stem and leaves are officinal. The taste is bitter and astringent. The plant contains a volatile oil, tannin, gum, and a phytosterol.[26] The drug is an excellent hemostatic, increasing the number of thrombocytes, increasing coagulation 40–50%, and apparently increasing the osmotic resistance of plasma membrane.[79]

Prescribed as astringent hemostatic in enterorrhagia, hematuria, metrorrhagia, gastrorrhagia, pulmonary tuberculosis; also as cardiotonic. Dose, 10–35 gm.

木瓜

CHAEOMELES SINENSIS Koeh.

(Rosaceae)

Chinese quince. A deciduous shrub 2–6 m. high, without spines. Leaves alternate, simple, elliptical-oval or elliptical, oblong, acuminate, 6–10 cm. long, denticulate, villous when young; stipules lanceolate. Flowers solitary, about 2.5 cm. wide, nearly sessile; March–April; calyx in 5 segments, finely serrate, reflected; petals 5, light pink; stamens numerous; carpels 5, depressed into the floral axis. Fruit a fleshy pome, 10–15 cm. long, deep yellow, firm when mature; October. Northern China, India, Iran. Cultivated. (Syn. *Cydonia sinensis* Thou., *Pseudocydonia sinensis* Schneider, *Pirus sinensis* Poir.)

The fruit is used medicinally. The taste is sour and astringent. The drug contains vitamin C, and malic, tartaric, and citric acids.[140] It may also contain hydrocyanic acid.[146]

Used as astringent in diarrhea; as analgesic in arthralgia, gout, cholera. Dose, 5–10 gm. Incompatible: iron.

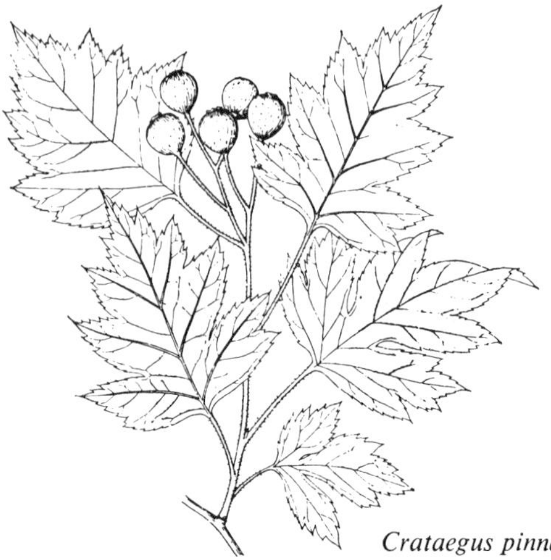

Crataegus pinnatifida

CRATAEGUS CUNEATA Sieb. et Zucc.

(Rosaceae)

山查

Chinese hill haw. A deciduous shrub 1.5 m. high, with thin spines 5–8 mm. long. Leaves obovate or obovate-oblong, narrowing gradually toward the petiole, incised or irregularly dentate, often trilobate at the tip, 2–6 cm. long, surface glabrous, underside lightly villous especially over the veins; stipules nearly oval, dentate. Inflorescence a small corymb; April. Calyx with a campanulate tube, the limb with 5 entire or lobed segments; petals 5, white or pink; stamens 20; anthers red; ovary inferior. Fruit drupaceous, red or yellow, rounded or elongate or pyriform, with the persistent sepals; September–October. Eastern China, Japan.

The fruits are used as aliment as well as medicinally. The taste is sweet and sour. The fruits contain 0.2% protein, 10% carbohydrate, fat, citric acid, and vitamin C.[140]

Used as digestant and antidiarrheic. Dose, 5–10 gm.

(The fruit of *C. pinnatifida* Bunge. [Syn. *C. pentagyna* Waldst. et Kit.] is similarly employed.)

枇杷葉

ERIOBOTRYA JAPONICA Lindl.

(Rosaceae)

Loquat. An evergreen tree 6 m. tall. Leaves alternate, briefly petiolate, elliptical-lanceolate, acuminate, 12–30 cm. long by 3–8 cm. wide, upper half dentate, thick, stiff, underside covered with an abundant grayish or yellowish tomentum. Inflorescence an agglomerate, pyramidal panicle, terminal, entirely covered with a thick, reddish tomentum. Flowers numerous, sessile or nearly so, odoriferous, 13–20 mm. in diameter; November; calyx cupuliform, united with the ovary, segments 5; petals 5, white, provided with long hairs inside; stamens 20; ovary partly inferior, 5-celled; styles 5, free. Fruit fleshy, nearly globular, somewhat tomentose, yellow at maturity, 3–4 cm. long; June; seeds very large, ovoid, tegument parchment-like. Southwestern China, Japan, Vietnam, India, Malay Archipelago, southern Europe. (Syn. *Crataegus bibas* Lour., *Mespilus japonica* Thunb., *Photinia japonica* Franch. et Sav.)

The leaves are officinal. The taste is bitter. The young leaves contain saponins; the seeds are slightly poisonous and contain amygdalin, hydrocyanic acid, and saponins; an infusion of the seeds contains over 0.1% hydrocyanic acid.[140, 151]

The leaves are employed as antitussive, expectorant. Dose, 10–15 gm.

石楠葉

PHOTINIA SERRULATA Lindl.

(Rosaceae)

An evergreen shrub 12 m. high. Leaves simple, oblong, acuminate, base rounded, dentate, 10–18 cm. long, glabrous, reddish when young; petiole 2–3 cm., reddish at the base. Inflorescence a corymb 10–16 cm. wide; May. Calyx with tube united with the ovary, limb with 5 segments, persistent; petals 5, white, unguiculate, oboval; stamens numerous;

ovary inferior but free at the top. Fruit globular, red, 5–6 mm. in diameter, endocarp coriaceous. China. (Syn. *Crataegus glabra* Lodd. non Thunb., *C. serratifolia* Desf.)

The leaves are used medicinally. The taste is bitter and pungent. The drug contains a glycoside of hydrocyanic acid, and tannin.[94 140]

Used as tonic and stimulant in neurasthenia, impotence, spermatorrhea, amenorrhea, infecundity. Dose, 5–10 gm.

(In Japan the leaves of *Rhododendron metternichii* Sieb. et Zucc. are employed.)

杏仁

PRUNUS ARMENIACA L.

(Rosaceae)

Apricot tree. A small tree 3–6 m. tall. Leaves oval-orbiculate, 5–10 cm. long, abruptly acuminate, base nearly cordate or rounded, twice dentate, glabrous; stipules caducous. Flowers solitary, white or pink, nearly sessile, blooming with or before the leaves; April; calyx with 5 segments, caducous; petals 5; stamens numerous; ovary at the base of the calyx tube, 1-celled. Fruit a large globular drupe, pubescent, velvety, fleshy-succulent, yellow or pale red, indehiscent; June; stone oval-compressed, surfaces smooth, one edge carinate and with 2 furrows, the other edge obtuse, with 1–2 bitter kernels. Northwestern China. (Syn. *Armeniaca vulgaris* Lam.)

The kernels of the fruit are officinal. They contain the bitter glycoside amygdalin ($C_{20}H_{27}NO_{11} \cdot 3H_2O$; orthorhombic columns; m.p. 200°, when anhydrous, about 220°, once melted and solidified, 125–130°; very soluble in boiling water; soluble in alcohol; insoluble in ether), and the enzyme emulsin (white or light yellow powder; soluble in water with turbidity).[140] Amygdalin, when pure, is almost entirely harmless; it is split up by the ferment emulsin in the presence of water, being decomposed in the body to yield hydrocyanic acid, glucose, and benzaldehyde; hydrocyanic acid (prussic acid; HCN; colorless gas or liquid; characteristic odor of bitter almonds; miscible with water, alcohol) is perhaps the most rapidly acting poison, producing death with asphyxial symptoms by hindering the oxidative processes of the tissues; it also interferes with most catalytic reactions and is therefore a general protoplasmic poison; symptoms of acute poisoning are vertigo, mental dimness, headache, palpitation, then dyspnea, unconsciousness accompanied by violent convulsions, respiration ceasing; the fatal dose of dilute HCN would be about 2.5 gm.[152] HCN has been used for its supposed antispasmodic and sedative action in spasmodic cough and asthma.[150]

Prescribed as antitussive and sedative in bronchitis, asthma. Dose, 3–5 gm. Incompatibles: *Astragalus hoantchy, Scutellaria baicalensis, Pueraria thunbergiana.*

桃仁

PRUNUS PERSICA (L.) Batsch.

(Rosaceae)

Peach. A tree 8 m. tall. Leaves alternate, petiolate, narrowly lanceolate or oblong-lanceolate, 8–15 cm. long, tip acuminate, glabrous, finely serrate, with glandular teeth at the tip. Flowers usually solitary, nearly sessile or very briefly pedicellate, blooming well before the leaves, pink, the base surrounded with brown scales; March–April; calyx a campanulate tube, 5-lobed; petals 5; stamens numerous, as long as the petals; ovary at the base of the calyx tube, 1-celled. Fruit a nearly globular drupe, 5–7 cm. in diameter, with a lateral furrow, covered with a velvety down; June; stone very solid, ovoid, compressed, deeply and irregularly furrowed. China. Cultivated. (Syn. *Amygdalus persica* L., *Persica vulgaris* Mill., *P. platycarpa* DC.)

The kernel of the stone is used medicinally. The taste is bitter. The drug is slightly poisonous. The kernels contain 0.4% volatile oil, amygdalin, emulsin.[151]

Used as antitussive, and sedative in hypertension. Dose, 5–10 gm.

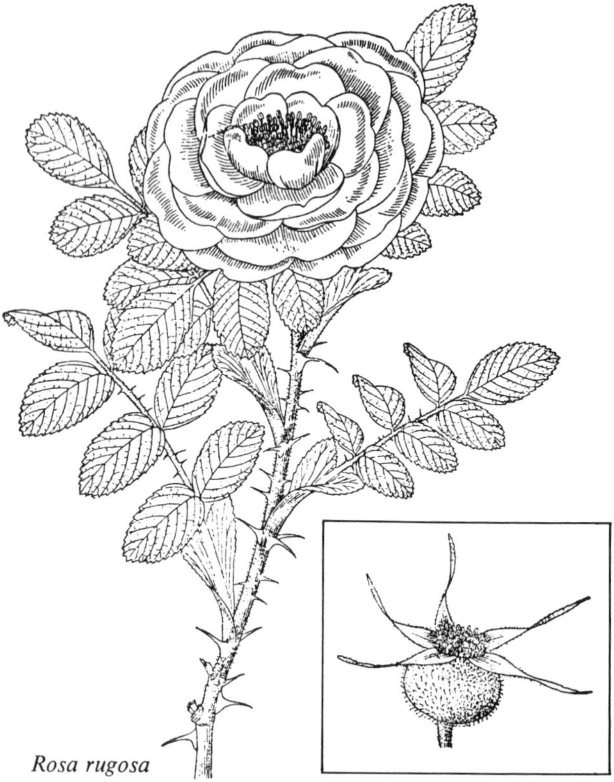

Rosa rugosa

ROSA CHINENSIS Jacq.

(Rosaceae)

China rose, Bengal rose. An upright, partly evergreen shrub 2 m. tall, the stems unarmed or with a few compressed, somewhat hooked prickles. Leaves alternate; leaflets 3–5, oval-oblong, 2.5–6.0 cm. long, acuminate, dentate, gla-

月季花

brous. Flowers solitary or in terminal corymbs, lengthily pedicellate, 5 cm. in diameter, red or pink; June–September; sepals refracted, tomentose inside, glabrous without, entire or provided with several lateral appendages; stamens numerous; styles more or less pilose; receptacle nearly globular; achenes numerous. Southeastern China, Japan. Cultivated. (Syn. *R. indica* Lindl., *R. sinica* L.)

The flowers are used medicinally. The taste is sweet. The petals contain an aromatic essential oil.[140]

Prescribed as tonic, circulatory stimulant, emmenagogue. Dose, 4–10 gm.

(*R. rugosa* Thunb. is used also.)

金櫻子

ROSA LAEVIGANA Michx.

(Rosaceae)

Cherokee rose. An evergreen, climbing shrub 5 m. tall. Leaflets 3, rarely 5, oval-elliptical or oval-lanceolate, 3–6 cm. long, acute or acuminate, finely dentate, glossy, the terminal leaflet larger and lengthily petiolate. Flowers solitary, odoriferous, white, rarely pink, 6–8 cm. in diameter; April–May; calyx a cupuliform tube covered with hairs; petals obcordate; stamens very numerous. Receptacle oblong, ovoid, or nearly globular, 1.5–3.0 cm. long by 1.0–1.5 cm. wide, reddish, covered with stiff hairs and crowned with the persistent calyx. Southern China, Japan, Vietnam, Taiwan. (Syn. *R. amygdalifolia* Ser., *R. cherokeansis* Donn., *R. cucumerina* Tratt., *R. hystrix* Lindl., *R. sinica* Ait., *R. ternata* Poir., *R. trifoliata* Bosc.)

The fruits are officinal. The taste is sour and astringent. The drug contains malic acid, citric acid, tannin, sugar, and resin.[140]

Prescribed as carminative and astringent in chronic enteritis, diarrhea, peritonitis; as tonic in enuresis, spermatorrhea. Dose, 10–18 gm.

薔薇

ROSA MULTIFLORA Thunb.

(Rosaceae)

Multiflora rose. A climbing or trailing shrub with stout, hooked prickles. Leaflets 5–9, generally oblongish, 2.5–3.5 cm. long. Flowers 2 cm. wide, often double, odoriferous, white or pink, in multifloral corymbs or panicles; July–August. China, Japan, Korea. (Syn. *R. linkii* Dehnh.)

The seeds are officinal. They contain 0.7% multiflorin ($C_{27}H_{36}O_{15}$), kaempferol, rhamnose, quercetin, and 8% fat.[134]

Used as diuretic and laxative. Dose, 7–15 gm.

地榆

SANGUISORBA OFFICINALIS L.

(Rosaceae)

Garden burnet. A perennial herb 0.4–1.0 m. tall. Leaves alternate, pinnate; leaflets 7–15, oblong, dentate. Inflorescence a terminal, compact spike, ovoid or oblong; July–September. Calyx with 4 petaloid segments, deep purple, caducous; petals none; stamens 4, as long as the calyx; gynoecium composed of separate carpels enclosed within the calyx tube. Fruit a tetragonal achene, enclosed in the persistent calyx, corners winged. China, northern Asia, Europe. (Syn. *S. carnea* Fisch., *Poterium officinale* Benth.)

The root is used medicinally. It occurs as long, fibrous pieces 7–8 cm. long by 1–2 cm. in diameter, the exterior brown, the interior reddish. The taste is bitter and astringent. The root contains 17% tannin, flavones, and sanguisorbin ($C_{38}H_{60}O_7$).[1, 32]

Employed as astringent hemostatic in hemoptysis, gastroenteric hemorrhage, dysentery, menorrhagia. Dose, 5–8 gm. Incompatible: *Liriope spicata.* A 5% decoction is used externally as lotion in eczema, pruritis.

Sanguisorba officinalis

CITRUS MEDICA L.

(Rutaceae)

Citron. A small tree 5–6 m. high, with or without horizontal spines which are stiff and attain 35 mm. in length. Leaves oval or lanceolate, 5–11 cm. long by 3.5–6.0 cm. wide, ser-

香櫞

rate, coriaceous; petiole without wings, articulate. Flowers solitary or in clusters of 2–3, white tinted with purple outside, fairly large; pedicel provided at its base with a small, lanceolate bract, glabrous or somewhat ciliate; sepals 5, triangular, mostly united, glabrous; petals 5, white, glabrous; stamens numerous, two-thirds as long as the petals; disk thick; ovary ovoid-elongate; style twice the length of the ovary; stigma somewhat capitate. Fruit a fleshy berry, lemon yellow, ovoid or oblong, terminated with a nipple, the pulp acid, skin thick and rough. China, India, Indochina. Cultivated. (Syn. *C. digitata seu chirocarpus* Lour.)

The rind of the fruit is officinal. It contains hesperidin ($C_{28}H_{34}O_{15}$; fine dentritic needles; m.p. 258–262°; freely soluble in pyridine, dilute alkalies; slightly soluble in methanol, hot glacial acetic acid; almost insoluble in acetone, benzene, chloroform; one gram dissolves in 50 l. water) and an essential oil comprising limonene, dipentene, citral.[140 149] Pure hesperidin provides no protection against capillary fragility; however certain water-soluble derivatives of it have such action, commonly attributed to vitamin P.[144] Addition of 1% hesperidin to the diet of rats produces no effect of any kind.[117]

Prescribed as aromatic stomachic. Dose, 3–5 gm.

橘皮

CITRUS NOBILIS Lour.

(Rutaceae)

King orange, mandarin orange. A small tree 5–8 m. tall, with or without short, straight spines. Leaves attenuate at the two extremities, entire or barely crenelate, somewhat coriaceous, articulate, oval, 5 cm. long by 2.5 cm. wide; petiole flattened on top, not winged. Flowers solitary, small, white, pedicels 3 mm. long, provided at their base with small, scaly bracts which are ciliate on the edges; sepals 5, nearly totally united; petals 5, oblong, 8–9 mm. long; stamens nearly as long as the petals, partly united; disk small; ovary globular; stigma capitate. Fruit nearly spherical, orange or reddish, flattened at the two ends, zest bruised but not warty, easily detached, pulp sweet and very aromatic, embryo greenish. Southeastern China, Vietnam. (Syn. *C. deliciosa* Tenore.)

The rind of the fruit is officinal. It contains vitamins A, B, and C, hesperidin, and an essential oil comprising limonene, citral, methyl anthranilate.[92 149]

Used as stomachic and digestant, expectorant, antitussive, antiemetic. Dose, 5 gm. The seeds have been employed as analgesic in colic, orchitis. The leaves have been used externally as antiphlogistic in mastitis and other swellings.

皮鮮白

DICTAMNUS ALBUS L.

(Rutaceae)

Dittany, fraxinella, burning bush. A strong-smelling, somewhat woody perennial herb 40–80 cm. tall, covered with glandular hairs. Leaves glandular, pinnate; leaflets 9–15, large, oval, sessile, denticulate; petiole somewhat winged. Inflorescence a terminal, erect raceme, pubescent-glandular. Flowers irregular, white or pink veined with purple; April; calyx with 5 sepals, somewhat connate at the base; petals 5, irregular, flat, entire, 3–4 times longer than the calyx, the 4 superior petals ascending, the 5th inferior petal reflected; stamens 10, directed below, longer than the petals; ovary stipitate. Fruit a cuspidate, wrinkled capsule, 5-divided, hard, almost woody. Northwestern China, northern Asia, Europe. (Syn. *Fraxinella dictamnus* Moench.)

The root epidermis is used medicinally. It occurs as yellowish white in color. The taste is bitter; the odor strong. The root contains the alkaloid dictamnine (dictamine; $C_{12}H_9NO_2$; prisms; m.p. 132–133°; soluble in hot alcohol, chloroform; slightly soluble in ether; insoluble in water).[4 108]

Used as antipyretic. Dose, 5–10 gm. A decoction is employed externally as antiseptic in scabies, eczema, impetigo.

Dictamnus albus

EVODIA RUTAECARPA Benth.

(Rutaceae)

A villous, woody shrub. Leaves opposite, pinnate, 30–45 cm. long; leaflets 5–7, winged, nearly sessile, oblong, acuminate, generally rounded at the base, entire, the underside villous. Inflorescence a terminal cyme, 7.5–10.0 cm. in diameter; August. Flowers fairly small, polygamous; pedicel very

萸茱吳

short; sepals 5; petals 5, the exterior nearly glabrous, the interior villous; stamens 5. Fruit a collection of dry pods, each 12 mm. in diameter, 2-valved, opening at the top. Southeastern China, Japan, India. (Syn. *Boymia rutaecarpa* Juss.)

The fruits are officinal. The taste is bitter and pungent. The drug is slightly poisonous. It contains the alkaloids evodiamine ($C_{19}H_{17}N_3O$; yellow plates; m.p. 278°; soluble in acetone; slightly soluble in alcohol, ether, chloroform; insoluble in water, benzene, petroleum ether) and rutaecarpine ($C_{18}H_{13}N_3O$; needles; m.p. 258°; soluble in alcohol, benzene, chloroform, ether; almost insoluble in water).[6] Evodiamine yields rutamine ($C_{10}H_{12}N_2O$), which is the beta isomer of indolethylamine.[7] Rutamine stimulates plain muscle, especially that of the uterus, and is also a central nerve stimulant; large doses produce intestinal hyperperistalsis, dyspepsia, and delirium.[91] Rutaecarpine causes increased arterial pressure.[144]

Used as stomachic and carminative, stimulant, uterotonic. Dose, 3–5 gm. Incompatible: *Salvia chinensis.*

柏 黃

PHELLODENDRON AMURENSE Rupr.

(Rutaceae)

Amur cork tree. A deciduous tree 10–15 m. tall, with gray, deeply fissured, corky bark. Leaves opposite, pinnate, 25–35 cm. long; leaflets 5–13, oval or oval-lanceolate, 5–10 cm. long, acute, base rounded, the underside glabrous. Inflorescence a somewhat contracted panicle, 6–8 cm. long, pubescent. Flowers dioecious, 6 mm. long, yellow green. Fruit an oval drupe 1 cm. in diameter, black, aromatic. Northern China, Siberia, Japan.

The bark is used medicinally. It occurs in pieces 7–12 cm. long, the color yellowish brown. The taste is bitter. The drug contains the alkaloids berberine ($C_{20}H_{19}NO_5 \cdot 5\frac{1}{2}H_2O$; long, silky yellow needles; m.p. 145° of the anhydrous salt; soluble in hot water, alcohol; slightly soluble in acetone, ether, benzene, chloroform) and palmatine ($C_{21}H_{23}NO_5$; forms addition products with acetone and chloroform as does berberine; orange-yellow needles; m.p. 241°); mucilage, and obacunone ($C_{28}H_{48}O_7$).[33] The obaculactone of Fujita and Wada has been identified as limonine.[96]

Prescribed as stomachic and antiseptic in typhoid fever, dysentery, enteritis, diarrhea, stomatitis, hepatitis, cystitis, urethritis. Dose, 5 gm. Used externally as antiphlogistic in skin diseases, conjunctivitis.

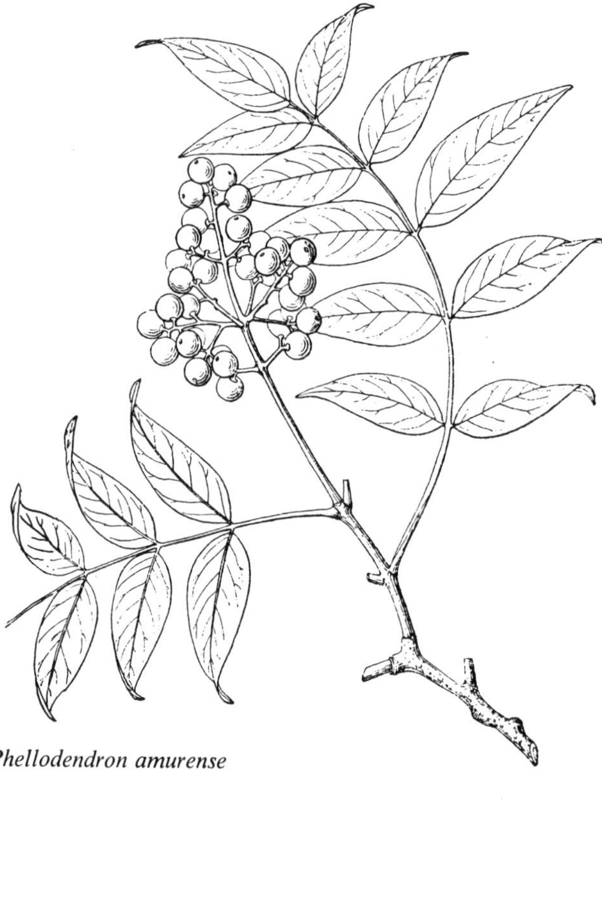

Phellodendron amurense

枳實 枳殼

PONCIRUS TRIFOLIATA Rafin.

(Rutaceae)

Trifoliate orange. A deciduous, glabrous tree, rarely over 6 m. tall; spines axillary and solitary, compressed at the base, rounded at the tip, 1.5–3.5 cm. long. Leaves alternate, trifoliate; leaflets elliptical, slightly crenelate, the central leaflet larger than the lateral leaflets, 4 cm. long by 2 cm. wide; petiole winged. Flowers white, flattish, 5 cm. wide; April–June; sepals 5; petals 5, oblong, longer than the sepals; stamens 8–10, free. Fruit a rugose berry covered with short, fine hair, greenish, 2–3 cm. in diameter, flesh dryish, very acid, fragrant, inedible; September–October. China, Japan. (Syn. *Citrus trifoliata* L., *C. triptera* Desf., *Aegle sepiaria* DC.)

The unripe fruits are officinal. The taste is bitter; the odor aromatic. The unripe fruits contain an essential oil comprising limonene, linalool, linalyl acetate, methyl anthranilate.[133]

Used as aromatic stomachic, diuretic, antidiarrheic. Dose, 5–10 gm.

川椒

XANTHOXYLUM PIPERITUM DC.

(Rutaceae)

Japanese prickly ash. A small, deciduous tree, the bark deep brown, prickly. Leaves alternate, odd-pinnate; leaflets opposite, lanceolate or ovate. Flowers dioecious, simple, small, axillary, yellowish green; spring. Fruit a collection of carpels, each 2-valved, with one black seed. China, Japan.

The fruits are used medicinally. The taste is pungent and bitter; the odor aromatic. The fruits contain 2–4% of an essential oil comprising phellandrene, limonene, citronellol, geraniol, sanshol; the seeds contain a large amount of limonene; the leaves contain a saponin and an essential oil comprising citral, citronellol, geraniol; the root contains berberine.[140] Xanthoxylin ($C_{10}H_{12}O_2$; white needles; m.p. 80°; soluble in alcohol, ether; insoluble in water) has been isolated from the fruit.[102]

Prescribed as stomachic, carminative, stimulant, diuretic. Dose, 3–5 gm.

香檀白

SANTALUM ALBUM L.

(Santalaceae)

White sandalwood. A tree 10 m. high. Leaves opposite, petiolate, entire, oblong, 3–7 cm. long, acuminate, coriaceous. Inflorescence an axillary or terminal panicle. Perianth a campanulate tube with 4 lobes, straw yellow at first, becoming purple; stamens 4; receptacle clothing the calyx tube; ovary free at first, becoming inferior, 1-celled. Fruit a globular drupe crowned with the remnants of the perianth, black. Southern China, India. (Syn. *S. verum* L., *S. myrtifolium* Roxb., *Sirium myrtifolium* L.)

The wood is used medicinally. It occurs as billets or broken pieces, texture fibrous, color light yellow to dark reddish brown, surface rough and furrowed. The taste is slightly sweet and pungent; the odor aromatic. The wood contains a volatile oil comprising at least 90% total alcohols calculated as alpha-santalol and beta-santalol; less important constituents are isovaleric aldehyde, santene, santenone, teresantol, santalone, and santalene.[144 148] Excessive doses of santal oil produce irritation of the urinary tract with kidney pain, albuminuria, and vesical tenesmus; the oil has been administered as urinary antiseptic.[152]

Prescribed as aromatic stomachic, carminative, analgesic in nervous gastralgia. Dose, 2–3 gm., powdered. The powdered drug is used externally in skin disorders.

荔枝核

LITCHI CHINENSIS Sonn.

(Sapindaceae)

Litchi. A tree 10–16 m. tall. Leaves alternate, pinnate, 10–15 cm. long, with 2–4 pair leaflets; leaflets lanceolate or oblong-lanceolate, base attenuate, tip acuminate, 6–10 cm. long by 2–3 cm. wide, coriaceous, surface shiny green, underside dull. Inflorescence a terminal panicle covered with brownish hairs. Flowers small, greenish white, unisexual or polygamous; March–April; calyx cupuliform, villous on both sides, barely lobate; no petals; stamens 6–10, lengthening after anthesis; ovary bilobate, villous. Fruit an ovoid drupe, 2.5 cm. long; seed arillate, partly free; aril fleshy. China, Vietnam, Thailand, India. (Syn. *Nephelium litchi* Cambess., *Dimocarpus litchi* Lour., *Scytalia chinensis* Gaertn.)

The seed is officinal. The taste is sweet and astringent. The fleshy aril contains citric acid, sugar, vitamins A, B, C.[151]

The seeds are employed as astringent and analgesic in gastralgia, colic, orchitis. Dose, 4–7 gm., powdered. The fresh fruit is used as tonic, antidiarrheic, antitussive.

龍眼肉

NEPHELIUM LONGANA Camb.

(Sapindaceae)

Longan, lungan. A tree 10–15 m. tall. Leaves alternate, irregularly pinnate, with 2–5 pair leaflets; leaflets oval-lanceolate, base cuneate, tip rounded or very briefly acuminate; limb 7–20 cm. long by 2.5–5.0 cm. wide. Inflorescence a small terminal or axillary panicle. Flowers polygamous-dioecious, small, yellowish white; April; calyx tomentose, with 5–6 segments; petals 5–6, spatulate, pubescent, nearly equalling the calyx; disk entire, villous; stamens 6–10. Fruit globular or ovoid, generally solitary through abortion, pericarp yellowish; seed spherical, enveloped in a fleshy, acid aril. Southern China, India, Réunion, Mauritius. (Syn. *Euphoria longana* Lam., *Dimocarpus longan* Lour.)

The dried aril and the kernel are both officinal. The aril contains 27% glucose, sucrose, tartaric acid, vitamins A, B; the kernel contains saponins, tannin, and fat.[140]

The dried aril is employed as nutrient tonic in neurasthenia, insomnia. Dose 10–15 gm. The ground kernel is employed as styptic.

草鯉魚

HOUTTUYNIA CORDATA Thunb.

(Saururaceae)

A perennial, stoloniferous herb, the stem erect, 30–40 cm. high. Leaves alternate, petiolate, 7 cm. long by 4 cm. wide, glabrous, rounded-oval, base cordate, tip acuminate; stipule intrapetiolar, brownish, scariose, fixed on the margin of the sheath. Inflorescence a terminal spike surrounded at the base with 4 free white bracts forming a persistent involucre. Flowers small, no perianth; May–August; stamens 3; ovary 1-celled. Fruit a capsule, dehiscent at the top. Southern China, Himalayas, Vietnam, Laos.

The entire plant is officinal. The taste is pungent. The stem and leaves are of a purplish red color; when in flower the plant has a fetid smell. The plant contains an essential oil comprising lauraldehyde, methyl nonyl ketone, and myrcene; quercitrin, flavones.[136]

Prescribed internally as diuretic and urinary antiseptic. Dose, 7–10 gm. The fresh leaves are used externally as vesicant in skin disorders.

山 常

DICHROA FEBRIFUGA Lour.

(Saxifragaceae)

A shrub 1–2 m. tall, the stem smooth, cylindrical, glabrous or pubescent, purplish. Leaves opposite, lanceolate or broadly linear, base attenuate, tip acuminate, 13–20 cm. long by 35–90 mm. wide, serrate, glabrous or lightly villous, purplish. Inflorescence a compact, axillary, or terminal panicle. Flowers numerous, compact, blue or pink, 8 mm. wide; May; calyx obconical, segments 4, 5, or 7, triangular; petals 4–7, blue or red; stamens 10 or 20; ovary nearly inferior; styles often 5. Fruit a blue berry, 5 mm. in diameter; seeds very numerous, pyriform, reticulate, small, barely 1 mm. long. Southern China, Himalayas, Philippines, Java. (Syn. *Adamia chinensis* Gard. et Champ., *A. cyanea* Wall., *A. versicolor* Fortune, *Cyanitis sylvatica* Reinw., *Dichroa cyanitis* Miq., *D. latifolia* Miq.)

The root is officinal. It occurs as flat, oval pieces 5 cm. long, without bark, the pith very apparent. The taste is bitter; the drug is poisonous. Three isomeric alkaloids, designated alpha-dichroine, beta-dichroine, and gamma-dichroine, have been isolated.[41] Alpha-dichroine is probably identical with isofebrifugine, while beta-dichroine and gamma-dichroine appear to be crystalline modifications of febrifugine.[144] Alpha-dichroine appears to be 100 times more effective as antimalarial than quinine; side effects include nausea and vomiting; toxic doses produce vomiting with diarrhea, gastrointestinal hypersecretion, hyperperistalsis, gastrointestinal hemorrhage, hypotension, tachypnea, death.[140] The crude infusion of the herb appears to be antipyretic, but the alkaloids alone show no such action.[71]

Used as antimalarial and antipyretic. Dose, 5–10 gm. in decoction. The emetic side effect may be controlled with the concurrent administration of 3–6 gm. *Pinellia tuberifera*.

BRUCEA JAVANICA Merr.

(Simarubaceae)

A small shrub. Leaves compound-paripinnate; leaflets 4–6 pair, opposite, lanceolate, serrate. Inflorescence a long cluster of small, polygamous flowers forming cymes; June. Sepals 4, connate at the base; petals 4, villous, glandular at the tips. In the male flowers, stamens 4, pistil reduced to a stigma; in the female, stamens 4, much reduced, ovary with 4 free carpels. Fruit a drupe containing a single flat seed. Southern China, India, Sumatra. (Syn. *B. sumatrana* Roxb.)

The seeds are used medicinally. They occur 6–10 mm. long by 5 mm. in diameter, ovoid, yellowish brown or russet, leathery. The taste is bitter. The seeds contain the alkaloid brucamarin (crystals; soluble in alcohol, benzene, chloroform; slightly soluble in water, ether; insoluble in petroleum ether), the glycoside kosamine, and formic acid.[151] Small doses of kosamine act as emetocathartic, cholagogue, anti-coagulant, and microbicide against Nematodia and *Taenia;* large doses inhibit respiratory movement, and induce bilious emesis, diarrhea, coma, death.[151]

Prescribed in acute amebic dysentery, and as anthelmintic. Since the drug is a gastrointestinal irritant, it is usually administered in compound as follows: powdered kernel of *B. javanica* with oil removed, 40 mg., bismuth nitrate 100 mg., tincture *Scopolia japonica* 0.1 cc., kaolin 250 mg. Dose, 400 mg. t.i.d.

STERCULIA SCAPHIGERA Wall.

(Sterculiaceae)

A tree 30–40 m. tall. Leaves coriaceous, glossy, glabrous, entire, base rounded or nearly truncate, often cordate, 6–20 cm. long by 4–10 cm. wide. Inflorescence a terminal panicle. Calyx deeply lobate, tube very short; staminal column longer than the calyx tube; stamens variable, generally more numerous in the male flowers. In the hermaphrodite flowers, ovary villous; carpels 2–5, membranous, monospermous; stigma sessile or nearly bilobate. Follicles 1–5, 15–20 cm. long by 4–5 cm. wide, attenuate toward the tip, membranous, distinctly veined, the veins villous, glabrous between. Laos, Malaysia, Thailand. (Syn. *Scaphium wallichii* Schott. et Endl.)

The seeds are officinal. They occur 2 cm. long, ovoid, glabrous, shiny. The taste is sweet. The seeds contain mucilage and traces of theobromine and caffeine.[151]

Prescribed as refrigerant, antiphlogistic, and expectorant in laryngeal and bronchial mucositis, atrophic pharyngitis. Dose, 3–6 seeds, macerated in water.

西河柳葉

TAMARIX CHINENSIS Lour.

(Tamaricaceae)

A deciduous shrub 3 m. tall, the branches slender. Leaves alternate, small, lanceolate, acuminate, carinate, greenish blue. Inflorescence a terminal panicle 3–5 cm., slender, dense; July–September; bracts linear, acuminate, longer than the pedicel. Sepals 5, shorter than the petals; petals 5; disk with 10 glands; stamens 5, equalling or twice as long as the petals; ovary 1-celled. Fruit a dehiscent capsule, valves 5. Northern China, Japan, Indochina. (Syn. *T. gallica* Thunb., *T. indica* Willd.)

The branchlets and leaves are officinal. The taste is bittersweet. The drug contains the glycoside salicin ($C_{13}H_{18}O_7$; orthorhombic crystals from water; m.p. 199–202°; soluble in alkalies, pyridine, glacial acetic acid; one gram dissolves in 23 ml. water, 3 ml. boiling water, 90 ml. alcohol; practically insoluble in ether, chloroform.)[140] Salicin yields upon hydrolysis saligenin; this in turn is oxidized to salicylic acid, but a part is excreted unchanged.[152] Salicin is a bitter tonic, antifermentive, antiseptic, highly destructive to low organisms, has slight antiperiodic power, and is feebly antipyretic; salicin and its derivatives have been chiefly used in acute rheumatism, to lower temperature, relieve pain, and reduce articular swelling.[150] Salicin is inferior to the salicylates because its conversion is often incomplete; it yields 45% salicylic acid, and is therefore at most half as effective.[152]

Used as antipyretic and analgesic in acute and chronic rheumatism; also used as carminative and diuretic. Dose, 5–10 gm.

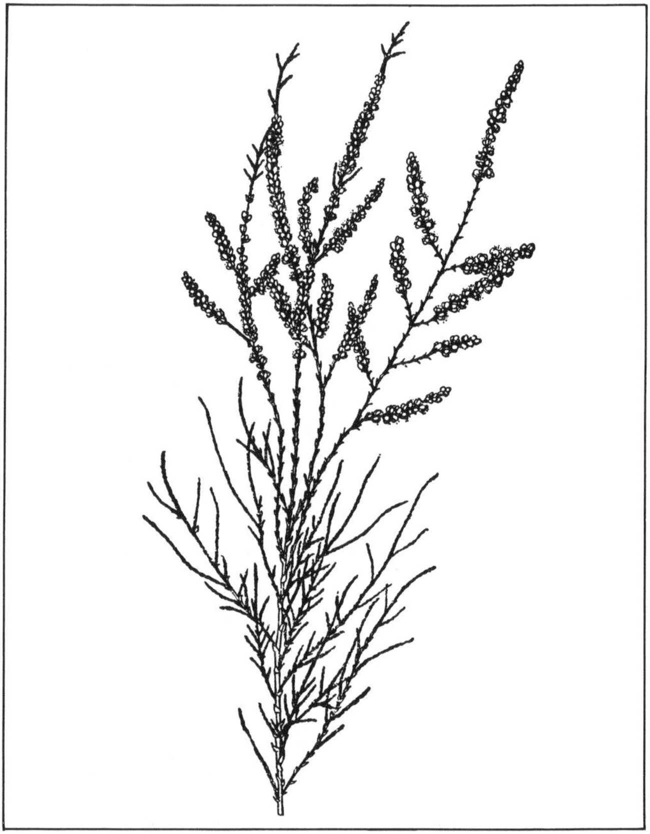

Tamarix chinensis

山茶花

CAMELLIA JAPONICA L.

(Theaceae)

Camellia. A shrub 2 m. high. Leaves simple, oval or elliptical, 5–10 cm. long, acuminate, coriaceous, surface glossy. Inflorescence a terminal cyme. Flowers red; October; calyx 5-lobed, the estivation quincuncial; corolla with a cylindrical tube somewhat enlarged at the top, limb 5-lobed; stamens 5; gynoecium consisting of 2 carpels, a single discoid style at the tip. Fruit a double samara, ligneous, winged, indehiscent. China, Japan.

The floral buds are used medicinally. The taste is sweet and slightly bitter.

Prescribed, apparently because of its red color, in hemoptysis, epistaxis, gastrointestinal hemorrhage, metrorrhagia. Dose, 5–10 gm. Used externally for burns and scalds, being ground to a powder and mixed with sesame oil.

茶

THEA SINENSIS L.

(Theaceae)

Tea plant. A shrub or small tree 10 m. tall in its natural habitat, but under 2 m. in cultivation. Leaves alternate, briefly petiolate, oval-oblong, acuminate, finely dentate, 2–15 cm. long by 1–6 cm. wide, slightly coriaceous. Flowers fragrant, nodding, axillary, solitary or agglomerate 3–4; calyx short, sepals 5; corolla white, petals 5; stamens numerous; ovary globular, 3-celled. Fruit a trigonal, ligneous capsule. China, Indochina, India. (Syn. *T. bohea* L., *T. cochinchinensis* Lour., *T. cantoniensis* Lour., *T. assamica* Mast., *T. chinensis* Sims., *T. viridis* L., *Camellia bohea* Griff., *C. theifera* Griff., *C. viridis* Link.)

The leaves are used medicinally. The taste is astringent and slightly bitter, the odor aromatic. Tea leaves contain 1.4–3.5% caffeine, 1–30% tannin, and traces of theobromine, theophylline, xanthine, adenine, and a volatile oil. Caffeine has the most powerful central nervous action, with relatively weak peripheral effects; the strongest diuretic action is produced by theophylline, which also causes the most marked cardiac stimulation and coronary dilation, its central effects and its action on muscle approaching those of caffeine; theobromine acts most powerfully on muscle, its effects on the heart and urine intermediate, causing little central stimulation. A cup of strong tea prepared from 5 gm. of leaves contains about 100 mg. caffeine; a quick infusion extracts practically all the caffeine, but only part of the tannin, which may be deleterious to digestion by precipitating proteins and albumoses, by lessening absorption, and by irritating the gastric mucosa. The action of the alkaloids consists in increased mental and physical efficiency by psychical stimulation, comfort, and relief from muscular and mental fatigue and from their attendant unpleasant sensations; chronic caffeine poisoning (5 cups of tea daily, corresponding to 600 mg. caffeine) exhibits dyspepsia, restlessness, nervous excitability, tremor, insomnia, anorexia, headache, vertigo, confusion, palpitation, and dyspnea; constipation is common, but not more so than in individuals not addicted to tea.[152]

Prescribed as cardiotonic, central nerve stimulant, diuretic, intestinal astringent. Dose, 4–7 gm.

沉香

AQUILARIA AGALLOCHA Roxb.

(Thymelaeaceae)

A tree 40 m. tall. Leaves alternate, petiolate, simple. Inflorescence a nearly sessile umbel. Flowers small; perianth villous, lobes 5; stamens 15, of which 10 are opposite the perianth lobes, the remaining 5 alternate; ovary nearly sessile, villous; style almost wanting; stigma broad. Fruit a capsule, surrounded by the persistent, accrete perigynous members, compressed; pericarp coriaceous, thick; seeds pyriform, with a long inferior appendage. Himalayas, Vietnam, northeast India.

The wood is used medicinally. The color is yellow, the texture hard; it sinks when immersed in water. The taste is pungent, sweet and bitter; the odor aromatic. The wood, known as Aloes wood, contains an essential oil which is used in perfumery.[155]

Prescribed as stomachic in gastralgia, colic, nervous emesis, hiccough. Dose, 1 gm.

Daphne genkwa

花 芫

DAPHNE GENKWA Sieb. et Zucc.

(Thymelaeaceae)

A shrub 1 m. high. Leaves opposite or occasionally alternate, oblong-elliptical, 3–5 cm. long, the veins pubescent. Flowers small, purplish, in clusters, the pedicel short, blooming before the leaves; March–April; petals none; calyx corolla-like, tubular; stamens 8, in 2 rows, not protruding; ovary 1-celled. Fruit a 1-seeded drupe. Eastern China, Japan. (Syn. *D. fortunei* Lindl.)

The flowers and root are officinal. The taste of the flowers is bitter and acrid. The drug is poisonous. The plant contains genkwanin, sitosterol, apigenin, benzoic acid.[151]

The flowers are prescribed as diuretic, stomachic, antitussive. Dose, 2–3 gm. The root is employed externally as vesicant.

皮白榆

ULMUS CAMPESTRIS L.

(Ulmaceae)

English elm. A tall tree. Leaves alternate, briefly petiolate, oval or elliptical, 6–10 cm. long, base very oblique, surface coarse, underside softly villous, margin doubly toothed. Flowers briefly pedunculate, blooming before the leaves; petals none; calyx bell-shaped, inconspicuous. Fruit a flat samara, nearly round, 2 cm. in diameter, not hairy. Central China, Himalayas, Iran, Syria, northern Africa, Europe. (Syn. *U. glabra* Mill.)

The bark is used medicinally. The taste is sweet. The bark contains mucilage, starch, phytosterol, sitosterol, phlobaphenes, hexylenaldehyde, lipase, butyric and capric acids.[151]

Employed as diuretic and demulcent in affections of the urinary tract. Dose, 10–15 gm.

荑 蕪

ULMUS MACROCARPA Hance.

(Ulmaceae)

A tree 10 m. tall. Leaves alternate, obovoid or elliptical, 3–7 cm. long by 5.5 cm. wide, briefly acuminate, base slightly cuneiform, margin doubly toothed, thick, the petiole pubescent. Flowers polygamous, apetalous; perianth campanulate; stamens 5–9, exserted; ovary sessile, 2-celled. Fruit an obovoid samara, 2.0–2.5 cm. long, pubescent. Northern China, Manchuria.

The fruit is officinal. The taste is pungent, the odor strong and fetid.

Prescribed as vermifuge. Dose, 2–5 gm.

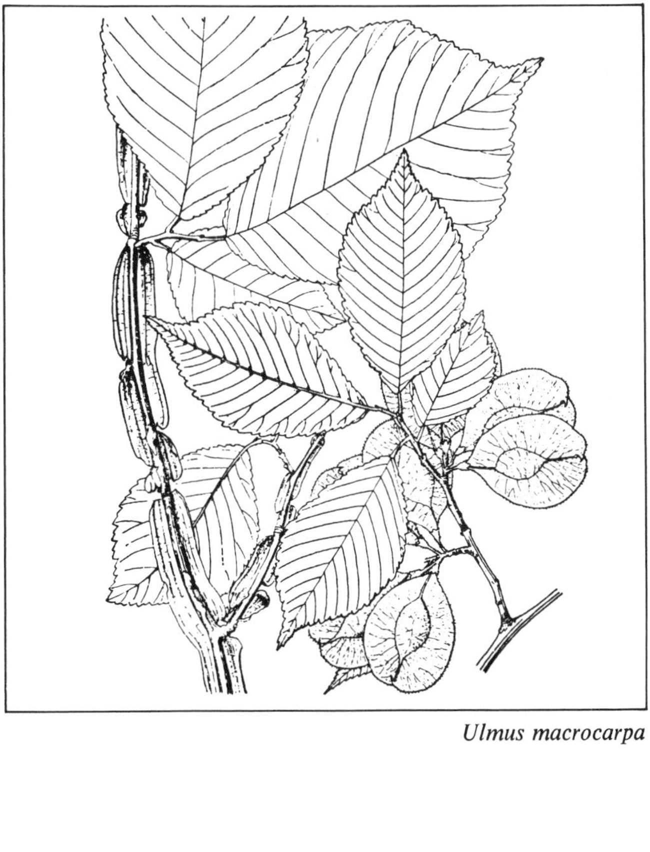

Ulmus macrocarpa

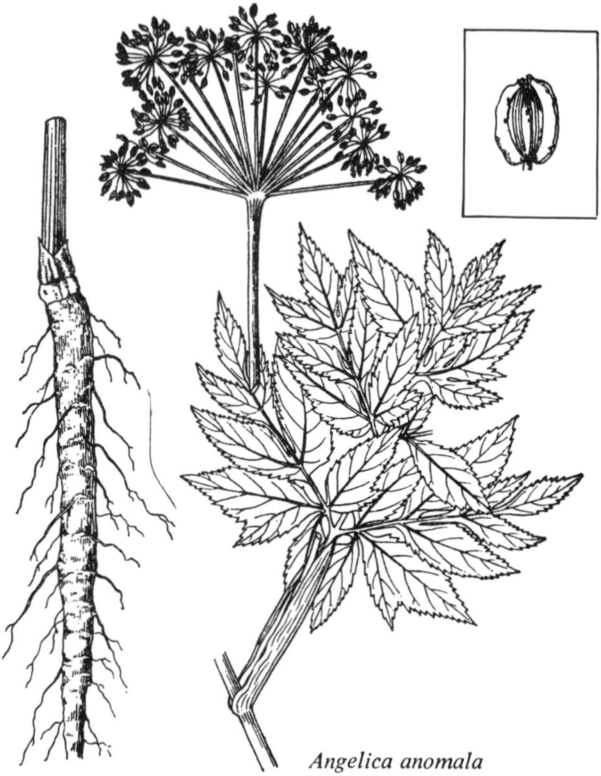

Angelica anomala

芷 白

ANGELICA ANOMALA Pall.

(Umbelliferae)

An alpine, perennial herb to 2 m. tall. Stem hollow, pubescent, often purplish. Leaves basal, broad, tripinnate; leaflets oval-elliptical, dentate, acute, underside powdery white; petiole broadly dilate at the base. Inflorescence a compound umbel, terminal. Flowers white; September; calyx with much-reduced teeth; petals 5, entire, incurvate at the tips. Fruit ovoid, compressed, edged with 4 membranous wings;

mericarps 5-ribbed, the 3 dorsal ribs filiform and close, the 2 marginal ribs dilate in membranous wings. China, Japan.

The root is used medicinally. It occurs in variable sizes, brownish yellow, covered with transversal wrinkles and resinous spots, the interior whitish. The odor is very aromatic, the taste bitter. The root contains a volatile oil comprising phellandrene.[151]

Prescribed as analgesic. Dose, 4–7 gm.

歸 當

ANGELICA POLYMORPHA Max.
(Umbelliferae)

A fragrant, perennial herb, the stem glabrous, lightly striate. Inferior leaves tripinnate, superior leaves often simply pinnate; segments oval or oval-lanceolate, dentate-incised, the teeth obtuse; petiole long, sheathed; bracts rudimentary, not prominent. Umbels multiflorous, 9–13, radiate, the rays irregular, interior margin uneven; bracteoles few, narrow-linear; pedicels slender, longer than the fruit. Carpophore bipartite. Carpels dorsally compressed, oblong or square-elliptical, the base cordiform, the tip rounded or lightly notched; dorsal veins 3, closely placed, elevated, the central vein barely winged, the marginal veins with very large wings; ducts oleaginous, solitary in each sinus, 2 in the commissure. Central China, Japan.

The root is used medicinally. It occurs divided into numerous rootlets, the exterior brownish, the interior white and spongy. The taste is bittersweet, the odor highly aromatic. The root contains 0.2–0.3% essential oil (comprising carvacrol, safrol, isosafrol, alcohols, sesquiterpenes, cadinene, n-dodecanol, n-tetradecanol, n-butylphalid),[124] 40% sucrose, and a non-glycosidal, non-alkaloid, and water-soluble crystalline substance.[140] Intravenous injection of the drug in rabbits and dogs produces diuresis, and excitation and contraction of smooth muscle of the bladder, intestine, and especially uterus.[99]

Prescribed as emmenagogue, sedative, analgesic. Dose, 5–10 gm.

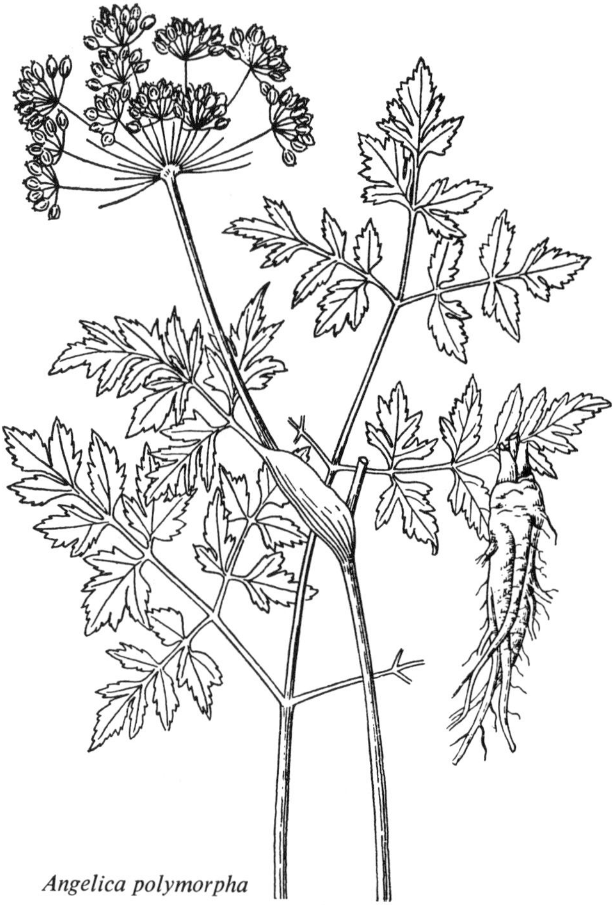

Angelica polymorpha

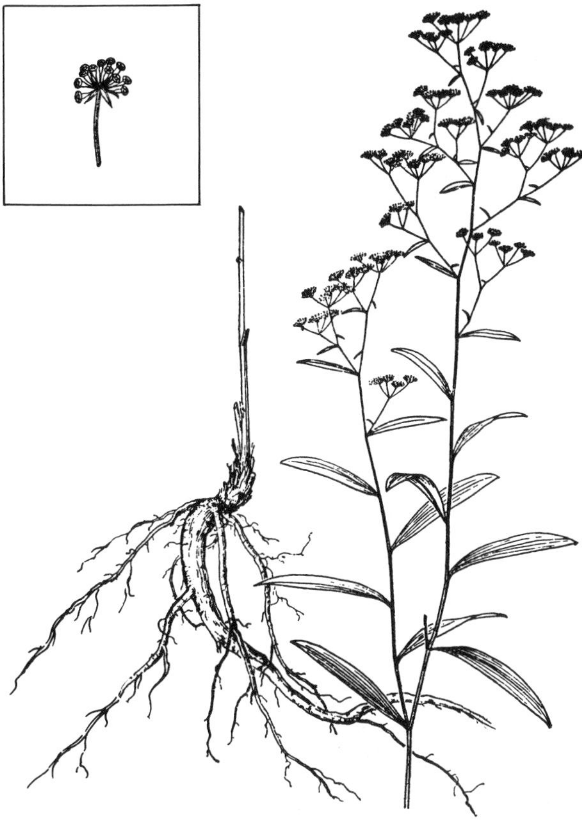

Bupleurum falcatum

BUPLEURUM FALCATUM L.

(Umbelliferae)

A perennial herb 30–80 cm. tall, the rhizome branching. Stem slender, flexuous, branches spreading. Leaves alternate, simple, entire, provided with a marginal vein; inferior leaves oval or oblong, the veins not prominent, mucronate, attenuate with the petiole; superior leaves linear-lanceolate,

柴胡

sessile. Umbels with 4–10 rays, nearly equal; involucre 1–4 linear leaflets, irregular; involucel 5–6 leaflets, lanceolate or linear, shorter than the umbels. Flowers yellow; July–October; calyx teeth almost wanting; petals with lobules inflected. Fruit ovoid, laterally compressed, crowned with the flat stylopodium and the reflected styles; carpel with 5 projecting ribs. Northern China, northern Asia, Europe. (Syn. *B. chinense* DC., *B. scorzoneraefolium* Willd.)

The root is officinal. It occurs pale red in color. The taste is bitter. The root contains furfurol, a sterol, and bupleurumol ($C_{37}H_{64}O_2$).[18] Large doses (50 gm. of a 20 % decoction) have been employed as antipyretic in malaria and blackwater fever.[140]

Prescribed as antipyretic, and in functional amenorrhea. Dose, 2–5 gm.

胡荽

CORIANDRUM SATIVUM L.

(Umbelliferae)

Coriander. An annual herb 30–60 cm. tall, glabrous, glossy, fetid, the stem erect, slender, striate. Inferior leaves pinnate, the segments oval, incised-dentate; superior leaves bipinnate or tripinnate, finely divided. Umbels with 3–8 rays; involucre none or one leaflet; involucel 3–5 linear leaflets, short, reflected, unilateral. Flowers white, the exterior flowers radiating; May; calyx with 5 lanceolate teeth, irregular, persistent; petals 5, emarginate with inflected lobules; stamens 5; styles longer than the conical stylopodium. Fruit aromatic, globular, 3–5 mm. in diameter, glabrous, brownish yellow; mericarp hemispherical, with 9 ribs, the 5 primary ribs flexuous and depressed, the 4 secondary ribs prominent, carinate; seed with concave, commissural surface. China, Japan, Indochina, India, Mediterranean.

The fruits are officinal. The taste is pungent and slightly

sour. The fruit contains about 1% volatile oil (comprising 45–65% coriandrol or l-linalool, d-pinene, terpinene, geraniol, borneol, decylaldehyde), fixed oils, malic acid, tannin, mucilage.[148] Coriander is aromatic, carminative, and stimulant and has been used as a corrective to griping purgatives.[144]

Employed as stomachic, carminative. Dose, 4–7 gm.

小茴香

FOENICULUM VULGARE Mill.

(Umbelliferae)

Fennel. An aromatic, perennial herb 1–2 m. high. Leaves alternate, 3 or 4 times pinnate, the ultimate leaflets very numerous, filiform, very elongate, the superior leaves with sheaths longer than the blade. Umbels compound, large, lengthily pedunculate, nearly regular. Flowers yellow, not involucrate; July–October; calyx with 5 very slight teeth; petals 5, entire, tips involute; stamens 5; ovary 2-celled; stylopodium large, conical. Fruit ovoid, 6 mm. long by 2 mm. in diameter, greenish, glabrous; mericarp compressed dorsally, semicylindrical, with 5 prominent, nearly regular ribs; seeds somewhat concave, with longitudinal furrows. Asia, Europe, northern Africa. (Syn. *F. officinale* All., *Anethum foeniculum* L.)

The fruits are used medicinally. The taste is sweet and pungent, the odor recalling anise. The fruits contain 3–4% volatile oil comprising 50–60% anethole ($C_{10}H_{12}O$; crystalline mass at 20–21°, liquid above 23°; m.p. 22–23°; soluble in benzene, chloroform, ether, acetone, petroleum ether; 1 part soluble in 5 parts alcohol; insoluble in water), about 20% fenchone ($C_{10}H_{16}O$; oily liquid; b.p. 193.5°; very soluble in absolute alcohol, ether; practically insoluble in water), pinene, limonene, dipentene, phellandrene.[148]

Prescribed as carminative, stomachic. Dose, 2–5 gm.

本 藁

NOTHOSMYRNIUM JAPONICUM Miq.

(Umbelliferae)

An alpine, perennial herb, the stem somewhat divaricate, striate, hollow, 30 cm. tall. Leaves oval-oblong, the inferior leaves bipinnate, the superior leaves smaller, clasping, pinnate. Umbels lengthily pedicellate, rays 9–14; involucre 3–4 persistent leaflets. Flowers in September; calyx without limb; petals white. Fruit didymous, ovoid, deep brown, tuberculate with 2 stylopodia somewhat compressed laterally; mericarps separate, ovoid-globular, with 5 much-reduced ribs, channels numerous. Southern China, Japan.

The root is officinal. The taste is bitter and pungent. The root contains 1.3% essential oil comprising nothosmyrnol ($C_{11}H_{14}O_2$) and dimethoxyallylbenzene.[131]

Prescribed as cerebral sedative, analgesic, antispasmodic. Dose, 3–5 gm.

胡 前

PEUCEDANUM DECURSIVUM Max.

(Umbelliferae)

An alpine, perennial herb. Leaves compound-pinnate; petiole expanded, clasping the stem. Inflorescence a compound umbel. Flowers small, purplish black, autumn. Eastern China, Japan.

The root is used medicinally. It occurs nodose, the epidermis blackish brown, the interior light yellow. The taste is bitter and pungent, the odor very strong. The root contains the glycoside nodakenin ($C_{20}H_{24}O_9$; thin, white leaflets; m.p. 215°; soluble in hot water, alcohol).[3]

Employed as analgesic, antipyretic, antitussive, expectorant in colds accompanied by fever and headache, bronchitis, asthma, pertussis. Dose, 5–10 gm.

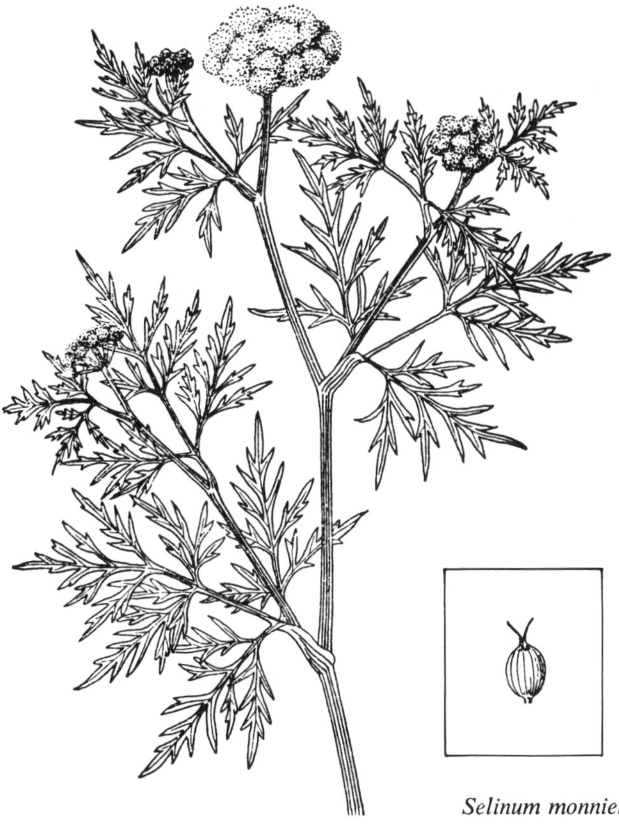

Selinum monnieri

SELINUM MONNIERI L.
(Umbelliferae)

An annual herb, the stem erect, 40–80 cm. high, branching, angular, furrowed. Leaves bipinnate, 5 cm. long; inferior segments pinnatifid, superior segments pinnatilobate or en-

子床蛇

tire, base cuneiform, tip acute. Inflorescence a compound umbel; involucre consisting of a few, very narrow bracts. Calyx without limb; petals oboval, white, 1 mm. across; July–August. Fruit oval, dorsally compressed, 2–3 mm. long by 2 mm. wide, brown; mericarp winged, surmounted with 2 styles. China, northern Vietnam, Laos, Siberia, eastern Europe. (Syn. *Athamanta chinensis* L., *Cicuta sinensis* Roem., *Cnidium monnieri* Cusson., *Seseli daucifolium* C. B. Clarke)

The seeds are officinal. They occur as grayish yellow, and resemble millet grains. The taste is bitter. The seeds contain 1.3% essential oil comprising borneol, pinene, camphene, terpineol.[123]

Prescribed as stimulant and aphrodisiac, as antirheumatic, and in renal disorders. Dose, 5–10 gm. Employed externally as an astringent vulnerary for hemorrhoids.

風 防

SILER DIVARICATUM Benth. et Hook.

(Umbelliferae)

A perennial herb 30–40 cm. tall, the stem erect, much-branched. Leaves pinnatifid; lobes 3–4, cuneiform, acute. No bracts; bracteoles 3–4, much shorter than the umbellules; calyx with 5 teeth; petals with lobules inflected; July–August. Fruit oblong, laterally compressed; mericarp with 5 primary and 4 secondary ribs, all regular, warted when immature. Northern China, Japan.

The roots are used medicinally. They occur as yellowish brown, 15 cm. long by 1 cm. in diameter, crowned at the tip with fragments of the stem. The taste is sweet and aromatic.

Used as antipyretic and analgesic. Dose, 4–7 gm.

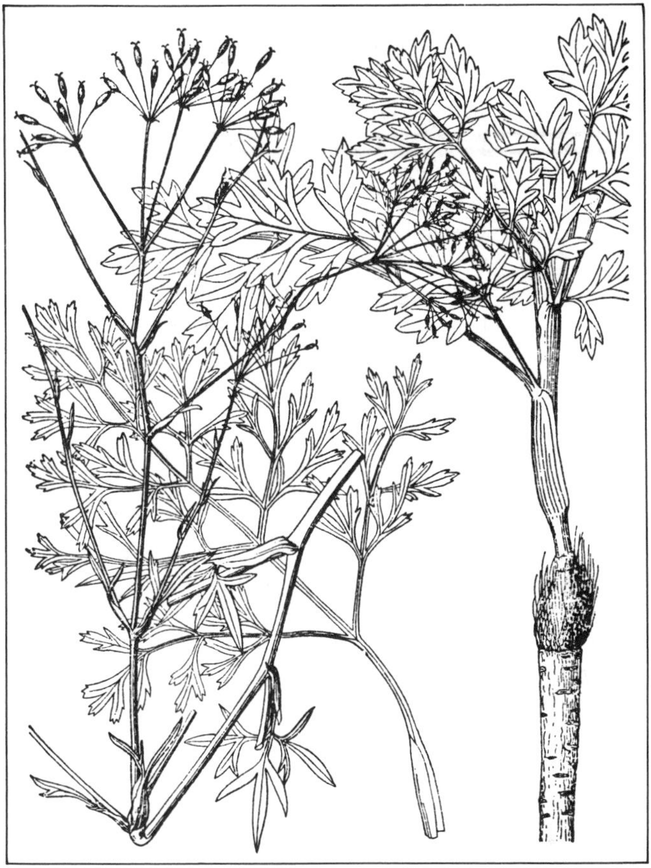

Siler divaricatum

BOEHMERIA NIVEA Gaudich

(Urticaceae)

China grass, ramie. A perennial herb 1–2 m. tall, stems hairy, ligneous at the base. Leaves alternate, lengthily petiolate, oval, dentate, tip acuminate, 7–15 cm. long by 4–8 cm. wide,

苧麻根

tomentose, the underside white; stipules linear, acuminate, rather caducous. Flowers small, monoecious or dioecious, axillary, in branching panicles; July–August. Male flowers with perianth in 4 segments; stamens 4. Female flowers with perianth tubular, corpulent, hirsute, 1.2 mm. long, with 3–4 teeth; ovary compressed, oval, nearly winged. Fruit an achene; September–November. Southern China, Japan, Korea, Vietnam, Laos, Australia. (Syn. *B. tenacissima* Gaudich, *Urtica tenacissima* Roxb., *U. utilis* Hort.)

The root is officinal. It occurs as yellowish white, not heavy. The taste is sweet. The root contains chlorogenic acid.[140]

Prescribed as diuretic, tonic. Dose, 5–10 gm.

紫花地丁

VIOLA PATRINII DC.

(Violaceae)

A perennial herb. Leaves alternate, petiolate, the inferior leaves generally oboval, the others narrowly oblong, base cuneate, truncate, or nearly cordate, crenelate-dentate, or nearly entire, 4 cm. long by 2 cm. wide, glabrous. Flowers axillary, solitary, violet; March–April; sepals 5; petals 5, the inferior petal spurred; stamens 5; ovary consisting of 3 carpels. Fruit an oblong capsule, 3-celled; seeds numerous. China, northern Vietnam, Laos, Japan, India, Afghanistan, Siberia. (Syn. *V. chinensis* G. Don., *V. averyi* Kell., *V. primulifolia* Lour., *V. prionantha* Bunge.)

The entire plant is used medicinally. The taste is bitter. The flowers contain a wax comprising 35% saturated acids (mainly cerotic), 5.8% unsaturated acids, 10% alcohols, 47% hydrocarbons.[140] The herbaceous portions of the plant are mucilaginous and emollient.[151]

Prescribed in suppurative inflammations, abscesses, ulcers. Dose, 5–10 gm. The fresh root is mashed and applied externally to abscesses.

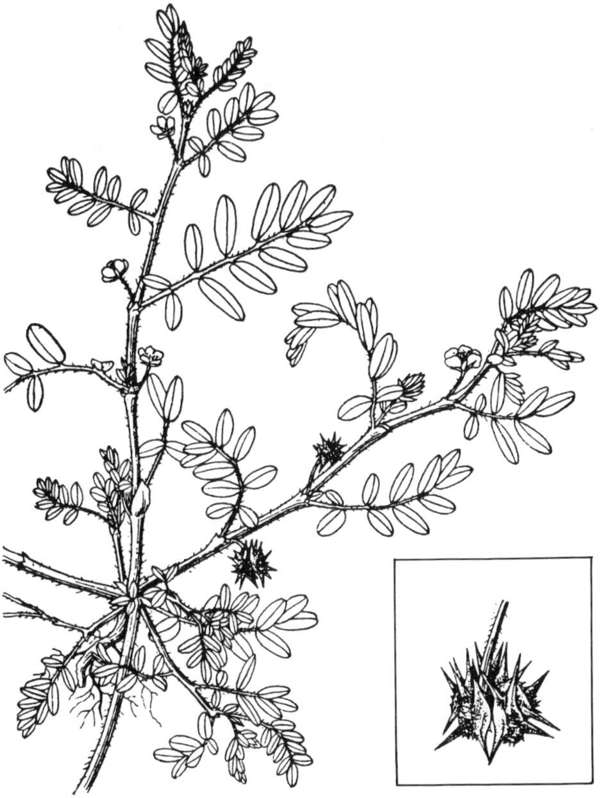

Tribulus terrestris

TRIBULUS TERRESTRIS L.

(Zygophyllaceae)

An annual herb 10–50 cm. tall, prostrate, villous. Leaves opposite, briefly petiolate, 4–5 cm. long; leaflets 5–8 pair, elliptical, somewhat oblique, 1 cm. long by 6 mm. wide; stipules very small. Flowers axillary, solitary, on peduncles which are shorter than the leaves, small, regular, yellow;

蒺藜刺

May–September; sepals 5, persistent; petals 5, caducous; disk thin; stamens 10, exserted; ovary sessile, 5-celled. Fruit a pentagonal capsule, depressed, splitting into 3 hulls arranged star-fashion, very hard, each provided with 4 spines, the 2 superior spines longer. China, Australia, Africa, tropics of the Old and New World.

The fruit is officinal. The taste is bitter and pungent. The drug contains a fixed oil, linoleic acid, an essential oil, tannin, phylloerythrin, vitamin A, a glycoside, phlobaphenes, peroxidase.[151]

Used as tonic in spermatorrhea, neurasthenia, vertigo; as astringent for oral inflammations. Dose, 7–10 gm.

ANGIOSPERMAE: Dicotyledonae:
Metachlamydeae

石絡

TRACHELOSPERMUM JASMINOIDES Lem.
(Apocynaceae)

Star jasmine. A high-climbing, woody vine. Leaves opposite, evergreen, briefly petiolate, ovalish, 5–7 cm. long, margin entire. Inflorescence a sparse, lengthily pedunculate cyme; April–May. Flowers white, 2 cm. wide, very fragrant; calyx 5-parted; corolla a short tube, lobes 5, oblong, twisted to the left; stamens 5, inserted on the corolla tube. Fruit consisting of 2 long, slender follicles. Southern China. (Syn. *T. divaricatum* Thunb., *Parechites adnascens* Hance., *P. thunbergii* A. Gray, *Echites saligna* Delile., *Nerium divaricatum* Thunb.)

The stem and leaves are officinal. The taste is bitter. The plant contains a resinous substance, a fatty matter, various tannins, glycosides; the stem is mildly toxic.[88]

Used as tonic, analgesic, emmenagogue. Dose, 5–10 gm.

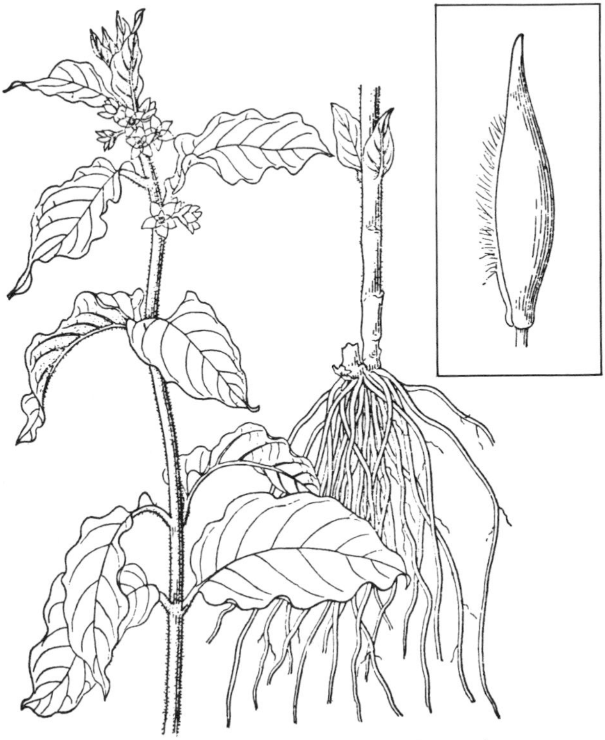

Cynanchum atratum

微 白

CYNANCHUM ATRATUM Bunge.

(Asclepiadaceae)

A perennial, alpine herb, the stem erect, tomentose. Leaves opposite, broadly oval, briefly petiolate, pubescent, base rounded or slightly cordate, tip acuminate. Inflorescence an axillary, umbellate cyme, sessile. Flowers brownish red; calyx in 5 segments; corolla rotate, lobes 5, elongate; stamens with filaments united in a tube. Fruit an acuminate follicle; seeds plumose. Northern China, Japan. (Syn. *Vince-*

toxicum atratum Moore et Decne., *V. acuminatum* Moore et Decne.)

The root is used medicinally. It occurs white tinged with yellow, fine, pliable, resembling that of *Achyranthes bidentata.* The taste is bitter and saline. The root contains cynanchin (vincetoxin; $C_{50}H_{82}O_{20}$).[140]

Prescribed as diuretic and antipyretic. Dose, 4–7 gm.

花葳紫

CAMPSIS CHINENSIS Voss.

(Bignoniaceae)

Chinese trumpet-creeper. A climbing vine with aerial rootlets, to 10 m. Leaves opposite, 0.5 cm. long, paripinnate; leaflets 5–9, oval-lanceolate, irregular, acute, serrate, glabrous, 7–8 cm. long by 3.0–3.5 cm. wide. Inflorescence a terminal cyme or panicle; July–August. Flowers large, nearly 7.5 cm. wide, scarlet; calyx coriaceous, campanulate, 5-lobed; corolla funnel-shaped, 5-lobed; stamens 4. Fruit a long-stalked capsule, somewhat curved, 20 cm. long by 1.5 cm. wide; seeds flattened, 2-winged. Southern China, Japan, northern Vietnam. (Syn. *C. adrepens* Lour., *Bignonia grandiflora* Thunb., *B. chinensis* Lam., *Incarvillea grandiflora* Poir., *Tecoma grandiflora* Loisel.)

The flowers are used medicinally. The taste is sour.

Prescribed as emmenagogue. Dose, 10–13 gm.

LITHOSPERMUM ERYTHRORHIZON Sieb. et Zucc.

(Boraginaceae)

A perennial herb, the stem erect, 30–80 cm. high, covered with coarse hairs. Leaves alternate, entire, sessile, lanceo-

草 紫

late, acuminate, the lateral veins protruding beneath. Inflorescence an axillary or terminal raceme; June. Flowers small, numerous, white; calyx in 5 segments; corolla funnel-shaped, barely surpassing the calyx, pubescent outside and at the throat; stamens 5. Fruit a collection of small, white nutlets within the persistent calyx. Northern China, Japan.

The root is officinal. The taste is bitter. "This plant is cultivated for the color yielded by its purple root; by a certain process a yellow color can be produced from the root."[138] The root contains 2 crystalline coloring matters, shikonin ($C_{16}H_{16}O_5$) and acetyl-shikonin ($C_{18}H_{18}O_6$).[140]

Prescribed as antipyretic and depurative in variola. Dose, 5–8 gm. Applied externally as ointment for eczema, boils, burns, and scalds.

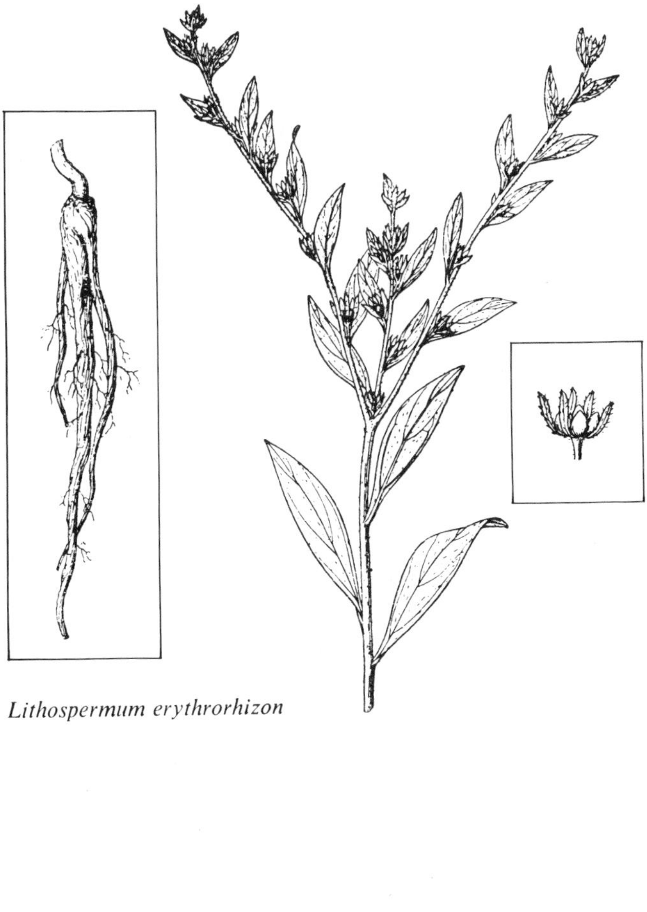

Lithospermum erythrorhizon

南沙參

ADENOPHORA VERTICILLATA Fisch.

(Campanulaceae)

An alpine, perennial herb, the stems numerous, erect. Leaves sessile or petiolate, lanceolate or oval, entire or dentate. Sepals 5, acute, entire or dentate; petals 5, deeply campanulate, glabrous, lilac blue; stamens shorter than the style, base spatulate; ovary inferior, 8-celled. Fruit a capsule. China, Japan.

The root is used medicinally. It occurs in pieces 8–9 cm. long, 1.5 cm. in diameter at the top, the color yellowish white, the interior spongy. The taste is bitter. The root contains saponins.[140]

Used as expectorant, sialagogue. Dose, 5–10 gm.

(*A. polymorpha* Ledeb. is similarly employed.)

黨參

CODONOPSIS TANGSHEN Oliv.

(Campanulaceae)

A perennial herb, the stem herbaceous, volubilate, 1 m. high, nearly glabrous. Leaves lengthily petiolate, oval-lanceolate, dentate, 3–5 cm. long by 1.5–2.5 cm. wide, tip acute, base rounded, the underside especially pubescent. Calyx deeply divided, persistent, ovoid, adnate with the ovary; corolla campanulate, 5-lobed, light green with violet streaks; stamens 5, free, opposite the segments of the involucre; ovary 5-celled; style with 5 stigmas. Fruit an obconical capsule dehiscent into 5 short valves; seeds numerous, small. Northern China.

The root is used medicinally. It occurs often bifurcate, 20–25 cm. long, yellowish brown, deeply wrinkled. The taste is sweet. The root contains saponin, starch, sugar.[140] Administered to rabbits, the drug augments the erythrocytes and hemoglobin, and diminishes the number of leukocytes; it possesses hypotensive properties.[48]

Prescribed as tonic in anemia, chronic enteritis, gastric atony, hyperacidity, diabetes mellitus, nephritis. Dose, 7–14 gm.

(The root of *Campanumaea pilosula* Franch. is similarly employed.)

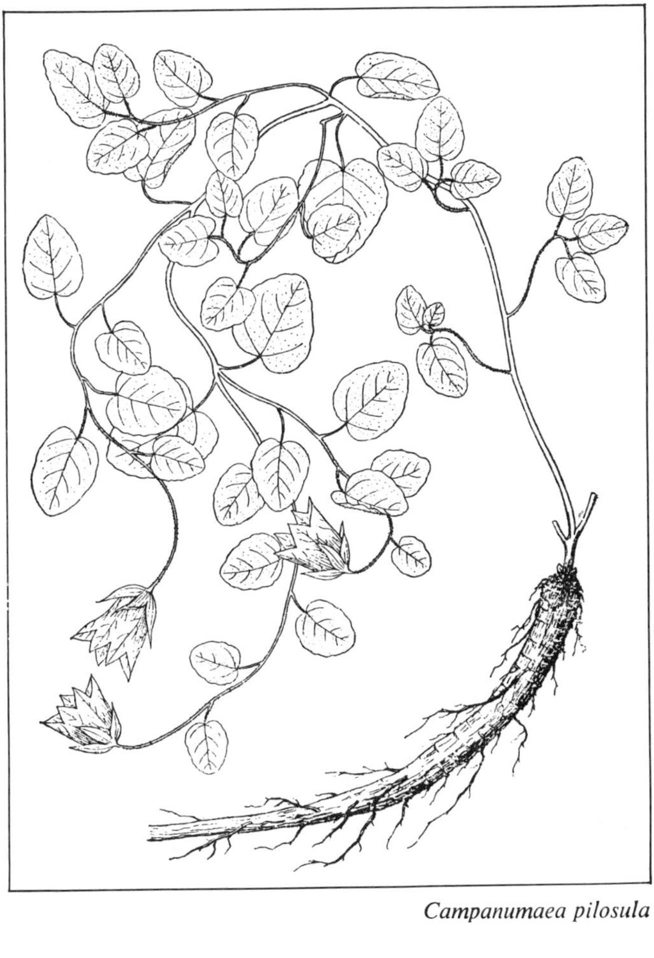

Campanumaea pilosula

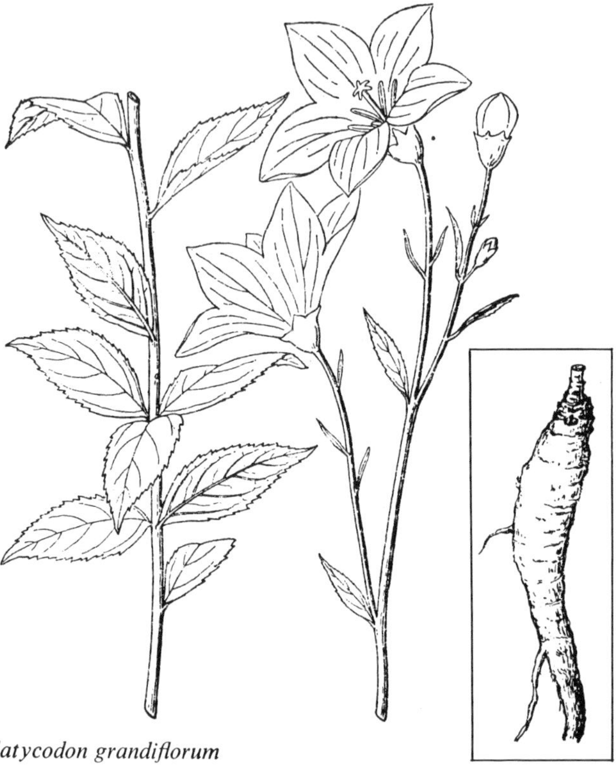

Platycodon grandiflorum

桔 梗

PLATYCODON GRANDIFLORUM DC.

(Campanulaceae)

Balloon-flower. A perennial herb, glabrous, more or less glaucous, the stem erect, 60–100 cm. high, containing an abundant latex. Leaves alternate, sessile, oval-lanceolate, acuminate, coarsely dentate, 3.0–5.5 cm. long by 2–3 cm. wide. Flowers solitary, lengthily pedunculate, broadly campanulate or deeply saucer-shaped; July–September; calyx in 5 segments; corolla 5-lobed, violet-blue, 4 cm. long; stamens

5; ovary many-celled. Fruit an ovoid capsule dehiscent at the top; September–October; seeds ovoid, compressed, obtuse, first violet then brown; albumen fleshy. China, Japan. (Syn *P. chinensis* Lindl., *P. autumnalis* Decne., *P. sinensis* Lem., *Campanula grandiflora* Jacq., *C. glauca* Thunb., *C. gentianoides* Lam.)

The root is officinal. It occurs in pieces 15 cm. long by 2 cm. in diameter, yellowish white, with rather deep longitudinal furrows, the leaf cicatrices visible in the upper portion. The taste is bittersweet. The root contains saponins, inulin, platycodigenin.[151]

Prescribed as expectorant. Dose, 2–5 gm. Incompatibles: *Gentiana scabra, Bletilla hyacinthina.*

花銀金

LONICERA JAPONICA Thunb.

(Caprifoliaceae)

Japanese honeysuckle. A volubilate shrub 6–9 m. tall, the branches slender, hairy. Leaves opposite, petiolate, oval-oblong, 3–8 cm. long by 1.5–4.0 cm. wide, tip acuminate, base rounded, pubescent especially beneath. Inflorescence a two-flowered cyme, in the axils of the terminal leaves; April–May. Flowers fragrant; calyx with ovoid tube, teeth 5, often irregular; corolla bilabiate, white tinged with purple, fading to yellow, 3–4 cm. long, the tube as long as the limb; stamens 3, exserted; ovary nearly globular, 3-celled. Fruit a black, fleshy berry. China, Japan, Korea, Taiwan. (Syn. *L. chinensis* Wats., *L. flexuosa* Thunb., *L. confusa* Miq., *L. brachypoda* DC., *L. japonica* var. *chinensis* Bak.)

The entire plant is used medicinally. The taste is bittersweet. The stem contains saponin; the leaves contain 8% tannin; the flowers 1% inositol.[130]

Prescribed as diuretic, refrigerant, antiphlogistic in acute infectious diseases; as antidiarrheic in dysentery and enteritis. Dose, 10–17 gm. An infusion of the floral buds is used topically for cutaneous infections.

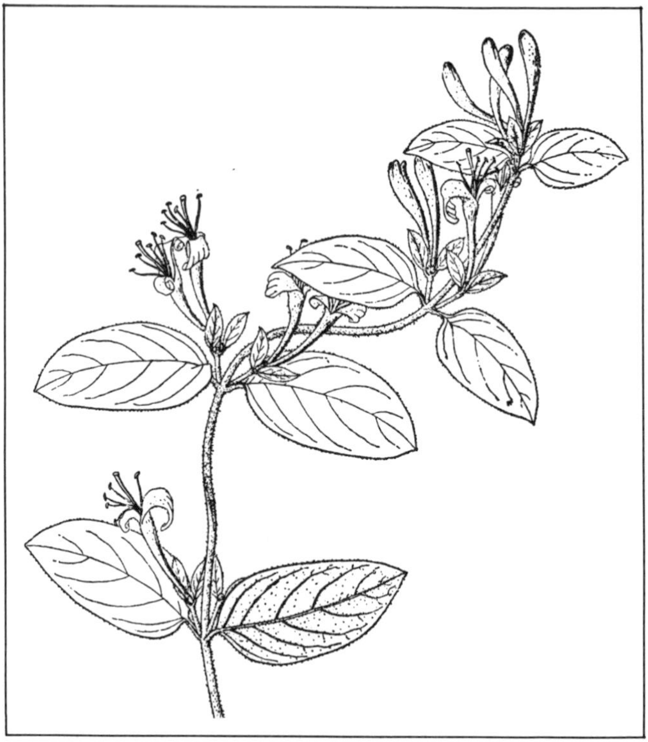

Lonicera japonica

217

惡實

ARCTIUM LAPPA L.

(Compositae)

Great burdock. A biennial herb, the stem sturdy, striate, branching, 0.8–1.2 m. tall. Leaves alternate, large; inferior leaves petiolate, often cordiform, surface glabrous, underside covered with white cottony hairs; superior leaves oval. Flowers grouped in heads which are disposed generally in corymbs at the tips of the branches, purple; July–August; involucre nearly globular, the bracts imbricate in several

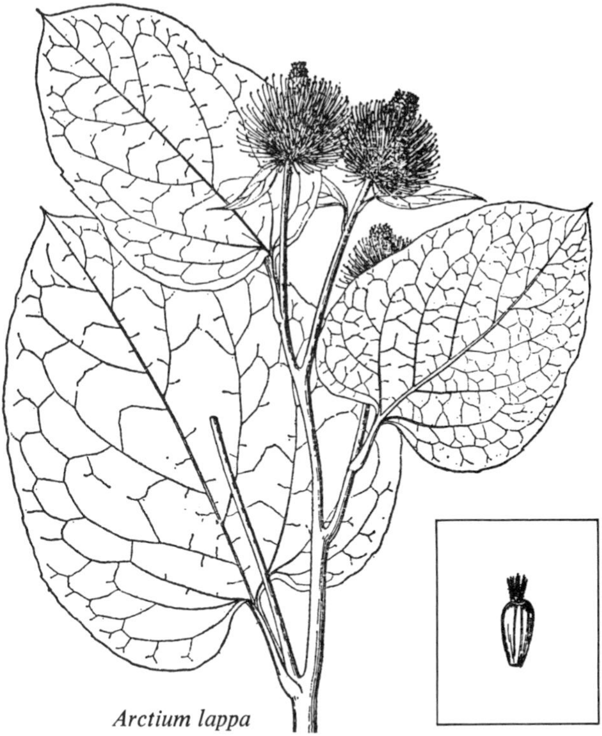

Arctium lappa

layers and awned; corolla tubular, 5-lobed. Fruit an achene, compressed, angular, surmounted with a pappus. Northern China, Asia, Europe. (Syn. *Lappa communis* Coss et Germ., *L. edulis* Sieb., *L. major* Gaerth., *L. minor* DC.)

The seeds and root are officinal. The seeds occur as oblong, slightly incurvate, 7 mm. long by 3 mm. wide, gray with black spots. The taste is pungent. The root occurs up to 30 cm. in length and to 25 mm. in diameter, texture resinous and horny, color grayish brown or white where the surface has been abraded, surface longitudinally furrowed and with slightly elevated root scars. The taste is sweet, mucilaginous, and slightly bitter. The seeds contain arctiin, arctigenin, gobosterin, essential oil, fatty oil; the root contains 40–70% inulin, lappine, the bitter principle lappatin, resin, essential oil, tannin.[151] The root promotes all the secretions and is considered aperient, diuretic, and diaphoretic without irritating qualities; it has been used in rheumatism, gout, pulmonary catarrh, and in chronic cutaneous affections; as an alterative in syphilis and scrofula; as an external application to swellings, hemorrhoids, chronic sores; a tincture of the seed has proved efficient as stomachic tonic, and has cured many cases of psoriasis inveterata.[150]

Prescribed as diuretic, antipyretic, expectorant, antiphlogistic in throat infections, pneumonia, scarlet fever, measles, smallpox, syphilis. Dose, 3–10 gm.

蒿 青

ARTEMISIA ANNUA L.

(Compositae)

An annual herb 30–90 cm. high, very fragrant. Leaves bipinnatifid, glabrous; segments linear, dentate. Inflorescence a terminal, compound panicle; September–November. Flower heads heterogamous, 2–3 mm. wide, globular; bracts linear, oval-acuminate or oval; marginal flowers female, corolla 4-lobed; disk flowers hermaphrodite, corolla 5-lobed, stamens 5, ovary sterile. Fruit an obovoid achene, smooth, 0.5 mm. long. China, northern Vietnam, Siberia, India.

The stem and leaves are officinal. The taste is bitter. The plant contains an essential oil comprising pinene, cineol, borneol, phenol, cuminic aldehyde, artemisia ketone.[151]

Used as antipyretic, and in chronic dysentery. Dose, 5–10 gm. Employed externally as bactericide for scabies, abscesses, and eye disorders.

Artemisia annua

ARTEMISIA CAPILLARIS Thunb.
(Compositae)

A perennial herb, the stem 40–80 cm. tall, purple. Leaves 2–3 times pinnatifid, the segments filiform or capillary, pubescent. Inflorescence loose, terminal; September. Flower

茵蔯

heads heterogamous, 2 mm. wide, purplish brown; marginal flowers female, disk flowers hermaphrodite. Northern China, Japan, Taiwan.

The stems and leaves are used medicinally. The taste is bitter and pungent; the odor highly aromatic. The plant contains an essential oil.[140]

Prescribed as diuretic and antipyretic in icterus. Dose, 3–10 gm.

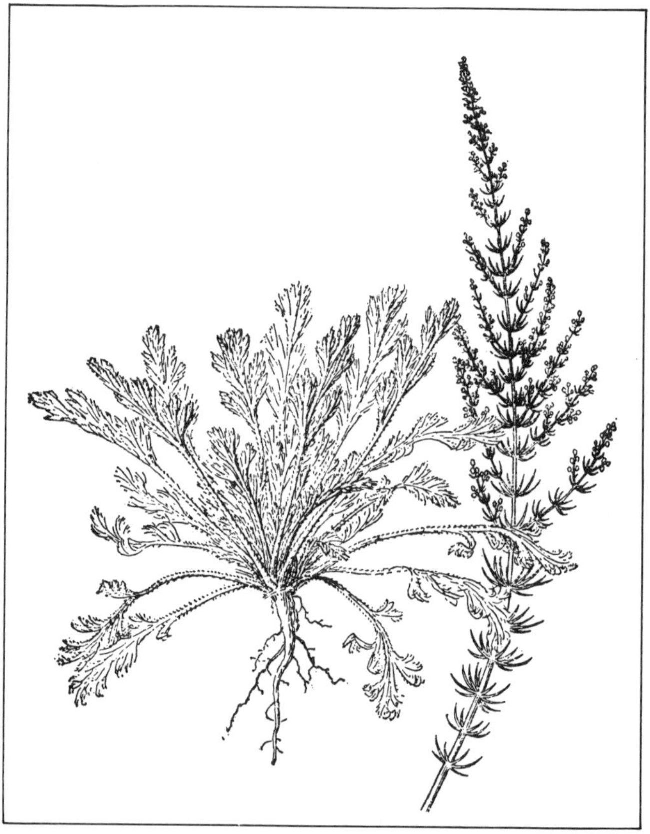

Artemisia capillaris

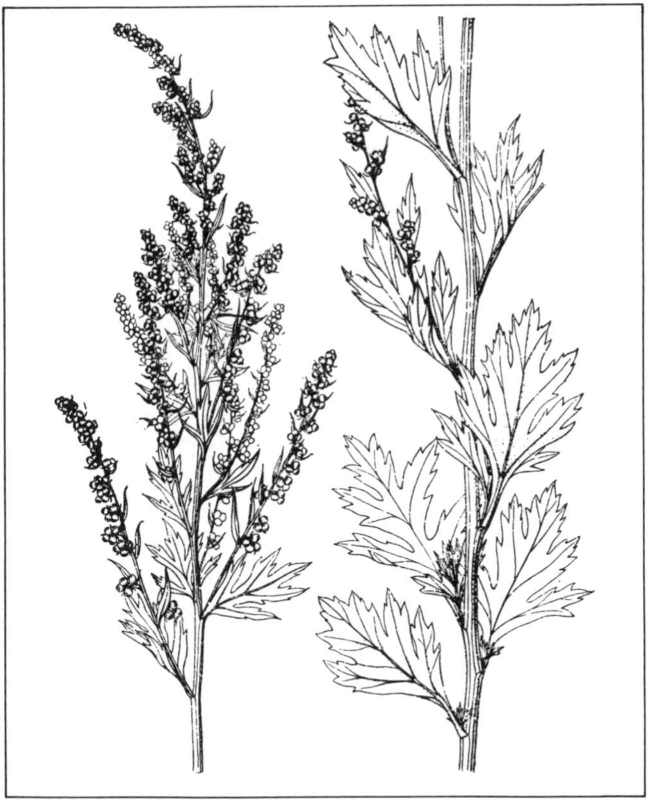

Artemisia vulgaris

艾葉

ARTEMISIA VULGARIS L.

(Compositae)

Mugwort. A perennial herb, the stem 7–12 cm. tall, striate, reddish, somewhat pubescent, branching. Leaves alternate, pinnatifid; segments oblong-lanceolate, acute, mostly dentate, surface glabrous, underside white and tomentose. Involucre white, tomentose; flower head ovoid-oblong, nearly sessile, in glomerules on the erect branches, yellow or reddish; July–September. China, Asia, Europe. (Syn. *A. integrifolia* L., *A. indica* Willd., *A. igniaria* Max., *A. lavandulaefolia* DC.)

The leaves are officinal. The taste is bitter, the odor aromatic. The leaves contain 0.02% essential oil (comprising mainly cineol and thujone), tannin, resinous matter, adenine, and the bitter principle artemisin ($C_{15}H_{18}O_4$; prismatic crystals; m.p. 203°; one gram dissolves in 60 ml. boiling water, in 3 ml. boiling alcohol).[151]

Used as hemostatic, stomachic. Dose, 2–3 gm. Employed in the preparation of moxas for cauterization.

Aster tataricus

紫菀

ASTER TATARICUS L.

(Compositae)

Tartarian aster. A perennial herb, the stem rigid, erect, angular, somewhat coarse, the branches slender, more or less divergent. Leaves alternate, lanceolate or lanceolate-oblong, acute, margin coarse, rather firm, usually broad, glabrous. Flower heads numerous, pedunculate; disk flowers yellow; marginal flowers blue or purplish blue; ligules lanceolate-oblong, narrow. Nutlet brown; pappus yellowish, rigid, one-third as long as the nutlet. Northern China, Siberia, Japan.

The root is officinal. It occurs as fasciculate, fibrous, reddish brown. The taste is bitter, the odor agreeable. The root contains saponins, shionon ($C_{34}H_{56}O_{10}$), quercetin, arabinose.[135]

Prescribed as antitussive, expectorant. Dose, 3–10 gm.

蒼朮

ATRACTYLIS OVATA Thunb.

(Compositae)

A perennial herb, glabrous, 30–60 cm. high, the stem erect, simple, lignified at the base. Cauline leaves alternate, simple or lobate-pinnate, base cuneiform, lobes 3–5, acuminate; terminal leaves elliptical, 5–8 cm. long, entire, margin ciliate; petiole short, slightly winged. Floral heads 3–4 in corymbs; September–October; peduncle 2.5 cm. in diameter; involucre with scariose bracts, firm, imbricate, acuminate, reddish; corolla of neuter flowers nearly radiant, corolla of fertile flowers tubular. Fruit an achene crowned with a silky pappus. China, Korea, Japan. (Syn. *A. lancea* Thunb., *A. chinensis* DC., *A. lyrata* Sieb. et Zucc., *Acarina chinensis* Bunge., *Atractylodes ovata* DC., *A. lancea* DC., *A. lyrata* Sieb. et Zucc.)

The root is used medicinally. It occurs in ramified pieces 7 cm. long by 2 cm. in diameter, reddish brown, furrowed. The taste is sweet. The root contains an essential oil comprising atractylon ($C_{14}H_{18}O$) and atractylol ($C_{15}H_{26}O$; white crystalline powder; m.p. 56°; soluble in ether, alcohol, chloroform).[105]

Prescribed as aromatic tonic in chronic gastroenteritis. Dose, 5–10 gm.

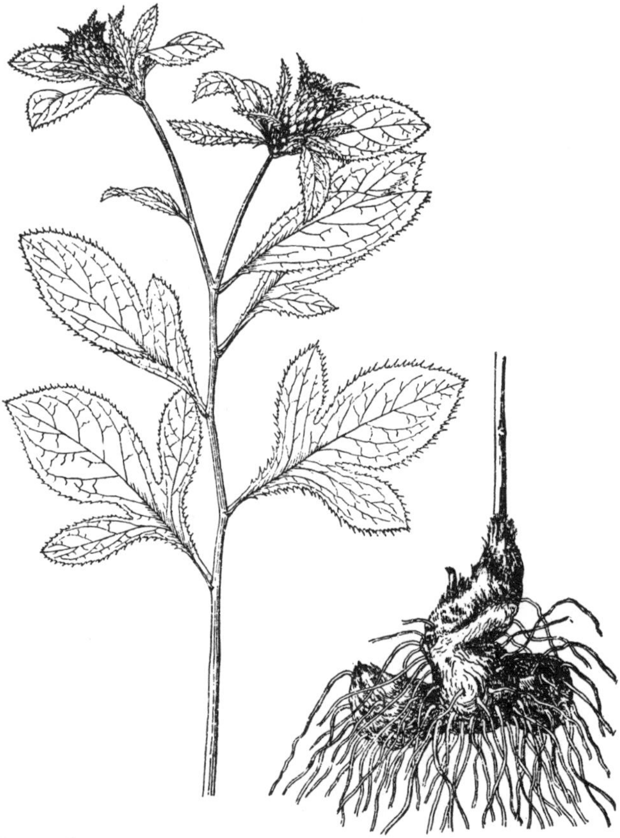

Atractylis ovata

精名天

CARPESIUM ABROTANOIDES L.

(Compositae)

An erect, rigid herb 0.6–1.2 m. tall, the stem simple or branching, striate. Leaves oblanceolate, base attenuate in a false petiole, tip more or less acuminate and acute, 5–12 cm. long by 1.5–5.0 cm. wide, villous, surface coarse, underside more villous and soft, margin irregularly dentate-crenelate. Floral heads often drooping, yellow, heterogamous, discoid; September–October; exterior bracts foliaceous, the others gradually more scariose, elliptical, rounded at the tip, margin ciliolate. Marginal flowers female, corolla tubular, teeth 3–5. Disk flowers hermaphrodite; corolla tubular, larger, teeth 5; stamens 5; anther sagittate at the base; auricles awl-shaped; ovary equalling the corolla, cylindrical, attenuate in a glandular beak. Fruit an achene, finely striate lengthwise. China, Japan, northern Vietnam, India, Europe. (Syn. *C. thunbergianum* Sieb. et Zucc.)

The stalk, leaves, and root are used medicinally. The taste is sweet. The plant contains an essential oil, and inulin.[140]

The stalk, leaves, and root are employed as expectorant and antiphlogistic in pharyngitis, laryngitis, trachitis. Dose, 4–10 gm. (The seeds have been used as anthelmintic.)

花 紅

CARTHAMUS TINCTORIUS L.

(Compositae)

Safflower. An annual, branching herb 0.6–1.0 m. high, glabrous, the stem whitish, striate. Leaves sessile, somewhat clasping, lanceolate-oblong, attenuate at both ends, strongly dentate, faintly spiny; venation pinnate and netted. Inflorescence a broad corymb, heads 3–5 borne on leafy peduncles. Floral head 5 cm. wide; exterior bracts whitish at the base, terminated with a green appendage; interior bracts much shorter, oval or linear, acuminate, terminated with 5–7

Carthamus tinctorius

spines. Flowers orange-red, surpassing the interior bracts; corolla 5-lobed, linear; stamens 5; style with branches entirely united, finely villous. Fruit a white achene. China, Laos, southern Vietnam, Cambodia.

The flowers are officinal. The taste is slightly bitter and pungent; the odor highly aromatic. The flowers contain carthamin (carthamic acid; $C_{21}H_{22}O_{11}$; dark red granular powder with green luster; soluble in alcohol; slightly soluble in water; insoluble in ether), and safflor-yellow ($C_{24}H_{30}O_{15}$; yellow coloring matter; soluble in water, alcohol; the aqueous solution rapidly decomposing).[148]

Prescribed as uterine astringent in dysmenorrhea. Dose, 2–5 gm.

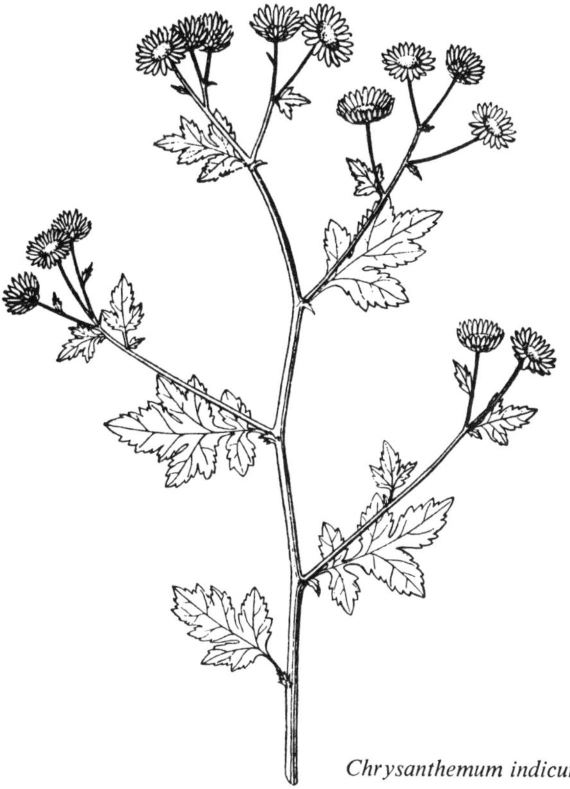

Chrysanthemum indicum

菊 野

CHRYSANTHEMUM INDICUM L.

(Compositae)

A perennial herb, the stems frutescent, branching, pubescent at the tips. Leaves petiolate, oval-acute, deeply lobate, tending to be pinnate; lobes elongate, teeth numerous. Inflorescence a many-flowered corymb, briefly pedunculate; October–November. Floral heads yellow, small; involucral scales oboval-oblong, completely scarious at the margin. Ray flowers with ligules 5 mm. long; disk flowers with tubular corolla, 2.5 mm. long, lobes triangular-acute. China, Japan. (Syn. *Ch. tripartium* Sw., *Ch. procumbens* Lour., *Pyrethrum indicum* Cass.)

The flowers are used medicinally. The taste is bitter. The plant contains an essential oil, tannin, and 7% chrysanthemine (colorless, syrupy liquid; gradually solidifies to a crystalline mass; freely soluble in water, alcohol; insoluble in chloroform, ether).[111] Chrysanthemine has been shown to be a mixture of stachydrine ($C_7H_{13}NO_2 \cdot H_2O$; deliquescent crystals, sweetish taste; m.p. 235° when anhydrous; soluble in water, alcohol; almost insoluble in ether, chloroform) and choline.[148]

Prescribed as digestive. Dose, 4–10 gm. The extracted juice of the fresh herb is applied topically as bactericide and antiphlogistic.

花菊甘

CHRYSANTHEMUM MORIFOLIUM Ram.

(Compositae)

A perennial or biennial herb, the stem erect, striate. Leaves petiolate, oval or rounded, base truncate or cordate-cuneiform, lobate-palmate, underside white and villous; lobes 3–5, oval, sinuate, dentate; petiole somewhat shorter than the limb, the base auriculate. Flower heads in terminal corymbs; October–November; ligulate flowers in 1–2 rows, white or purple, female; central flowers tubular, numerous, yellow, stamens 5. Fruit a glabrous, obovoid achene. China, Japan. (Syn. *Ch. sinense* Sabine., *Pyrethrum sinense* DC.)

The flowers are officinal. The taste is bitter. The plant contains an essential oil, adenine, choline, stachydrine.[140]

Used as sedative, refrigerant in headache, influenza. Dose, 4–10 gm. An infusion is employed as collyrium in conjunctivitis.

Chrysanthemum morifolium

CIRSIUM JAPONICUM DC.

(Compositae)

A perennial herb, the stem 40 cm. or more, tomentose. Basal leaves 20–40 cm. long, bipinnate-lobate, 5–10 cm. wide, oboval, margin very spiny; primary lobes 6–10 pair, the superior larger, decreasing toward the base where they are represented by groups of 2–3 spines; secondary lobes 3–5 with 2–3 strong, separate spines, divergent. Cauline leaves 5 or more, sessile, auriculate, becoming more reduced and simplified, the superior leaves once-pinnate. Inflorescence an axillary and terminal head; bracts imbricate in numerous layers, the exterior spiny; receptacle hairy. Flowers very numerous, hermaphrodite, red or white; pappus dirty white, plumose; corollas tubular, 5-lobed; stamens 5. Fruit an oblong achene, compressed, smooth. China, Japan, Vietnam. (Syn. *C. littorale* Max., *C. brevicaule* A. Gray., *C. maakii* Max., *Carduus japonicus* Franch., *Car. acaulis* Thunb., *Cnicus japonicus* Max.)

The stems and leaves are used medicinally. The taste is sweet and pungent. The plant contains an essential oil, a glycoside, and a bitter principle.[140]

Prescribed as hemostatic. Dose, 4–10 gm.

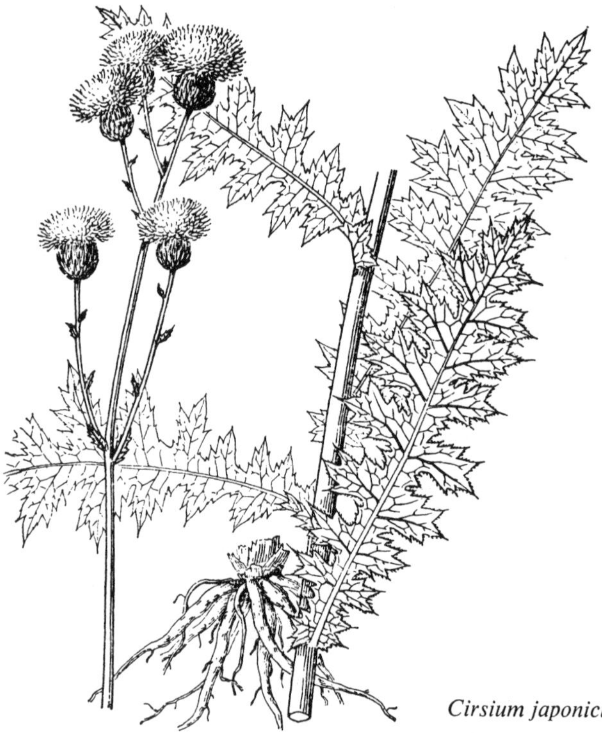

Cirsium japonicum

漏盧

ECHINOPS DAHURICUS Fisch.

(Compositae)

A perennial herb, the stem 1 m. high, divaricate, base pubescent, the upper part heavily tomentose. Leaves alternate, broad, pinnatifid, spiniferous, 12–26 cm. long; rachis dentate-spiny, limb heavily tomentose below, pubescent above; involucral bracts setaceous, elongate, distinct. Floral heads small, uniflorous, united, numerous on a common receptacle; involucre of numerous imbricate bracts, acute, rigid. Flowers deep blue; August–September; corolla regular, achene with pappus. Northern China, Mongolia, Japan. (Syn. *E. grijsii* Hance., *E. gmelini* Ledeb., *E. sphaerocephalus* Miq.)

The root and lower portion of the stem are used medicinally. The taste is saline. The plant contains 0.1% essential oil.[140]

Prescribed as hemostatic, and in the treatment of abscesses, mastitis, boils, and contusions. Dose, 5–10 gm.

鱧腸

ECLIPTA ALBA Hassk.

(Compositae)

An annual herb, erect or diffuse, 80 cm. high, villous. Leaves opposite, linear-lanceolate, base attenuate, tip acuminate-acute, villous, dentate, 2–8 cm. long by 5–15 mm. wide, nearly sessile. External flowers ligulate, female, white; disk flowers hermaphrodite, tubular, 4-lobed, stamens 4; July–September. Fruit an achene 3 mm. long by 1.5 mm. wide, compressed, somewhat winged, tip truncate. China, Taiwan, Indochina, India, Japan, Philippines. (Syn. *E. erecta* L., *E. prostrata* L., *E. thermalis* Bunge., *E. marginata* Boiss.)

The entire plant is officinal. The taste is sweet-sour. The plant contains nicotine.[80]

Eclipta alba

Prescribed as astringent hemostatic. Dose, 5–10 gm. The extracted juice of the fresh herb is applied to the scalp to promote hair growth; taken internally it blackens the hair and beard.

GNAPHALIUM MULTICEPS Wall.

(Compositae)

An annual herb, the stem 40 cm. tall, white, cottony. Leaves alternate, entire, oboval-linear, tip obtuse and mucronate,

鼠麴草

base lengthily attenuate, somewhat decurrent, 4–7 cm. long by 5–15 mm. wide, tomentose; bracts oboval and linear, the back cottony. Floral heads yellow-gold, grouped in heterogamous corymbs, multiflorous; April–May. Corolla filiform, tridentate; disk flowers hermaphrodite, teeth 5; stamens 5. Achene oblong-ovoid, the pappus consisting of a row of capillary hairs. Southern China, Japan. (Syn. *G. luteo-album* L. var. *multiceps* Hook., *G. javanum* DC., *G. ramigerum* DC., *G. confusum* DC., *G. arenarium* Thunb.)

The young stems and leaves are used medicinally. The taste is sweet. The plant contains fat, resin, phytosterol, and a large amount of carotene.[140]

Employed as antitussive and expectorant. Dose, 4–7 gm.

三七

GYNURA PINNATIFIDA Vanniot

(Compositae)

A perennial herb, the stem erect, 1 m. tall. Leaves alternate, petiolate, pinnatilobate, dentate, hispid. Floral heads solitary or in corymbs, orange-yellow, the base with bracteoles; involucre oblong. Flowers yellow, regular; September–October; corolla tubular, 5-segmented; stamens 5, inserted on the corolla and alternate with the petals. Achene cylindrical, ribbed, with several rows of silky white pappula. China, Japan. (Syn. *G. japonica* Mak., *G. segetum* Merr., *Senecio japonica* Thunb., *Cacalia pinnatifida* Lour., *Kleinia japonica* Less., *Porophyllum japonicum* DC.)

The root is officinal. It occurs in pieces 2.5 cm. long by 1 cm. in diameter, grayish, the surface furrowed. The taste is bittersweet. The drug contains saponins.[128]

Prescribed as hemostatic. Dose, 5–8 gm. Used externally as styptic.

Gynura pinnatifida

INULA BRITANNICA L.

(Compositae)

A perennial herb, more or less villous, the stem 30–80 cm. high, erect, simple. Leaves alternate, faintly dentate, narrowly lanceolate, 3.5–5.0 cm. long by 4–8 mm. wide, acute, the underside pubescent and evenly silky, often glabrous, clasp-

Inula britannica

旋覆花

ing, the inferior leaves attenuate in petiole. Floral heads terminal, solitary; July–September; flowers all yellow, fertile; involucre of smooth leaflets, linear, villous-silky. Marginal flowers female, ligulate; disk flowers hermaphrodite, corolla tubular, teeth 5. Achene hairy, pappus white. China, Japan, Siberia, Europe.

The flowers are used medicinally. The taste is saline. The drug contains inulin (alantin, dahlin; $[C_6H_{10}O_5]n$; white, starch-like powder; soluble in hot water, slightly soluble in cold water; only slightly soluble in organic solvents), and flavone.[140]

Prescribed as expectorant and stomachic. Dose, 5–8 gm.

香 木

SAUSSUREA LAPPA Clarke

(Compositae)

Costus. A perennial herb, the stem simple, 2 m. high, sturdy, the superior part pubescent. Basal leaves triangular, the terminal lobe attaining 30 cm. in length; petiole winged; cauline leaves shortly petiolate or sessile, auriculate, lyrate, 15–30 cm. long. Floral heads axillary or terminal, grouped 2–3, nearly lobular, sessile, 3–4 cm. in diameter; bracts numerous, oval, lanceolate, acuminate, stiff, purple, pubescent when young, glabrous at maturity. Corollas tubular, 5-lobed, deep purple. Fruit an oblong achene, glabrous, compressed, with pappus consisting of hairs in several rows. India. (Syn. *Aplotaxis lappa* Decne., *Aucklandia costus* Falc.)

The root is officinal. It occurs in fragments 4 cm. long by 1 cm. in diameter, the exterior light brown, the interior white. The root contains the alkaloid saussurine, and an essential oil comprising costulactone, costol, costene, camphene, and phellandrene.[35] A fluid extract of the root appears to be useful in the treatment of asthma.[127]

Prescribed as stomachic.

草簽豨

SIEGESBECKIA ORIENTALIS L.

(Compositae)

An annual herb 30–90 cm. tall, branching. Leaves opposite, triangular or lanceolate-diamond, attenuate in petiole, acuminate-obtuse, sinuate-dentate and even shortly lobular, 4–7 cm. long by 2–5 cm. wide. Floral heads 6–7 mm. wide, in leafy corymbs; July–October; marginal flowers female, with short tube and ligular limb; disk flowers hermaphrodite, tubular; stamens 5. Fruit an obovoid achene with 4–5 angles, blackish. China, Indochina, Philippines, Java, India.

The root and young plants are used medicinally. The root occurs as fasciculate, the exterior yellowish brown, the interior white. The taste is bitter and pungent. The plant contains the bitter principle darutin, and an essential oil.[151]

Prescribed as analgesic and antirheumatic. Dose, 5–7 gm. Used externally for ulcers, abscesses, boils.

Siegesbeckia orientalis

蒲公英

TARAXACUM OFFICINALE Weber.

(Compositae)

Dandelion. A perennial, acaulose herb with milky juice. Leaves basal, in rosette, glabrous, base attenuate, runcinate, pinnatifid, the segments triangular-lanceolate. Scapes hollow, 6–30 cm., erect, with 1 solitary floral head. Involucre leaflets entire or denticulate at the tips, provided or not with callosity, the exterior extended or reflected; flowers completely ligular, yellow; April–October. Achene oblong, grayish. Temperate Zone. (Syn. *T. ceratophorum* DC., *T. corniculatum* DC., *T. sinense* DC., *T. dens-leonis* Desf., *Leontodon taraxacum* L., *L. sinense* Lour.)

The rhizome and root are used medicinally. The drug occurs as a mixture of entire and broken fragments measuring up to 16 cm. in length and 3 cm. in diameter at the crown, texture waxy, color light gray to dark reddish brown, irregularly wrinkled longitudinally. The taste is bittersweet. The drug contains 24% inulin, an essential oil, resinous matter, fatty acids, p-hydroxyphenylacetic acid;[83] taraxasterol, choline, levulin, pectin.[148] An extract of the drug has been reported to stimulate bile flow in rats.[12] The drug has been used in dyspepsia with hepatic torpor; as found in the shops it is usually inert.[150]

Employed as stomachic, cholagogue, lactagogue. Dose, 10–30 gm. The juice of the fresh plant is applied to snake bites.

TUSSILAGO FARFARA L.

(Compositae)

Coltsfoot. A perennial herb 1–2 dm. high, the stem downy, scaly. Leaves appearing after the flowers, all basal, petiolate, nearly orbiculate, cordate, sinuate-dentate, surface green, underside white and tomentose. Floral heads erect, solitary,

花冬款

terminal on the stem, drooping after flowering. Involucre leaflets in a single row. Flowers yellow; March–April; marginal female, ligulate, arranged in several rows; disk flowers male. Northern China, Europe, Africa.

The young floral buds are officinal. The taste is pungent. The drug contains a glycoside, saponins, gallic acid, inulin, phytosterols, stearin, palmitin, choline, sitosterol.[151] The leaves and other parts of the plant have been used as a demulcent in pulmonary affections associated with cough.[144]

Prescribed as antitussive, expectorant. Dose, 5–10 gm.

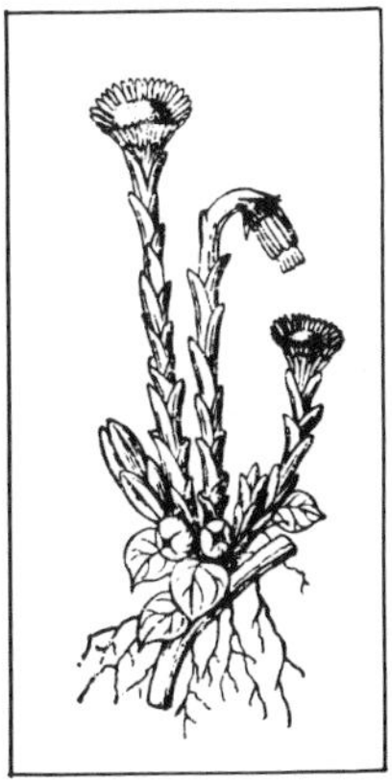

Tussilago farfara

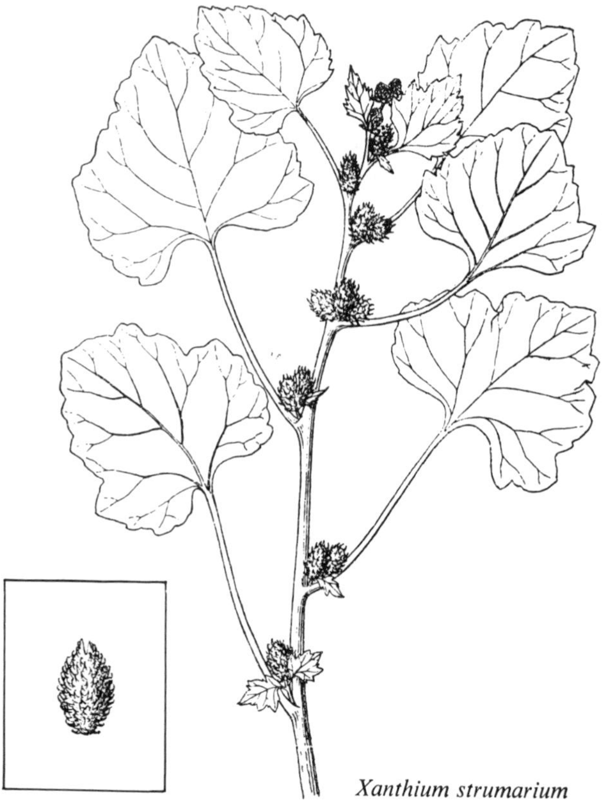

Xanthium strumarium

XANTHIUM STRUMARIUM L.

(Compositae)

An annual herb 30–80 cm. high. Leaves alternate, lengthily petiolate, oval-triangular, lobes 3–5, 4–10 cm. long by 5–12 cm. wide, base somewhat cordate, coarsely dentate, pubescent. Floral heads monoecious, grouped 2–5; May–June. Male with involucre rather short, corolla tubular, 5-toothed,

耳 蒼

filaments monodelphous; female heads biflorous, involucre nearly globular, consisting of conical bracts, covered with hooked prickles, corolla none. Fruit an achene enclosed in the persistent involucre which has become coriaceous, oblong, 1.5 cm. long by 7 mm. wide, covered with spines; August–September. China, Indochina, India, Europe, America. (Syn. *X. indicum* Koen., *X. chinense* Mill.)

The fruits are used medicinally. They contain 39% of the glycoside xanthostrumarin, resin, vitamin C, and fatty oil comprising oleic and linoleic acids.[13]

Prescribed as diuretic, antispasmodic, analgesic in rheumatism, arthralgia. Dose, 5–10 gm.

子絲菟

CUSCUTA JAPONICA Choisy

(Convulvulaceae)

An annual, parasitic plant, the stem volubilate, filiform, attaining 2 mm. in diameter, often reddish, deprived of leaves. Inflorescence a lateral, loose cluster; June–August; bracts and bracteoles scaly; pedicels 2–3 mm. Calyx 5-segmented; corolla tubular, 5-lobed, white; stamens 5; ovary superior, 2-celled. Fruit an ovoid capsule 5 mm. long; seeds 1–2, glabrous, greenish or reddish. China, Japan.

The seeds are used medicinally. They occur as globular, 1 mm. in diameter, brown. The taste is sweet and slightly pungent. The drug contains the glycoside cuscutin (yellow, amorphous powder; soluble in hot water, alcohol; slightly soluble in ether; insoluble in cold water).[140]

Prescribed as tonic in impotence, spermatorrhea, prostatitis, neurasthenia. Dose, 7–15 gm.

(*C. chinensis* Lam. is similarly employed.)

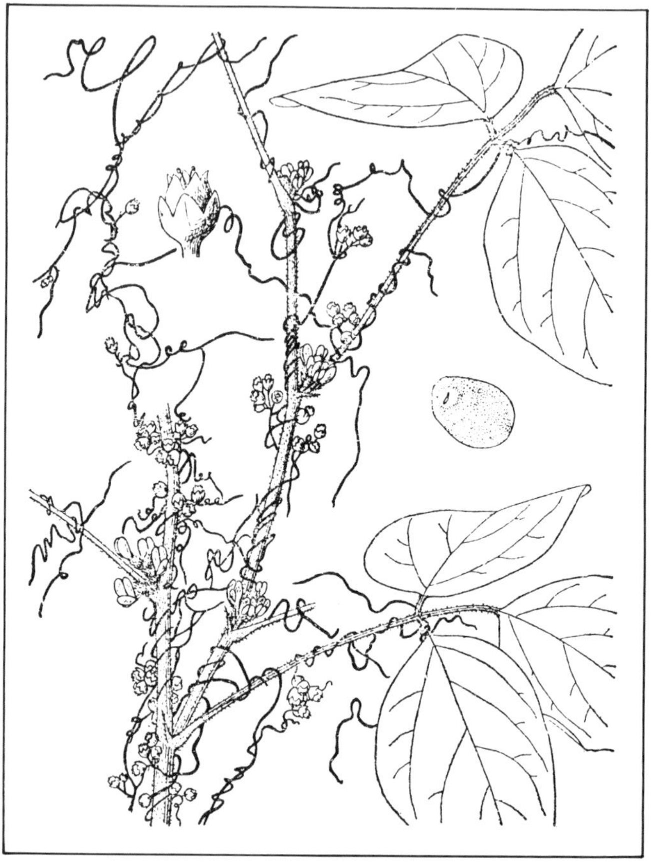

Cuscuta chinensis

PHARBITIS HEDERACEA Choisy

(Convulvulaceae)

An annual herb, the stem volubilate. Leaves petiolate, trilobate or entire, base cordate, 5 cm. long by 7 cm. wide. Inflorescence axillary, pedunculate; flowers 1–3; July–September; tube pale, throat pink or blue; corolla campanulate, 7 cm.

牛 牽

long; sepals 5; ovary 3-celled. Fruit a globular capsule, 8 mm. in diameter, surrounded and surpassed by the sepals; seeds 2–4. China, India, tropical and subtropical regions. (Syn. *Ph. triloba* Miq., *Ph. diversifolia* Lindl., *Convolvulus nil* L., *Ipomoea hederacea* Jacq., *I. triloba* Thunb., *I. caerulea* Koeh., *I. barbata* Both.)

The seeds are officinal. They occur as trigonal, 6 mm. long by 4 mm. wide, smooth, deep violet. The taste is bitter. The drug is poisonous. The seeds contain pharbitin ($C_{54}H_{96}O_{27}$; white amorphous powder; soluble in alcohol; insoluble in water, benzene, ether), rhamnose, angelic acid, pelargonin, cyanin.[151] Pharbitin is closely related chemically and physiologically to convolvulin.[148]

Used as cathartic, diuretic, anthelmintic. Dose, 1–2 gm.

Pharbitis hederacea

山茱萸

CORNUS OFFICINALIS Sieb. et Zucc.

(Cornaceae)

A deciduous shrub 10 m. tall. Leaves opposite, elliptical or oval, rarely oval-lanceolate, 5–12 cm. long, acuminate, briefly petiolate, surface somewhat lanate, underside even more so. Inflorescence a sessile umbel; March–April; bracts dark. Flowers yellow; calyx with 4 teeth; petals 4; stamens 4; ovary adherent. Fruit an oblong drupe 1.5 cm. long, red at maturity, fleshy, 1-seeded; August. Eastern China, Korea, Japan.

The fruits are used medicinally. The taste is sour and astringent. The fruits contain the bitter principle cornin (bitter needles, silky luster; soluble in water, alcohol; very slightly soluble in ether), tannin, resin, and tartaric acid.[140] The related *C. florida,* indigenous to the U.S., contains the same constituents; it has been used as a simple bitter and has had a reputation as an efficient remedy in malarial fever; heat destroys the active principle, hence a decoction is useless.[150]

Prescribed as an astringent tonic in impotence, spermatorrhea, lumbago, vertigo, night sweats. Dose, 5–10 gm. Incompatibles: *Platycodon grandiflorum, Siler divaricatum,* Menispermaceae fam.

冬瓜

BENINCASA CERIFERA Savi.

(Cucurbitaceae)

Chinese preserving melon, wax gourd, white gourd, winter melon. An annual, long-trailing vine, the stem brown-hairy, elongate, branching. Leaves lobate-palmate, villous, with stiff hairs, round-reniform, 10–25 cm. in diameter, deeply cordate, dentate or crenelate; lobes triangular or oval, often acute, sometimes reaching the middle of the limb; petiole sturdy, hirsute; tendrils 2–4. Flowers solitary, yellow. Male flowers with broadly campanulate calyx tube, the lobes nearly foliaceous, lobate-dentate; petals 5, oboval, entire; stamens 3; anthers exserted, thick. Female flowers with 3 staminodia; pistil with ovoid or cylindrical ovary, covered with long hairs; ovules very numerous, horizontal; style thick, with 3 undulate stigmas. Fruit large, melon-like, but without a hard rind, oval-oblong, 25–40 cm. long by 10–15 cm. thick, hispid, covered with a pruinose wax, green marbled with white, indehiscent. China, Japan, India, Indochina, tropical Africa. (Syn. *B. hispida* Cogn., *Cucurbita hispida* Thunb., *Lagenaria dasystemon* Miq.)

The seeds are officinal. They occur as yellowish white, 10–11 mm. long by 5–7 mm. wide, ovoid-oblong, compressed, margin inflated. The taste is sweet. The seeds contain urease.[140]

Used as diuretic. Dose, 10–30 gm.

瓜 西

CITRULLUS VULGARIS Schrad.

(Cucurbitaceae)

Watermelon. An annual, tender vine, the stem prostrate, smoothly villous, especially at the tip and at the nodes. Leaves alternate, petiolate, simple, oval-oblong, 8–20 cm. long; segments 3–7, narrow, villous as well as the petiole; tendrils bifid. Inflorescence monoecious, the flowers axillary, solitary, yellow, briefly pedicellate; June–July. Male flowers with calyx campanulate, segments 5, narrow; corolla with 5 deep lobes, obtuse; stamens 3. Female flowers with similar perianth; staminodia 3, short; ovary ovoid, inferior; stigmas 3. Fruit an oblong pepo, smooth, greenish, often marbled; August–September; flesh white or reddish; seeds varying in color, compressed, smooth. Southern China, Russia, a native of tropical Africa. (Syn. *C. edulis* Spach., *Cucurbita citrullus* L., *C. anguria* Duch.)

The rind of the fruit is used medicinally. The taste is sweet. The juice of the fruit contains the amino acid citrulline ($C_6H_{13}N_3O_3$; prisms; m.p. 222°; soluble in water; insoluble in methanol, ethanol);[112] aminoacetic acid, arginine, betaine, lycopene, carotene, vitamin C, bromine, fructose, dextrose, sucrose, malic acid, phosphoric acid.[140] Citrulline is believed to be involved in the formation, in the liver, of urea from ammonia and carbon dioxide; it is an intermediate between ornithine and arginine, two other amino acids involved in producing urea.[144]

Prescribed as diuretic in nephritis, diabetes, alcoholic poisoning. Dose, 10–30 gm.

蔕 瓜

CUCUMIS MELO L.
(Cucurbitaceae)

Melon. An annual, prostrate vine, the stem coarse. Leaves orbiculate or reniform, slightly lobate, dentate, base cordate, coarse, hairy, 6–15 cm. long; tendrils simple. Male flowers fasciculate, briefly pedicellate; calyx tube hirsute on the outside, lobate and narrow, villous, awl-shaped; petals united at least one-third; anthers inserted in the middle of the tube. Female flowers solitary; pistil with a villous ovary, ovoid; style columnar; stigmas sessile, somewhat united at the base, deeply emarginate at the top. Fruit fleshy, polymorphous, without prickles. China, tropical Asia.

The seeds and the immature footstalk of the fruit are used medicinally. The seeds occur as oboval, compressed, 7 mm. long by 2 mm. wide, white, smooth. The seeds contain myristic acid, phosphates, galactan, lysine, citrulline, histidine, tryptophane, cystine.[125] The taste of the footstalk is bitter. It contains the neutral principle elaterin ($C_{20}H_{28}O_5$; white crystalline powder, very bitter taste, poisonous; one gram dissolves in 100 ml. boiling water, in 325 ml. alcohol, in 16 ml. chloroform).[140] Elaterin is one of the most powerful of the hydragogue cathartics, producing continuous watery stools, and, when given in large doses, intense irritation, hyperemia, nausea, and dangerous prostration.[150]

The seeds are prescribed as digestive, refrigerant, antitussive. Dose, 10–18 gm. The footstalk is used as expectorant and emetic. Dose as expectorant, 750–1,000 mg.; as emetic, 2–10 gm.

南瓜

CUCURBITA PEPO L.

(Cucurbitaceae)

Pumpkin. An annual, prostrate vine, the stems and petioles prickly. Leaves triangular-oval, lengthily petiolate, usually prominently 5-lobed, 15–30 cm. long, tip acuminate. Flowers large, yellow, axillary, monoecious; corolla lobes pointed, erect or spreading, not recurved. Fruit large, furrowed, usually orange, the stalk enlarged at the point of attachment. Cultivated worldwide.

The seeds are officinal. They occur as yellowish or grayish white, up to 3.5 cm. long by 2 cm. wide by 5 mm. thick, base rounded, tip tapering and irregularly truncate, margin entire, ovate to oval to elliptical, surface convex, smooth. The taste is sweet and oily. The seeds contain fixed oil, acrid resin, myosin, vitellin, sugar.[148] The fresh seeds of the pumpkin are actively vermicidal, this action residing in the lipoids which may be extracted by ether or alcohol.[87]

Prescribed as anthelmintic. Dose, 30–60 gm., shelled, bruised, stirred into an emulsion in thick syrup; follow with cathartic.

LAGENARIA VULGARIS Ser.

(Cucurbitaceae)

Calabash. An annual herbaceous vine, musky-scented, the stem sticky-hairy. Leaves alternate, nearly orbiculate, cordate, dentate; tendrils bifid. Flowers solitary, monoecious,

盧 壺

white. Male flowers lengthily pedunculate; calyx campanulate; petals 5; stamens 3, attached to the calyx tube. Female flowers with cupuliform calyx; staminodia 3, rudimentary; ovary ovoid or cylindrical. Fruit indehiscent, very variable in form and size, rind ligneous; seeds obovate, compressed, marginate, often bicornuate. Southern China, southern Asia, Africa, America.

The rind of the mature fruit is officinal. The taste is sweetish. The fruit contains 6% sugar, fat, vitamin C, saponin.[140]

Employed as diuretic. Dose, 19–38 gm.

瓜 絲

LUFFA CYLINDRICA Roem.

(Cucurbitaceae)

An annual, herbaceous vine. Leaves alternate, petiolate, triangular, sinuate, dentate, base cordate, 15–25 cm. wide, lobes 5–7; tendrils elongate, sturdy, often trifid. Male flowers in pedunculate clusters; calyx campanulate, segments 5, petals 5, expanded, yellow-brown; stamens 3. Female flowers solitary. July–September. Fruit dry, fusiform, cylindrical or vaguely trigonal, 15–30 cm. long by 6–10 cm. thick, interior fibrous, October; seeds compressed, brown, 12 mm. long by 8–9 mm. wide, surmounted with a wing 0.5–1.0 mm. China, Vietnam, Thailand, Laos, Philippines, Japan. (Syn. *L. aegyptiaca* Mill., *L. faetida* Sieb. et Zucc., *L. petola* Ser., *Momordica cylindrica* L.)

The fibers of the fruit are used medicinally. The taste is sweet. The fruit contains xylose, mannosan, galactan, saponins, vitamins A, B, and C.[151]

Prescribed as hemostatic and analgesic in enterorrhagia, dysentery, metrorrhagia, orchitis, hemorrhoids; also used to treat variola, boils. Dose, 5–10 gm.

仁蔞栝

TRICHOSANTHES KIRILOWII Max.

(Cucurbitaceae)

A perennial vine 3–10 m., the root tuberous. Leaves alternate, orbiculate, 10–12 cm. in diameter, often 3-lobed; lobes oblong, often mucronate and lobular, separated by obtuse sinuses reaching one-fourth the limb, often dotted with white spots; tendrils three- to five-branched. Flowers dioecious, white, solitary; June–July; calyx tubular, dilated below the throat, 5-lobed; petals 5; in the male stamens 3; in the female ovary inferior, 1-celled. Fruit fleshy, ovoid or

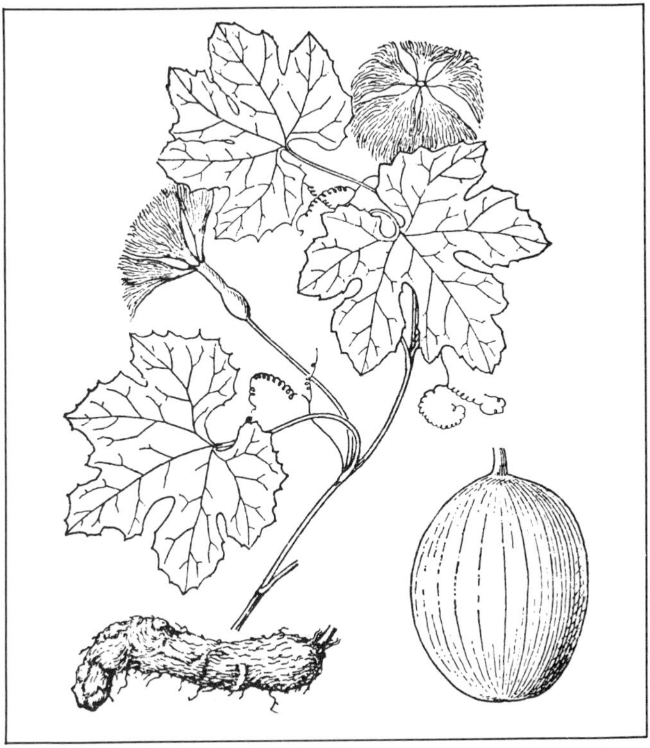

Trichosanthes kirilowii

oblong, pale yellow, glabrous and smooth; August–September; seeds compressed, oblong, marginate. Southern China, Vietnam. (Syn. *T. palmata* Hance., *Eopepon aurantiacus* Naud., *E. vitifolius* Naud.)

The root and the kernel of the seed are officinal. The taste of the kernel is sweet; that of the root bittersweet and sour. The root contains a large amount of starch; the seeds contain fatty oil.[140] The plant contains trichosanthine.[151]

The kernel is prescribed as antitussive, expectorant, and as emollient for skin swellings, icterus. Dose, 7 gm. The root is considered antipyretic. Dose, 6–10 gm. Incompatibles with the root: *Achyranthes bidentata, Rhus vernicifera, Zingiber officinalis, Aconitum* gen.

柿

DIOSPYROS KAKI L.

(Ebenaceae)

Japanese persimmon. A deciduous tree 6–20 m. Leaves alternate, petiolate, elliptical-oval, acuminate, 3–16 cm. long by 2–9 cm. wide. Flowers rather lengthily pedicellate, dioecious or polygamous; May–June. Male flowers in axillary cymes; calyx in 4 segments, shorter than the corolla; corolla urceolate, yellowish white, externally villous, lobes 4; stamens 14–24, often 16, in pairs; ovary reduced to a small central prominence. Female flowers generally solitary, axillary, pedicel bibracteolate; calyx in 4 segments, accrete under the fruit; corolla with 4 oval lobes, curved outward; staminodia 8, often to 16, villous; ovary glabrous; style villous; stigmas 4. Fruit glabrous or nearly so, yellow or reddish, ovoid or globular; August–November. China, Japan, Vietnam, Annam, eastern India. (Syn. *D. chinensis* Blume., *D. schitze* Bunge., *D. roxburgii* Carr., *D. costata* Carr., *Embryopteris kaki* G. Don.)

The fruit and peduncle are used medicinally. The taste of

the ripe fruit is sweet and astringent; that of the peduncle, bitter and astringent. The fruit contains sugar, tannin, malic acid, trioxybenzoic acid, arabinose, lycopene, carotene, zeaxanthin, oxidase, pentosans, vitamins A, B, and C.[151] The peduncle contains a non-nitrogenous, crystalline substance, m.p. 275°.[140]

The ripe fruit is prescribed as stomachic, astringent in enterorrhagia, diarrhea, hemorrhoids. Dose, ad lib. The peduncle is used to treat hiccough and cough. Dose, 4–5 gm. The extracted juice of the unripe fruit is employed in hypertension.

躅躑羊

RHODODENDRON SINENSE Sw.

(Ericaceae)

A deciduous shrub 1.5 m. tall. Leaves oblong-lanceolate, 6.0–8.5 cm. long, tip obtuse, ciliate, coriaceous, entire, underside gray and hairy. Flowers 5–10 in umbels; May; calyx small, segments 5; corolla funnel-shaped, lobes 5, yellow or red-orange; stamens 5, shorter than the corolla. Fruit an ovoid-oblong capsule, deeply furrowed, shiny, lightly villous. Northern China, Japan. (Syn. *R. molle* Sieb. et Zucc., *Azalea japonica* A. Gray., *A. mollis* Blume., *A. pontica* var. *sinensis* Lindl.)

The flowers are used medicinally. The taste is acrid. The drug is poisonous. The flowers contain andromedotoxin ($C_{31}H_{50}O_{10}$; crystals or amorphous vitreous substance; m.p. about 120°; soluble in water, alcohol, chloroform, ether; insoluble in benzene).[140] Andromedotoxin has potent hypotensive action, and induces convulsions, labored respiration, and cardiac paralysis.[22] The toxin appears to belong in action to the group of veratrine alkaloids.[152]

Prescribed as sedative, analgesic, anesthetic in rheumatism. Dose, 500–1,000 mg.

Gentiana scabra

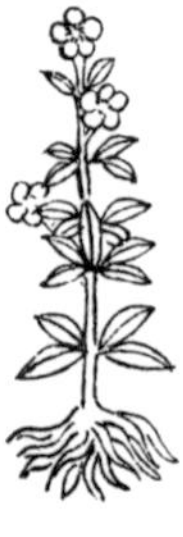

草胆龍

GENTIANA (gen.)

(Gentianaceae)

Various species of Gentiana are employed, including *G. scabra* Bunge., *G. barbata* Frocl., and *G. olivieri* DC. China, Japan.

The roots are officinal. The taste is bitter. The root of *G. scabra* contains the bitter glycosides gentiopicrin ($C_{16}H_{20}O_9$; white needles; m.p. 191° when anhydrous; soluble in water, alcohol; insoluble in ether), gentiamarin ($C_{16}H_{22}O_{10}$; yellowish powder; soluble in water, alcohol), gentiin ($C_{25}H_{28}O_{14}$; small yellow needles; m.p. about 274°; slightly soluble in alcohol; insoluble in water), and the trisaccharide gentianose.[132] The root of *G. lutea* L., whose composition is similar to the above, is a simple bitter free from aromatic oils or tannin, and hence without astringency.

Prescribed as bitter stomachic. Dose, 5 gm. Incompatible: *Rehmannia glutinosa.*

薷 香

ELSHOLTZIA CRISTATA Willd.

(Labiatae)

An aromatic undershrub 30–45 cm. high, nearly glabrous, the stem erect or procumbent. Leaves opposite, petiolate, membranous, 5–8 cm. long by 3 cm. wide, oblong, acute, base cuneiform, dentate. Inflorescence terminal, unilateral, compact; September–October; bracts broad, nearly orbiculate, acuminate, green, membranous, surpassing the small, sessile flowers. Calyx tubular, teeth 5; corolla pale violet, bilabiate; superior lip trilobate, the median lobe emarginate; inferior lip somewhat longer; stamens 4; style longer than the stamens, glabrous, bifid; stigmas subulate, smooth. Fruit a collection of nutlets 0.5 mm. long, oblong, smooth. China, Korea, Japan, northern Vietnam, Laos, India. (Syn. *E. argyi* Lev., *E. feddei* Lev., *E. souliei* Lev., *Hyssopus ocymifolius* Lam., *Perilla polystachya* D. Don., *Mentha ovata* Cav.)

The entire herb is officinal. The taste is pungent. The plant contains an essential oil comprising elsholtzia ketone ($C_{10}H_{14}O_2$; aromatic colorless liquid; b.p. 210°; insoluble in alcohol, chloroform; decomposes to isovalerianic acid), elsholtzianic acid ($C_{10}H_{14}O_3$; white crystalline powder, odor agreeable; m.p. 134°; soluble in all organic solvents), furylmethyl ketone ($C_6H_{33}O$; colorless volatile liquid; b.p. 161°; soluble in alcohol, ether, chloroform), furylpropyl ketone ($C_9H_{39}O$; colorless liquid; b.p. 207°; soluble in usual solvents), furylisobutyl ketone ($C_{10}H_{14}O_2$; colorless liquid darkening quickly; b.p. 221°; soluble in alcohol, ether, chloroform), furane, pinene, terpene.[8]

Prescribed as stomachic, carminative, diuretic. Dose, 4–8 gm.

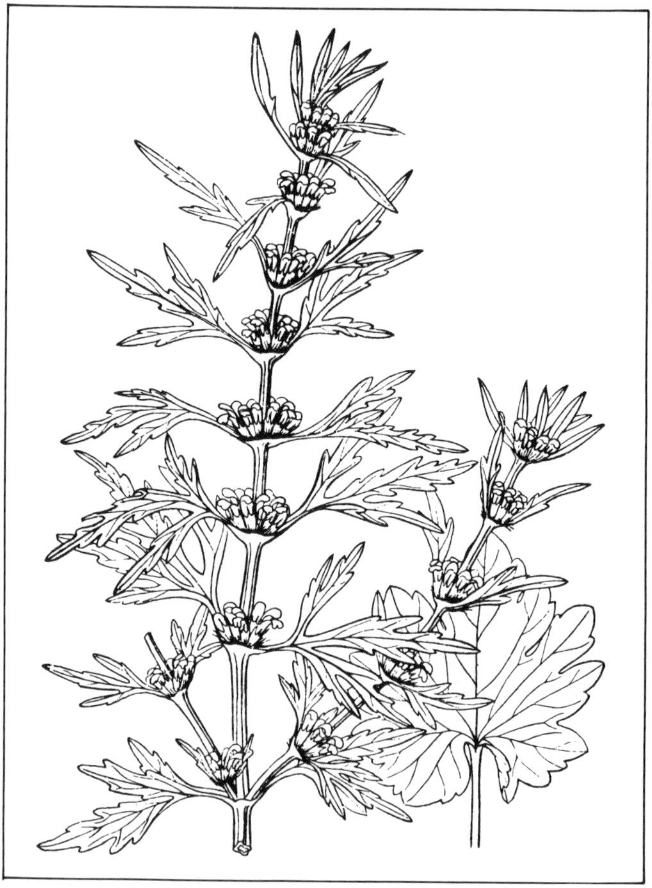

Leonurus heterophyllus

蔚 茺

LEONURUS SIBIRICUS L.
(Labiatae)

Siberian motherwort. An annual herb, the stem 0.4–1.2 m. tall, branching. Leaves petiolate, palmate-tripartite, the lobes themselves coarsely divided into 3–4 parts, 7 cm. long by 4 cm. wide. Inflorescence a compact, axillary verticil; June–August. Calyx campanulate, teeth 5; corolla exserted, 10–15 mm. long, white or red, tube equalling the limb, straight, superior lip oboval, curved, concave, inferior lip equally long, expanded trilobate, median lobe truncate, broad, obcordate, lateral lobes smaller, rounded; stamens 4. Fruit a collection of smooth, triquetrous nutlets. China, Manchuria, Siberia, Indochina, India, Africa, America.

The seeds are used medicinally. They occur small, oblong, triangular. The taste is sweet and pungent. The plant contains 0.5% essential oil, and the alkaloid leonurin ($C_{13}H_{19}N_4O_4$; m.p. 238°; reddish yellow amorphous powder; soluble in alcohol, chloroform; insoluble in water, benzene).[66]

Prescribed as emmenagogue, diuretic, vasodilator. Dose, 5–10 gm.

(Also used, *L. heterophyllus* Sweet.)

香 藿

LOPHANTHUS RUGOSUS Fisch. et Mey.
(Labiatae)

An annual plant 1.0–1.5 m. tall. Leaves opposite, petiolate, base truncate or cordate, tip acute, crenelate, 5 cm. long by 3 cm. wide. Inflorescence a dense, terminal spike, cylindrical, 7–10 cm. long. Flowers purple; calyx campanulate, teeth 5, irregular; corolla tube as long as the calyx, limb bilabiate, the superior lip erect, bilobate, the inferior lip expanded, 3-lobed, the median lip broader and crenelate; stamens 4, didymous, the superior pair declined; style bifid. Nutlets smooth. China, Japan, northern Vietnam, Laos. (Syn. *L. chinensis* Walp., *Agastache rujosa* Kye.)

The leaves are officinal. The taste is sweet; the odor highly aromatic. The plant contains an essential oil.[122]

Prescribed as carminative, stomachic. Dose, 5–7 gm.

荷薄

MENTHA ARVENSIS L.

(Labiatae)

Field mint, corn mint, wild pennyroyal. A perennial herb 10–60 cm., more or less villous, odoriferous, the stem erect or running. Leaves opposite, petiolate, oval-acute or oval-lanceolate, base attenuate, serrate, 2–4 cm. long by 8–10 mm. wide, slightly downy. Inflorescence an axillary verticil, multiflorous, compact. Flowers pink; September; calyx campanulate, teeth 5, regular; corolla 4-lobed; stamens 4. Fruit a collection of ovoid, smooth nutlets. China, Vietnam, Annam, India, Europe.

The leaves are used medicinally. The taste is pungent; the odor aromatic. The plant contains a volatile oil comprising menthol ($C_{10}H_{20}O$; crystals or granules; peppermint taste and odor; m.p. 41–43°, b.p. 212°; very soluble in alcohol, ether, chloroform; slightly soluble in water), menthone ($C_{10}H_{18}O$; bitter liquid, slight peppermint odor; b.p. 207°; soluble in organic solvents; slightly soluble in water), d-piperitone ($C_{10}H_{16}O$; liquid, camphor-like odor), limonene, hexenolphenylacetate, ethylamylcarbinol, neomenthol.[151]

Prescribed as stomachic, carminative, stimulant, diaphoretic. Dose, 2–4 gm.

Lophanthus rugosus

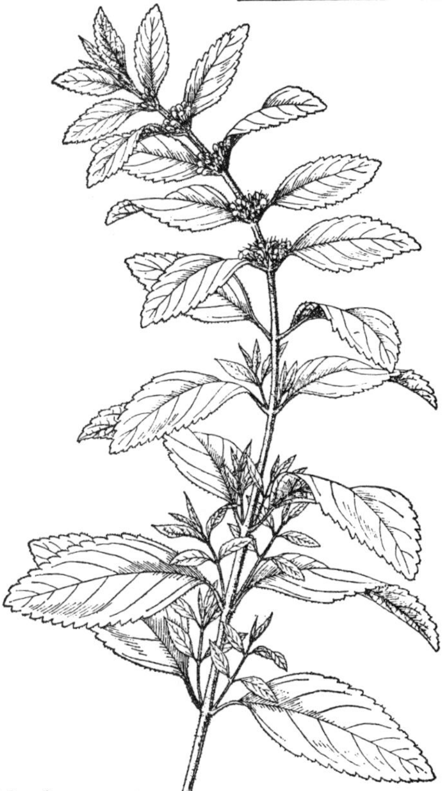

Mentha arvensis

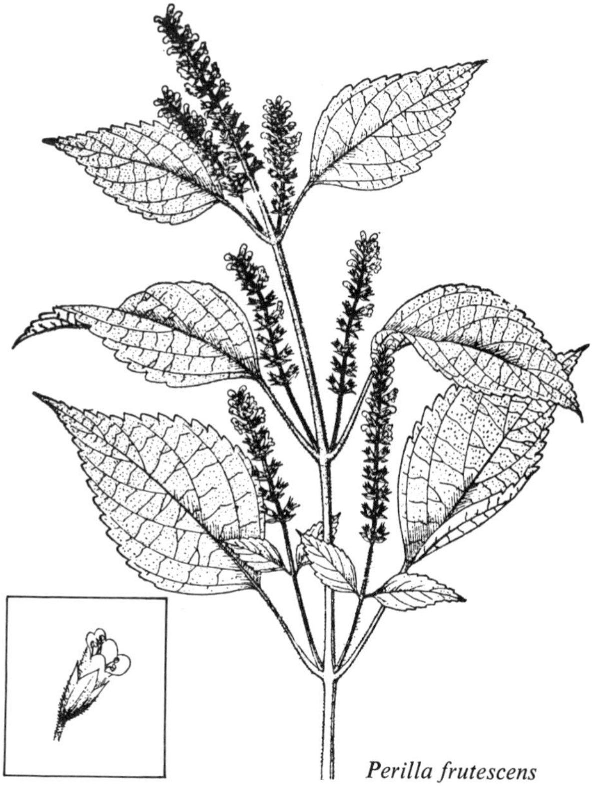

Perilla frutescens

蘇 紫

PERILLA FRUTESCENS Britt.

(Labiatae)

An annual herb, the stem branching, tomentose, 0.5–1.5 m. high. Leaves opposite, lengthily petiolate, oval, acuminate, pubescent, dentate, crenelate, limb 14 cm. long by 6 cm. wide, green occasionally marked reddish brown. Inflorescence an axillary and terminal raceme, 6–20 cm. long; September–October. Flowers small, 3–8; calyx campanulate, teeth 5; corolla campanulate, white or violet, 5-lobed; stamens 4. Fruit a collection of globular nutlets, 2 mm. in diameter, reticulate, light brown. Southern China, Taiwan, Japan, northern Vietnam, Laos, Thailand, India, Burma. (Syn. *P. arguta* Benth., *P. ocymoides* L., *P. ocymoides* var. *crispa* Benth., *Dentidia nankinensis* Lour., *Plectranthes nankinensis* Spreng., *Mentha reticulosa* Hance.)

The leaves and seeds are officinal. The taste is pungent; the odor aromatic. The plant contains 0.5% essential oil comprising perilla aldehyde, d-pinene, l-limonene, perillanine.[140] The seeds are the source of a drying oil resembling linseed oil and comprising glycerides of linoleic, oleic, and palmitic acids.[151]

Prescribed as antitussive, stomachic, antiseptic. Dose of the leaves, 7–10 gm.; of the seeds, 5–8 gm.

草枯夏

PRUNELLA VULGARIS L.

(Labiatae)

Self-heal, heal-all. A low or sprawling perennial herb, 45 cm. high, faintly pubescent. Leaves petiolate, opposite, simple, elliptical or oval, base rounded or wedge-shaped, entire or dentate, 3 cm. long by 1 cm. wide, faintly nervate. Inflorescence a compact head provided with broad, persistent bracts; June–September. Flowers violet-blue, rather small; calyx oblong, deeply bilabiate, the superior lip with 3 teeth, not pronounced, the inferior lip split halfway into 2 finely ciliate lobes; corolla 10–14 mm., gradually widening; limb bilabiate, the superior lip entire, arched, the inferior lip expanded, trilobate, the median lobe concave, dentate; stamens 4, didymous. Fruit a collection of ovoid nutlets, smooth, 2-celled when young, splitting into 4 parts when mature, each part containing 1 seed. Northern China, Northern Hemisphere.

Prunella vulgaris

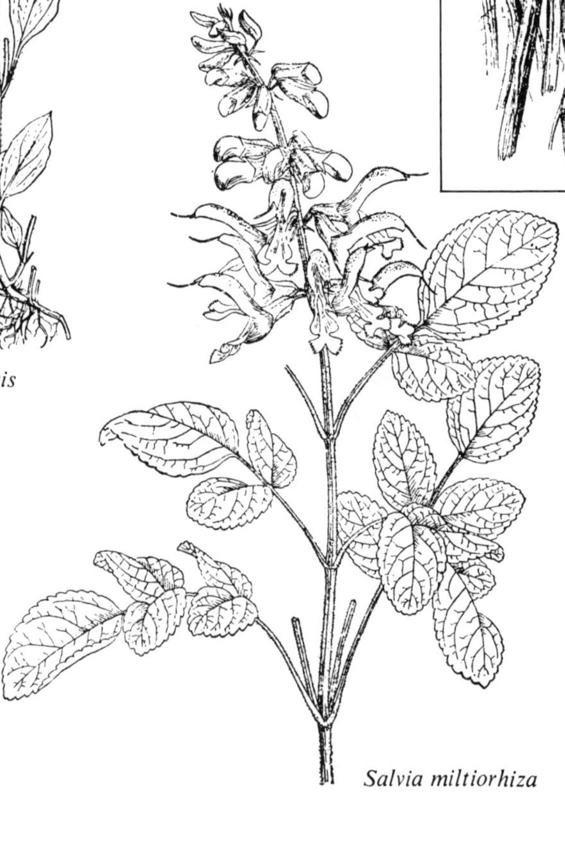

Salvia miltiorhiza

The stem, leaves, and inflorescence are all used medicinally. The taste is bitter and pungent. The plant contains an essential oil and a bitter principle.[114]

Prescribed as alterative, antipyretic, diuretic in scrofula, gout. Dose, 5–7 gm.

參 丹

SALVIA MILTIORHIZA Bunge.

(Labiatae)

An annual herb 40–80 cm. tall, villous, the stem square. Leaves opposite, petiolate, generally simple, base rounded or cordate, dentate, tip acuminate, often pinnate with 3–4 leaflets. Flowers grouped 4–5 in spikes, blue, pink, or yellow, to 2 cm. in length; May–October. Calyx purple, bilabiate, the superior lip entire, the inferior bidentate; corolla bilabiate; the superior lip longer than the tube, bifid, the inferior lip 3-lobed; stamens 2, longer than the corolla; style bifid. Fruit a collection of oblong nutlets, obtuse, 3 mm. long. Northeastern China, Manchuria, Japan. (Syn. *S. pogonocalyx* Hance.)

The root is officinal. It occurs as forked, brick red in color, slender, wrinkled, very irregular, texture solid and almost brittle. The taste is bitter and astringent. The root contains 3 coloring principles, including tanshinone.[151]

Employed as female tonic in amenorrhea, metrorrhagia, gastralgia, mastitis. Dose, 5–10 gm.

SCUTELLARIA BAICALENSIS Georgi.

(Labiatae)

Baical skullcap. A spreading perennial 30–60 cm. high, the stems erect, branching near the base, glabrous, entire, pubescent at the corners. Leaves opposite, sessile, entire, oblong

芩 黄

or oblong-lanceolate, tip obtuse, 2–3 cm. long by 5 mm. wide. Flowers blue, in racemes; May; calyx campanulate, bilabiate, the superior lip provided on the back with a crest; corolla tube long, enlarged toward the top, much longer than the calyx, swelling at the base, limb bilabiate; stamens 4, didymous, fertile, ascending under the superior lip; anthers ciliate; ovary superior. Fruit a collection of small tuberculate nutlets, nearly globular, leathery. Northern China, Manchuria, Siberia. (Syn. *S. macrantha* Fisch., *S. grandiflora* Adams., *S. lanceolaria* Miq.)

The root is used medicinally. It occurs as long, fibrous,

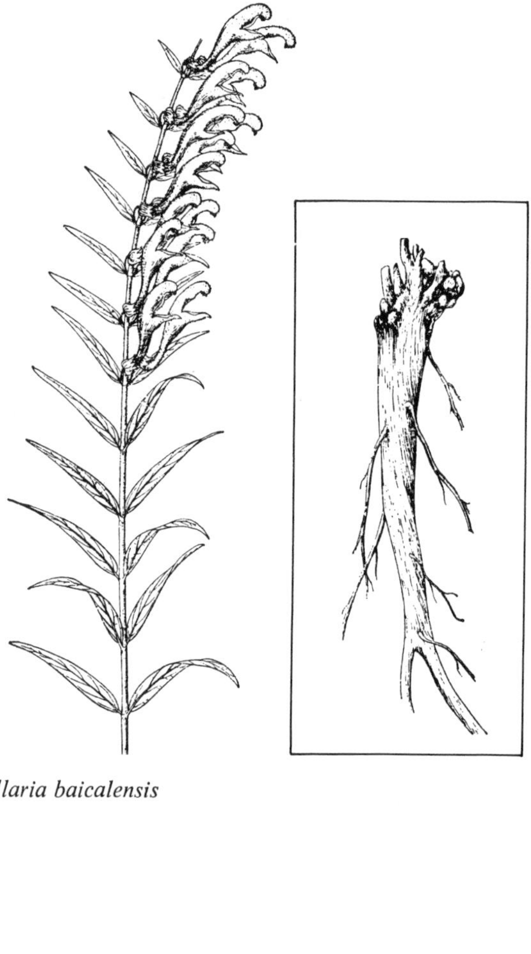

Scutellaria baicalensis

yellow. The taste is bitter. The root contains an essential oil, and the flavone derivatives scutellarin ($C_{21}H_{18}O_{12} \cdot 2\frac{1}{2}H_2O$; light yellow needles; m.p. 310°; soluble in glacial acetic acid; very slightly soluble in organic solvents; insoluble in water) and baicalein ($C_{15}H_{10}O_5$; yellow prisms; m.p. 264–265°; soluble in alcohol, methanol, ether; sparingly soluble in chloroform; insoluble in water).[151] Scutellarin upon hydrolysis gives scutellarein ($C_{15}H_{10}O_6$) and glucuronic acid.[148]

Employed as stomachic, antipyretic, expectorant; in dysentery, diarrhea, hypertension, mastitis, jaundice. Dose, 5–8 gm. Incompatible: *Paeonia moutan.*

花蒙密

BUDDLEIA OFFICINALIS Max.

(Longaniaceae)

A shrub to 2 m. tall, the branchlets round and gray-scurfy. Leaves opposite, oval or oblong-lanceolate, tip acute or acuminate, base attenuate, entire or dentate, 6–11 cm. long by 2–4 cm. wide, surface glabrous, underside pubescent, membranous or somewhat coriaceous; stipules membranous and auriculate, or wanting. Inflorescence a terminal thyrse consisting of multiflorous, pedunculate cymes, 15 cm. long, often narrow, compressed; April. Flowers fragrant, pale lilac with a yellow-orange throat, 8 mm. long, briefly pedicellate; bracteoles linear, lanceolate, shorter than the calyx; calyx campanulate, lobes 4; corolla a campanulate tube, 4-lobed; stamens 4; ovary 2-celled; style filiform; stigma club-shaped. Fruit a crustaceous capsule, oblong-ellipsoid, twice as long as the calyx. China, northern Vietnam. (Syn. *B. madagascariensis* Hance.)

The floral buds are used medicinally. They contain the yellow alkaloid buddlein.[140]

Prescribed as ophthalmic in nyctalopia, asthenopia, cataract. Dose, 4–8 gm.

鼈木番

STRYCHNOS NUX-VOMICA L.

(Longaniaceae)

Strychnine tree. Height 12 m. Leaves opposite, entire, orbiculate or oval, 6–12 cm. long by 3.5–8.5 cm. wide, coriaceous, often membranous. Inflorescence a terminal, corymbose cyme, 3–5 cm. long. Calyx in 5 segments; corolla campanulate, 5-lobed; stamens 5; ovary free, 2-celled. Fruit a globular berry 4 cm. in diameter, pericarp reddish yellow; seeds about 15, thrust into a white pulp, flat, orbiculate, 1.5 cm. wide, surface silky-brown. India, Thailand, southern Vietnam.

The seeds, *Nux Vomica,* are officinal. They occur as flat, lenticular to oblong, to 30 mm. wide by 6 mm. thick, texture bony, color gray to yellowish gray or green, surface smooth and shiny. The taste is very strong and persistently bitter. The seeds contain 4% fatty matter, the glycoside longanin ($C_{25}H_{34}O_{14}$ or $C_{26}H_{36}O_{14}$; crystals; m.p. 215°; soluble in water, alcohol, chloroform, ether), chlorogenic acid, mannosan, galactan, 0.24% copper, and the alkaloids strychnine ($C_{21}H_{22}N_2O_2$; orthorhombic, sphenoidal prisms; m.p. 268–290°; one gram dissolves in 6,400 ml. water, 3,100 ml. boiling water, 150 ml. alcohol, 35 ml. boiling alcohol, 5 ml. chloroform; very slightly soluble in ether) and brucine ($C_{23}H_{26}N_2O_4 \cdot 4H_2O$; monoclinic prisms, very bitter taste; m.p. 178°; one gram dissolves in 1.3 ml. alcohol, 5 ml. chloroform, 187 ml. ether, 1,320 ml. water, 750 ml. boiling water).[151] Strychnine, the main alkaloid of *Nux Vomica,* increases the reflex excitability of the spinal chord and the medullary centers; therapeutic doses produce a tonic effect on the alimentary canal, and a limited amount of respiratory and vasomotor stimulation; toxic doses cause characteristic tetanus, spasmodic respiration, violent changes in blood pressure, death occurring from asphyxia and from the paralysis which succeeds the stimulations.[152]

Prescribed as bitter stomachic, nerve tonic, spinal stimulant, and in laryngitis and laryngoparalysis. Dose, 60 mg.

Forsythia suspensa

FORSYTHIA SUSPENSA Vahl.

(Oleaceae)

Weeping golden bell. An upright shrub 2.5–3.5 m. tall, the branches erect or hanging, slender, the young branches angular, the mature cylindrical, stem hollow between the nodes. Leaves petiolate, oval or oval-acuminate, glabrous, underside glaucous, dentate, often with 3 leaflets, the terminal leaf larger and resembling the simple leaves, the 2 lateral leaflets small and oval-lanceolate. Flowers in axillary clus-

翹 連

ters of 1–3, nearly sessile, about 2.5 cm. long; March–April; calyx 4-lobed, oval or oval-lanceolate, pointed, half as long as the corolla; corolla golden yellow, streaked with orange on the interior of the tube which is very short; stamens 2, as long as the tube; ovary 2-celled. Fruit an ovoid capsule, acuminate; seeds brown. Northern China, Japan. (Syn. *Syringa suspensa* Thunb.)

The fruit is used medicinally. The taste is bitter and astringent. The drug contains saponins and the glycoside phillyrin (phyllyrin; $C_{27}H_{34}O_{11}$; needles or leaflets, tasteless then bitter; m.p. 162°; freely soluble in hot water, in alcohol, chloroform; almost insoluble in ether).[28] Phillyrin has been used as antipyretic.[144]

Prescribed as antipyretic and antiphlogistic in infectious fevers, suppurative inflammations, phlegmon, variola, erysipelas, measles. Dose, 5–10 gm.

皮 秦

FRAXINUS BUNGEANA DC.

(Oleaceae)

A shrub 4–5 m. tall. Leaves opposite, pinnate, leaflets 3–7, oval, elliptical, 3 cm. long by 2 cm. wide, acuminate, crenelate, glabrous. Flowers monoecious or dioecious, small, pink, in terminal panicles; May; calyx with 4 teeth; petals 4, linear. Fruit an oblong samara, compressed, winged; wings 3 cm. long by 3 mm. wide. Northern China. (Syn. *F. floribunda* Bunge., *F. obovata* Blume., *F. ornus* L. var. *bungeana* Hance.)

The bark is officinal. It occurs as whitish brown, fibrous. The taste is bitter and astringent.

Employed as astringent, stomachic in enteritis, diarrhea. Dose, 5–8 gm. Incompatibles: *Evodia rutaecarpa, Euphorbia pekinensis*. A decoction is used as an antiphlogistic ophthalmic wash.

(Also used, *F. rhynchophylla* Hce.)

Fraxinus rhynchophylla

女貞子

LIGUSTRUM JAPONICUM Thunb.
(Oleaceae)

Japanese wax privet. An evergreen shrub 3–5 m. tall. Leaves opposite, petiolate, oval-oblong, 8–11 cm. long by 5–6 cm. wide, tip obtuse or acute, base rounded, central vein reddish, coriaceous. Inflorescence a terminal panicle, 6–16 cm. long, pyramidal; May. Calyx small, teeth 4; corolla infundibulate, longer than the calyx, limb 4-lobed, spreading; stamens 2,

Ligustrum japonicum

somewhat longer than the lobes; ovary 2-celled. Fruit a globular berry, black, 9 mm. long by 6 mm. wide when dried. Southern China, Korea, Japan.

The berries are officinal. The taste is bitter. The berries contain syringin (ligustrin; $C_{17}H_{24}O_9 \cdot H_2O$; small acicular crystals; m.p. 192°; soluble in hot water, alcohol; slightly soluble in cold water; insoluble in ether) and invertin.[140]

Prescribed as nutrient tonic. Dose, 5–15 gm.

肉蓯蓉

OROBANCHACEAE (fam.)

Various plants of the family Orobanchaceae are employed, including *Orobanche epithymum* DC., *Boschniakia glabra* C. A. Mey., *Aeginetia japonica* Sieb. et Zucc., *Phelypaea salsa* C. A. Mey. They are annual parasitic herbs, the rootstalk tuberous, the stem fleshy, cylindrical, leaves scaly. The plant was believed to have sprouted from the semen of the wild horse.[138] Siberia, Mongolia, northern China.

The fleshy stems, salted and pressed dry, are used medicinally. The taste is sweet-sour and salty. The drug contains orobanchin (bitter, crystalline powder; m.p. 160°; soluble in alcohol, water; insoluble in chloroform, ether).[140]

Prescribed as aphrodisiac, and tonic in spermatorrhea, impotence. Dose, 5–10 gm.

胡麻

SESAMUM INDICUM L.

(Pedaliaceae)

Sesame. An annual herb 1 m. tall. Leaves opposite, petiolate, hastate; the superior leaves nearly entire, 7–12 cm. long by 3–7 cm. wide; the median leaves strongly dentate; the inferior leaves trilobate. Flowers axillary, solitary, white with yellow or red spots, briefly pedicellate; July–August. Calyx small, 5-lobed; corolla with curved tube, enlarged toward the top, limb 5-lobed, the 2 posterior lobes shorter; stamens 4; ovary superior, 2-celled; style filiform, bifid at the tip. Fruit an oblong capsule, prismatic, with 4 ribs, 2.5 cm. long by 6 mm. wide, erect, pubescent; September–October; seeds numerous, compressed, oval, nearly smooth. Tropical Asia; cultivated in warm regions of the Old and New World. (Syn. *S. orientale* L.)

The seeds are officinal. Two varieties exist, black and white. They occur as compressed, oval, nearly smooth, 3 mm. long. The taste is sweet. The seeds contain 47–56% fatty oil (comprising 48% olein, 37% linolein, 8% palmitin, 5% stearin, myristin), the resinoid matter sesamin ($C_{20}H_{18}O_6$), sesamol ($C_{20}H_{18}O_7$), pentosan, phytin, lecithin, choline, 1% calcium oxalate, chlorogenic acid, vitamins A and B.[151] Sesame oil (pale yellow, bland taste, almost odorless; solidifies about $-5°$; soluble in chloroform, ether; slightly soluble in alcohol; insoluble in water) is employed externally to soften the skin, as dressing for burns, as vehicle for liniments; internally it is used similarly to olive oil, as nutrient, laxative, and in hyperchlorhydria.[152]

Prescribed as lenitive in scybalous constipation; as nutrient tonic in degenerative neuritis, neuroparalysis. Dose, 10–15 gm.

車前子

PLANTAGO MAJOR L.

(Plantaginaceae)

A perennial herb 10–15 cm. tall. Leaves basal, in rosettes, entire, thick, ribbed, broadly oval; petiole rather long, somewhat winged. Inflorescence an erect spike, elongate, cylindrical, somewhat loose at the base; May–June. Flowers small; calyx in 4 segments; corolla grayish, 4-lobed; ovary 2-celled. Fruit a membranous pyxidium, opening circularly toward the base; seeds small, angular. Cosmopolitan. (Syn. *P. major* var. *asiatica* DC., *P. asiatica* L., *P. exaltata* Horn., *P. loureiri* Roem. et Schult.)

The seeds are used medicinally. The taste is sweet. The entire herb contains sugar, citric and oxalic acids, emulsin, invertin, aucubin ($C_{15}H_{24}O_9 \cdot H_2O$; needles; m.p. 181°; soluble in water, alcohol; insoluble in ether, chloroform).[151] A decoction of the seed is diuretic, increasing excretion of urea, uric acid, and sodium chloride.[55]

Employed as diuretic, expectorant. Dose, 5–10 gm.

(Also employed, *P. depressa* Willd.)

Plantago depressa

栀子

GARDENIA FLORIDA L.
(Rubiaceae)

Gardenia, Cape jasmine. An evergreen shrub 2 m. high. Leaves opposite or ternate, oblong-elliptical, 7–14 cm. long by 2–5 cm. wide, coriaceous, occasionally variegated. Flowers solitary, terminal or axillary, broad, white, very fragrant; June; calyx tubular, in 6 segments; corolla salver-shaped or short-tubular, limb with 6–12 fleshy lobes, spreading, more or less twisted; stamens 6–12; ovary 1-celled. Fruit ovoid, rather large, surmounted with the rigid and acute sepals, provided with 6–7 longitudinal ribs which are more or less winged; seeds numerous, oblong, compressed, 5 mm. long by 3 mm. broad, reddish, adhering to the placenta, which is yellow-orange. China, Japan, Taiwan. (Syn. *G. radicans* Thunb., *G. pictorum* Hassk., *G. maruba* Sieb., *G. grandiflora* Sieb. et Zucc., *G. jasminoides* Ellis)

The fruit is officinal. The taste is bitter. The drug contains gardenin ($C_{14}H_{12}O_6$ or $C_{23}H_{30}O_{10}$; golden yellow crystals; m.p. 163–164°; soluble in alcohol, chloroform), crocin ($C_{44}H_{64}O_{24}$; brownish red needles; m.p. 186°; freely soluble in hot water; sparingly soluble in absolute alcohol, ether), chlorogenin, tannin, mannitol.[140]

Prescribed as antipyretic, hemostatic, antiphlogistic; and in jaundice. Dose, 5–10 gm.

鈎藤鈎

NAUCLEA SINENSIS Oliv.

(Rubiaceae)

A shrub, the branches small, bearing compressed, curved spines occasionally. Leaves oval-elliptical, tip acute, base rounded, 10–14 cm. long by 5.0–7.5 cm. wide. Inflorescence an axillary capitulum. Flowers white; calyx in 5 segments; corolla infundibular, with 5 lobes which are much smaller than the tube; stamens 5; ovary 2-celled. Fruit a dry capsule. Central China.

The stem and spines are officinal. The taste is bitter and astringent. The drug contains the alkaloid rhynchophylline ($C_{22}H_{28}N_2O_4$; crystals; m.p. 216°; freely soluble in organic solvents except petroleum ether).[140] Rhynchophylline lowers blood pressure and paralyzes sympathetic nerve endings.[144]

Employed as sedative, antispasmodic in infantile nervous disorders. Dose, 5–10 gm.

(In Japan, *N. rhynchophylla* Miq. [Syn. *Uncaria rhynchophylla* Miq., *Ourouparia rhynchophylla* Miq.] is used.)

Rubia cordifolia

RUBIA CORDIFOLIA L.

(Rubiaceae)

India madder. A perennial, creeping herb, the stem tetragonal. Leaves verticillate by 4, 2–4 cm. long by 2.5–3.0 cm. wide, oval-lanceolate, acute, base cordate, margin provided with small prickles. Inflorescence a paniculate cyme, terminal

草 茜

and axillary, 3–20 cm. long; August–September. Flowers small, yellowish white; calyx tube nearly globular, no limb; corolla rotate, 5-lobed; stamens 5. Fruit a small berry, October. China, India, Africa. (Syn. *R. cordifolia* Thunb., *R. mungista* Roxb.)

The root is used medicinally. It occurs as orangish brown, very fibrous. The taste is bitter. The root contains ruberythric acid (rubianic acid; $C_{25}H_{26}O_{13}$; yellow prisms, silky, lustrous; m.p. 258–260°; soluble in hot water, alkalies; slightly soluble in cold alcohol, ether; insoluble in benzene), purpurin ($C_{14}H_8O_5$; long orange needles; anhydrous at 100°, m.p. 257°; freely soluble in alcohol, ether; soluble in benzene, toluene, xylene), munjistin ($C_{15}H_8O_6$; yellow crystals; m.p. 229–230°; soluble in boiling water or hot alcohol, in chloroform, ether; slightly soluble in cold water).[140 151] On hydrolysis ruberythric acid yields alizarin and dextrose; purpurin is formed during storage, as no appreciable amount is found in the fresh root.[148]

Prescribed as emmenagogue; as hemostatic in hemorrhoidal hemorrhage; in jaundice, rheumatism. Dose, 5–10 gm. Incompatible with iron preparations.

連黃胡

PICRORHIZA KURROA Royle.

(Scrophulariaceae)

An herbaceous, suckering plant, the root thick, stem short. Leaves in rosettes near the base of the stem, narrowing toward the petiole, oblong, crenelate-dentate, 5–10 cm. long. Inflorescence a terminal spike, peduncle scapiform. Flowers sessile, purple, provided with lanceolate bracts; calyx in 5 segments; corolla shorter, 4-lobed; stamens 4. Fruit an acute capsule with 4 coriaceous valves, 12 mm. long. Himalayas, China.

The root is used medicinally. It occurs in pieces 3–5 cm.

long, 1 cm. in diameter, epidermis brownish yellow, interior black. The taste is bitter, the odor hay-like. The root contains cathartic acid, and the glycoside picrorhizin.[151]

Prescribed as antipyretic, stomachic. Dose, 2–5 gm.

黄地生

REHMANNIA GLUTINOSA Lib.

(Scrophulariaceae)

A perennial, hirsute herb, the stem 15–50 cm., erect, purplish, branching at the base. Basal leaves fasciculate, superior leaves alternate, oval or spatulate, tapering to a short petiole, coarsely dentate, pubescent, the underside often reddish, 7–26 cm. long by 3–9 cm. wide. Axillary flowers solitary or in cymes, terminal flowers in few-blossomed cymes, violet-orange tinted with purple; May–June. Calyx tube inflated, in 5 segments, bent, oval; corolla 3 cm. long, villous, tube compressed, limb broad, bilabiate, the superior lip bilobate, the inferior trilobate; stamens 4; disk hypogynous, very small; ovary 2-celled. Fruit a globular capsule; seeds numerous, small, oval, reticulate. Northern China. (Syn. *R. chinensis* Fisch. et Mey., *Digitalis glutinosa* Gaertn.)

The root is officinal. It occurs as large, fleshy, brownish yellow. The taste is sweet. The root contains glycosides, saponins, tannin, resins, coloring matter, and a principle as yet undetermined but which appears analogous to myrtillin.[151] An extract of the drug is cardiotonic in medium doses, large doses producing ventricular stoppage; intravenous injection induces mild, temporary hypertension; small doses produce distinct vasoconstriction, larger doses vasodilation; the extract has a diuretic effect and very obviously lowers blood sugar.[53]

Prescribed as cardiotonic, diuretic, hemostatic; in diabetes mellitus. Dose, 5–8 gm. Incompatibles: *Fritillaria verticillata, Ulmus macrocarpa,* iron preparations.

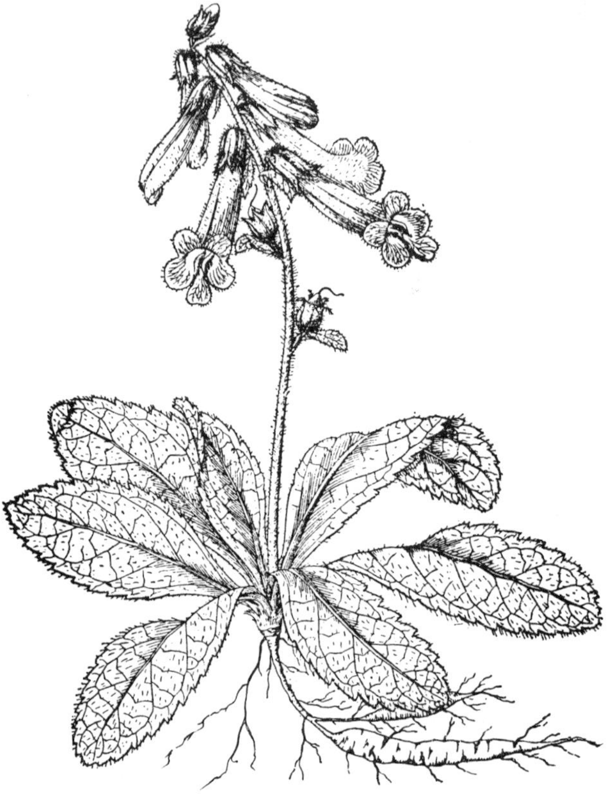

Rehmannia glutinosa

參 元

SCROPHULARIA OLDHAMI Oliv.

(Scrophulariaceae)

A perennial herb 6–12 cm. high, the stem square. Leaves opposite, petiolate, oval-lanceolate, acuminate, base rounded or nearly cuneiform. Inflorescence a terminal thyrse, elongate. Flowers small, numerous, greenish or yellowish; calyx in 5 segments; corolla irregular, tubular, 5-lobed; stamens 4; ovary superior. Fruit an obovoid capsule, 2-celled; seeds dispersed through pores. Northern China, Japan. (Syn. *S. puergeriana* Miq.)

The root is employed medicinally. It occurs 12 cm. long by 3.5 cm. wide, flat, brownish, irregularly furrowed, fleshy, the interior blackish. The taste is bittersweet. The dried root contains a volatile oil, a phytosterol, alkaloids not yet identified, and perhaps dextrose.[23] Small doses of the drug

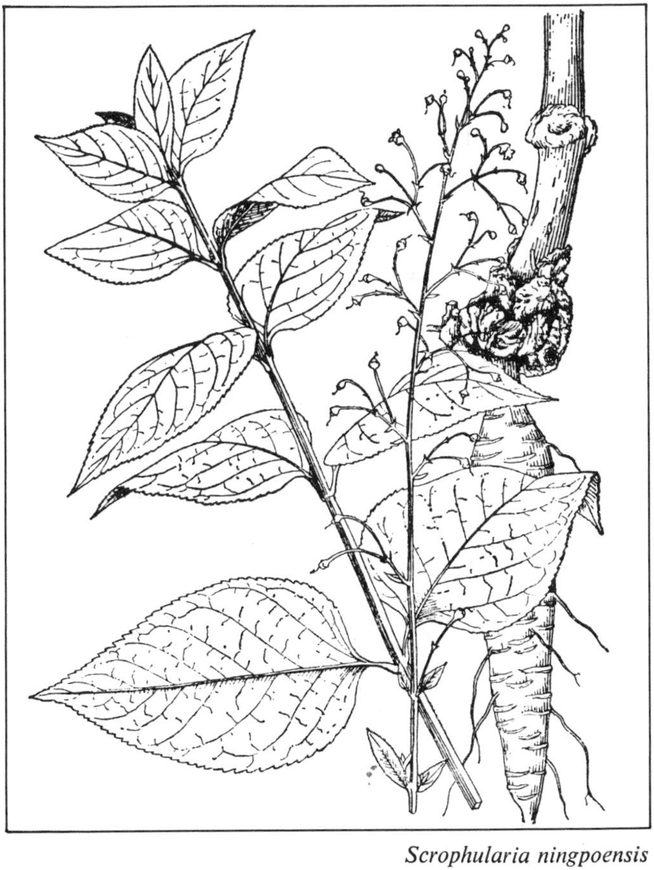

Scrophularia ningpoensis

are mildly cardiotonic, larger doses paralyzing cardiac movement; vasodilation is noted; large doses produce temporary mild hypotension, augmentation of respiratory movement; the blood sugar is lowered.[54]

Prescribed as cardiotonic; as antipyretic and antiphlogistic in laryngitis, tonsillitis, pharyngalgia, diphtheria, scarlet fever, erysipelas. Dose, 7–10 gm.

(*S. ningpoensis* Hemsl. is used also.)

花羅陀曼

DATURA ALBA Nees.

(Solanaceae)

An annual herb, erect, glabrous or lightly pubescent, the stem nearly ligneous. Leaves petiolate, oval, acute or briefly acuminate, entire or irregularly sinuate, 9–18 cm. long. Flowers solitary on very short terminal or lateral pedicels, large, white; calyx tubular, segments 5, 6 cm. long; corolla infundibular, limb 5-lobed, acuminate, 15 cm. long. Fruit a globular capsule, 3.5 cm. in diameter, covered with short spines. Southern China, southern Asia. (Syn. *D. fastuosa* L. var. *alba* Clark)

The leaves and seeds are officinal. The taste is pungent. The drug is poisonous. The leaves and seeds contain about 0.5% hyoscine (scopolamine; $C_{17}H_{21}NO_4$; viscous liquid; freely soluble in hot water, in alcohol, ether, chloroform, acetone; sparingly soluble in benzene), traces of hyoscyamine ($C_{17}H_{23}NO_3$; silky tetragonal needles; m.p. 108.5°; freely soluble in alcohol, dilute acids; one gram dissolves in 281 ml. water, 69 ml. ether, 150 ml. benzene, 1 ml. chloroform) and atropine ($C_{17}H_{23}NO_3$; long orthorhombic prisms; m.p. 114–116°; one gram dissolves in 455 ml. water, 90 ml. water at 80°, 2 ml. alcohol, 25 ml. ether, 1 ml. chloroform; soluble in benzene, dilute acids); the seeds also contain resin and fixed oil.[148] Atropine produces complete paralysis of the peripheral distribution of the parasympathetic nerves, dilating and drying the bronchial tubes, dilating the pupils, and relaxing intestinal spasm.[152] Toxic doses cause motor restlessness, excitement, delirium, and coma.[144]

Prescribed as antispasmodic in spastic cough, as bronchodilator in asthma. Dose, 112.5–225.0 mg.

Datura alba

Hyoscyamus niger

HYOSCYAMUS NIGER L.

(Solanaceae)

Black henbane. A biennial or annual herb 30–80 cm. tall, villous, viscid. Leaves alternate, the basal leaves petiolate, the cauline sessile, clasping, oval-oblong, sinuate, pinnatifid, 15–20 cm. long; lobes irregular, triangular, lanceolate. Flow-

莨菪子

ers in terminal, scorpioid cymes, or axillary, nearly entirely sessile; June; calyx tubular-campanulate, segments 5, mucronate, persistent, accrete; corolla infundibular, 5-lobed, irregular, dirty yellow veined with violet, the throat purplish black; stamens 5, barely exserted; ovary 2-celled. Fruit a capsule, enclosed in the persistent and enlarged calyx; seeds small, compressed, nearly ovoid, slightly reniform, 1 mm. in diameter, brownish gray, surface reticulate. Northwestern China, Asia, Europe, North Africa.

The leaves and flowering tops are used medicinally. The taste is bitter. The drug is poisonous. The leaves contain about 0.04% alkaloids (chiefly hyoscyamine and scopolamine), the glycoside hyoscypicrin, and choline.[148] The therapeutic effects of the drug are similar to those of belladonna but are less intense because of lower alkaloid content; the presence of scopolamine imparts a central narcotic effect; the drug is uncertain in its action.[144]

Prescribed as antispasmodic, analgesic, narcotic in asthma, gastralgia, gastrospasm, sciatica, pertussis, neuralgia. Dose, 130–320 mg.

(In Japan, *Scopolia japonica* Max. is employed.)

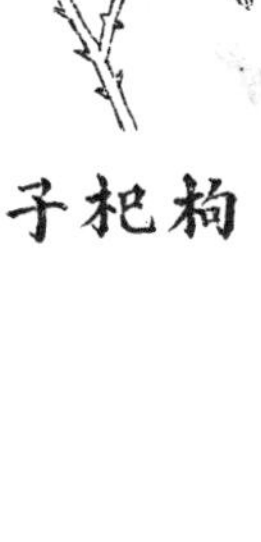

枸杞子

LYCIUM CHINENSE Mill.

(Solanaceae)

Chinese wolfberry. A shrub 1 m. high, the branches hanging, often spiny. Leaves petiolate, alternate, oval-lanceolate, entire, acute or obtuse. Flowers small, borne singly or clustered in the leaf axils, purple; June–September; calyx campanulate; corolla tube rather long, limb broadly campanulate; deeply 5-lobed, lobes 4-5 mm. long; stamens 5, exserted; ovary 2-celled. Fruit an ovoid berry, orange-red, 1.5–2.5 cm. long; August–October. China, Japan. (Syn. *L. barbatum* L. var. *chinense* Ait., *L. megistocarpum* Dun., *L. ovatum*

Loisel., *L. trewianum* G. Don., *L. barbatum* Thunb., *L. turbinatum* Loisel.)

The fruit and root epidermis are officinal. The taste of the fruit is sweet; of the root epidermis, bitter. The plant contains betaine (lycine; $C_5H_{11}NO_2$; deliquescent scales or prisms; m.p. 293°; one gram dissolves in 160 ml. water, 9 ml. alcohol; sparingly soluble in ether), a polyterpene, physaline, vitamin A.[151] Betaine is nearly inactive by mouth.[152]

The fruit is prescribed as nutrient tonic in diabetes mellitus, pulmonary tuberculosis. Dose, 6–10 gm. The root epidermis is considered antipyretic, antitussive in pulmonary tuberculosis. Dose, 5–8 gm.

Lycium chinense

Physalis alkekengi

漿 酸

PHYSALIS ALKEKENGI L.

(Solanaceae)

Strawberry tomato, winter cherry, Chinese lantern plant. A perennial herb 20–60 cm. tall, the stock creeping, stem erect, angular, pubescent, simple or branching. Leaves geminate, petiolate, oval, acuminate, sometimes deltoid, entire or lightly sinuate, glabrous. Inflorescence a drooping, axillary peduncle; June–July. Flowers solitary, rather large, whitish; calyx floriferous, much inflated, oval, veined, at maturity orange-red and enveloping the fruit without touching it; corolla rotate, 5-lobed; stamens 5; 2-celled ovary; style short, terminated with a very small, convex stigma. Fruit a berry supported on a reflected pedicel, globular, smooth, glabrous, red, succulent, 2-celled; July–September; seeds reniform, flattened. China, Japan, southern Europe.

The entire plant is used medicinally. The taste is bitter. The taste of the berries is acid. The entire plant contains physalin (physalien, zeaxanthin dipalmitate; $C_{72}H_{116}O_4$; fine yellow or red needles; m.p. 97°), zeaxanthin (zeaxanthol; $C_{40}H_{56}O_2$; yellow rhombic plates with steel blue metallic luster; m.p. 207° or 215.5°; soluble in benzene, chloroform; slightly soluble in petroleum ether, methanol; insoluble in water), resinous and pectic matter; the berries contain citric acid and vitamin C.[151] One kilogram of the air-dried petals yields 4 gm. zeaxanthin, after saponification of the dipalmitate.[67]

Prescribed as antitussive, antiphlogistic, antipyretic in trachitis, bronchitis, pharyngitis, pertussis. Dose, 5–10 gm. The berries are employed as diuretic, laxative.

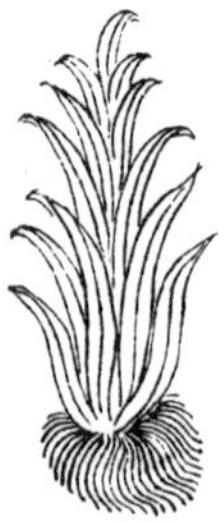

香松甘

NARDOSTACHYS JATAMANSI DC.

(Valerianaceae)

An alpine perennial herb, the stem thick, fragrant, surrounded at the base with the remains of the old leaves. Leaves opposite, 30–90 mm. long, oblong, glabrous or lightly pubescent, the cauline leaves sessile. Inflorescence a terminal, capitate panicle consisting of cymes, provided with opposite bracts. Flowers reddish, somewhat irregular; calyx tube sacciform, segments 5; corolla nearly campanulate, 5-lobed; stamens 4; ovary inferior. Fruit dry, surmounted with the indehiscent calyx, villous. Himalayas, Yunnan.

The root is officinal. The taste is sweet and slightly bitter; the odor aromatic. The root contains 1–2% essential oil.[140]

Prescribed as aromatic stomachic, sedative, antispasmodic. Dose, 4–8 gm.

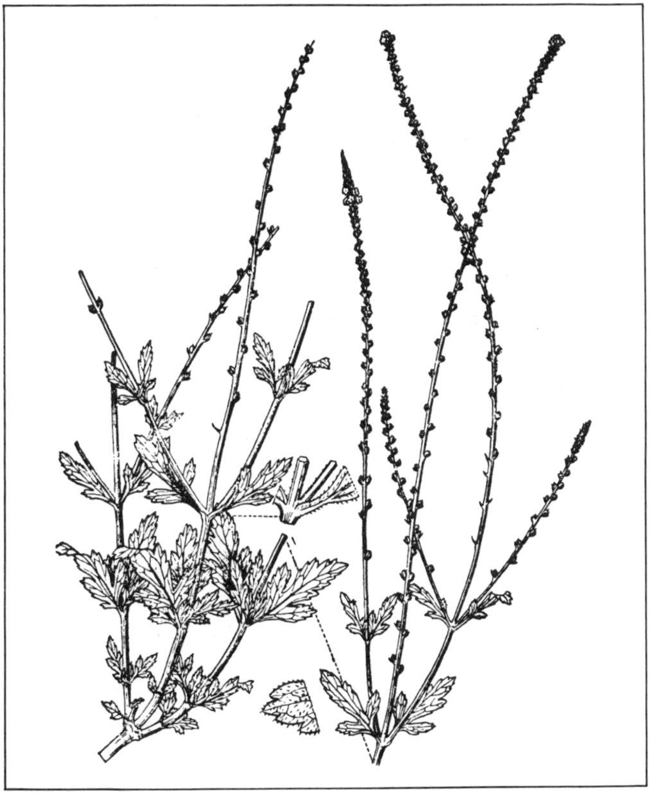

Verbena officinalis

馬鞭

VERBENA OFFICINALIS L.
(Verbenaceae)

A perennial herb 40–80 cm. high. Leaves opposite; inferior leaves petiolate, oboval; superior leaves narrow, cuneiform, pinnatifid, the segments incised-crenelate, petiole nearly foliaceous. Inflorescence a long, terminal spike, filiform; May–July. Calyx tubular, teeth 5, nearly regular; corolla tubular, narrow, opening salver-wise, lobes 5; stamens 4, in pairs, enclosed; ovary superior, 4-celled. Fruit a capsule enclosed within the calyx, oblong, dividing into 4 parts. Cosmopolitan.

The leaves are used medicinally. The taste is bitter. The plant contains an essential oil (comprising citral, geraniol, limonene, verbenone), invertin, a bitter principle, verbenalol ($C_{11}H_{14}O_5$; long prismatic needles; m.p. 133°; soluble in ether, acetic acid; poorly soluble in water) and the glycoside verbenalin ($C_{17}H_{25}O_{10}$; bitter needles; m.p. 178°; freely soluble in water; slightly soluble in alcohol, acetone; insoluble in chloroform, ether).[17] [151] Verbenalin in frogs produces mucosal excoriation.[43]

Prescribed as emmenagogue. Dose, 10–18 gm.

APPENDICES

APPENDIX I
SUPPLEMENTARY BOTANICAL DRUGS

The following comprises a list of additional plants used in Chinese *materia medica*, descriptions and analyses of which were insufficient for inclusion in the main section of this work.

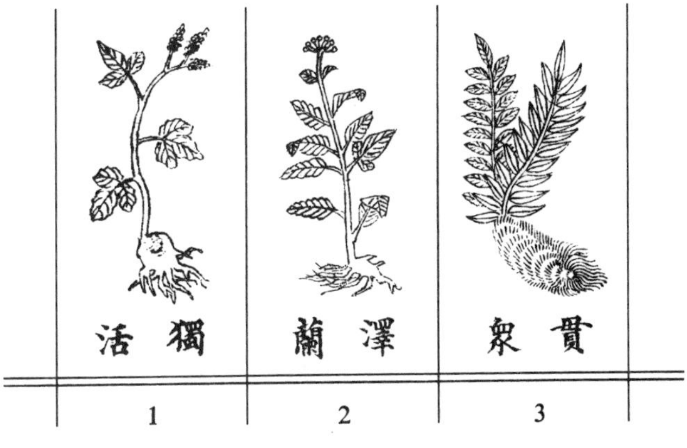

1. **Angelica grosserrata Maxim.** (Umbelliferae)
   Root. Bitter, pungent; fragrant. Essential oil. Antispasmodic, analgesic, diaphoretic, diuretic. Dose, 4–11 gm.

2. **Arethusa japonica A. Gr.** (Compositae)
   Leaves. Bittersweet. Essential oil, tannin. Diuretic, emmenagogue. Dose, 5–10 gm.

3. **Aspidium falcatum Sw.** (Polypodiaceae)
   Root. Bitter. Slightly poisonous. Filicic acid, tannin, essential oil, starch, resin, sugar. Anthelmintic, hemostatic, antidote. Dose, 5–7 gm.

省藤	没藥	芎藭	薰草零陵香
4	5	6	7

4. **Calamus margaritae Hance.** (Palmaceae)
Stem. Bitter. Anthelmintic, carminative, analgesic. Dose, 10–19 gm. Decoction used for toothache.

5. **Commiphora myrrha Engler.** (Burseraceae)
The resin. Bitter. 25–40% resin, 60% gum, 5% myrrhol; also yomniphoric acid, myrrholic acid, arabinose, oxydase, galactose, xylose. Exsiccant, stomachic, antispasmodic. Dose, 3–5 gm.

6. **Conioselinum univittatum Turcz.** (Umbelliferae)
Root. Bitter, very fragrant. 1–2% essential oil. Emmenagogue, sedative, analgesic. Dose, 4–11 gm.

7. **Coumarouna odorata Aubl.** (Leguminosae)
Stem and leaves. Bitter, pungent. Essential oil, coumarin. Aromatic stomachic, diaphoretic, antipyretic.

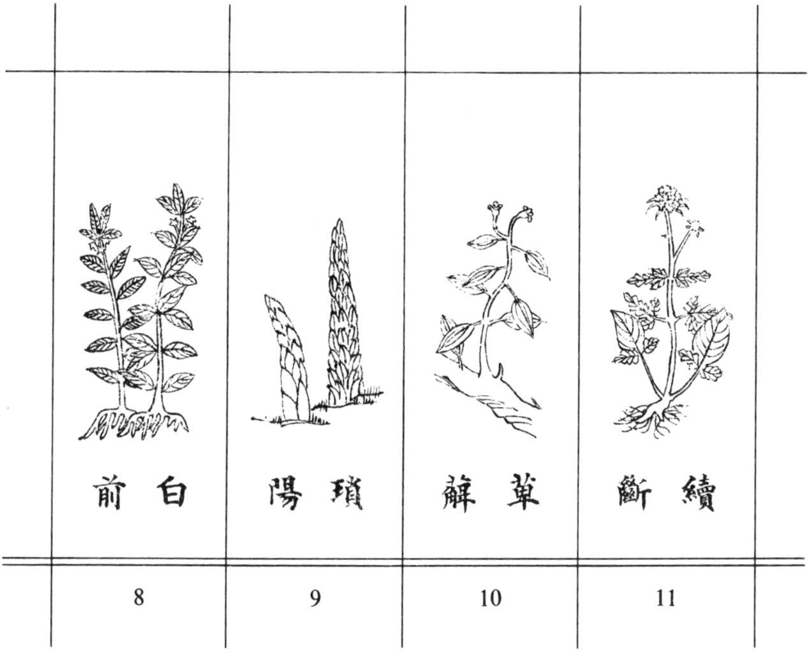

8. **Cynanchum japonicum Moore et Decne**. (Asclepiadaceae)
Root. Bitter, pungent. Antitussive, expectorant. Dose, 4–6 gm. (Syn. *Vincetoxicum purpurascens* Moore et Decne.)

9. **Cynomorium coccineum L.** (Balanophoraceae)
Stem. Sweet. Enzyme, fatty oil, sugar. Tonic, aphrodisiac, spermatopoietic. Dose, 4–11 gm.

10. **Dioscorea sativa L.** (Dioscoreaceae)
Root. Bitter. Dioscin, dioscoreasapotoxin. Alterative in syphilis, gonorrhea; diuretic. Dose, 5–10 gm.

11. **Dipsacus asper Wall.** (Dipsacaceae)
Root. Bitter, slightly pungent. Essential oil, alkaloid lamine. Tonic, analgesic, hemostatic. Dose, 5–10 gm.

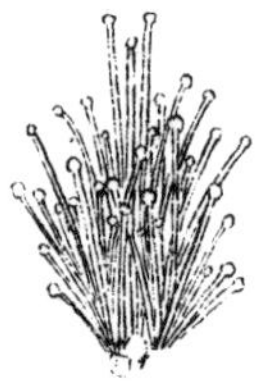			
穀精草	山豆根	阿魏	砂仁
12	13	14	15

12. **Eriocaulon sieboldianum Stend.** (Eriocaulaceae)
Entire plant. Pungent, sweet. Antiphlogistic, ophthalmic. Dose, 5–10 gm.

13. **Euchresta japonicum Benth.** (Leguminosae)
Root. Bitter. Antipyretic, antiphlogistic, antidote. Dose 4-8 gm.

14. **Ferula assafoetida L.** (Umbelliferae)
The gum-resin. Bitter, pungent, fetid. 69% asaresinotannol, 4–6% sulfuretted volatile oil; also ferulic acid, vanillin, mucilage, bassorine. Vermicide, sedative, antispasmodic, digestive. Dose, 2–4 gm.

15. **Hedychium coronarium Koen.** (Zingiberaceae)
Seed. Pungent, aromatic. Essential oil (borneol, bornyl acetate, l-camphor, linalool, nerolidol), carbohydrate 24%, fat 4%. Aromatic stomachic, carminative. Dose, 2-4 gm.

打得落	青 大	艽 秦	蒁莪蓬
16	17	18	19

16. **Inula helenium L.** (Compositae)
Rhizome. Pungent, bitter, aromatic. Alantolactone (helenin), alantol (in fresh root only), inulin. Aromatic stomachic, anthelmintic, disinfectant and antiseptic, expectorant. Dose, 4–11 gm.

17. **Isatis oblongata DC.** (Crucifereae)
Fruit. Bitter, slightly saline. Isatin. Antiphlogistic, antipyretic, antidote. Dose, 7–15 gm.

18. **Justicia gendarussa L.** (Acanthaceae)
Root. Bitter, pungent. Alkaloid justicine, essential oil. Diuretic, antipyretic, sedative. Dose, 4–10 gm.

19. **Kaempferia pandurata Roxb.** (Zingiberaceae)
Tuber. Bitter, pungent. Essential oil (cineol, camphor, d-borneol, d-pinene, sesquiterpene, zingiberene), curcumin, zedoarin, resin, starch. Emmenagogue, aromatic stomachic, expectorant, analgesic. Dose, 2–7 gm.

百合	蘇合	狗骨	冬葵子
20	21	22	23

20. **Lilium japonicum Thunb.** (Liliaceae)
Bulb. Sweet, slightly bitter. 4% protein, 0.1% fat, starch, colchiceine. Nutrient, antitussive, expectorant. Dose, 10–19 gm.

21. **Liquidambar orientalis Mill.** (Hamamelidaceae)
The resin. Pungent, sweet. Essential oil (styrol, vanillin, styrocamphor), balsam (cinnamic acid, cinnamein, styrocin, storesinol). Aromatic stimulant, expectorant. Dose, 1–2 gm. Externally for skin diseases, frostbite.

22. **Mahonia japonica DC.** (Berberidaceae)
Leaf and seed. Bitter. Nutrient tonic, antipyretic. Dose, 7–15 gm.

23. **Malva verticillata L.** (Malvaceae)
Seed. Sweet. 1% essential oil. Demulcent, diuretic. Dose, 8–15 gm. (Syn. *M. chinensis* Mill., *M. pulchella* Berhn.)

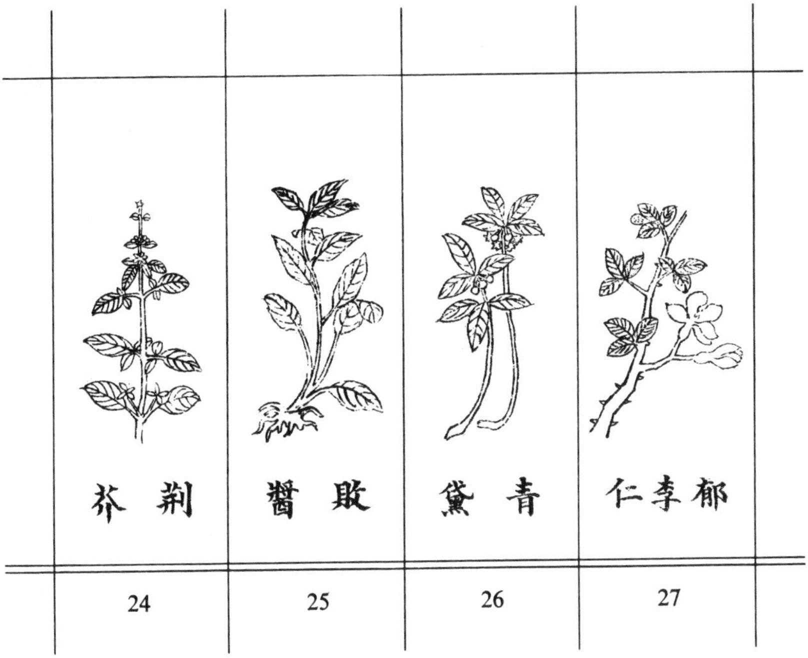

24. **Nepeta japonica Maxim.** (Labiatae)
Flowers and leaves. Pungent, slightly bitter, aromatic. 2% essential oil (menthone, limonene). Diaphoretic, antipyretic. Dose, 4–11 gm.

25. **Patrinia scabiosaefolia Link.** (Valerianaceae)
Root. Bitter, fetid. 8% essential oil. Resolvent, antiphlogistic, diuretic. Dose, 8–15 gm.

26. **Polygonum tinctorium Lour.** (Polygonaceae)
Stem and leaves. Slightly saline. Indigotin. Antiphlogistic, antidote, antipyretic. Dose, 400–1,000 mg.

27. **Prunus japonica Thunb.** (Rosaceae)
Kernel of seed. Pungent, bitter, slightly sour. Diuretic, laxative. Dose, 4–7 gm. (Syn. *P. glandulosa* Thunb., *P. sinensis* Pers., *P. chinensis* Blume., *P. domestica* Thunb., *Amygdalus pumila* Sims., *Cerasus japonica* Loisel., *C. dulosa* Loisel.)

 烏梅	 覆盆子	 芸香	 荊三稜
28	29	30	31

28. **Prunus mume Sieb. et Zucc.** (Rosaceae)
Unripe fruit. Sour, astringent. Hydrocyanic acid. Stomachic, antipyretic, astringent. Dose, 4–7 gm. (Syn. *P. armeniaca* Thunb., *Armeniaca mume* Sieb., *A. nana* Thunb.)

29. **Rubus coreanus Miq.** (Rosaceae)
Unripe seed. Sweet-sour, bitter. Tartaric acid, citric acid. Tonic, astringent. Dose, 5–10 gm. (Syn. *R. tokkura* Sieb.)

30. **Ruta graveolens L.** (Rutaceae)
Entire herb. Pungent, fragrant. 0.6% essential oil (80–90% methyl-n-nonyl ketone, methyl ketone, methyl-n-heptyl carbinol, nonyl carbinol, methyl acetate, pinene, cineol), rutin, flavonol. Antispasmodic, carminative, emmenagogue. Dose, 2–4 gm.

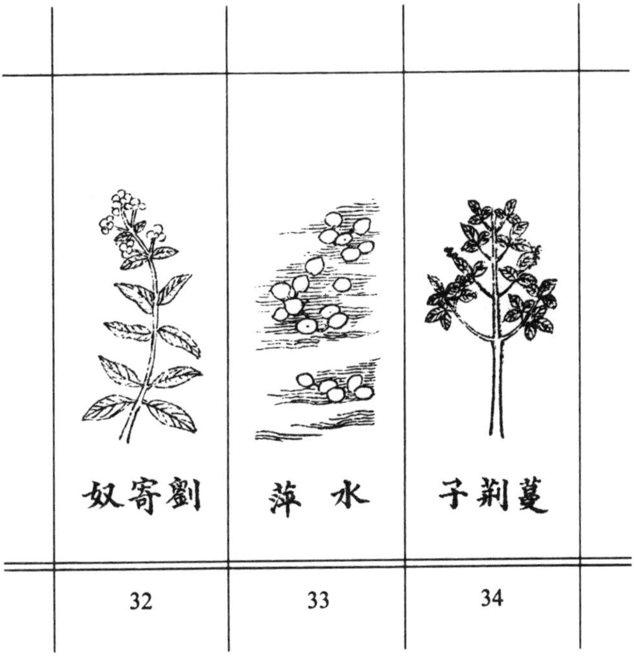

31. **Scirpus maritimus L.** (Cyperaceae)
Tuber. Bittersweet, aromatic. Emmenagogue, analgesic, laxative. Dose, 4–7 gm.

32. **Senecio palmatus Pall.** (Compositae)
Entire plant. Bitter. 0.5% essential oil, saponin. Hemolytic, emmenagogue, diuretic, hemostatic. Dose, 5–10 gm.

33. **Spirodela polyrhiza Schleid.** (Lemnaceae)
Entire plant. Pungent. Diaphoretic, diuretic. (Syn. *Lemna polyrhiza* L.)

34. **Vitex trifolia L.** (Verbenaceae)
Seed. Bitter, pungent. Essential oil (55% camphene, 20% limonene, pinene), acetic acid. Sedative, analgesic. Dose, 5–10 gm.

APPENDIX II

MINERAL DRUGS

Employed in Chinese Medicine

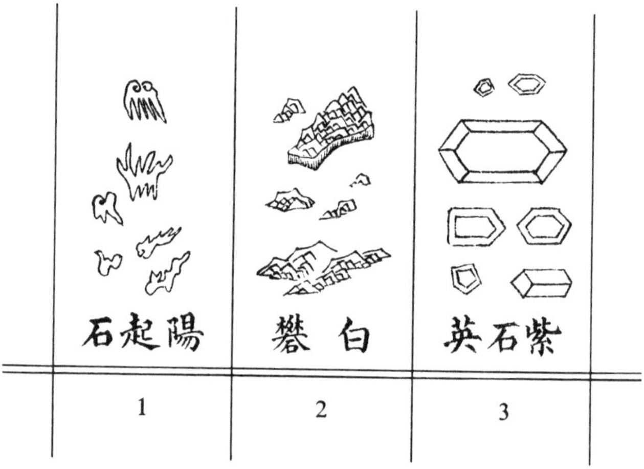

1. **Actinolite** (Calcium and Magnesium Silicates)
Taste saline. Used as tonic and antispasmodic in colic, prostatitis, cystospasm, cystoparalysis, amenorrhea, endometritis, uterine spasm, impotence, spermatorrhea. Dose, 4–6 gm.

2. **Alum, Potassium** (Aluminium Potassium Sulfate) $AlK(SO_4)_2 \cdot 12H_2O$
Sour, astringent. Used as styptic, astringent. Dose, 100–1,000 mg. Externally, 5–10% solution.

3. **Amethyst** (Silica with trace of Manganese Oxide)
Taste sweet. Used as tonic, sedative in tachycardia, singultus, gastralgia, infantile night terrors. Dose, 7–10 gm.

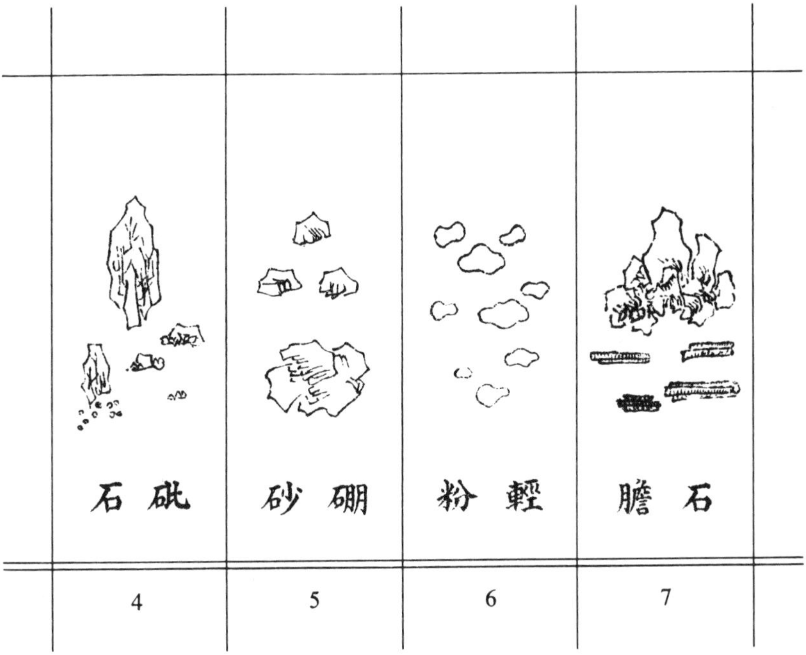

4. **Arsenic Trioxide** As_2O_3
Very poisonous. Blood tonic and purifier in anemia, anemic cardiasthenia, cyanosis, pernicious malaria; also in skin diseases and asthma. Dose, 3 mg.

5. **Borax** (Sodium Borate) $Na_2B_4O_7 \cdot 10H_2O$
Taste bitter. Astringent, antiphlogistic in stomatitis, pulpitis, tonsillitis. 1–2% solution. Topically as ophthalmic.

6. **Calomel** (Mercurous Chloride) HgCl
Taste pungent. Poisonous. Used as cathartic, diuretic, antisyphilitic. Dose, 180–250 mg. Externally for scabies and other skin diseases.

7. **Chalcanthite** (Copper Sulfate Pentahydrate, Blue Vitriol) $CuSO_4 \cdot 5H_2O$
Taste pungent, sour. Poisonous. Emetic in phosphorous poisoning. As collyrium, 6% solution.

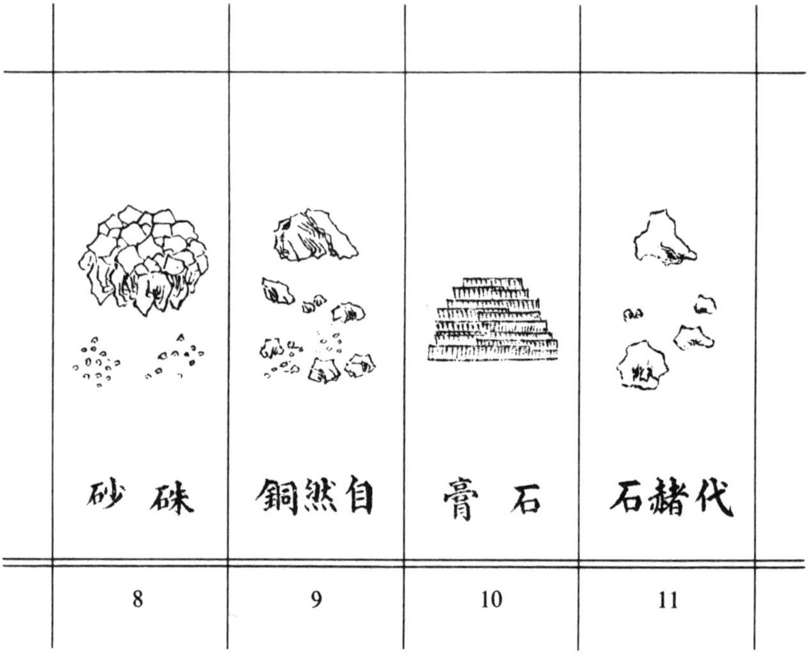

8. **Cinnabar** (Red Mercuric Sulfide) HgS
Taste sweet. Poisonous. Antispasmodic, sedative in nervous tachycardia, infantile convulsions. Dose, 400–1,800 mg.

9. **Copper, Native**
Taste pungent. Analgesic, decongestant for bruises, contusions, fractures, dislocations. Dose, 5–10 gm.

10. **Gypsum** (Native Calcium Sulfate, Alabaster, Selenite, Satinite, Terra Alba) $CaSO_4 \cdot 2H_2O$
Tasteless. Antipyretic, antiphlogistic. Dose, 10–37 gm.

11. **Hematite** (Native Brown Iron Oxide) Fe_2O_3 and Clay
Taste bitter. Used as hematonic, antiemetic, hemostatic, astringent. Dose, 2–5 gm. powdered, 10–15 gm. in decoction.

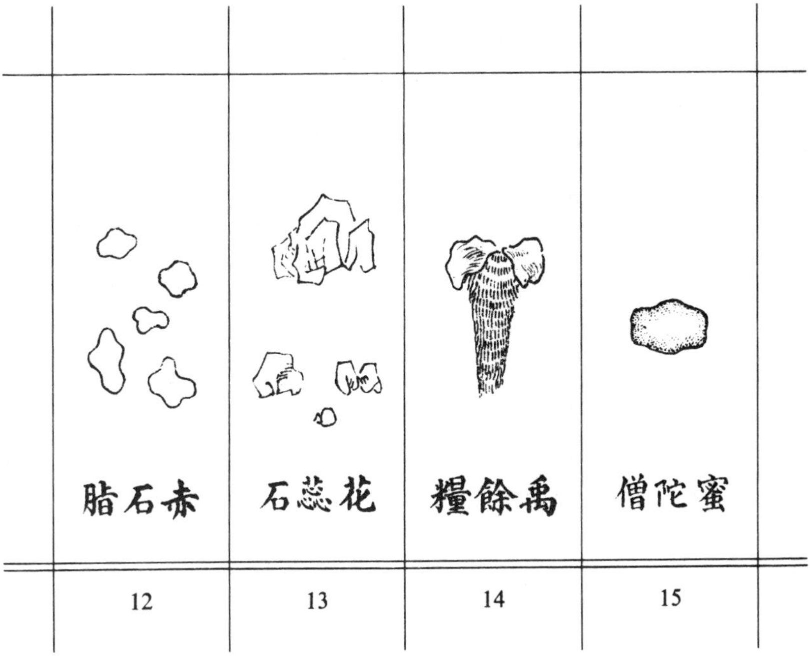

12. **Kaolin** (Essentially Hydrated Aluminum Silicate)
Taste sweet-sour, astringent. Absorbent, astringent in chronic diarrhea, gastroenterorrhagia, and in phosphorous and mercury poisoning.

13. **Limestone** (Mainly Calcium Carbonate)
Taste sour, astringent. As source of calcium in athrombia. Dose, 4–11 gm.

14. **Limonite** (Hydrated Ferric Oxide) $2Fe_2O_3 \cdot 3H_2O$
Taste sweet, astringent. Astringent, antidiarrheic, hemostatic. Dose, 5–15 gm.

15. **Litharge** (Lead Monoxide) PbO
Poisonous. External astringent, hemostatic for ulcers, scabies, hemorrhoidal hemorrhage, incised wounds.

		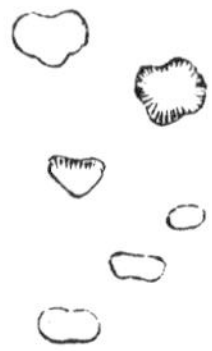	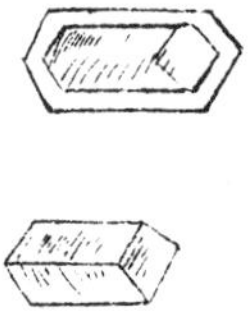
慈石	綠礬	鉛丹	朴硝
16	17	18	19

16. **Loadstone** (Lodestone, Magnetic Magnetite, Ferrosoferric Oxide) Fe_3O_4
Taste pungent. Hematonic, sedative in tachycardia, asthma. Dose, 7–15 gm.

17. **Melanterite** (Green Vitriol, Ferrous Sulfate) $FeSO_4 \cdot 7H_2O$
Taste sour, astringent. Mildly poisonous. Hematonic. Dose, 100–250 mg.

18. **Minium** (Red Lead Oxide) Pb_3O_4
Taste pungent. Poisonous. Externally as disinfectant, antiphlogistic in conjunctivitis, cuts, and burns.

19. **Mirabilite** (Glauber's Salt, Sodium Sulfate Decahydrate) $Na_2SO_4 \cdot 10H_2O$
Taste saline, bitter. Cathartic. Dose, 10–18 gm. Employed topically as ophthalmic, gargle.

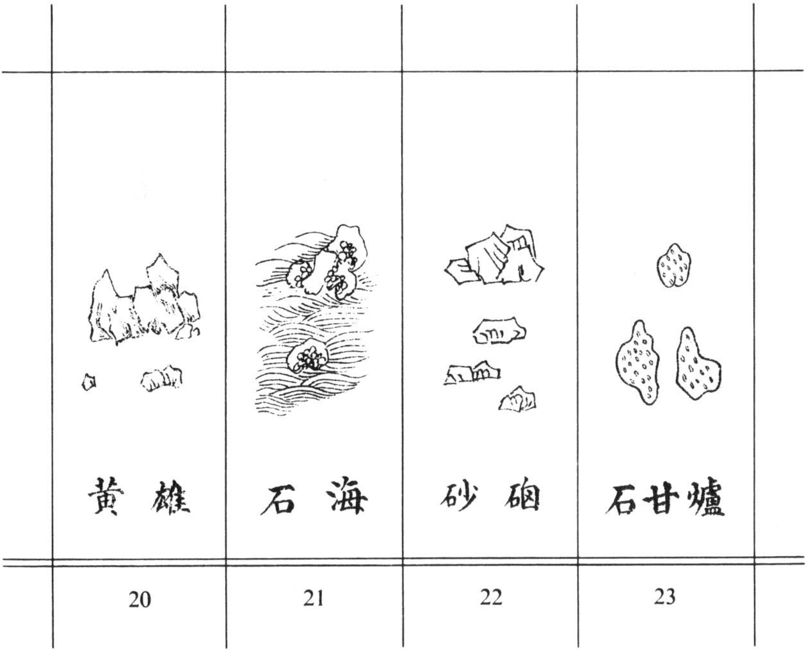

20. **Orpiment** (Native Arsenic Trisulfide) As_2S_3
Pungent-bitter. Poisonous. In chronic malaria. Dose, 250–375 mg. Externally as antidote for snake and scorpion bites, and for ulcers and scabies.

21. **Pumice** (Mainly Complex Silicates of Aluminum, Sodium, Potassium)
Taste saline. Sedative, alterative, expectorant in asthma, cough, gravel, hematuria, urethral stricture, lymphoma. Dose, 4–11 gm.

22. **Sal Ammoniac** (Ammonium Chloride) NH_4Cl
Taste saline, bitter, pungent. Mildly poisonous. Expectorant. Dose, 400–1,000 mg. Externally as corrosive for ulcers.

23. **Smithsonite** (Native Zinc Carbonate) $ZnCO_3$
Taste sweet. Externally as astringent, antiseptic in inflammatory skin diseases.

乳 鍾	黄硫石	石 滑	肝龍伏
24	25	26	27

24. **Stalactites** (Chiefly Calcium Carbonate)
Used as a tonic and source of calcium. Dose, 4–10 gm.

25. **Sulfur** S
Taste sour, pungent. Poisonous. Laxative, blood tonic, for rheumatism. Dose, 1.0–1.8 gm. Externally in parasitic skin diseases.

26. **Talc** (Native Hydrous Magnesium Silicate)
Taste sweet. Antiphlogistic, hemostatic, diuretic in urethritis, strangury, vesical calculus, hematuria. Dose, 5–10 gm.

27. **The Hardened Earth found on the interior bottom of wood-burning kitchen stoves after several years of use** (Mainly Silicic Acid, Aluminum Oxide, Ferric Oxide)
Taste pungent. Antiemetic, sedative, hemostatic, antidiarrheic. Dose, 18–37 gm.

APPENDIX III

DRUGS OF ANIMAL ORIGIN

Employed in Chinese Medicine

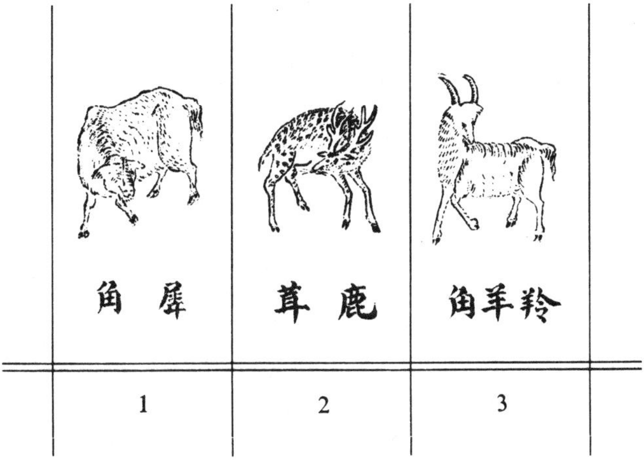

1. **Horn of the Rhinoceros**
   Taste saline. Contains keratin, thiolactic acid, tyrosine, cystine, calcium carbonate, calcium phosphate. Cardiotonic, antipyretic, antidote, hemostatic. Dose, 1–2 gm.

2. **Horn of the Stag,** *Cervus sika*
   Taste sweet-pungent-saline. Contains hartshorn spirit, ammonium carbonate, protein, collagen, cartilage. Tonic, stimulant. Dose, 3–5 gm.

3. **Horn of the Antelope,** *Nemorhaedus cripus*
   Taste saline-bitter. Keratin, calcium phosphate. Antispasmodic, antipyretic, tonic. Dose, 1–3 gm.

龍骨	龜板	虎骨	熊膽
4	5	6	7

4. **Fossilized Bones of Dinosaurs and Other Reptiles**
   Sedative. Dose, 10–18 gm.

5. **Shell of the Turtle,** *Clemmys chinensis*
   Taste sweet. Contains calcium salts, fat, gelatin. Nutrient tonic. Dose, 10–18 gm.

6. **Bones of the Tiger**
   Contain calcium phosphate. Tonic. Dose, 4–10 gm.

7. **Gall Bladder of the Bear,** *Ursus torquatus*
   Taste bitter. Contains glycocholic acid, taurocholic acid, cholesterol, bilirubin. Antiphlogistic, antipyretic, analgesic, antispasmodic. Dose, 400–1,100 mg.

麝香	阿膠	牛黄
8	9	10

8. **Musk** (Dried Secretion from Preputial Follicles of the Musk-Deer) *Moschus moschiferous*
   Contains the odorous substance muskone, cholesterol, fat, wax, albumins. Cardiotonic, stimulant. Dose, 200–375 mg.

9. **Glue Prepared from the Hide of Black Asses**
   Taste sweet, fetid. Contains lysine, arginine, histidine, cystine, calcium, sulfur. Hemostatic. Dose, 5–10 gm.

10. **Bezoar from Gall Bladder of the Rhinoceros**
    Taste bitter. Antitoxin, cardiotonic, antipyretic, sedative, diuretic. Dose, 200–375 mg.

 狗	 馬	 狒 狒	 皮 猬
11	11	12	13

11. **Bezoar from Horses, Dogs**
    Taste saline. Calcium carbonate, magnesium carbonate, magnesium phosphate. Sedative, antispasmodic in convulsions, insomnia, spastic cough, also antitoxin in measles. Dose, 1–4 gm.

12. **Bezoar from Gall Bladder of Apes and Monkeys**
    Taste saline-bitter. Antispasmodic, sedative. Dose, 1–2 gm.

13. **Hide of the Hedgehog,** *Erinaecus koreanus*
    Astringent, hemostatic in hemorrhoids, enterorrhagia, involuntary emissions, peptic ulcer.

14. **Scales of the Anteater,** *Manis pentadactyla*
    Taste saline, fetid. Lactagogue, to hasten suppuration in skin diseases, and analgesic in arthralgia. Dose, 5–10 gm.

 鯉 鯪	 臍肭膃	 肝 獺	 雞
14	15	16	17

15. **Genitalia of the Male Sea Lion,** *Callotaria ursina*
Taste saline. Contains 16% protein, androsterone. Tonic in impotence, sterility, neurasthenia. Dose, 2–4 gm.

16. **Liver of the Otter,** *Lutra vulgaris*
Odor fetid. Contains glycogen, vitamins A and B. For pulmonary cough, nictalopia. Dose, 4–7 gm.

17. **Gastric Tissue of Domestic Fowl**
Taste bitter. Stomachic, digestive. Dose, 4–7 gm.

18. **Egg, Chicken**
Egg white as nutrient, demulcent in chronic throat disorders. Egg yolk in heart disease. Eggshell in gastritis, rachitis, pulmonary tuberculosis, scrofula. Membrane in asthma.

蟾蜍	五靈脂	瑇瑁	鱉甲
19	20	21	22

19. **Dried Venom of the Toad,** *Bufo vulgaris*
Taste sweet, pungent. Poisonous. Contains bufotoxins, bufogins, bufotolins. Cardiotonic, analgesic, diuretic in cardiac edema, venous stasis, cardiasthenia, as antidote for ulcers, abscesses, tumors, septicemia. Dose, 22–37 mg.

20. **Guano of the Bat,** *Pleropus pselaphon*
Taste sweet-bitter-saline, odor fetid. Analgesic, emmenagogue. Dose, 4–10 gm.

21. **Shell of the Tortoise,** *Chelonia imbricata*
Taste sweet. Antidote, antipyretic, antispasmodic in blood poisoning, smallpox, heat convulsions, febrile delirium. Dose, 3–8 gm.

22. **Shell of the Tortoise,** *Trionyx sinensis*
Taste saline. Contains gelatin, iodine, copper, vitamin D. Antipyretic, tonic. Dose, 10–18 gm.

	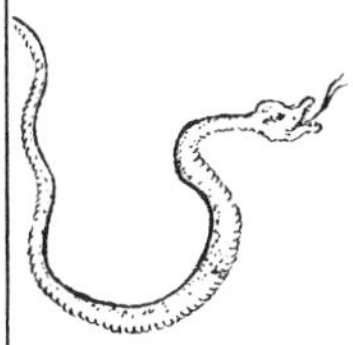		
蚧 蛤	蛇花白	蠶殭白	蚓蚯頸白
23	24	25	26

23. **Tail of the Red Spotted Lizard,** *Phrynosoma cornuta*
Taste saline. Mildly poisonous. Stimulant, tonic in asthma, pulmonary tuberculosis, neurasthenia. Dose, the tail of one male and of one female together.

24. **Body of the Viper** (head discarded) *Agkistrodon acutus*
Taste sweet, astringent. Poisonous. Antisyphilitic, anthelmintic. Dose, 4–10 gm.

25. **The Silkworm,** *Bombyx mori*
Stiffened silkworm used in infantile convulsions, night cries, tonsillitis, trachitis, in apoplexy, deafness. Silkworm moth as nerve stimulant, and in impotence. Silkworm excreta as sedative, analgesic in arthritis, paralysis, headache. Silkworm chrysalis in dyspepsia, malnutrition, diabetes mellitus. Silkworm cocoon as antiemetic, anthelmintic, and in diabetes mellitus.

26. **The Earthworm,** *Perichaeta communissma*
Taste saline. Antipyretic, bronchodilator, hypotensor. Dose, 5–10 gm.

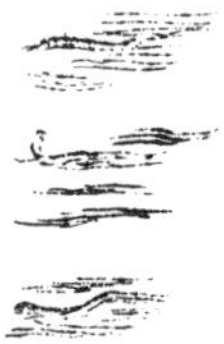		
水蛭	桑螵蛸	蟬蛻
27	28	29

27. **Dried Leech,** *Hirudo nipponica*
Taste bitter-saline. Poisonous. Contains hirudin. Anticoagulant. Dose, 3–4 gm.

28. **Chrysalis of the Praying Mantis,** *Tenodera aridifolia*
Taste sweet-saline. Tonic in impotence, spermatorrhea, enuresis. Dose, 4–7 gm.

29. **Exuviae of the Cicada,** *Cryptotympana pustulata*
Taste saline-sweet. Antipyretic, antispasmodic in febrile headache, colds, convulsions. Dose, 3–5 gm.

30. **The Cricket,** *Gryllodes berthellus*
In cystoparalysis, urethrospasm. Dose, 1–2 pair (male and female).

 蛄 螻	 蠍	 房蜂露	 蜜 蜂
31	32	33	34

31. **The Mole-Cricket,** *Gryllotalpa africana*
Taste saline. Diuretic. Dose, 4–10 gm.

32. **Tail of the Scorpion**
Taste saline-pungent. Poisonous. Antispasmodic, nerve tonic. Dose, 40–100 mg.

33. **Nest of the Wasp or Hornet**
Taste pungent. Antispasmodic, anthelmintic, in prurigo, eczema. Dose, 1–2 gm.

34. **Honey**
20% water, 39% fructose, 35% dextrose, 1% sucrose, formic acid, coloring matter, aromatic substances, vitamins B_1 and C. Nutrient, demulcent, lenitive in chronic bronchitis, chronic constipation, peptic ulcer. Dose, 10–75 gm.

	 斑貓	 蝱虫	 海馬	 海螵蛸
	35	36	37	38

35. **Chinese Cantharides,** *Mylabris sidae, Cicindela chinensis*
Taste pungent. Poisonous. Contains cantharidin. Externally as vesicant.

36. **Body of the Gadfly** (wings removed) *Tabanus bovinui*
Taste bitter-saline. Emmenagogue. Dose, 2–4 gm.

37. **The Sea Horse,** *Hippocampus coronatus*
Taste saline. Tonic, stimulant. Dose, 4–10 gm.

38. **Vertebrae of the Cuttlefish,** *Sepia esculenta*
Taste saline, astringent. Calcium phosphate, calcium chloride. In hyperchlorhydria, peptic ulcer. Dose, 5–10 gm.

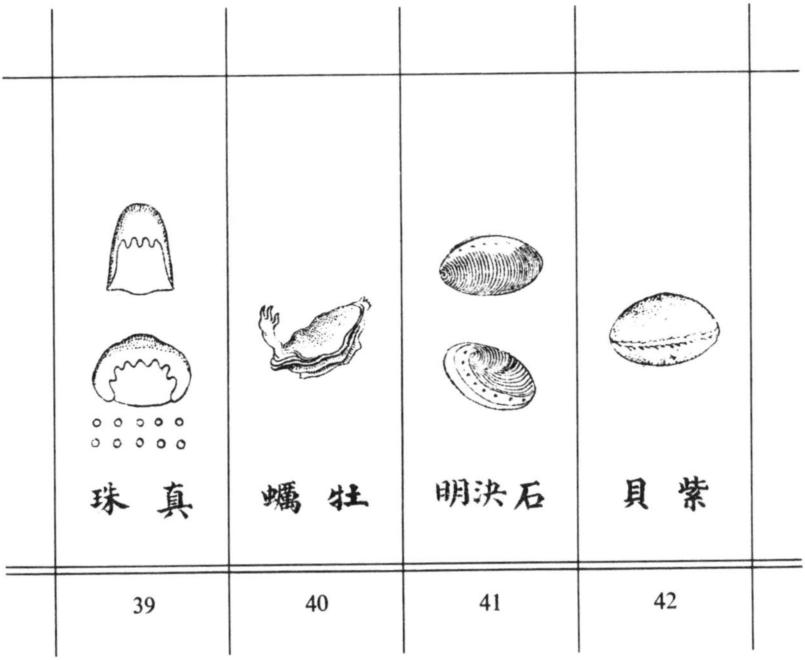

39. **Pearl of the Pearl Oyster**
91.72% calcium carbonate, 2.23% water, 5.94% organic matter. Taste saline. Sedative in insomnia, headache, convulsions. Dose, 400–1,100 mg. Topically in leukoma.

40. **Shell of the Oyster**
Taste saline. 75% calcium carbonate, 2% calcium phosphate. In hyperchlorhydria. Dose, 5–10 gm.

41. **Shell of the Sea-ear,** *Haliotis gigantea*
Taste saline. Sedative, alterative, hypotensor. Dose, 7–15 gm.

42. **Shell of the Cowrie,** *Cypraea macula*
Calcium salts. Sedative, antidote, antiphlogistic in insomnia, measles. Dose, 8–18 gm.

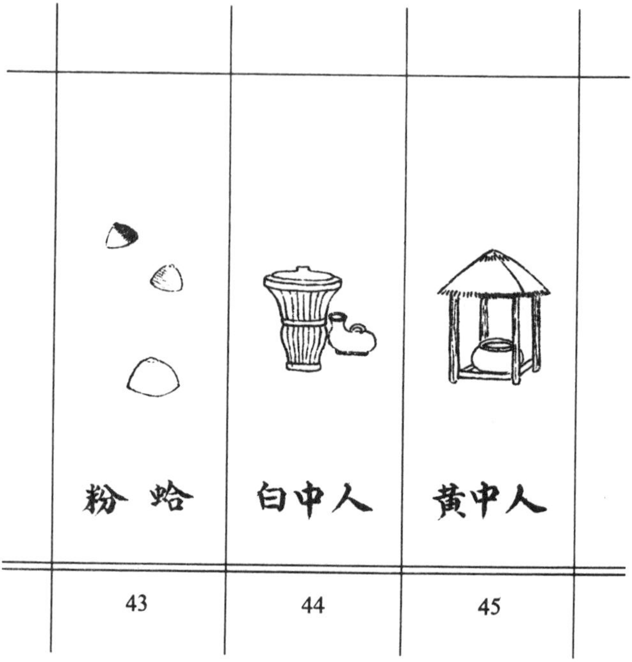

43. **The Shell of Bivalves**
Taste saline. Calcium. As source of calcium in hyperchlorhydria, tuberculosis, asthma. Dose, 7–15 gm.

44. **The Dried White Precipitate found in Urinary Chamber Pots**
Taste saline, fetid. Tonic, antiphlogistic in pulmonary tuberculosis, hematuria. Dose, 2–4 gm. Externally in epistaxis, gum boil, mouth sores, laryngitis, eczema.

45. **Powdered Licorice Root which has been enclosed in a bamboo case and buried in a cesspool for one winter, the case being hung to dry thoroughly, and the Licorice extracted**
Taste sweet-saline. Antipyretic, antidote in septicemia. Dose, 2–4 gm. in pills.

童便	人胞	髮
46	47	48

46. **The Clear Urine of healthy boys under 12 years of age**
Nutrient tonic, hemostatic in pulmonary tuberculosis, chronic cough, neurasthenia.

47. **Dried Human Placenta**
Taste sweet-saline, fetid. In neurasthenia, impotence, infecundity, pulmonary tuberculosis. Dose, 3–5 gm.

48. **Human Hair, Calcined and Powdered**
Astringent, hemostatic in hematemesis, hematuria, menorrhagia, leukorrhea. Dose, 2–15 gm. Externally for epistaxis, bleeding gums.

APPENDIX IV
A COLLECTION OF CHINESE PRESCRIPTIONS

The following prescriptions, taken from Chinese medical books and dispensatories, are presented here as informative matter only, and are not intended by the author to be construed by the reader as reliable or in some instances even safe treatment of the corresponding maladies.

ABSCESS, PULMONARY

Take equal parts of:

Fritillaria verticillata
Croton tiglium, seed expressed of oil
Platycodon grandiflorum

Grind to powder. Dose, 375 mg. with hot water.

ALCOHOLIC POISONING

1. Prepare a decoction with one or more of the following:
   Coptis teeta, 3 gm.
   Pueraria thunbergiana, 4 gm.
   Sophora flavescens, 3 gm.
   Hovenia dulcis, q.s.
   Nelumbium nelumbo, rhizome, q.s.
2. Take of the following, ad lib.:
   Schizandra chinensis, fresh seed
   Amomum globosum, kernel
   Morus alba, juice of fresh fruit
3. In inebriation, prepare a decoction of:
   Areca catechu, 3 gm.
   Thea sinensis, q.s.
   Or take the following, ad lib.:
   Prunus mume, powdered

ALOPECIA

1. Prepare a paste of:
   Anemone cernua, fresh root
   Apply to the scalp daily.
2. Take equal quantities of the following:
   Abelmoschus manihot, flower
   Rheum officinale
   Scutellaria baicalensis
   Grind to a powder, add sesame oil to form an ointment. Apply to the scalp daily.
3. Take of:
   Brassica campestris, fresh seed

Grind to a pulp, mix in vinegar, strain. Apply this lotion to the scalp three times daily.

4. Prepare a lotion with:
   Morus alba, wood ashes, and juice of fresh fruit

   Apply to the scalp, allow to dry under sunlight.

ANEMIA

Atractylis ovata, 15 gm.
Angelica polymorpha, 15 gm.
Conioselinum univittatum, 15 gm.
Leonurus sibiricus, 8 gm.
Rubia cordifolia, 10 gm.
Lithospermum erythrorhizon, 8 gm.

Chop fine, add water 650 cc., decoct to 600 cc. Dose, 100 cc. three times a day.

ANHIDROSIS

1. Of colds. Take of the following:
   Pueraria thunbergiana, 2.5 gm.
   Zingiber officinale, fresh root, 1.5 gm.
   Cinnamomum cassia, 1.0 gm.
   Glycyrrhiza uralensis, 0.5 gm.
   Ephedra sinica, 1.5 gm.
   Zizyphus jujuba, 1.5 gm.
   Paeonia albiflora, 1.0 gm.

   Chop fine, add water 350 cc., decoct to 300 cc. Dose, 100 cc. three times a day.
2. Diaphoretics. Prepare a 300-cc. decoction with any one of the following:
   Imperata cylindrica, 9 gm.
   Angelica anomala, 5 gm.
   Asarum sieboldi, 5 gm.
   Picrorrhiza kurroa, 3 gm.

   Dose, 100 cc. three times daily.

ANTIDOTES

Prepare a decoction of one or more of the following:

Glycyrrhiza uralensis
Leonurus sibiricus
Phragmites communis
Cimicifuga foetida
Black soybeans

APOPLEXY

1. Combine the following:
   Polygonatum officinale, 5 gm.
   Paeonia moutan, root epidermis, 5 gm.
   Clematis chinensis, 5 gm.
   Angelica grosserrata, 5 gm.
   Pueraria thunbergiana, 7 gm.
   Ephedra sinica, 3 gm.
   Mentha arvensis, 1.5 gm.

   Chop fine, add water 350 cc., decoct to 300 cc. Dose, 100 cc. three times daily.
2. In spastic paralysis, hemiplegia. Combine:
   Ephedra sinica, 2 gm.
   Astragalus hoantchy, 2 gm.
   Scutellaria baicalensis, 1.5 gm.
   Angelica grosserrata, 4 gm.

   Chop fine, add water 350 cc., decoct to 300 cc. Dose, 100 cc. three times daily.

ASCITES

Combine and chop fine:

Ephedra sinica, 5 gm.
Rheum officinale, 2 gm.
Menispermaceae fam., 6 gm.
Alisma plantago, 7 gm.
Taraxacum officinale, 6 gm.
Cryptomeria japonica, wood, 10 gm.

Caesalpinia sappan, wood, 5 gm.
Add water 350 cc., decoct to 300 cc. Dose, 100 cc. three times a day.

ASTHMA

1. Combine:
   Ephedra sinensis, 2.5 gm.
   Asarum sieboldi, 1 gm.
   Zingiber officinale, 3 gm.
   Schizandra chinensis, 2 gm.
   Cinnamomum cassia, 5.5 gm.
   Pinellia tuberifera, 11 gm.
   Paeonia albiflora, 11 gm.
   Glycyrrhiza uralensis, 4 gm.
   Chop fine, add water 350 cc., decoct to 300 cc. Dose, 100 cc. three times daily.
2. Expectorant in emphysema. Combine equal parts of:
   Euphorbia pekinensis
   Euphorbia sieboldiana
   Sinapis alba
   Grind to a fine powder, add excipient, make into pills. Dose, 1 gm.

ATELECTASIS

Panax ginseng, 7.5 gm.
Angelica polymorpha, 7.5 gm.
Schizandra chinensis, 2 gm.
Citrus nobilis, 7.5 gm.
Polygala tenuifolia, 7.5 gm.
Paeonia albiflora, 7.5 gm.
Atractylis ovata, 5.5 gm.
Astragalus hoantchy, 7.5 gm.
Cinnamomum cassia, 2 gm.
Poria cocos, 11 gm.
Glycyrrhiza uralensis, 4 gm.
Rehmannia glutinosa, 11 gm.

Combine the above, chop fine, add water 350 cc., decoct to 300 cc. Dose, 100 cc. three times a day.

BERIBERI

1. Dry and wet types. Combine and chop fine:
   Areca catechu, 7.5 gm.
   Perilla frutescens, 5.5 gm.
   Poria cocos, 11 gm.
   Citrus medica, 5.5 gm.
   Chaenomeles sinensis, 11 gm.
   Poncirus trifoliata, 5.5 gm.
   Talc, 11 gm.
   Add water 350 cc., decoct to 300 cc. Dose, 100 cc. three times a day.
2. Fulminating type. Prepare a 300-cc. decoction from the following:
   Cinnamomum cassia, 7.5 gm.
   Paeonia albiflora, 5.5 gm.
   Anemarrhena asphodeloides, 7.5 gm.
   Atractylis ovata, 7.5 gm.
   Glycyrrhiza uralensis, 4 gm.
   Aconitum, secondary tuber, 7.5 gm.
   Siler divaricatum, 7.5 gm.
   Zingiber officinale, 7.5 gm.
   Dose, 100 cc. three times daily.

BLISTERS

Take one or both of the following:
Bletilla hyacinthina
Pinellia tuberifera

Grind to a fine powder, adding a quantity of wheat flour. Mix in water to form a smooth paste. Apply to the affected part.

BLOOD CLEANSER

Nelumbium nelumbo, leaves, 5 gm.
Conioselinum univittatum, 5 gm.
Paeonia albiflora, 5 gm.
Rehmannia glutinosa, 3 gm.
Paeonia moutan, 3 gm.

Leonurus sibiricus, 5 gm.
Artemisia vulgaris, 3 gm.
Carthamus tinctorius, 3 gm.
Rubia cordifolia, 4 gm.
Nepeta japonica, 3 gm.
Angelica anomala, 5 gm.
Thuja orientalis, leaf, 3 gm.
Caesalpinia sappan, wood, 5 gm.

Combine and chop fine. Add water 350 cc., decoct to 300 cc. Dose, 100 cc. three times a day.

BOILS, ULCERS, TUMORS, and SWELLINGS

As an internal remedy, prepare a decoction from one or more of the following:

Conioselinum univittatum, 10 gm.
Leonurus sibiricus, 10 gm.
Carthamus tinctorius, 5 gm.
Lithospermum erythrorhizon, 5 gm.
Nepeta japonica, 10 gm.
Angelica anomala, 10 gm.

Dose, 100 cc. three times a day.

BRONCHITIS

1. Prepare a 300-cc. decoction with one of the following prescriptions:
   a. *Polygonatum cirrhifolium*, 10 gm.
      Lycium chinense, 5 gm.
      Zizyphus jujuba, 3 gm.
      Anemarrhena asphodeloides, 5 gm.
      Belamcanda chinensis, 3 gm.
   b. *Polygonatum officinale*, 10 gm.
      Pinellia tuberifera, 3 gm.
      Poria cocos, 5 gm.
      Prunus armeniaca, kernel, 2 gm.
   c. *Thuja orientalis*, 5 gm.
      Polygala tenuifolia, 10 gm.
      Diospyros kaki, 2 each
   d. *Aster tataricus*, 10 gm.
      Typha latifolia, 5 gm.
      Prunus armeniaca, kernel, 2 gm.
      Fritillaria verticillata, 5 gm.
2. In catarrhal bronchitis, prepare a 300-cc. decoction from one of the following prescriptions:
   a. *Coix lachryma-jobi*, 10 gm.
      Polygonatum cirrhifolium, 5 gm.
      Adenophora verticillata, 5 gm.
   b. *Astragalus hoantchy*, 10 gm.
      Schizandra chinensis, 2 seeds
      Lycium chinense, 10 seeds
      Polygala tenuifolia, 5 gm.
   c. *Liriope spicata*, 10 gm.
      Ephedra sinica, 5 gm.
      Anemarrhena asphodeloides, 3 gm.

BRUISES

1. Mash to a pulp any of the following fresh herbs and apply to the affected part:
   Gynura pinnatifida
   Sambucus racemosa, root epidermis
   Raphanus sativus, root or leaves
2. For the bruising and swelling of fractures, powder and take mixed with wine:
   Bletilla hyacinthina, 7 gm.
   Mash and apply externally:
   Dipsacus chinensis, fresh leaf
   Gleditschia sinensis, pod
3. In metastasis, fever, gastralgia:
   Typha latifolia, 18 gm.
   Angelica polymorpha, 2 gm.
   Cinnamomum cassia, 2 gm.
   Combine and grind to a fine powder. Dose, 3.5 gm. mixed with wine.

BUBO

1. Prepare a decoction with one or both of the following:
   Belamcanda chinensis, 7 gm.
   Lycoris radiata, 5 gm.
   Dose, 100 cc. three times daily.
2. Grind to a fine powder:
   Musa basjo, leaf
   Add sesame oil to form an ointment, and apply to the affected part.

BURNS and SCALDS

1. Grind the following to a fine powder:
   Camellia japonica
   Bletilla hyacinthina
   Mix in sesame oil to form a smooth ointment. Apply to the affected part.
2. Prepare a concentrated decoction of:
   Panax ginseng
   Glycyrrhiza uralensis
   Apply as lotion to the affected part.
3. As analgesic, apply the fresh, mashed seeds of:
   Pyrus communis

CANITIES

1. Prepare a 300-cc. decoction with:
   Rehmannia glutinosa, 7 gm.
   Ligustrum japonicum, 6 gm.
   Nelumbium nelumbo, stamina, 10 gm.
   Dose, 100 cc. three times a day.
2. Take one or more of the following ad lib.:
   Polygonum multiflorum, steamed
   Rubus tokkura, mashed and steamed in wine
   Morus alba, fresh fruit, steamed in wine

CARBUNCLE and ANTHRAX

1. Combine the following:
   Angelica polymorpha, 7 gm.
   Polygonum multiflorum, 10 gm.
   Leonurus sibiricus, 8 gm.
   Lithospermum erythrorhizon, 6 gm.
   Cirsium japonicum, 8 gm.
   Rosa multiflora, root, 10 gm.
   Dianthus superbus, 6 gm.
   Cyperus rotundus, 6 gm.
   Echinops dahuricus, 7 gm.
   Caesalpinia sappan, 5 gm.
   Citrus nobilis, aged rind, 6 gm.
   Chop fine, add water 350 cc., decoct to 300 cc. Dose, 100 cc. three times daily.
2. Apply one or more of the following, mashed smooth, to the affected part:
   Arisaema thunbergii, fresh root
   Gynura pinnatifida, fresh root
   Boehmeria nivea, fresh root
   Musa basjo, fresh root

CARDIOTONICS

Prepare a decoction with one or more of the following:
Polygonatum cirrhifolium, 8 gm.
Polygonatum officinale, 8 gm.
Liriope spicata, 7 gm.
Rehmannia glutinosa, 7 gm.
Cinnamomum cassia, 6 gm.
Poria cocos, 7 gm.
Angelica polymorpha, 7 gm.

CARIES, DENTAL

Grind to a fine powder:

Xanthoxylum piperitum
Piper nigrum
Pistachia lentiscus, resin
Phaseolus mungo var. *subtrilobata*, bean

Mix into melted beeswax. Press into the affected cavity.

CEREBRAL HYPEREMIA

1. Combine and chop fine:
   Bupleurum falcatum, 10 gm.
   Clematis chinensis, 8 gm.
   Add water 350 cc., decoct to 300 cc. Dose, 100 cc. three times a day.
2. Cerebral anemia. Chop fine:
   Arisaema thunbergii, 10 gm.
   Poria cocos, 7 gm.
   Prepare a 300-cc. decoction. Dose, 100 cc. three times a day.

CHAPPING

Apply one or more of the following to the affected part:

Bletilla hyacinthina, powdered and mixed with water to a paste
Solanum melongana, root, decoction
Melia azedarach, fruit macerated in wine
Trichosanthes cucumeroides, seed macerated in wine

CHLOROSIS

Take one or more of the following:

Lilium japonicum, powdered, made into pills, dose 10–18 gm.
Trichosanthes japonica, juice of fresh root mixed with honey
Evonymus alata, branchlets, 4 gm.

CHOLERA

Prepare a 300-cc. decoction with the following:

Artemisia vulgaris, 10 gm.
Peucedanum decursivum, 7 gm.
Artemisia capillaris, 10 gm.
Elsholtzia cristata, 10 gm.
Lophanthus rugosus, 10 gm.
Cyperus rotundis, 6 gm.
Chaenomeles sinensis, 8 gm.
Magnolia officinalis, 7 gm.

Dose, 100 cc. three times a day.

CHOLOLITHIASIS

Prepare a decoction with the following:

Angelica polymorpha
Paeonia albiflora
Poncirus trifoliata
Tribulus terrestris
Melia azedarach, seed
Pinellia tuberifera
Commiphora myrrha
Citrus nobilis
Talc

CLAVUS, CALLOSITIES, and CORNS

1. Mash one or more of the following and apply to the affected part:
   Pinellia tuberifera, fresh tuber
   Bletilla hyacinthina, fresh root
   Nelumbium nelumbo, fresh rhizome
2. To soften corns on the foot, prepare a decoction with:
   Brassica campestris, fresh leaf
   Raphanus sativus, fresh leaf
   Add alum. Soak repeatedly to soften corn.

COLDS

1. Prepare a 300-cc. decoction with the following:
   Phragmites communis, 7 gm.
   Nepeta japonica, 7 gm.
   Angelica anomala, 8 gm.
   Asarum sieboldi, 7 gm.
   Cimicifuga foetida, 7 gm.
   Picrorrhiza kurroa, 5 gm.
   Cornus officinalis, 6 gm.
   Vitex trifolia, 5 gm.
   Phyllostachys puberula, 10 gm.
   Dose, 100 cc. three times daily.
2. Cold with anhidrosis, oliguria, chest pains. Prepare a decoction with:
   Pueraria thunbergiana, 5 gm.
   Cinnamomum cassia, 3 gm.
   Glycyrrhiza uralensis, 3 gm.
   Zizyphus jujuba, 4 gm.
   Ephedra sinica, 4 gm.
   Paeonia albiflora, 3 gm.
   Zingiber officinale, 4 gm.
   Dose, 100 cc. three times daily.
3. General body aches. Prepare a decoction with:
   Ephedra sinica, 4 gm.
   Glycyrrhiza uralensis, 3 gm.
   Atractylus ovata, 5 gm.
   Cinnamomum cassia, 3 gm.
   Prunus armeniaca, 7 kernels
   Dose, 100 cc. three times daily.
4. Children's colds. Take the following:
   Trichosanthes kirilowii, 1.5 gm.
   Powder the root, mix with milk.

COMEDONES

Apply one or more of the following nightly:
Bletilla hyacinthina, fresh root
Vitis serianaefolia, fresh root
Spirodela polyrhiza, fresh herb
Portulaca oleracea, decoction

CONCUSSION, CEREBRAL

Prepare a 300-cc. decoction with one or more of the following:
Ephedra sinica, 10 gm.
Aralia cordata, 12 gm.
Angelica grosserrata, 10 gm.
Artemisia capillaris, 8 gm.
Dose, 100 cc. three times daily.

CONJUNCTIVITIS

1. Prepare a 300-cc. decoction with the following:
   Plantago major, 8 gm.
   Ephedra sinica, 5 gm.
   Dose, 100 cc. three times daily.
2. Prepare a decoction with one or both of the following and use topically:
   Erythrina indica
   Sophora japonica

CONSTIPATION

1. Prepare a 300-cc. decoction with:
   Leonurus sibiricus, 7 gm.
   Carthamus tinctorius, 5 gm.
   Lithospermum erythrorhizon, 6 gm.
   Clematis chinensis, 7 gm.
   Rheum officinale, 2 gm.
   Dose, 100 cc. three times daily.
2. Scybalous constipation. Prepare a decoction with the following:
   Prunus amygdalis, kernel, 11 gm.
   Prunus persica, kernel, 7.5 gm.
   Pinus gen., seed, 11 gm.
   Thuja orientalis, seed, 11 gm.

Prunus japonica, kernel, 11 gm.
Citrus nobilis, 5.5 gm.
Dose, 100 cc. three times daily.

3. Constipation of senile hypomyxia. Prepare pills of equal quantities of:
Astragalus hoantchy
Poncirus trifoliata, unripe fruit
Clematis chinensis
Dose, ad lib.

CONTUSIONS

Apply one or more of the following fresh roots, mashed:
Achyranthes bidentata
Dipsacus chinensis
Drynaria fortunei
Boehmeria nivea
Vitis serianaefolia
Gynura pinnatifida

CONVULSIONS

1. Prepare a 300-cc. decoction with one of more of the following:
Acorus gramineus, 5 gm.
Arisaema thunbergii, 8 gm.
Asarum sieboldi, 6 gm.
Angelica grosserrata, 8 gm.
Dose, 100 cc. three times daily.
2. Infantile convulsions. Extract the juice from fresh leaves of:
Saxifraga sarmentosa
Add salt.

COUGH

1. Antitussive. Prepare a 300-cc. decoction with one or more of the following:
Asarum sieboldi, 6 gm.
Poria cocos, 6 gm.
Poncirus trifoliata, unripe fruit, 8 gm.
Trichosanthes kirilowii, kernel, 8 gm.
2. Powder the following:
Aster tataricus, 35 gm.
Tussilago farfara, 35 gm.
Stemona tuberosa, 20 gm.
Take 10 gm. of the above mixture with a decoction of:
Prunus mume, fruit
Zingiber officinale
3. Antitussive and expectorant. Prepare a 300-cc. decoction with:
Peucedanum decursivum, 7 gm.
Mentha arvensis, 5 gm.
Anemarrhena asphodeloides, 7 gm.
Magnolia officinalis, 8 gm.
Phyllostachys puberula, fresh leaf
Dose, 100 cc. three times a day.
4. Chronic dry cough. Prepare a decoction with:
Liriope spicata, 19 gm.
Pinellia tuberifera, 7.5 gm.
Adenophora verticillata, 11 gm.
Platycodon grandiflorum, 5.5 gm.
Peucedanum decursivum, 7.5 gm.
Arctium lappa, 5.5 gm.
Rice, 19 gm.
Dose, 100 cc. three times a day.

CUTS and INCISED WOUNDS

1. Prepare a decoction with one or more of the following and apply as lotion:
Achyranthes bidentata
Dipsacus asper
Drynaria fortunei
Boehmeria nivea
Vitis serianaefolia
2. Grind to a powder and apply to the affected part:

Pistachia lentiscus, resin
Caesalpinia sappan, wood
Amber

CYSTOPATHY

In retention of urine. Prepare a 300-cc. decoction of the following:

Gentiana gen., 5 gm.
Alisma plantago, 10 gm.
Dianthus superbus, 5 gm.
Kochia scoparia, 10 gm.
Phellodendron amurense, 5 gm.
Ulmus campestris, 10 gm.

Dose, 100 cc. three times daily.

DIABETES INSIPIDUS

Prepare a 300-cc. decoction with the following:

Phragmites communis, 10 gm.
Akebia quinata, 7 gm.
Alisma plantago, 8 gm.
Trichosanthes cucumeroides, root, 7 gm.
Asparagus lucidus, 7 gm.
Rosa multiflora, 8 gm.
Picrorrhiza kurroa, 5 gm.

Dose, 100 cc. three times daily.

DIABETES MELLITIS

Chop the following:

Quercus dentata, leaf, 5 gm.
Allium fistulosum, fresh white part, 3 gm.

Add water 200 cc., decoct to 150 cc. Dose, 150 cc.

DIAPHORESIS

1. Prepare a 300-cc. decoction with the following:

   Aconitum, prepared (?), 11 gm.
   Paeonia albiflora, 7.5 gm.
   Zingiber officinale, 3 slices
   Poria cocos, 11 gm.
   Atractylis ovata, 7.5 gm.

   Dose, 100 cc. three times daily.
2. Night sweats. Combine equal amounts of:

   Astragalus hoantchy
   Atractylis ovata
   Siler divaricatum

   Chop fine, take 10 gm. and add water 250 cc. Decoct to 200 cc. Dose, 100 cc.

DIARRHEA

1. Prepare a 300-cc. decoction with one or more of the following:

   Panax ginseng, 7 gm.
   Pueraria thunbergiana, 10 gm.
   Anemarrhena asphodeloides, 7 gm.
   Smilax china, 8 gm.
   Poria cocos, 7 gm.

   Dose, 100 cc.
2. Watery stools. Prepare a decoction with:

   Rosa multiflora, 12 gm.
   Evodia ruaecarpa, 8 gm.
3. Diarrhea with gastralgia. Prepare a 300-cc. decoction with the following:

   Coptis teeta, 10 gm.
   Rheum officinale, 3 gm.
   Sophora japonica, 7 gm.
   Punica granatum, 5 gm.

   Dose, 100 cc. three times daily.
4. Chronic diarrhea. Prepare a decoction with:

   Sanguisorba officinalis, 7 gm.
   Cimicifuga foetida, 7 gm.

   Dose, 100 cc. three times daily.

DIURETICS

1. Prepare a 300-cc. decoction with the following:
   Leonurus sibiricus, 7 gm.
   Lithospermum erythrorhizon, 5 gm.
   Taraxacum officinale, 7 gm.
   Imperata cylindrica, 5 gm.
   Clematis chinensis, 7 gm.
   Rheum officinale, 1 gm.
   Artemisia capillaris, 5 gm.
   Dose, 100 cc. three times daily.
2. Prepare a decoction with:
   Poria cocos, 10 gm.
   Atractylis ovata, 5 gm.
   Zingiber officinale, 1 gm.
   Glycyrrhiza uralensis, 1 gm.
   Dose, 100 cc. three times daily.
3. Combine and grind to a fine powder:
   Rehmannia glutinosa, 10 gm.
   Cornus officinalis, 5 gm.
   Paeonia moutan, 4 gm.
   Dioscorea japonica, 5 gm.
   Poria cocos, 4 gm.
   Alisma plantago, 4 gm.
   Cinnamomum cassia, 2.5 gm.
   Aconitum, secondary tuber, 2.5 gm.
   Achyranthes bidentata, 1.5 gm.
   Plantago major, 2.5 gm.
   Make pills. Dose, 12 gm.

EDEMA, DROPSY

Prepare a 300-cc. decoction with the following:

Leonurus sibiricus, 10 gm.
Lithospermum erythrorhizon, 5 gm.
Phragmites communis, 5 gm.
Rheum officinale, 2 gm.
Elsholtzia cristata, 10 gm.
Poria cocos, 7 gm.
Poncirus trifoliata, 10 gm.
Evodia rutaecarpa, 6 gm.

Dose, 100 cc. three times daily.

DYSENTERY

Prepare a 300-cc. decoction with one or more of the following:

Conioselinum univittatum, 10 gm.
Rubia cordifolia, 8 gm.
Sanguisorba officinalis, 10 gm.
Pueraria thunbergiana, 10 gm.
Cimicifuga foetida, 10 gm.
Sophora flavescens, 7 gm.
Rheum officinale, 3 gm.
Cyperus rotundus, 7 gm.
Anemone cernua, 10 gm.
Thuja orientalis, 10 gm.
Hibiscus syriacus, 8 gm.

Dose, 100 cc. three times daily.

DYSPEPSIA

Prepare a 300-cc. decoction with one of the following prescriptions:

a. *Picrorrhiza kurroa*, 10 gm.
   Pueraria thunbergiana, 5 gm.
   Rheum officinale, 0.5 gm.
   Platycodon grandiflorum, 5 gm.
b. *Rheum officinale*, 1 gm.
   Magnolia officinalis, 5 gm.
   Poncirus trifoliata, 2 gm.
   Mirabilite, 1 gm., added after decocting

EARACHE

Imbue cotton with a paste of one or more of the following fresh herbs, and insert into the affected ear:

Acorus gramineus
Melia azedarach, fruit

Phytolacca acinosa
Arctium lappa

ECZEMA

1. Prepare a decoction with one or more of the following and use as lotion:
   Nepeta japonica
   Spirodela polyrhiza
   Xanthium strumarium, seed
   Sophora japonica, seed
2. Grind to a fine powder and apply externally:
   Phellodendron amurense, 10 gm.
   Portulaca oleracea, 20 gm.

EDEMA, PULMONARY

Prepare a 300-cc. decoction with one of the following prescriptions:

a. *Ephedra sinica*, 5 gm.
   Pinellia tuberifera, 3 gm.
   Asarum sieboldi, 3 gm.
   Schizandra chinensis, 10 gm.
b. *Draba nemorosa*, 5 gm.
   Ulmus campestris, 10 gm.
   Asparagus lucidus, 5 gm.
c. *Atractylis ovata*, 5 gm.
   Vitis serianaefolia, 5 gm.
   Asparagus lucidus, 10 gm.
   Imperata cylindrica, 3 gm.

Dose, 100 cc. three times daily.

ENTERITIS

Poncirus trifoliata, 7.5 gm.
Rheum officinalis, 5.5 gm.
Crataegus cuneata, 7.5 gm.
Scutellaria baicalensis, 5.5 gm.
Poria cocos, 11 gm.
Coptis teeta, 3 gm.
Magnolia officinalis, 4 gm.
Citrus nobilis, 7.5 gm.

Prepare a 300-cc. decoction. Dose, 100 cc.

ENTERORRHAGIA

Prepare a decoction with one or more of the following:

Sanguisorba officinalis, 7 gm.
Nepeta japonica, 8 gm.
Angelica anomala, 10 gm.
Equisetum hyemale, 6 gm.
Punica granatum, 5 gm.

Dose, 100 cc. three times daily.

ENURESIS

Prepare a 225-cc. decoction with one of the following prescriptions:

a. *Rosa multiflora*, 5 gm.
   Prunella vulgaris, 3 gm.
b. *Dioscorea sativa*, 5 gm.
   Angelica anomala, 3 gm.

Dose, 75 gm. three times daily.

EPILEPSY

1. Grind to a fine powder:
   Thuja orientalis, kernel, 10 gm.
   Picrorrhiza kurroa, 6 gm.
   Amber, 7 gm.
   Dose, 7.5 gm. three times daily, dispersed in liquid.
2. Grind to a fine powder:
   Perilla frutescens, seed, 50 gm.
   Arctium Lappa, seed, 30 gm.
   Stiffened silkworms, 20 gm.
   Cinnabar, 10 gm.
   Mix with fresh juice of:
   Zingiber officinale
   Dose, 1 teaspoonful.

EPISTAXIS

1. Prepare a 300-cc. decoction with one or more of the following:

Rehmannia glutinosa, 5 gm.
Cirsium japonicum, 10 gm.
Imperata cylindrica, 10 gm.
Nepeta japonica, 10 gm.
Nelumbium nelumbo, leaf, 10 gm.
Dose, 100 cc. three times daily.

2. Grind to a fine powder and inhale as snuff:
   Sanguisorba officinalis
   Typha latifolia
   Lycoperdaceae fam.
   Trachycarpus fortunei, calcined fiber

ERYSIPELAS

1. Prepare a 300-cc. decoction with:
   Belamcanda chinensis, 10 gm.
   Echinops dahuricus, 5 gm.
   Polygonum aviculare, 5 gm.
   Spirodela polyrhiza, 10 gm.
   Dose, 100 cc. three times daily.
2. Apply one or more of the following fresh herbs externally:
   Boehmeria nivea
   Portulaca oleracea
   Brassica campestris
   Sedum purpureum
   Sambucus javanica

EXPECTORANTS

1. Prepare a 300-cc. decoction with one or more of the following:
   Platycodon grandiflorum, 10 gm.
   Fritillaria verticillata, 10 gm.
   Rubia cordifolia, 5 gm.
   Citrus nobilis, rind, 3 gm.
   Dose, 100 cc. three times a day.
2. Take of the following:
   Poria cocos, 1.5 gm.
   Zingiber officinale, fresh root, 2 slices
   Pinellia tuberifera, 2 gm.
   Add water 150 cc. Decoct to 100 cc. Take as one dose.

FACIAL ERUPTIONS

1. Combine and powder equal parts of the following:
   Xanthium strumarium
   Magnolia officinalis
   Citrus nobilis, rind
   Add water to form a smooth paste and apply topically.
2. Take the fresh flowers of:
   Hibiscus mutabilis
   Bruise and apply to the affected area. Or use the dried flower, powdered and mixed with egg albumen.

MELANODERMA, FACIAL

Prepare a 300-cc. decoction with:
Angelica anomala
Apply as needed.

FAVUS

Prepare a paste with one of the following and apply externally:
Stemona tuberosa, fresh root
Bletilla hyacinthina, fresh root
Gardenia florida, fresh fruit

FEVER

Prepare a 300-cc. decoction with one or more of the following:
Imperata cylindrica
Phragmites communis
Nepeta japonica
Pueraria thunbergiana
Bupleurum falcatum
Ephedra sinica
Rheum officinale

Artemisia capillaris
Melia azedarach
Dose, 100 cc. three times a day.

FRECKLES

Combine and powder equal parts of:
Arctium lappa
Tulipa edulis
Prunus persica, flower
Benincasa cerifera, kernel
Poria cocos
Mix with egg albumen, apply daily before retiring.

FROSTBITE

Extract the juice of one or more of the following and apply as lotion:
Vitis serianaefolia, fresh root
Zingiber officinale, fresh root
Dioscorea japonica, fresh root
Nelumbium nelumbo, fresh rhizome

FURUNCLE

Apply one or more of the following:
Ulmus macrocarpa, fresh kernel grated and combined with suet
Arctium lappa, bruised leaves
Leonurus sibiricus, grated seed

GASTRALGIA

1. Combine and powder equal parts of the following:
   Alpinia officinarum
   Cyperus rotundus
   Citrus nobilis
   Angelica polymorpha
   Conioselinum monnieri
   Paeonia albiflora
   Dose, 5 gm. before meals.
2. Gastralgia of cholera. Prepare a 300-cc. decoction with:
   Lophanthus rugosus, 5 gm.
   Dose, 100 cc. three times a day.
3. Colic. Prepare a 300-cc. decoction with the following:
   Equisetum hyemale, 5 gm.
   Platycodon grandiflorum, 3 gm.
   Foeniculum vulgare, 5 gm.
   Dose, 100 cc. three times a day.
4. Flatulence. Prepare a 300-cc. decoction with the following:
   Sanguisorba officinalis, 5 gm.
   Sophora flavescens, 2 gm.
   Dose, 100 cc. three times daily.

GASTRIC ATONY

Prepare a 300-cc. decoction with the following:
Codonopsis tangshen, 3 gm.
Atractylis ovata, 2 gm.
Poria cocos, 3 gm.
Glycyrrhiza uralensis, 2 gm.
Citrus nobilis, 2 gm.
Pinellia tuberifera, 2 gm.
Angelica polymorpha, 3 gm.
Paeonia albiflora, 2 gm.
Dose, 100 cc. three times a day.

GASTROSPASM

1. Prepare a 300-cc. decoction with the following:
   Trichosanthes japonica, kernel, 5 gm.
   Allium odorum, 10 gm.
   Pinellia tuberifera, 5 gm.
   Dose, 100 cc. three times daily, with wine added.
2. Prepare a 300-cc. decoction with the following:
   Poncirus trifoliata, unripe fruit, 5 gm.
   Magnolia officinalis, 10 gm.

Allium odorum, white portion, 10 gm.
Cinnamomum cassia, 2 gm.
Trichosanthes japonica, kernel, 3 gm.
Dose, 100 cc. three times a day.

GINGIVITIS

Combine and powder the following:
Rheum officinale, 5 gm.
Gardenia florida, 10 gm.
Forsythia suspensa, 10 gm.
Scutellaria baicalensis, 10 gm.
Glycyrrhiza uralensis, 4 gm.
Mentha arvensis, 7 gm.
Phyllostachys puberula, 10 gm.
Mirabilite, 5 gm.
Dose, 6 gm. three times daily, taken with honey.

GLOSSITIS

1. Prepare a 200-cc. decoction with the following and use as mouthwash:
   Bupleurum falcatum, 4 gm.
   Lycium chinense, 4 gm.
2. Use as mouthwash:
   Citrullus vulgaris, juice of fresh fruit

GOITER

1. Prepare a 300-cc. decoction with the following:
   Laminaria japonica, 5 gm.
   Sargassum siliquastrum, 5 gm.
   Prunella vulgaris, 7 gm.
   Pinellia tuberifera, 7 gm.
   Dose, 100 cc. three times daily.
2. Apply one or more of the following to the affected area:
   Ricinus communis, seed powdered and mixed with flour and water
   Portulaca oleracea, charred, powdered, and mixed with suet
   Anemone cernua, fresh root minced to a paste

GONORRHEA

1. Prepare a 600-cc. decoction with the following:
   Leonurus sibiricus, 5 gm.
   Imperata cylindrica, 5 gm.
   Phragmites communis, 7 gm.
   Juncus effusus, 8 gm.
   Plantago major, 7 gm.
   Dianthus superbus, 7 gm.
   Kochia scoparia, 7 gm.
   Lygodium japonicum, 5 gm.
   Echinops dahuricus, 5 gm.
   Taraxacum officinale, 7 gm.
   Dose, 100 cc. three times a day.
2. Painful urination. Take of the following ad lib.:
   Portulaca oleracea, succus of fresh herb
   Cirsium japonicum, juice of fresh root
   Coix lachryma-jobi, decoction
   Imperata cylindrica, decoction
3. Gleet. Combine the following:
   Humulus japonicum, juice of fresh root, 400 cc.
   Vinegar, 50 cc.
   Dose, ad lib.

HEADACHE

1. Prepare a 200-cc. decoction with the following:
   Cimicifuga foetida, 3 gm.
   Xanthium strumarium, 3 gm.
   Nelumbium nelumbo, 1 leaf

Dose, 100 cc. or 200 cc., as needed.

2. Prepare a 100-cc. decoction with the following:
   Asarum sieboldi, 2 gm.
   Cyperus rotundus, 2 gm.
   Conioselinum univittatum, 2 gm.
   Dose, 100 cc.
3. Combine and powder equal parts of the following:
   Conioselinum univittatum
   Angelica polymorpha
   Xanthium strumarium
   Dose, 3 gm. before retiring.

HELMINTHIASIS

1. Prepare a decoction with one or more of the following:
   Artemisia vulgaris, 10 gm.
   Thuja orientalis, 10 gm.
   Erythrina indica, 7 gm.
   Gleditschia sinensis, 7 gm.
   Xanthoxylum piperitum, 3 gm.
   Dose, 100 cc. three times daily.
2. Taeniasis. Combine and powder:
   Pharbitis hederacea, 20 gm.
   Areca catechu, 20 gm.
   Mylitta lapidescens, 5 gm.
   Aspidium falcatum, 0.750 gm.
   Inula helenium, 5 gm.
   Dose, 10–15 gm. before breakfast.
   To prevent nausea, add:
   Hematite, 10 gm.
   Paeonia albiflora, 10 gm.
3. Ascariasis. Combine and powder equal parts of:
   Punica granatum
   Melia azedarach
   Aspidium falcatum
   Areca catechu
   Dose, 7.5–10.0 gm. before breakfast.
4. Enterobiasis. Combine and powder equal quantities of:
   Torreya grandis
   Areca catechu
   Ulmus macrocarpa
   Dose, 10 gm. before breakfast.
5. Ancylostomiasis. Combine and powder:
   Quisqualis indica, 10 gm.
   Punica granatum, 2.5 gm.
   Areca catechu, 2.5 gm.
   Dose, 7.5 gm. before breakfast.

HEMATEMESIS

1. Prepare a 300-cc. decoction with one or more of the following:
   Artemisia vulgaris, 3 gm.
   Rubia cordifolia, 3 gm.
   Sanguisorba officinalis, 7 gm.
   Imperata cylindrica, 2 gm.
   Plantago major, 5 gm.
   Dose, 100 cc. three times daily.
2. As follow-up medication, prepare a 400-cc. decoction with:
   Thuja orientalis, 10 gm.
   Zingiber officinalis, 3 gm.
   Artemisia vulgaris, 5 gm.
   Dose, 100 cc.

HEMORRHOIDS

1. Prepare a 300-cc. decoction with one or more of the following:
   Rubia cordifolia, 3 gm.
   Lithospermum erithrorhizon, 3 gm.
   Cimicifuga foetida, 5 gm.
   Equisetum hyemale, 2 gm.
   Aster trinervius, 3 gm.
   Anemone cernua, 5 gm.
   Dose, 100 cc. three times daily.
2. Prepare a decoction with one or

more of the following and employ as lotion to the affected part:

Sophora japonica
Cirsium japonicum
Portulaca oleracea

HOARSENESS

1. Combine and powder:
   Prunus armeniaca, toasted, 1 gm.
   Cinnamomum cassia, 0.4 gm.
   Make into pills with honey as excipient. Dose, ad lib.
2. Combine and powder equal parts of:
   Mentha arvensis
   Polygonum tinctorium
   Make into pills with honey. Dose, ad lib.

HYPERCHLORHYDRIA and HYPOCHLORHYDRIA

1. Hyperchlorhydria. Combine and powder:
   Coptis teeta, 6 gm.
   Evodia rutaecarpa, 1 gm.
   Dose, 2.5 gm. as pills.
2. Hypochlorhydria. Combine and powder equal parts of the following:
   Prunus mume
   Asarum sieboldi
   Zingiber officinalis
   Angelica polymorpha
   Coptis teeta
   Xanthoxylum piperitum
   Cinnamomum cassia
   Panax ginseng
   Phellodendron amurense
   Dose, 1.5 gm. as pills, three times daily.

HYSTERIA

Prepare a 300-cc. decoction with one of the following:

Arisaema Thunbergii, 7 gm.
Menispermaceae fam., 8 gm.

Dose, 100 cc. three times daily.

IMPOTENCE

Prepare a 300-cc. decoction with one or more of the following:

Selinum monnieri, 8 gm.
Epimedium macranthum, 7 gm.
Achyranthes bidentata, 7 gm.
Cimicifuga foetida, 7 gm.
Dioscorea sativa, 5 gm.
Acanthopanax spinosum, 6 gm.
Asparagus lucidus, 10 gm.

Dose, 100 cc. three times daily.

INCONTINENCE of URINE

1. Prepare a decoction with one or more of the following:
   Cimbotium barometz, 10 gm.
   Achyranthes bidentata, 7 gm.
   Trichosanthes kirilowii, 8 gm.
   Rosa multiflora, 7 gm.
   Sophora flavescens, 6 gm.
   Dioscorea sativa, 6 gm.
   Curculigo ensifolia, 5 gm.
   Dose, 100 cc. three times daily.
2. Take of the following, dispersed in rice water:
   Lyndera strychnifolia, 7 gm.

INSOLATION

Prepare a 200-cc. decoction with one or more of the following:

Artemisia vulgaris, 3 gm.
Coptis teeta, 5 gm.
Elsholtzia cristata, 5 gm.
Lophanthus rugosus, 5 gm.

Dose, 100 cc. twice daily.

INSOMNIA

Prepare a 300-cc. decoction with one or more:

Hybiscus syriacus, 10 gm.
Juncus effusus, 5 gm.
Ulmus campestris, 10 gm.

Dose, 100 cc. three times daily.

JAUNDICE

1. Combine and powder the following:
   Artemisia capillaris, 7.5 gm.
   Cinnamomum cassia, 5.5 gm.
   Atractylis ovata, 5.5 gm.
   Poria cocos, 18 gm.
   Alisma plantago, 7.5 gm.
   (No dose given)
2. Prepare a 300-cc. decoction with one or more:
   Rubia cordifolia, 4 gm.
   Imperata cylindrica, 3 gm.
   Clematis chinensis, 5 gm.
   Rheum officinale, 1 gm.
   Artemisia capillaris, 4 gm.
   Phellodendron amurense, 2 gm.
   Dose, 100 cc. three times daily.

LACQUER POISONING

Prepare a decoction with one or more and employ as lotion:

Melia azedarach
Nelumbium nelumbo, leaf
Xanthoxylum piperitum

LARYNGITIS

1. Prepare a 400-cc. decoction with:
   Belamcanda chinensis, 15 gm.
   Dose, 50 cc. Gargle well, then swallow.
2. Laryngeal swelling. Combine, toast, and powder:
   Scrophularia oldhami, 3.5 gm.
   Arctium lappa, 3.5 gm.
   Dose, 3.5 gm. twice daily, dispersed in liquid.

LEPROSY

1. Prepare a 300-cc. decoction with one or more of the following:
   Acorus gramineus, 10 gm.
   Sophora flavescens, 7 gm.
   Kochia scoparia, 10 gm.
   Gleditschia sinensis, 6 gm.
   Dose, 100 cc. three times daily.
2. Combine and powder:
   Rheum officinale, 20 gm.
   Gleditschia sinensis, thorns, 20 gm.
   Dose, 3.5 gm. before meals.
3. Prepare a decoction with:
   Nepeta japonica, 3 gm.
   Mentha arvensis, 2 gm.
   Add to the decoction:
   Verbena officinalis, powdered, 3.5 gm.
4. Employ as topical medication:
   Hydnocarpus anthelmintica, oil
   Spirodela polyrhiza, decoction

LEUCODERMA

1. Prepare a 300-cc. decoction with the following:
   Bletilla hyancinthina, 5 gm.
   Gardenia florida, two seeds
   Dose, 100 cc. three times daily.
2. Combine:
   Green hull of *Juglans regia*, mashed
   Sulfur
   Employ topically.

LIVER TONIC

Prepare a 300-cc. decoction with one or more:

Pinellia tuberifera, 5 gm.
Prunella vulgaris, 3 gm.
Polygonum multiflorum, 6 gm.
Ligustrum japonicum, 3 gm.
Conioselinum univittatum, 5 gm.
Eucommia ulmoides, 7 gm.
Paeonia albiflora, 6 gm.
Carthamus tinctorius, 4 gm.
Lycium chinense, 7 gm.

LUMBAGO

1. Prepare a 300-cc. decoction with one or more:
   Paeonia albiflora, 8 gm.
   Angelica grosserrata, 10 gm.
   Salvia multiorhiza, 10 gm.
2. Prepare a 100-cc. decoction with the following:
   Corydalis ambigua, 3 gm.
   Piper nigrum, 3 gm.
   Mix with rice wine and take as a single dose.
3. Combine and powder:
   Foeniculum vulgare, 10 gm.
   Poncirus trifoliata, 10 gm.
   Commiphora myrrha, 5 gm.
   Dose, 3 gm. dispersed in hot rice wine.

MACULAE

Prepare a salve from one or more of the following fresh botanicals by grinding until smooth and incorporating vinegar. Apply to the affected part.

Gynura pinnatifida
Arisaema thunbergii
Euphorbia lathyris (poisonous)

The above may also be used in dried form, by powdering and mixing with flour and making into a paste, or by making into ointment.

MARASMUS, INFANTILE

1. Prepare a 100-cc. decoction with:
   Picrorrhiza kurroa, 1 gm.
   Add honey 10 gm. Divide into three doses daily.
2. Prepare a 100-cc. decoction with one of the following:
   Bupleurum falcatum, 3 gm.
   Peucedanum decursivum, 3 gm.
   Dose, 33 cc. three times daily.
3. Combine and powder equal parts of:
   Aloe vera
   Quisqualis indica
   Add Glycyrrhiza powder, q.s. Dose, 3–5 gm. in broth.

MEASLES

1. Prepare a 300-cc. decoction with one or more:
   Cimicifuga foetida, 10 gm.
   Scrophularia oldhami, 10 gm.
   Ephedra sinica, 5 gm.
   Phyllostachys puberula, 10 gm.
   Aspidium falcatum, 8 gm.
   Dose, 100 cc. three times daily.
2. Fever of Measles. Prepare a 300-cc. decoction with:
   Cimicifuga foetida, 8 gm.
   Pueraria thunbergiana, 5 gm.
   Paeonia albiflora, 3 gm.
   Glycyrrhiza uralensis, 1 gm.
   Dose, 100 cc. three times daily.
3. Fever with cough. Prepare a 300-cc. decoction:
   Morus alba, 10 gm.

Arctium lappa, 3 gm.
Platycodon grandiflorum, 3 gm.
Nepeta japonica, 5 gm.
Spirodela polyrhiza, 2 gm.
Lycium chinense, root epidermis, 5 gm.
Glycyrrhiza uralensis, 1 gm.

Dose, 100 cc. three times daily.

4. Lesions. Prepare a 300-cc. decoction:

Panax ginseng, 3 gm.
Anemarrhena asphodeloides, 1 gm.
Arctium lappa, 1 gm.
Cimicifuga foetida, 5 gm.
Phyllostachys nigra, 5 gm.
Glycyrrhiza uralensis, 1 gm.
Forsythia suspensa, 2 gm.
Lycium chinense, root epidermis, 3 gm.
Gypsum, 1 gm.
Glutinous rice, q.s.

Dose, 100 cc. three times daily.

5. For the final stages of the disease, after rash and fever have declined. Prepare a 300-cc. decoction:

Panax ginseng, 3 gm.
Asparagus lucidus, 5 gm.
Schizandra chinensis, 5 gm.
Rehmannia glutinosa, 2 gm.
Ligustrum japonicum, 3 gm.
Anemarrhena asphodeloides, 1 gm.
Paeonia albiflora, 2 gm.
Citrus nobilis, 1 gm.
Glycyrrhiza uralensis, 1 gm.

Dose, 100 cc. three times daily.

MENSTRUAL DISORDERS

1. Amenorrhea. Prepare a 300-cc. decoction with one or more:

Achyranthes bidentata, 7 gm.
Belamcanda chinensis, 7 gm.
Paeonia albiflora, 7 gm.
Paeonia moutan, 6 gm.
Carthamus tinctorius, 8 gm.

Dose, 100 cc. three times daily.

2. Irregular menstruation. Grind to a powder:

Scutellaria baicalensis, soaked in rice wine until it turns purple, then toasted until dry, 7 gm.

Disperse the powder in a decoction of:

Angelica polymorpha, 5 gm.

Take as a single dose.

3. Dysmenorrhea. Powder equal parts of the following:

Angelica polymorpha
Corydalis ambigua
Carthamus tinctorius

Dose, 7 gm. dispersed in warm rice wine.

4. Menopause. Prepare a 300-cc. decoction:

Rubia cordifolia, 6 gm.

Dose, 100 cc. three times daily.

5. Leucorrhea. Prepare a 300-cc. decoction with one or more of the following:

Acorus gramineus, 10 gm.
Polygonum multiflorum, 8 gm.
Angelica anomala, 7 gm.
Cyperus rotundis, 7 gm.
Althaea rosea, 7 gm.
Leonurus sibiricus, 8 gm.
Artemisia vulgaris, 10 gm.
Rubia cordifolia, 8 gm.
Cirsium japonicum, 7 gm.
Cimicifuga foetida, 7 gm.
Fraxinus bungeana, 6 gm.
Caesalpinia sappan, 5 gm.

Punica granatum, 6 gm.
Dose, 100 cc. three times daily.
Or take one of the following, powdered:
Trachycarpus fortunei, 5 gm.
Celosia argentea var. *cristata*, 7 gm.
Prunella vulgaris, 7 gm.

6. Metrorrhagia, menorrhagia. Powder the following:
   Typha latifolia, 35 gm.
   Scutellaria baicalensis, 35 gm.
   Nelumbium nelumbo, leaf, 18 gm.
   Dose, 7 gm. before meals, dispersed in rice wine.

MENTAL DISORDERS

Prepare a 300-cc. decoction with the following:
Lilium japonicum, 10 gm.
Coptis teeta, 5 gm.
Anemarrhena asphodeloides, 10 gm.
Dose, 100 cc. three times daily.

MILIARIA (PRICKLY HEAT)

Apply one or more of the following:
Trichosanthes kirilowii, starch of root, powdered
Xanthium strumarium, ash, powdered and mixed with salt
Morus alba, ash, powdered
Prunella vulgaris, concentrated decoction

MOLES

Apply one of the following nightly:
Brassica campestris, seed, ground into a paste
Morus alba, ash, prepared into a concentrated decoction

NAUSEA

1. Prepare a 300-cc. decoction with the following:
   Evodia rutaecarpa, 10 gm.
   Panax ginseng, 5 gm.
   Zingiber officinale, 1 gm.
   Zizyphus jujuba, 2 gm.
   Dose, 100 cc. three times daily.
2. Prepare a 225-cc. decoction with:
   Phragmites communis, 10 gm.
   Elsholtzia cristata, 5 gm.
   Dose, 75 cc. three times daily.
3. Emesis with resultant thirst. Prepare a 300-cc. decoction:
   Poria cocos, 5 gm.
   Cinnamomum cassia, 2 gm.
   Atractylis ovata, 2 gm.
   Alisma plantago, 10 gm.
   Glycyrrhiza uralensis, 1 gm.
   Zingiber officinale, 1 gm.
   Dose, 100 cc. three times daily.
4. Gastric fever. Prepare a 300-cc. decoction:
   Pinellia tuberifera, 3 gm.
   Phyllostachys puberula, 10 gm.
   Zingiber officinale, 1 gm.
   Pueraria thunbergiana, 2 gm.
   Glycyrrhiza uralensis, 1 gm.
   Zizyphus jujuba, 1 gm.
   Dose, 100 cc. three times daily.
5. Nausea. Prepare a 300-cc. decoction:
   Pinellia tuberifera, 10 gm.
   Phragmites communis, 5 gm.
   Bupleurum falcatum, 5 gm.
   Dose, 100 cc. three times daily.
6. Prepare a 300-cc. decoction:
   Magnolia officinalis, 10 gm.
   Coptis teeta, 5 gm.
   Phragmites communis, 5 gm.
   Dose, 100 cc. three times daily.

NEURALGIA

1. Prepare a 300-cc. decoction with one or more:
   Conioselinum univittatum, 8 gm.
   Paeonia moutan, 7 gm.
   Siegesbeckia orientalis, 7 gm.
   Akebia quinata, 7 gm.
   Thuja orientalis, 6 gm.
   Acanthopanax spinosum, 8 gm.
   Erythrina indica, 8 gm.
   Dose, 100 cc. three times daily.
2. Powder equal parts of the following:
   Corydalis ambigua
   Angelica polymorpha
   Cinnamomum cassia
   Dose, 3 gm. dispersed in liquid.
3. Combine and apply topically to the affected area:
   Phyllostachys bambusoides, powdered
   Egg white

NYCTALOPIA

Combine and grind to powder the following:
Rehmannia glutinosa, 25 gm.
Dioscorea japonica, 22 gm.
Cornus officinalis, 12 gm.
Poria cocos, 10 gm.
Alisma plantago, 10 gm.
Paeonia moutan, 10 gm.
Cinnamomum cassia, 3 gm.
Cyperus rotundis, 3 gm.
Make into pills the size of soybeans. Dose, 15 to 30 pills, twice daily.

OPHTHALMIA

1. Prepare a 300-cc. decoction with one or more:
   Sophora flavescens, 7 gm.
   Asarum sieboldi, 6 gm.
   Celosia argentea, seed, 5 gm.
   Angelica anomala, 7 gm.
   Dose, 100 cc. three times daily.
2. Prepare a decoction with one or more of the following and employ topically:
   Rhus cotinus
   Schizandra chinensis
   Vitex trifolia

ORCHITIS

1. Prepare a powder with:
   Nepeta japonica
   Dose, 5 gm.
2. Apply one or more of the following topically:
   Brassica campestris, juice of fresh root
   Raphanus sativum, juice of fresh root
   Nelumbium nelumbo, leaf, decoction
   Vinegar

OTORRHEA

Express the juice of one of the following fresh herbs and employ as lavage to the ear:
Mentha arvensis
Artemisia annua
Leonurus sibiricus
Saxifraga sarmentosa

PARALYSIS

1. Prepare a 300-cc. decoction with one or more:
   Atractylis ovata, 7 gm.
   Angelica polymorpha, 8 gm.
   Conioselinum univittatum, 8 gm.
   Rehmannia glutinosa, 7 gm.

Siegesbeckia orientalis, 8 gm.
Akebia quinata, 6 gm.
Phellodendron amurense, 6 gm.
Erythrina indica, 6 gm.
Dose, 100 cc. three times daily.

2. Combine and powder the following:
Dioscorea sativa, 10 gm.
Eucommia ulmoides, 3 gm.
Dose, 7 gm. dispersed in liquid.

PAVOR NOCTURNUS (NIGHT TERRORS)

1. Prepare a decoction with:
Coptis teeta, 3 gm.
Glycyrrhiza uralensis, 1 gm.
Bamboo leaves, 20
2. Disperse the following in milk:
Angelica polymorpha, 0.5 gm.

PEDICULOSIS

Prepare a concentrated decoction with one or more of the following and apply externally:
Pharbitis hederacea
Stemona tuberosa
Erythrina indica
Gleditschia sinensis

PEMPHIGUS

Apply one or more of the following externally:
Cunninghamia sinensis, concentrated decoction
Phellodendron amurense, powdered
Portulaca oleracea, powdered
Hibiscus mutabilis, fresh flowers, ground to paste
Prunus persica, leaves, ground to paste and mixed with vinegar

PERITONITIS

1. Prepare a decoction with one or more of the following:
Paeonia albiflora, 7 gm.
Plantago major, 8 gm.
Aspidium falcatum, 7 gm.
Cinnamomum cassia, 7 gm.
Poncirus trifoliata, 10 gm.
Gleditschia sinensis, 8 gm.
Dose, 100 cc. three times daily.
2. Combine and powder the following:
Thuja orientalis, kernel, 15 gm.
Amber, 9 gm.
Dose, 8 gm. three times daily.

PERTUSSIS

1. Take one of the following powders three times daily:
Trichosanthes japonica, 4 gm.
Anemarrhena asphodeloides, 3 gm.
Draba nemorosa, 5 gm.
2. Powder:
Prunus armeniaca, 7 gm.
Aster tataricus, 10 gm.
Form into 10 pills with honey. Dose, 1 pill every 2 hours, taken with a decoction of:
Schizandra chinensis
3. Take the following decoction several times daily:
Peucedanum decursivum, 3 gm.
Phyllostachys nigra, ad lib.
4. Powder:
Anemarrhena asphodeloides, 15 gm.
Glycyrrhiza uralensis, 7 gm.
Stir into honey. Divide into 10 doses daily.

PHALLALGIA

1. Prepare a 300-cc. decoction with:
   Dioscorea sativa, 5 gm.

   Dose, 100 cc. three times daily.
2. Powder equal parts of the following:
   Evodia rutaecarpa
   Foeniculum vulgare
   Areca catechu

   Form into pills. Dose, several pills before meals taken with salt water.
3. Combine and employ topically:
   Selinum monnieri, powdered
   Egg yolk

PLEURISY

1. Dry pleurisy. Prepare a 300-cc. decoction:
   Bupleurum falcatum, 10 gm.
   Peucedanum decursivum, 3 gm.
   Conioselinum univittatum, 5 gm.

   Dose, 100 cc. three times daily.
2. Powder the following:
   Morus alba, root epidermis, 11 gm.
   Lycium chinense, root epidermis, 11 gm.
   Glycyrrhiza uralensis, 4 gm.
   Rice, 7.5 gm.

   Dose, 9 gm.
3. Purulent pleurisy. Prepare a 300-cc. decoction with:
   Trichosanthes japonicum, starch of root, 5 gm.
   Menispermaceae, 10 gm.
   Clematis chinensis, 5 gm.
   Cinnamomum cassia, 3 gm.

   Dose, 100 cc. three times daily.
4. Purulent pleurisy with edema. Prepare a 300-cc. decoction:
   Menispermaceae, 10 gm.
   Magnolia officinalis, 5 gm.
   Poncirus trifoliata, 5 gm.
   Ephedra sinica, 3 gm.

   Dose, 100 cc. three times daily.

PNEUMONIA

Prepare a 300-cc. decoction with one of the following formulas. Dose, 100 cc. three times daily.

1. *Imperata cylindrica*, 5 gm.
   Polygonatum cirrhifolium, 10 gm.
   Poria cocos, 5 gm.
2. *Morus alba*, root epidermis, 10 gm.
   Stemona tuberosa, 5 gm.
   Lycium chinense, 5 gm.
   Ephedra sinica, 3 gm.
3. *Imperata cylindrica*, 5 gm.
   Morus alba, root epidermis, 5 gm.
   Asparagus lucidus, 10 gm.
   Anemarrhena asphodeloides, 3 gm.

POLYPUS, NASAL

1. Employ a concentrated decoction of one of the following as a lavage:
   Tribulus terrestris
   Coptis teeta
2. Powder equal quantities of:
   Lagenaria vulgaris
   Cucumis melo

   Add a small amount of:
   Musk, powdered

   Employ as snuff.

POLYURIA

Powder the following:

Lycium chinense, 15 gm.
Rubus tokkura, 20 gm.
Cuscuta japonica, 20 gm.
Plantago major, 20 gm.
Schizandra chinensis, 5 gm.

Make into pills Dose, 12 gm. twice daily.

PREGNANCY and CHILDBIRTH

1. Morning sickness. Powder equal quantities of:
   Cyperus rotundis
   Lophanthus rugosus
   Glycyrrhiza uralensis
   Dose, 7 gm.
2. Vaginal discharge. Prepare a 300-cc. decoction with one of the following:
   Acorus gramineus, 8 gm.
   Angelica polymorpha, 10 gm.
   Conioselinum univittatum,10 gm.
   Anemarrhena asphodeloides, 8 gm.
   Gynura pinnatifida, 5 gm.
   Eucommia ulmoides, 8 gm.
   Dose, 100 cc. three times daily.
3. Constipation of pregnancy. Take of the following ad lib.:
   Perilla frutescens, juice of fresh herb
   Cannabis sativa, seed
   Barley malt
4. Puerperal fever. Prepare a 300-cc. decoction with one:
   Bupleurum falcatum, 7 gm.
   Pueraria thunbergiana, 8 gm.
   Angelica anomala, 10 gm.
   Dose, 100 cc. three times daily. Or take of the following, dispersed in rice wine:
   Sophora japonica, seed, 3 gm.
5. Dystocia. Take one of these, powdered:
   Anemarrhena asphodeloides, 8 gm.
   Abelmoschus mannihot, 7 gm.
   Or take of the following, in decoction:
   Leonurus sibiricus, 10 gm.
6. To guard against miscarriage. Prepare a decoction with:
   Cirsium japonicum, 10 gm.
   Anemarrhena asphodeloides, 10 gm.
   Take two to three times daily. Or prepare the following decoction:
   Angelica polymorpha, 10 gm.
   Ulmus campestris, 10 gm.
   Zingiber officinale, q.s.
   Take two to three times daily.
7. After miscarriage. Take one of the following powders, dispersed in rice wine:
   Carthamus tinctorius, 10 gm.
   Malva verticillata, 3 gm.
   Or prepare a 100-cc. decoction with:
   Angelica polymorpha, 3 gm.
   Conioselinum univittatum, 1.5 gm.
8. Postpartum gastralgia. Prepare a 300-cc. decoction with the following:
   Aspidium falcatum, 7 gm.
   Arethusa japonica, 7 gm.
   Dose, 100 cc. three times daily. Or prepare equal parts of the following, powdered:
   Lindera strychnifolia
   Angelica polymorpha
   Dose, 10 gm. before meals.
9. Postpartum hemorrhage. Prepare a 200-cc. decoction with:
   Evodia rutaecarpa, 10 gm.
   Artemisia vulgaris, 10 gm.
   Zingiber officinale, 10 gm.

Dose, 100 cc. twice daily.

10. Puerperal night sweats. Prepare a 100-cc. decoction with:
    Evodia rutaecarpa, 5 gm.

    Take with rice wine.
11. Puerperal diarrhea. Take one or more of the following ad lib.:
    Xanthium strumarium, juice of fresh herb, mixed with wine
    Amaranthus mangostanus, leaves, cooked in cereal
    Duchesnea indica, seed, decoction

PROLAPSUS ANI

1. Prepare a 300-cc. decoction with one of the following:
    Cimicifuga foetida, 7 gm.
    Equisetum hyemale, 10 gm.

    Dose, 100 cc. three times daily.
2. Prepare a concentrated decoction of:
    Punica granatum

    Add alum. Employ as lotion to the affected area.

RENAL TONICS

1. Prepare a 300-cc. decoction with one or more of the following:
    Schizandra chinensis, 7 gm.
    Pinellia tuberifera, 7 gm.
    Rehmannia glutinosa, 7 gm.
    Alisma plantago, 10 gm.
    Cyperus rotundis, 8 gm.
    Cornus officinalis, 6 gm.
    Lycium chinense, 7 gm.
    Eucommia ulmoides, 8 gm.
    Ligustrum japonicum, 7 gm.
    Phellodendron amurense, 5 gm.
    Nelumbium nelumbo, stamina, 8 gm.
    Artemisia vulgaris, 8 gm.
    Cassia tora, 6 gm.
    Rhododendron metternichii, 8 gm.

    Dose, 100 cc. three times daily.
2. Disperse one or more of the following powdered drugs in 300 cc. liquid:
    Thuja orientalis, kernel, 6 gm.
    Euryale ferox, 7 gm.
    Polygonum multiflorum, 10 gm.

    Dose, 100 cc. three times daily.

RETENTION of URINE

Powder the following:
Anemarrhena asphodeloides, 20 gm.
Phellodendron amurense, 20 gm.
Cinnamomum cassia, 2 gm.

Dose, 8 gm. as pills.

RHEUMATISM

Prepare a 300-cc. decoction with one or more:
Prunella vulgaris, 7 gm.
Conioselinum univittatum, 10 gm.
Paeonia albiflora, 8 gm.
Siegesbeckia orientalis, 5 gm.
Nepeta japonica, 7 gm.
Angelica anomala, 8 gm.
Xanthium strumarium, fruit, 7 gm.
Akebia quinata, 8 gm.
Cinnamomum cassia, 7 gm.
Eucommia ulmoides, 8 gm.
Morus alba, 10 gm.
Rhododendron metternichii, 7 gm.
Gleditschia sinensis, 7 gm.

Dose, 100 cc. three times daily.

RHINITIS and SORE THROAT

Prepare a 300-cc. decoction with:

Allium fistulosum, fresh, 11 gm.
Platycodon grandiflorum, 5.5 gm.
Gardenia florida, 5.5. gm.
Glycyrrhiza uralensis, 4 gm.
Mentha arvensis, 5.5 gm.
Forsythia suspensa, 11 gm.
Salted black soybeans, 11 gm.
Phyllostachys, fresh leaves, 30 each

Dose, 100 cc. three times daily

RHINOCLEISIS

1. Prepare a 300-cc. decoction with one or more:
   Platycodon grandiflorum, 10 gm.
   Asarum sieboldi, 5 gm.
   Akebia quinata, 15 gm.
   Magnolia liliflora, 10 gm.
   Phyllostachys puberula, epidermis, 10 gm.
   Dose, 100 cc. three times daily.
2. Powder and employ as snuff:
   Gleditschia sinensis

RINGWORM

Powder one or more of the following, mix into an ointment base, and apply to the affected area:

Selinum monnieri
Ulmus macrocarpa
Lycium chinense, root epidermis

SCABIES

1. Prepare a 300-cc. decoction with one or more of the following:
   Salvia miltiorhiza, 7 gm.
   Lonicera japonica, 8 gm.
   Mentha arvensis, 7 gm.
   Artemisia apiacea, 8 gm.
   Selinum monnieri, 6 gm.
   Dose, 100 cc. three times daily.
2. Prepare a concentrated decoction with one or more of the following and apply topically:
   Stemona tuberosa
   Coptis teeta
   Celosia argentea
   Polygonum multiflorum
   Artemisia vulgaris

SCROFULA

Prepare a 300-cc. decoction with one or more:

Polygonum multiflorum, 5 gm.
Nepeta japonicum, 3 gm.
Mentha arvensis, 3 gm.
Xanthium strumarium, 5 gm.
Tulipa edulis, 7 gm.
Anemone cernua, 5 gm.
Voila patrinii, 3 gm

Dose, 100 cc. three times daily.

SCROTAL ECZEMA

Powder one or more of the following and apply as a dusting powder:

Selinum monnieri
Acorus gramineus
Typha latifolia

SINGULTUS and SPASTIC DIAPHRAGM

1. Prepare a 300-cc. decoction with the following:
   Citrus nobilis, 1.5 gm.
   Phyllostachys puberula, epidermis, 2 gm.
   Glycyrrhiza uralensis, 1 gm.
   Panax ginseng, 2 gm.
   Pinellia tuberifera, 2 gm.
   Liriope spicata, 3 gm.
   Poria cocos, 2 gm.

Eriobotrya japonica, 2 gm.
Coptis teeta, 0.75 gm.
Evodia rutaecarpa, 0.50 gm.
Dose, 100 cc. three times daily.

2. Prepare a decoction of the following and take ad lib.:
   Diospyros kaki, peduncle
   Zingiber officinale
3. Grind into a powder and take as snuff to induce sneezing:
   Gleditschia horrida

SLEEPING SICKNESS

Prepare a 300-cc. decoction with the following:
Akebia quinata, 10 gm.
Thea sinensis, 6 gm.
Dose, 100 cc. three times daily.

SMALLPOX

1. Prepare a 300-cc. decoction with one or more of the following:
   Astragalus hoantchy, 10 gm.
   Carthamus tinctorius, 7 gm.
   Lithospermum erythrorhizon, 8 gm.
   Pueraria thunbergiana, 10 gm.
   Bupleurum falcatum, 8 gm.
   Cimicifuga foetida, 8 gm.
2. Prepare a 300-cc. decoction with the following:
   Paeonia moutan, 2 gm.
   Paeonia albiflora, 2 gm.
   Rehmannia glutinosa, 7 gm.
   Rhinoceros horn, 1 gm.
   Dose, 100 cc. three times daily.

SORE THROAT

1. Prepare a 300-cc. decoction with the following:
   Gypsum, 2 gm.
   Gardenia florida, 3 gm.
   Phyllostachys puberula, 30 leaves, fresh
   Anemarrhena asphodeloides, 4 gm.
   Scrophularia oldhami, 5 gm.
   Alisma plantago, 2 gm.
   Nelumbium nelumbo, 1 leaf, fresh
   Dose, 100 cc. three times daily.
2. Prepare a decoction with the following and employ as gargle:
   Glycyrrhiza uralensis, 2 gm.
   Platycodon grandiflorum, 2 gm.
   Mentha arvensis, 3 gm.
   Rehmannia glutinosa, 5 gm.
   Gypsum, 10 gm.

SORES and INFLAMMATIONS

Prepare a decoction with one or more and apply as lotion:
Anemarrhena asphodeloides
Punica granatum

SPERMATORRHEA

1. Combine and powder the following:
   Panax ginseng, 5 gm.
   Asparagus lucidus, 5 gm.
   Rehmannia glutinosa, 10 gm.
   Phellodendron amurense, 15 gm.
   Hedychium coronarium, 5 gm.
   Glycyrrhiza uralensis, 5 gm.
   Dose, 8 gm. as pills.
2. Combine and powder:
   Nelumbium nelumbo, seed, 14 gm.
   Euryale ferox, seed, 2 gm.
   Xanthoxylum piperitum, 6 gm.
   Typha latifolia, 14 gm.
   Allium odorum, seed, 14 gm.
   Dose, 7 gm. three times daily, dispersed in liquid.

3. Prepare a 300-cc. decoction with one or more of the following:
   Nelumbium nelumbo, staminae, 10 gm.
   Artemisia vulgaris, 7 gm.
   Dioscorea sativa, 6 gm.
   Echinops dahuricus, 7 gm.
   Poria cocos, 6 gm.
   Dose, 100 cc. three times daily.

STOMATITIS

1. With fever and oliguria. Prepare a 300-cc. decoction with:
   Rehmannia glutinosa, 6 gm.
   Poria cocos, 3 gm.
   Paeonia moutan, 1.5 gm.
   Juncus effusus, 8 gm.
   Nelumbium nelumbo, seed, 2 gm.
   Liriope spicata, 5 gm.
   Phyllostachys puberula, 3 gm.
   Talc, 2 gm.
   Glycyrrhiza uralensis, 1 gm.
   Cinnabar, 750 mg.
   Dose, 100 cc. three times daily.
2. Vincent's gingivitis. Combine and powder:
   Mirabilite, 3 gm.
   Rheum officinale, 3 gm.
   Gardenia florida, 6 gm.
   Forsythia suspensa, 6 gm.
   Scutellaria baicalensis, 6 gm.
   Glycyrrhiza uralensis, 2 gm.
   Mentha arvensis, 4 gm.
   Phyllostachys puberula, 6 gm.
   Dose, 6 gm. three times daily, taken with honey.
3. Gangrenous stomatitis. Prepare a 300-cc. decoction with:
   Aloe vera, 2 gm.
   Bupleurum falcatum, 2 gm.
   Picrorrhiza kurroa, 2 gm.
   Arctium lappa, 2 gm.
   Scrophularia oldhami, 2 gm.
   Platycodon grandiflorum, 2 gm.
   Gardenia florida, 2 gm.
   Mentha arvensis, 2 gm.
   Phyllostachys puberula, 2 gm.
   Gypsum, 2 gm.
   Antelope horn, 2 gm.
   Dose, 100 cc. three times daily.

SYPHILIS

Prepare a 300-cc. decoction with:
Smilax china, 10 gm.
Lonicera japonica, 10 gm.
Dose, 100 cc. three times daily.

TABEFACTION

Prepare a 300-cc. decoction with one or more:
Astragalus hoantchy, 7 gm.
Panax ginseng, 7 gm.
Polygala tenuifolia, 6 gm.
Liriope spicata, 8 gm.
Angelica polymorpha, 8 gm.
Bupleurum falcatum, 7 gm.
Dose, 100 cc. three times daily.

TETANUS

Prepare a 300-cc. decoction with one or more:
Carthamus tinctorius, 8 gm.
Lithospermum erythrorhizon, 8 gm.
Drynaria fortunei, 5 gm.
Dose, 100 cc. three times daily.

THIRST

Prepare a 300-cc. decoction with one or more:
Polygonatum officinale, 5 gm.
Imperata cylindrica, 3 gm.
Phragmites communis, 3 gm.

Boehmeria nivea, 6 gm.
Pueraria thunbergiana, 8 gm.
Anemarrhena asphodeloides, 5 gm.
Morus alba, 8 gm.
Hibiscus syriacus, root epidermis, 7 gm.

Dose, 100 cc. three times daily.

THRUSH

Prepare a concentrated decoction of one of the following and apply topically:

Rosa multiflorum, root
Castanea sp., involucre
Phellodendron amurense

To the above may be added:

Borax, 5 gm.
Cinnabar, 3 gm.

TINNITUS

1. Prepare a 300-cc. decoction with one or more:
   Bupleurum falcatum, 10 gm.
   Asarum sieboldi, 7 gm.
   Akebia quinata, 8 gm.
   Dose, 100 cc. three times daily.
2. Express the fresh juice from one of the following and apply in the ear:
   Rehmannia glutinosa
   Drynaria fortunei
   Acorus gramineus

TONICS for GENERAL VIGOR

1. Prepare a 300-cc. decoction with one or more:
   Artemisia vulgaris, 7 gm.
   Kochia scoparia, 7 gm.
   Selinum monnieri, 7 gm.
   Epimedium macranthum, 8 gm.
   Sophora flavescens, 7 gm.
2. Combine and powder:
   Plantago major, 10 gm.
   Kochia scoparia, 12 gm.
   Selinum monnieri, 12 gm.
   Eugenia caryophyllata, 10 gm.
   Dose, 5 gm.

TONICS for LONGEVITY

Take one or more of the following powders:

Panax ginseng, 5 gm.
Ligustrum japonicum, 6 gm.
Polygonum multiflorum, 3 gm.
Polygonatum cirrhifolium, 2 gm.
Plantago major, 7 gm.
Cuscuta japonica, 5 gm.
Epimedium macranthum, 6 gm.
Cornus officinalis, 8 gm.
Nelumbium nelumbo, staminae, 5 gm.
Lycium chinense, seed, 6 gm.

TOOTHACHE

Prepare a decoction with one or more of the following and employ as mouthwash:

Anemone cernua
Rosa multiflorum
Angelica anomala
Selinum monnieri
Asarum sieboldi
Quercus dentata

TUBERCULOSIS

1. Prepare a 300-cc. decoction with one or more:
   Arisaema thunbergii, 8 gm.
   Sargassum siliquastrum, 10 gm.
   Scirpus maritimus, 8 gm.
   Clematis chinensis, 8 gm.
   Achyranthes bidentata, 10 gm.

Draba nemorosa, 8 gm.
Tulipa edulis, 7 gm.
Belamcanda chinensis, 8 gm.
Dose, 100 cc. three times daily.

2. Pulmonary tuberculosis. Prepare a 300-cc. decoction:
   Adenophora verticillata, 5 gm.
   Artemisia annua, 3 gm.
   Fritillaria verticillata, 10 gm.
   Angelica polymorpha, 5 gm.
   Dose, 100 cc. three times daily.
   Or the following:
   Polygonum multiflorum, 5 gm.
   Cimicifuga foetida, 10 gm.
   Liriope spicata, 5 gm.
   Conioselinum univittatum, 3 gm.
   Or the following:
   Forsythia suspensa, 5 gm.
   Bletilla hyacinthina, 10 gm.
   Artemisia annua, 5 gm.
   Imperata cylindrica, 3 gm.
   Or the following:
   Phyllostachys puberula, epidermis, 10 gm.
   Ligustrum japonicum, 5 gm.
   Ephedra sinica, 3 gm.
   Platycodon grandiflorum, 3 gm.
   Or the following:
   Clematis japonica, 5 gm.
   Angelica anomala, 3 gm.
   Menispermaceae fam., 10 gm.
   Panax ginseng, 5 gm.
3. To encourage regrowth of connective tissue. Combine and powder:
   Panax ginseng, 5 gm.
   Bletilla hyacinthina, 5 gm.
   Fritillaria verticillata, 5 gm.
   Paeonia albiflora, 5 gm.
   Coix lachryma-jobi, 5 gm.
   Lilium japonicum, 5 gm.
   Pearl, 5 gm.
   Stalactite, 5 gm.
   Dose, 4 gm. dispersed in cooked cereal.
4. Expectorant. Prepare a 300-cc. decoction with:
   Adenophora verticillata, 3 gm.
   Lilium japonicum, 4 gm.
   Cynanchum atratum, 2 gm.
   Lycium chinense, root epidermis, 2 gm.
   Bupleurum falcatum, 1.5 gm.
   Zizyphus jujuba, kernel, 3 gm.
   Polygonatum officinale, 4 gm.
   Platycodon grandiflorum, 1.5 gm.
   Peucedanum decursivum, 1.5 gm.
   Arctium lappa, 1.5 gm.
   Aster tataricus, 2 gm.
   Poria cocos, 3 gm.
   Dose, 100 cc. three times daily.

ULCER, DERMAL

1. Prepare a concentrated decoction with one or more and apply to the affected area:
   Rosa multiflorum, root
   Boehmeria nivea
   Bletilla hyacinthina
   Anemarrhena asphodeloides
2. Powder one or more and prepare an ointment:
   Typha latifolia
   Phellodendron amurense
   Artemisia vulgaris, ash

ULCER, PEPTIC

Prepare a 300-cc. decoction with:
Laminaria japonica, 20 gm.
Cinnamomum cassia, 2 gm.
Allium odorum, fresh leaf, 10 gm.
Dose, 100 cc. three times daily.
Or use the following:

Hedychium coronarium, 5 gm.
Cinnamomum cassia, 5 gm.
Evodia rutaecarpa, 3 gm.

URETHRITIS

Prepare a 300-cc. decoction with:
Poria cocos, 6 gm.
Atractylis ovata, 5 gm.
Zingiber officinale, 2 gm.
Glycyrrhiza uralensis, 1 gm.
Dose, 100 cc. three times daily.

VERRUCA

Prepare a concentrated decoction with:
Kochia scoparia, 5 gm.
Artemisia vulgaris, 5 gm.
Add alum, 3 gm. Apply as lotion.

VERTIGO

1. Prepare a 300-cc. decoction with the following:
   Pinellia tuberifera, 2 gm.
   Bupleurum falcatum, 2 gm.
   Arisaema thunbergii, 1.5 gm.
   Siler divaricatum, 2 gm.
   Akebia quinata, 2 gm.
   Poria cocos, 1.5 gm.
   Dose, 100 cc. three times daily.
2. Prepare a 75-cc. decoction with:
   Sambucus javanica, 1.5 gm.
   Angelica grosserrata, 1.5 gm.
   Gypsum, 1 gm.
   Add rice wine, 25 cc. and take as a single dose.

VULVITIS

1. Prepare a concentrated decoction with one or more and apply topically:
   Lycium chinense, seed
   Chrysanthemum indicum
   Selinum monnieri
   Poncirus trifoliata
   Aegle sepiaria
2. Pruritis vulvae. Prepare a concentrated decoction and employ as lotion:
   Acanthopanax spinosum
   Selinum monnieri
   Cirsium japonicum
   Allium scorodoprasum

APPENDIX V

TABLE OF TOXIC HERBS

The following is a classification, after the Chinese pharmacists, of the degrees of toxicity of the poisonous botanicals.

1. **MILDLY POISONOUS**
   Anemone cernua
   Aspidium falcatum
   Curculigo ensifolia
   Dichroa febrifuga
   Ginkgo biloba
   Melia azedarach
   Mylitta lapidescens
   Pinellia tuberifera
   Prunus armeniaca
   Prunus persica
   Ricinus communis
   Tulipa edulis

2. **GENERALLY POISONOUS**
   Aconitum gen.
   Daphne genkwa
   Datura alba
   Euphorbia pekinensis
   Hydnocarpus anthelmintica
   Lycoris radiata
   Narcissus tazetta
   Papaver somniferum
   Paris polyphylla
   Pharbitis hederacea
   Phytolacca acinosa
   Rhododendron sinense
   Rhus vernicifera
   Strychnos nux-vomica
   Veratrum nigrum

3. **EXTREMELY POISONOUS**
   Croton tiglium
   Hyoscyamus niger

4. **POISONOUS ONLY WHEN FRESH** (before desiccation)
   Arisaema thunbergii
   Belamcanda chinensis

GLOSSARY OF BOTANICAL TERMS

acaulose: acaulescent; apparently stemless; the proper stem, bearing the leaves and flowers, being very short or subterranean
accrete: accrescent; growing larger after flowering
achene: a one-seeded, seed-like fruit
acuminate: taper-pointed
acute: merely sharp-pointed, or ending in a point less than a right angle
adnate: growing fast to; born adherent; the anther is adnate when fixed by its whole length to the filament or its prolongation
albumen: nourishing matter stored up with the embryo of a seed, but not within the embryo
alternate: one after another; petals are alternate with the sepals, or stamens with the petals, when they stand over the intervals between them
amylaceous: starch-like
annulate: marked by rings
anther: the essential part of the stamen, which contains the pollen
anthesis: the period of the act of the expansion of a flower
apetalous: destitute of petals
arborescent: tree-like, in size or form
aril: a fleshy growth forming a false coat or appendage to a seed
arillate: furnished with an aril
aristate: awned; *see* awn
articulate: jointed
attenuate: tapering gradually
auriculate: furnished with auricles or ear-like appendages
awl-shaped: sharp-pointed from a broader base
awn: the bristle or beard of barley, oats, etc., or any similar bristle-like appendage
axile: belonging to the axis, or occupying the axis

axillary: occurring in an axil (the angle on the upper side between a leaf and the stem)
axis: the central line of any body; the organ round which others are attached; the root and stem

bacciform: shaped like a berry
basal: belonging to or attached to the base
beaked: ending in a prolonged narrow tip
berry: a fruit pulpy or juicy throughout
bicornuate: having two horns
bidentate: having two teeth (not twice or doubly dentate)
biennial: of two years' continuance; springing from the seed one season, flowering and dying the next
bifid: divided into two equal lobes or parts
biflorous: with flowers in pairs
bifurcate: twice forked; forked into two branches
bilabiate: two-lipped
bilobate: two-lobed
bilocular: two-celled, as most anthers, which develop and contain pollen
bipartite: divided into two parts almost to the base, as a leaf
bipinnate: twice pinnate; *see* pinnate
bract: in general the leaves of an inflorescence, more or less different from ordinary leaves; specially, the small leaf or scale from the axil of which a flower or its pedicel (stalk) proceeds
bracteolate: furnished with bracteoles (bractlets), leaves or scales from whose axil flowers or stalks proceed
bracteole: bractlet; a bract seated on the pedicel or flower-stalk
bulbous: bulb-like in shape

caducous: dropping off very early, compared with other parts
callose: hardened; furnished with callosities or thickened spots
calycle: an involucre resembling the calyx (the external, usually leafy part of a flower) but consisting of a whorl of bracts below the calyx or resulting from the union of the sepal appendages
campanulate: bell-shaped
capillary: hair-like in shape
capitate: having a globular apex, like the head on a pin; or forming a head
capitulum: a close, rounded dense cluster or head of sessile flowers (those on no stalk, directly attached to the base)
carina: a keel; the two anterior petals of a papilionaceous (butterfly-shaped) flower, which are combined to form a body shaped somewhat like the keel of a vessel

carinate: keeled; furnished with a sharp ridge or projection on the lower side
carpel: a simple pistil, or one of the parts or leaves of which a compound pistil is composed
carpophore: the stalk or support of a fruit or pistil within the flower
cartilaginous: firm and tough, like cartilage
caryopsis: a small one-seeded dry indehiscent (closed at maturity) fruit in which the fruit and seed fuse in a single grain, as in wheat, barley, etc.
catkin: a scaly deciduous spike of flowers; an ament, such as willow, birch, poplar
cauline: of or belonging to a stem
ciliate: beset on the margin with a fringe of cilia or hairs like the eyelashes
ciliolate: minutely ciliate
cirrose: having ringlets
cladophyll: a branch assuming the form of and closely resembling an ordinary foliage leaf and often bearing leaves or flowers on its margins
club-shaped: clavate; slender below and thickened upwards
columnar: shaped like a column or pillar
commissure: joint, seam, the line of junction, of union of two carpels
compound leaf: a leaf in which the blade is divided to the midrib, forming two or more leaflets on a common axis
compressed: flattened on two opposite sides
cone: the fruit of the pine family
connate: congenitally united or grown together (of leaves)
connivent: converging, or brought close together
contiguous: touching or adjoining
cordate: cordiform; heart-shaped
coriaceous: resembling leather in texture
corneous: of a horny consistency or appearance
corolla: the leaves of the flower within the calyx; the inner highly colored portion of the flower
corollate: having a corolla
corymb: a sort of flat or convex flower cluster
creeping: growing flat on or beneath the ground and rooting
crenelate: crenate; crenelled; the edge scalloped into rounded teeth
crustaceous: hard and brittle in texture; crust-like
cuneate: cuneiform; wedge-shaped
cupula: cupule; a little cup; the cup to the acorn
cupuliform: shaped like or provided with a cupula
cuspidate: tipped with a sharp and stiff point
cyme: any arrangement or disposition of flowers with main and secondary axes always terminating in a single flower

deciduous: falling off, or subject to fall; said of leaves which fall in autumn, and of a calyx and corolla (outer and inner leaves of a flower, respectively) which fall before the fruit forms
decumbent: reclined on the ground, the summit tending to rise; of stems or shoots
decurrent: leaves extending downward along the stem beneath the insertion
dehiscence: a bursting open, as of a capsule, pod at maturity
dehiscent: opening wide, gaping; used especially of ripe fruit
deltoid: of a triangular shape
dentate: toothed
denticulate: furnished with very small teeth
depressed: flattened, as if pressed down from above; flattened vertically
diadelphous: stamens united by their filaments in two sets
diaphanous: transparent or translucent
dichotomous: two-forked
didymous: twin
didynamous: having four stamens in two pairs, one pair shorter than the other
diffuse: spreading widely and irregularly
digitate: leaflets of a compound leaf borne on the apex of the petiole, resembling the fingers of the hand
dioecious: location of the stamens in the flowers of one plant and pistils in the flowers of a different plant
disk: the face of any flat body; the central part of a head of flowers as opposed to the ray or margin; a fleshy expansion of the receptacle of a flower
divaricate: straddling; very widely divergent
drupaceous: like or pertaining to a drupe
drupe: a stone-fruit
ducts: the so-called vessels of plants

echinate: armed with prickles
ellipsoid: approaching an elliptical figure
elliptical: oval or oblong, with the ends regularly rounded
emarginate: notched at the summit, as a leaf
embryo: the rudimentary undeveloped plantlet in a seed
endocarp: the inner layer of a pericarp or fruit
entire: the margins not at all toothed, notched, or divided, but even
epidermis: the skin of a plant
epiphyte: a plant growing on another plant, but not nourished by it
estivation: the arrangement of parts in a flower bud
exocarp: epicarp; the outermost layer of a fruit
exserted: protruding out of, as the stamens out of the corolla

falciform: falcate; scythe-shaped; a flat body curved, its edges parallel
farinaceous: mealy in texture
fasciate: banded; also applied to monstrous stems which grow flat
fascicle: a close cluster
fasciculate: growing in a bundle or tuft, as the leaves of the pine or the roots of the peony
filamentose: bearing or formed of slender threads
filiform: thread-shaped; long, slender, and cylindrical
fimbriate: fringed; furnished with fringes
flexuose: flexuous; bending gently in opposite directions, in a zigzag way
floriferous: blooming freely
foliaceous: belonging to, or of the texture or nature of, a leaf
follicle: a simple pod, opening down the inner suture or seam
free: not united with any other parts of a different sort
frond: corresponds to leaves in ferns; the stem and leaves fused into one body, as in duckweed
frutescent: somewhat shrubby; becoming a shrub
fusiform: spindle-shaped

gamosepalous: formed of united sepals
geminate: twin; in pairs
glabrous: smooth, having no hairs, bristles or other pubescence
glands: small cellular organs which emit oily or aromatic secretions or other products; they are sometimes sunk in the leaves or rind; sometimes on the surface as small projections; sometimes raised on hairs or bristles. The name is also given to any small swellings, whether they secrete anything or not.
glandular: furnished with glands, or gland-like
glaucous: covered with a bloom or fine white powder that rubs off
globose: spherical in form, or nearly so
globular: nearly globose
glomerule: a dense head-like cluster
glume: the husks or floral coverings of grasses; particularly, the outer husks or bracts of each spikelet
glumelles: the inner husks, or paleae, of grasses
granular: composed of grains
gynoecium: a general term for the pistils of a flower

hastate: shaped like a halberd; furnished with a spreading lobe on each side at the base
herbaceous: of the texture of common herbage; not woody
hermaphrodite: having both stamens and pistils in the same blossom; perfect

heterogamous: bearing flowers of two different kinds as to their stamens and pistils
hilum: the scar of the seed; its place of attachment
hirsute: hairy with stiffish or beard-like hairs
hispid: bristly; beset with stiff hairs
hypogamous: inserted under the pistil

imbricate: overlapping one another, like tiles or shingles on a roof; in aestivation, where some leaves of the calyx or corolla are overlapped on both sides by others
incised: cut rather deeply and irregularly
incurvate: incurved; gradually curving inwards
indehiscent: not splitting open; not dehiscent
indusium: the shield or covering of a fruit dot of a fern
inferior: growing below some other organ
inflated: turgid and bladdery
inflexed: bent inwards
inflorescence: the arrangement and disposition of flowers on the stem
infundibular: funnel-shaped
integument: something that covers or encloses
introrse: turned or facing inwards
involucre: a whorl or set of bracts around a flower, umbel, or head

keel: a projecting ridge on a surface, like the keel of a boat; the two anterior petals of a papilionaceous corolla

labiate: bilabiate or two-lipped
labium: the lower lip of a labiate corolla
lacerate: having the edges deeply and irregularly cut
lanceolate: lance-shaped
ligneous: woody in texture
ligulate: furnished with a ligule
ligule: the strap-shaped corolla in many Compositae; the little membranous appendage at the summit of the leaf sheaths of most grasses
limb: the blade of a leaf, petal, etc.
linear: narrow and flat, the margins parallel
lip: the principal lobes of a bilabiate corolla or calyx; the odd and peculiar petal in the orchid family
lobate: having lobes
lobe: any projection or division, especially a rounded one, of a leaf, etc.
lyrate: lyre-shaped; a pinnatifid leaf of an obovate or spatulate outline, the end lobe large and roundish, and the lower lobes small, as in the radish

mammilla: any structure resembling a nipple
membranous: of the texture of membrane; thin and more or less translucent
mericarp: one carpel (pistil) of the fruit of an umbelliferous plant
midrib: the middle or main rib of a leaf
monadelphous: having stamens united by their filaments into one set
monoecious: having stamens or pistils only
monospermous: one-seeded
mucronate: tipped with an abrupt short point
mycelium: the spawn of fungi; the filaments from which mushrooms originate

navicular: boat-shaped, like the glumes of most grasses
netted: furnished with branching veins forming network
node: a knot; the joints of a stem, or the part whence a leaf or a pair of leaves springs
nodose: knotty or knobby
nut: a hard, mostly one-seeded indehiscent fruit
nutlet: a little nut; or the stone of a drupe

ob-: as a prefix, signifies inversion
obcordiform: heart-shaped with the broad and notched end at the apex instead of the base
oblique: as applied to leaves, not equal-sided
oblong: from two to four times as long as broad, and more or less elliptical in outline
obovoid: ovoid with the broad end towards the apex
obtuse: blunt, or round at the end
ocrea: a tubular sheath around the base of a leafstalk
octamerous: parts in eights
odoriferous: yielding a fragrance
operculate: furnished with a lid or cover, as the capsules of mosses
orbiculate: orbicular; circular in outline or nearly so
oval: broadly elliptical
ovoid: ovate or oval in a solid form
ovulate: ovular; relating to or being an ovule
ovule: the body which is destined to become a seed

palmate: leaflets or the divisions of a leaf all spreading from the apex of the petiole, like a hand with fingers spread
panicle: any pyramidal loosely branched flower cluster, like a raceme
paniculate: arranged in panicles; branching like a panicle
papilionaceous: butterfly-shaped
pappus: thistledown; the down crowning the achenium of the thistle and other

Compositae, representing the calyx. The scales, teeth, chaff, as well as bristles, or whatever takes the place of the calyx in this family, is called the pappus.
pedicel: the stalk of each particular flower of a cluster
pedicellate: furnished with a pedicel
peduncle: a flower stalk, whether of a single flower or of a flower cluster
pedunculate: furnished with a peduncle
peltate: shield-shaped; said of a leaf, whatever its shape, when the petiole (leafstalk) is attached to the lower side, somewhere within the margin
pepo: a fruit like the melon and cucumber
perennial: lasting from year to year
perfect: having both stamens and pistils
perianth: the leaves of the flower generally, especially when we cannot readily distinguish them into calyx and corolla
pericarp: the ripened ovary; the walls of the fruit
perigynous: the petals and stamens borne on the calyx
persistent: remaining beyond the period when such parts commonly fall, as the leaves of evergreens, and the calyx of such flowers as remain during the growth of the fruit
petal: a leaf of the corolla
petaloid: petal-like; resembling or colored like petals
petiolate: furnished with a petiole
petiole: a footstalk of a leaf; a leafstalk
pinna: a primary branch of the petiole of a bipinnate or tripinnate leaf
pinnate: leaflets arranged along either side of a common petiole, resembling a feather
pinnatifid: pinnately cleft
pinnatilobate: pinnatifid
pinnule: a secondary branch of the petiole of a bipinnate or tripinnate leaf
pistil: the seed-bearing organ of the flower
pith: the cellular center of an exogenous stem (growing from or on the outside)
placenta: the surface or part of the ovary to which the ovules are attached
plicate: plaited
plumose: feathery
polygamous: having some perfect and some separated flowers, on the same or on different individuals
polygonal: many-angled
pome: the apple, pear, and similar fleshy fruits
prismatic: prism-shaped; having three or more angles bounding flat or hollowed sides
procumbent: trailing on the ground
prostrate: lying flat on the ground

prunose: frosted; covered with a powder-like frost
pubescent: hairy or downy, especially with fine and soft pubescence
pyriform: having the shape of a pear
pyxis: pyxidium; a pod opening into an upper and lower half

quincuncial: in a quincunx; the parts in aestivation number five, two of them outside, two inside, and one half-out and half-in

raceme: a flower cluster, with one-flowered pedicels arranged along the sides of a general peduncle
rachis: a rhachis; the axis of a spike, or other body
radiant: furnished with ray flowers
ramiform: branched
ramose: full of branches
ray: the marginal flowers of a head or cluster, when different from the rest, especially when ligulate, and diverging like sunbeams; the branches of an umbel, which diverge from a concentrated center
receptacle: the axis or support of a flower; the common axis or support of a head of flowers
reflected: bent outwards or backwards
reniform: kidney-shaped
reticulate: the veins forming a network
rhizome: a rootstock
rostrate: bearing a beak or a prolonged appendage
rotate: wheel-shaped
rugose: wrinkled, roughened with wrinkles
runcinate: coarsely saw-toothed or cut, the pointed teeth turned towards the base of the leaf

sac: any closed membrane, or a deep purse-shaped cavity
sagittate: arrowhead-shaped
salver-shaped: with a border spreading at right angles to a slender tube
samara: a winged fruit or key, as in the ash, elm, maple
scabrous: rough or harsh to the touch
scales: a modified leaf protecting a seed plant bud before expansion; a thin, membranous, chaffy or woody bract
scaly: furnished with scales, or scale-like in texture
scape: a peduncle rising from the ground, or near it
scapiform: scape-like
scariose (also scarious): thin, dry, and membranous
scorpioid: curved or circinate at the end, like the tail of a scorpion
segment: a subdivision or lobe of any cleft body

sepal: a leaf or division of the calyx
serrate: the margin cut into teeth pointing forwards towards the apex
sessile: without any stalk, as a leaf destitute of petiole, or an anther destitute of filament
setaceous: bristle-like
sheath: the base of such leaves as those of grasses, which are wrapped around the stem
silicle: a pouch or short pod of the family Cruciferae
silique: a longer pod of the family Cruciferae
simple: of one piece, opposed to compound
sinuate: strongly wavy; with the margin alternately bowed inwards and outwards
sinus: a recess or bay; the re-entering angle or space between two lobes or projections
solitary: single; not associated with others
sorus: the proper name for fruit dots on ferns; a cluster of spores, sporangia, or analogous reproductive bodies
spadix: a fleshy spike of flowers
spathaceous: resembling or furnished with a spathe
spathe: a bract which inwraps an inflorescence
spatulate: shaped like a spatula
spiciform: in shape resembling a spike
spike: an inflorescence like a raceme, except that the flowers are sessile (without a stalk)
spine: a thorn
spiniferous: thorny
sporangia: spore cases of ferns, mosses, etc.
spore: a body resulting from the fructification of cryptogamous plants, taking the place of a seed
spur: any projecting appendage of the flower, looking like a spur
spurred: having one or more spurs
stamen: the organ of a flower that produces the male gamete, consisting of an anther and a filament
staminate: furnished with stamens
staminode: an abortive stamen, or other body resembling a sterile stamen
sterile: barren or imperfect
stigma: the part of the pistil which receives the pollen
stipitate: furnished with a stipe, or stalk of a pistil
stipules: the appendages on each side of the base of certain leaves
stoloniferous: producing stolons
stolons: shoots developing a bud and root at the tip or at both the node and tip

striate: marked with slender longitudinal grooves or channels
strobilus: a multiple fruit in the form of a cone or head, as that of the hop and pine
style: a part of the pistil which bears the stigma
stylopodium: an epigynous disk, or an enlargement at base of the style, found in umbelliferous and some other plants
sub-: as a prefix means "about," "nearly," "somewhat"
succulent: juicy or pulpy
suckers: shoots from subterranean branches
sword-shaped: vertical leaves with acute parallel edges, tapering above to a point

tegument: integument; *see above*
tendril: a thread-shaped body used for climbing; it is either a branch or a part of a leaf
terminal: borne at, or belonging to, the extremity or summit
ternate: in threes
testa: the outer, and usually the harder, coat or shell of the seed
tetragonal: four-angled
throat: the opening or gorge of a monopetalous corolla, where the border and the tube join, and a little below
thyrse: a compact and pyramidal panicle
tomentose: clothed with matted woolly hairs or tomentum
toothed: furnished with teeth or short projections of any sort on the margin, used especially when these are sharp, like saw-teeth, and do not point forwards
tortuous: marked by repeated twists or bendings
tridentate: three-toothed
trifid: three-cleft
trifoliate: three-leaved
trigonal: three-angled or triangular
trilobate: three-lobed
tripartite: three-part
tripinnate: thrice pinnate
triquetrous: sharply triangular, especially with the sides concave, like a bayonet
truncate: as if cut off at the top, the end square or even
tube: the narrow basal portion of a gamopetalous corolla or a gamosepalous calyx
tuber: a thickened portion of a subterranean stem or branch, provided with eyes, or buds, on the sides
tubercle: a small excrescence

tuberculate: bearing excrescences or pimples
tuberiferous: bearing tubers
tuberiform: having the shape of a tuber
tunicate: coated; invested with layers, like an onion

umbel: rays appearing to spring from the same point, forming a flat or rounded flower cluster
umbelliferous: bearing umbels
umbellule: a secondary umbel in a compound umbel
undulate: wavy, or wavy-margined
unguiculate: furnished with a claw, i.e. a narrow base, as the petals of the rose, where the claw is very short, and those of Dianthus, where the claw is very long
uniflorous: one-flowered
unilateral: one-sided
urceolate: urn-shaped
utricle: a small, thin-walled, one-seeded fruit

valve: one of the pieces into which a dehiscent pod splits
valvular: opening by valves
veins: the small ribs or branches of the framework of leaves, etc.
vermiculate: shaped like worms
verticil: a whorl
verticillate: whorled
vexillum: the standard of a papilionaceous flower
villous: shaggy with long and soft hairs
volubilate: twining, as the stem of beans

whorl: leaves arranged in a circle around the stem
winged: furnished with a membranous expansion

zest: the peel of the orange, lemon, etc.

REFERENCES

The standard scientific journal abbreviations listed below are those found in the *Index Catalog of the Library of the Surgeon-General's Office, U.S. Army*, Washington, D.C., and in the *Quarterly Cumulative Index Medicus* of the American Medical Association, Chicago. Bold numerals indicate volume numbers.

1. ABE, KOTAKE: Science Papers Inst. Phys. Chim. Res., 1933, **23**, 44.
2. ABE, SAITO: Jap. Med. World, 1922, **2**, 166.
3. ARIMA: Bull. Chem. Soc. Japan, 1929, **4**, 16, 113.
4. ASAHINA et al.: Ber., 1930, **63**, 2045.
5. ASAHINA, FUJITA: Acta Phytochim. Japan, 1922, **1**, 1.
6. ASAHINA, MANSKE, ROBINSON: J. Chem. Soc., 1927, 1708.
7. ASAHINA, OTA: C. A., 1927, **21**, 2134.
8. ASHIMA, MURAYAMA: Arch. Pharm., 1914, **252**, 435; J. Pharm. Soc. Japan, 1914, **390**, 885; 1915, **398**, 261; 1916, **415**, 781; 1918, **451**, 1; 1922, **485**, 565.
9. BAILEY, NORRIS: Biochem. J., 1932, **26**, 1609.
10. BOEHM: Arch. Exp. Path. Pharmakol., 1915, **79**, 138.
11. BOEHM, FLASCHENTRAGER: Apoth. Ztg., 1930, **45**, 1401.
12. BUSSEMAKER: Arch. Exper. Path. Pharmakol., 1936, **181**, 512.
13. CHEATHAM: Chin. J. Physiol., 1935, **9**, 47.
14. CHEN, CHEN: J. Pharmacol., 1935, **55**, 319.
15. CHEN, HOU: Am. J. Med. Sci., 1926, **172**, 113.
16. CHEN, SCHMIDT: Medicine, 1930, **9**, 1–117.
17. CHEYMOL: J. Pharm. et Chimie, 1937, **25**, 110.
18. CHI, MA: Chin. Chem. Soc., 1935, **3**, 78.
19. CHI, WONG: J. Chin. Chem. Soc., 1934, **2**, 329.
20. CHOU et al.: Chin. J. Physiol., 1928, **2**, 203; 1929, **3**, 69, 301; 1933, **7**, 35;

1934, **8**, 155; 1935, **10**, 107; 1937, **11**, 7; J. Pharm. Soc. Japan, 1920, **463**, 763; **547**, 711; 1929, **49**, 125.
21. Chu: Chin. J. Physiol., 1927, **1**, 7.
22. Chu, How: Chin. J. Physiol., 1931, **5**, 115.
23. Chuang, Ma: Trans. Sci. Soc. China; 1932, **7**, 187.
24. Daels: J. Pharm. Belg., 1928, **10**, 353.
25. Davenport, Schweitz: Apoth. Ztg., 1918, **56**, 522.
26. Dragendorf: Heilpflanzen, 1898, p. 280.
27. Dutt et al.: Arch. Pharm., 1938, **276**, 343.
28. Eijkman: Rec. Trav. Chim. Pays-Bas, 1886, **5**, 127.
29. Elborne: Pharm. J., 1889, **3**, 242.
30. Finnemore: Pharm. J., 1910, **31**, 145.
31. Freudenberg, Frick: Ber., 1920, **53**, 1728.
32. Fuji, Shimada: J. Pharm. Soc. Jap., 1933, **53**, 1920.
33. Fujita, Wada: J. Pharm. Soc. Jap., 1931, **51**, 52.
34. Fujitani: Arch. Intern. Pharmaco. Therap., 1905, **14**, 355.
35. Ghosh et al.: J. Indian Chem. Soc., 1929, **6**, 517.
36. Gosh et al.: Arch. Pharm., 1938, **276**, 351–353.
37. Goto: Ann., 1935, **521**, 175.
38. Greshoff, Boorsma: Mededeel. Lands Plant, 1899, **31**, 125.
39. Hamet: Bull. Sci. Pharmacol., 1928, **21**, 1848.
40. Hanbury: Science Papers, 1875, pp. 209–277.
41. Hartwich: Neue Arzneidrogen, 1897, 127.
42. Holste: Compt. rend. Soc. de biol., 1928, **99**, 1257.
43. Holtste: Arch. exp. Path. Pharmakol., 1924, **101**, 46.
44. Jaretsky, Lier: Arch. Pharm., 1938, **276**, 138.
45. Jarisch, Henze: Arch. f. exper. Path. u. Pharmakol., 1937, **187**, 706, 1938, **191**, 30.
46. Kaku et al.: J. Pharm. Soc. Japan, 1936, **56**, 361.
47. Kimoto: Bull. Coll. Physic. Tokyo, 1902, **5**, 253.
48. King: Contrib. Inst. Physiol. Peiping, 1934–35, **2**, 61, 145.
49. ———: Contrib. Inst. Physiol. Peiping, 1935, **2**, 189.
50. King et al.: Contrib. Inst. Physiol. Peiping, 1936, **4**, no. 2, 19.
51. King, Li: Contrib. Inst. Physiol. Peiping, 1936, **4**, 1.
52. King, Shih: Contrib. Inst. Physiol. Peiping, 1935, **3**, 9.
53. ———: Contrib. Inst. Physiol. Peiping, 1935, III, **6**, 95.
54. ———: Contrib. Inst. Physiol. Peiping, 1936, IV, **3**, 39.
55. King, Wou: Contrib. Inst. Physiol. Peiping, 1935, II, **5**, 133.
56. Kitasato: J. Pharm. Soc. Japan, 1925, **522**; 1926, **535**, 80; Bull. Chem. Soc. Japan, 1930, **5**, 348.
57. ———: C. A., 1927, **21**, 2700; J. Pharm. Soc. Japan, 1927, **542**, 48.

58. KONDO: Chem. Zentr., 1929, II, **752**, 1012.
59. ———: Arch. Pharm., 1937, **275**, 493.
60. KONDO et al.: J. Pharm. Soc. Japan, 1923, **497**, 511.
61. KONDO, KEIMATSU: Ber., 1935, **68**, 1503.
62. KONDO, NAKAZATO: J. Pharm. Soc. Japan, 1924, **511**, 1; 1926, **532**, 40.
63. KONDO, OCHIAI: Ann., 1929, **470**, 224.
64. KONDO, TAKEDA: J. Pharm. Soc. Japan, 1939, **59**, 162.
65. KONDO, TOMITA: J. Pharm. Soc. Japan, 1930, **50**, 633; 1935, **55**, 637; Arch. Pharm., 1936, **274**, 73.
66. KUBOTA, NAKASHIMA: Fol. Pharm. Jap., 1930, **11**, 153.
67. KUHN, WINTERSTEIN, KAUFMANN: Ber., 1930, **63**, 1489.
68. KUWADA, YOSHIKI: J. Pharm. Soc. Japan, 1939, **59**, 203.
69. LEHMAN, CHASE: Fed. Proc., 1942, **1**, 157.
70. LOBSTEIN, TRENSZ: Bull. Sci. Pharmacol., 1935, **42**, 343.
71. MA: Contr. Inst. Physiol. Peiping, 1935, **11**, no. 7.
72. MACHT, COOK: J. Am. Pharm. Assn., 1932, **21**, 324.
73. MAIJIMA et al.: Ber. d. deutsch. Chem. Gesellsch., 1922, **55**, 172.
74. MARANON, SANTOS: Philipp. J. Sci., 1932, **48**, 563.
75. NAGAI: Deutschen Chemis. Gesell., XXIV, p. 2847.
76. NAKAYAMA: Pharm. Soc. Japan, 1924, **509**, 551.
77. OHTA: Japan Med. World, 1923, **3**, 268.
78. ———: Physiol. Chem., 1940, **263**, 221.
79. OU, CHIU: Bull. Med. Univ. Aurore, Shanghai, 1938, 1941.
80. PAL, NARASIMBAN: J. Ind. Chem. Soc., 1943, **20**, 181.
81. PANICKER et al.: J. Indian Inst. Sci., 1926, **9**, A, 133.
82. POHL: Arch. exptl. Path. Pharmakol., 1892, **29**, 282.
83. POWER: Chemist and Druggist, 1912, 822.
84. POWER, Lees: Pharm. J., 1903, **17**, 183.
85. POWER et al.: J. Chem. Soc., 1904–1907.
86. POWER, SALWAY: Am. J. Pharm., 1908, **80**, 251, 563.
87. RATH: Arch. f. exper. Path. u. Pharmakol., 1929, **142**, 157.
88. RAZIMBAUD: Étude de quelques drogues utilisées comme cardiotoniques en Extreme-Orient, These Univ. Toulouse, 1939.
89. READ: Chin. Med. J., 1924, **38**, 25.
90. RICHTER, SCHROCKSNADEL: Arch. f. exper. Path. u. Pharmakol., 1938, **191**, 23.
91. RYO: Folia Pharmacol. Japon, 1927, **6**, 232, 247.
92. SAH, HSIUNG: J. Chin. Chem. Soc., 1933, **1**, 96.
93. SAKAI: Tokyo Igakukai Zasshi, 1917, **31**, 1; Jap. Med. Lit., 1918, **3**, 27.
94. SALGUES: Compt. Rend. Acad. Sci., 1936, **202**, 971.
95. SANTESSON: Skandinav. Arch. f. Physiol., 1938, **80**, 361.

96. SCHECHTER, HALLER: J. Am. Chem. Soc., 1940, **62**, 1307.
97. SCHLOSSBERGER: Handb. d. Exp. Pharmak., Erg., 1937, **5**.
98. SCHMIDT: Chin. Med. J., 1926, **40**, 415.
99. SCHMIDT et al.: Chin. Med. J., 1924, **38**, 362.
100. SCHREDER: Ber. v. Schim., 1898, **4**, 57; 1929, **7**.
101. SHERMAN: Philipp. J. Sci., 1929, **38**, 9.
102. STENHOUSE: Ann., 1854, **89**, 251; 1857, **104**, 236.
103. STEVENS: J.A.M.A., 1945, **127**, 912.
104. STILLMARK: Arb. Pharmak. Inst. Dorpat, 1889, 59.
105. TAKAGI, HONGO: J. Pharm. Soc. Japan, 1924, **504**, 539.
106. TANG, PENG: J. Pharm. Soc. China, 1943, **1**, 1.
107. ———: J. Pharm. Soc. China, 1943, **1**, 17.
108. THOMS, DAMBERGIS: Arch. Pharm., 1930, **268**, 39.
109. TSUCHIRASHI, TASAKI: J. Chem. Industr. Japan, 1919, **22**, 288.
110. TUTIN, CLEWER: J. Chem. Soc., 1911, **99**, 946.
111. VALYASHKO, TSVEIBAHK: Farmatsiya, 1940, **1**, 14.
112. WADA: Biochem. Z., 1930, **224**, 420.
113. WANG, HU: J. Chin. Soc., 1936, **4**, 89; 1944, 307.
114. WASICKY: Pharm. Post., 1913, **46**, 625.
115. WAUD: J.P.E.T., 1934, **50**, 100.
116. WEHMER: Die Planzenstoffen, second edition, 1929, Jena.
117. WILSON; DE EDS: Food Research, 1940, **5**, 89.
118. YAGI: Arch. Pharm., 1878, **213**, 335.
119. ———: Arch. Int. Pharmac., 1913, **23**, 277.
120. YONG: Am. J. Pharm., 1886, **58**, 417.

UNAUTHORED PAPERS APPEARING IN JOURNALS

121. Ber., 1939, **72**, 519.
122. Ber. v. Schim., 1915, Apr. 35.
123. Ber. v. Schim., 1921, 46.
124. Ber. v. Schim., 1924, 3.
125. Chin. J. Physiol., 1927, **1**, 33; 1928, 164; 1935, **9**, 47.
126. Deutschen chemis. Gesell. XXIV.
127. Ind. J. Med. Res., 1929, **17**, 351.
128. J. Chin. Chem. Soc., 1939, **23**, 185.
129. J. Chin. Chem. Soc., 1944, **11**, 99.
130. Jap. J. Med. Sci., 1930, **5**, 71.
131. J. Tokyo Chem. Soc., **49**, 534.
132. J. Pharm. Soc. Jap., 1913, **33**, 1175; 1914, **34**, 912.
133. J. Pharm. Soc. Jap., 1928, **48**, 1064, 1178.

134. J. Pharm. Soc. Jap., 1929, **49**, 182.
135. J. Pharm. Soc. Jap., 1929, **49**, 184, 1169; 1932, **52**, 499.
136. J. Pharm. Soc. Jap., 1936, **56**, 441.

IN CHINESE

137. HAN PAO-SHENG: *Shu Pen-ts'ao*, mid-tenth century.
138. LI SHI-CHEN: *Pen-ts'ao Kang-mu*, sixteenth century.
139. LIU HAN, MA CHI: *Kai-pao Pen-ts'ao*, tenth century.
140. LU KUEI-SHENG: *Chung-yo-k'o Hsueh-hua Ta-tz'u-tien*, 1954, Hong Kong.
141. SU KUNG: *T'ang Pen-ts'ao*, seventh century.
142. SU SUNG: *T'u-king Pen-ts'ao*, eleventh century.
143. TAO HUNG-KING: *Ming-i Pie-lu*, sixth century.

IN ENGLISH AND FRENCH

144. *Blackiston's New Gould Medical Dictionary*, second edition, 1956.
145. BRETSCHNEIDER: *Botanicum Sinicum*, 1895.
146. HURRIER: *Matière médicale et pharmacopée sino-annamites*, 1907.
147. MANSFIELD: *Squibb's Atlas of the Official Drugs*, 1919.
148. *The Merck Index*, sixth edition, 1952.
149. PARRY: *The Chemistry of Essential Oils and Artificial Perfumes*, second edition, 1908.
150. POTTER: *Materia Medica and Therapeutics*, seventh edition, 1899.
151. ROI: *Traité des plantes médicinales chinoises*, 1955.
152. SOLLMANN: *A Manual of Pharmacology*, seventh edition, 1948.
153. SOUBEIRAN: *La matière médicale chez les chinois*, 1874.
154. TABER: *Cyclopedic Medical Dictionary*, sixth edition, 1955.
155. UPHOF: *Dictionary of Economic Plants*, 1959, Weinheim.

INDEX

As a child growing up in San Francisco, **John D. Keys** was intrigued by the mysterious medicinal shops common in the city's Chinatown district. This interest in Chinese herbs provided the motivation for his study of Chinese, Japanese, and French, languages he discovered were essential for the study of original works on herbs. The full extent of the author's knowledge of herbs will be readily apparent to readers of this book.